TUTTLE

Beginner's Mandarin Chinese Dictionary

LI Dong 李冬

TUTTLE Publishing

Tokyo | Rutland, Vermont | Singapore

Published by Tuttle Publishing, an imprint of Periplus Editions (HK) Ltd.

www.tuttlepublishing.com

Copyright © 2016 by Periplus Editions (HK) Ltd

ISBN 978-0-8048-4668-4

North America, Latin America and Europe
Tuttle Publishing
364 Innovation Drive,
North Clarendon,
VT 05759-9436 USA.
Tel: 1(802) 773-8930
Fax: 1(802) 773-6993
info@tuttlepublishing.com
www.tuttlepublishing.com

Asia Pacific
Berkeley Books Pte. Ltd.
61 Tai Seng Avenue #02-12,
Singapore 534167
Tel: (65) 6280-1330
Fax: (65) 6280-6290
inquiries@periplus.com.sg
www.periplus.com

18 17 16   6 5 4 3 2 1   1610MP
Printed in Singapore

TUTTLE PUBLISHING® is a registered trademark of Tuttle Publishing, a division of Periplus Editions (HK) Ltd.

Contents

A Guide for Learners of Chinese

This dictionary is for learners of Chinese as a foreign or second language. It is designed to be a teaching/learning aid to the growing communities of teaching and learning the language. More specifically, this dictionary aims to help those learners who wish to sit for the New Chinese Proficiency Test (New HSK 新汉语水平考试), the Chinese government-sponsored, international standardized test, as it gives detailed treatment of all the 2,500 words in the prescribed Word Lists from Level 1 to Level 5. A further 1,000 very useful words are covered in the dictionary to allow for flexibility of the vocabulary requirement of the HSK.

In the following pages I offer the essentials of the Chinese language and, along the way, advice on how to make the best use of this dictionary.

1   PRONUNCIATION

1.1 The Pinyin Romanization System
The pronunciation of Chinese words is transcribed in this dictionary using the internationally recognized Chinese romanization scheme called pinyin. Every Chinese word in this dictionary is accompanied by its *pinyin* spelling so users will know how it is pronounced.

Pronouncing Chinese syllables normally involves three elements: vowels, consonants and tones. Modern standard Chinese, known as *Putonghua*, uses about 419 syllables without tones and 1,332 syllables with tones.

1.2 Vowels

1.2.1 Single Vowels
There are seven basic single vowels:
a   similar to *a* in *ah*
e   similar to *a* in *ago*
ê   similar to *e* in *ebb* (this sound never occurs alone and is transcribed as **e**, as in **ei, ie, ue**)
i   similar to *ee* in *cheese* (spelled **y** when not preceded by a consonant)

o   similar to *oe* in *toe*
u   similar to *oo* in *boot* (spelled **w** when not preceded by a conso-
        nant)
ü   similar to German *ü* in *über* or French *u* in *tu*; or you can also get
        ü by saying *i* and rounding your lips at the same time (spelled **u**
        after **j**, **q**, **x**; spelled **yu** when not preceded by a consonant)

1.2.2 Vowel Combinations

These single vowels enter into combinations with each other or the
consonants of **n** or **ng** to form what are technically known as *diphthongs*. These combinations are pronounced as a single sound, with a
little more emphasis on the first part of the sound.

You can learn these combinations in four groups:

Group 1:   diphthongs starting with **a/e/ê**
   ai   similar to *y* in *my*
   ao   similar to *ow* in *how*
   an
   ang
   en
   eng
   ei   similar to *ay* in *may*

Group 2:   diphthongs starting with **i**
   ia
   ie   similar to *ye* in *yes*
   iao
   iou   similar to *you* (spelled **iu** when preceded by a consonant)
   ian
   ien   similar to *in* (spelled **in** when preceded by a consonant)
   ieng   similar to *En* in *English* (spelled **ing** when preceded by a
                             consonant)
   iang   similar to *young*
   iong

Group 3:   diphthongs starting with **u/o**

    ua

    uo

    uai   similar to *why* in British English

    uei   similar to *way* (spelled **ui** when preceded by a consonant)

    uan

    uen   (spelled **un** when preceded by a consonant)

    ueng

    uang

    ong

Group 4:   diphthongs starting with **ü**

    üe   used only after **j**, **q**, **x**; spelled **ue**

    üen   used only after **j**, **q**, **x**; spelled **un**

    üan   used only after **j**, **q**, **x**; spelled **uan**

1.3   Consonants

Consonants may be grouped in the following ways.

Group 1:   These consonants are almost the same in Chinese and English.

    m   *m*

    n   *n*

    f   *f*

    l   *l*

    s   *s*

    r   *r*

    b   pronounced as hard *p* (as in *speak*)

    p   *p* (as in *peak*)

    g   pronounced as hard *k* (as in *ski*)

    k   *k* (as in *key*)

    d   pronounced as hard *t* (as in *star*)

    t   *t* (as in *tar*)

Group 2:   Some modification is needed to get these Chinese sounds from English.

    j   as *j* in *jeep* (but unvoiced, not round-lipped)

    q   as *ch* in *cheese* (but not round-lipped)

x	as *sh* in *sheep* (but not round-lipped)
c	as *ts* as in *cats* (make it long)
z	as *ds* as in *beds* (but unvoiced, and make it long)

Group 3:   No English counterparts
Chinese **zh**, **ch**, and **sh** have no English counterparts. You can learn to say **zh**, **ch** and **sh** starting from **z**, **c** and **s**. For example, say **s** (which is almost the same as the English *s* in *sesame*) and then roll up your tongue to touch the roof of your mouth. You get **sh**.

1.4 Tones
Chinese is a tonal language, i.e. a sound pronounced in different tones is understood as different words. So the tone is an indispensable component of the pronunciation of a word.

1.4.1 Basic Tones
There are four basic tones. The following five-level pitch graph shows the values of the four tones:

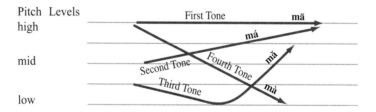

The **First Tone** is a high, level tone and is represented as ¯, e.g. 妈 **mā** (meaning *mother*, *mom*).

The **Second Tone** is a high, rising tone and is represented by the tone mark ´, e.g. 麻 **má** (*hemp* or *sesame*).

The **Third Tone** is a falling and rising tone. As you can see from the pitch graph it falls from below the middle of the voice range to nearly the bottom and then rises to a point near the top. It is represented by the tone mark ˇ, e.g. 马 **mǎ** (*horse*).

The **Fourth Tone** is a falling tone. It falls from high to low and is represented by the tone mark ` , e.g. 骂 **mà** (*curse*).

In Chinese speech, as in English speech, some sounds are unstressed, i.e. pronounced short and soft. They do not have any of the four tones. Such sounds are said to have **Neutral Tone**. Sounds with the neutral tone are not marked. For example in 爸爸 **bàba** (*daddy*) the first syllable is pronounced in the fourth tone and the second syllable in the neutral tone, i.e. unstressed.

1.4.2 Tone Changes
Tones may undergo changes in actual speech ("tone sandhi"). The third tone, when followed by a first, second, fourth or neutral tone sound, loses its final rise and stops at the low pitch. Followed by another third tone sound, it becomes the second tone. This is a general rule and the notation of third tone sounds remains unchanged.

For example, in 所以 **suǒyǐ** (*therefore, so*), notation remains the third tone for both syllables, but the word is actually pronounced like **suóyǐ**.

Two important words 不 **bù** (*no*) and 一 **yī** (*one*) also undergo tone changes. You will find the details of their tone changes under these entries.

1.5   Syllables

1.5.1 Chinese Syllables: Distinct Units
Normally a consonant and a vowel merge to form a syllable in Chinese. Every syllable is a distinct unit in speech. Learners should say each syllable clearly and give full value to most syllables in speech. The general impression of Chinese speech, described in musical terms, is staccato rather than legato (which could be used to describe English).

1.5.2 Syllable Division Mark
As Chinese syllables are distinct units and should not be liaised with preceding or following syllables, a syllable division mark (') is sometimes used to avoid confusion, e.g. **shí'èr**, **píng'ān**, **tiān'é**.

2   WRITTEN CHINESE

2.1 "Chinese characters," a Unique Writing System

Chinese is not written in letters, like **a**, **b**, **c**, nor does it use an alphabet. Chinese is written in logograms, known as 汉字 (**Hànzì**) and generally referred to as "Chinese characters."

Each Chinese character is pronounced as a syllable and, with few exceptions, has distinctive meaning or meanings. Though there are tens of thousands of Chinese characters, only a couple of thousands are in frequent use – the first 1,000 Chinese characters cover about 90% of daily communication.

2.2 The Composition of Chinese Characters: Meaningful Components

Chinese characters may be composed of parts, some of which convey certain meanings. The presence of such components gives you some clue to the meaning of characters. The ability to **recognize** these components is both useful and interesting. See List 1 Meaningful Character Components on page xix.

2.3 The Writing of Chinese Characters

STROKES

Each Chinese character is written by a number of strokes, with the sole exception of 一 (which means "one"). The table below shows the basic strokes.

Stroke	Writing the stroke	Examples
Héng	left to right 一	千 主 女
Shù	top to bottom 丨	千 山 北
Piě	top (right) to bottom (left) 丿	千 人 么

Stroke	Writing the stroke	Examples
Nà	top (left) to bottom (right) ＼	人 木 又
Diǎn	top to bottom ＼	主 心 习
Tí	Bottom (left) to top (right) ╱	习 打 北
Strokes with hook	left to right, top to bottom ⟍⎟⎞⎞	买 打 以 心
Strokes with turn(s)	⎿ ⎤ ⟨ ⎠	山 马 女 么 又
Strokes with turn(s) and hook	⎣ ⎤ ⟍⎞ 乙	北 习 认 马

STROKE ORDER

For the character to look correct, its strokes should be written in the correct order. Knowing the order will also help you remember characters. The general rules of stroke order are as follows.

Rule	Example	Stroke order
Top before bottom	三	一 二 三
Left before right	什	丿 亻 仁 什
Horizontal before vertical/downward	天	一 二 チ 天
"Enter the room, then close the door"	日	丨 冂 冃 日
Vertical stroke before sides/bottom	小	亅 小 小

2.4 Simplified and Traditional Characters

The Chinese government simplified hundreds of Chinese characters in mid-1950s by reducing the numbers of their strokes. Such simplified characters are called 简体字 **jiǎntǐzì**. This dictionary uses *jiantizi*. Traditional versions (also known as complicated characters) are still used in Taiwan and Hong Kong, and they are shown where applicable, e.g.:

    xué 学 TRAD 學

3 VOCABULARY

3.1 Words in This Dictionary

This dictionary gives detailed description of the 2,500 words prescribed for Level 1 to Level 5 of **the New Chinese Proficiency Test (New HSK** 新汉语水平考试 **Xīn Hànyǔ Shuǐpíng Kǎoshì)**, the Chinese government-sponsored, international standardized test. Over 1,000 more words are covered, to further develop learners' vocabulary power.

3.2 The Importance of Chinese Characters

Most Chinese words are made up of two or more characters; the component characters usually determine the meaning of words. It is widely accepted by teachers and students of Chinese that in order to understand the meaning of a word, one should first of all learn the meanings of its component characters. This dictionary treats Chinese characters as individual items and gives them clear definitions, with the exception of a very few which are not used alone in Modern Chinese.

3.3 Word-formation Methods

Chinese words are very transparent, i.e. the way a word is formed tells a lot about its meaning. Therefore it is very helpful to know the ways words are formed, as it facilitates understanding of words and makes learning more interesting.

This dictionary analyzes word-formation methods of headwords, whenever it is practical to do so. We recognize five methods of word-formation.

- **Compounding** (shortened to "comp"): the components of a word are complementary to each other in meaning and are of the same status. For example:

  cáifǎng 采访 [comp: 采 gather + 访 visit] **v** (of mass media) interview

- **Modification** ("modif"): one component modifies the other. For example:

  báitiān 白天 [modif: 白 white + 天 day] **N** daytime

- **Verb+object** ("v+obj"): the word has a verb-and-object relationship. For example:

  chànggē 唱歌 [v+obj: 唱 sing + 歌 song] **v** sing songs, sing

- **Verb+complementation** ("v+compl"): the word has a verb-and-complement relationship, that is, the first component is a verb and the second one modifies it. For example:

  kànjiàn 看见 [v+compl: 看 look + 见 see] **v** see, get sight of

- **Suffixation** ("suffix"): the word contains a suffix. For example:

  bēizi 杯子 [suffix: 杯 cup + 子 nominal suffix] **N** cup, mug, glass (只 **zhī**)

3.4 Definitions

In most cases English equivalents or near equivalents are given as definitions. For example:

bāngmáng 帮忙 **v** help, help out

For grammatical words that have no English equivalents, concise explanations are given in brackets. For example:

de 的 PARTICLE (attached to a word or phrase to indicate that it is an attribute. 的 **de** is normally followed by a noun.)

After the definition of a noun, the specific measure word used with the noun is shown, if it is one of headwords in the dictionary. For example:

diànnǎo 电脑 [modif: 电 electricity + 脑 brain] **N** computer (台 **tái**)

When no measure word is shown for a noun, you can use the default measure word 个 **gè**.

The dictionary also show antonyms after the definition of common adjectives and some nouns. For example:

gāo 高 ADJ tall, high (ANTONYMS 矮 **ǎi**, 低 **dī**)

3.5 Example Sentences

Words become really meaningful only when used in sentences. **Where appropriate, example sentences to amply illustrate the meaning and usage of words are included.** Great attention was paid to the composition of the sentences to make sure they are

(1)   idiomatic,
(2)   communicatively useful, and
(3)   within the controlled vocabulary of this dictionary.

These sentences are accompanied by their *pinyin* and English translations. In some cases a second translation is provided in brackets to aid comprehension and idiomatic expression.

All this makes this dictionary an essential aid to teaching and learning Chinese.

4   GRAMMAR: Main Features

4.1   Topic+Comment Structure

The basic principle in making Chinese sentences is to follow the "topic+comment" structure. "Topic" means the subject matter you want to talk about, and "comment" is the information you give about the subject matter. To make a Chinese sentence, you simply first mention the subject matter you want to talk about, and then add what you have to say about it. For example, you can say 这件事 **zhè jiàn shì** (*this matter/affair*) first as the "topic" and then add "comment":

这件事　我不清楚。 **Zhè jiàn shì wǒ bù qīngchǔ.**
I'm not clear about this matter.

这件事 我很了解。 **Zhè jiàn shì wǒ hěn liǎojiě.**
I know this matter well.

这件事 谁都不知道。 **Zhè jiàn shì shuí dōu bù zhīdào.**
Nobody knows this matter.

这件事 我不感兴趣。 **Zhè jiàn shì wǒ bù gǎn xìngqu.**
I'm not interested in this matter.

这件事 最近社交网站都在谈。 **Zhè jiàn shì zuìjìn shèjiāo dōu zài tán.** *Social media are all talking about this matter these days.*

4.2 Ellipsis of Sentence Elements

Chinese speakers may leave out words that are supposed to be understood, and therefore need not be spoken. Subjects and conjunctions are often omitted. For example, you may translate the English sentence:
If you like it, you may buy it, but if you don't like it, you don't have to,
into the Chinese sentence 喜欢就买， 不喜欢就别买。 **Xǐhuan jiù mǎi, bù xǐhuan jiù bié mǎi.**

Compare the two sentences, and you will find that some English words, such as *if*, *you*, *it*, and *but* are not translated.

4.3 Word Classes: Flexibility, No Inflection

Chinese words do not have inflections, i.e. they do not change to indicate grammatical categories. For example, the verb 做 **zuò** (*to do*) is invariably 做 **zuò**; there is no past form or any other inflected form of this verb. Neither do Chinese words normally have formal markers of word class. Consequently, it is rather easy for a word to be used in more than one word class. This relative flexibility in word classes, however, does not mean that Chinese does not have word classes (see Section 4.5).

4.4 Measure Words and Particles

Measure words (量词 **liàngcí**) and particles (助词 **zhùcí**) are two word classes found in Chinese but not in English and most other languages.

Measure words are usually required when a noun is modified by a numeral. For example, 两书 **liǎng shū** is unacceptable; you must use the measure word 本 **běn** between the numeral and the noun: 两本书 **liǎng běn shū** (*two books*). Furthermore, Chinese nouns require specific measure words to go with them. For example, the noun 书 **shū** (*book*) must be used with the measure word 本 **běn**. See List 2 Measure Words.

In Chinese grammar, particles are words attached to other words or at the end of a sentence to indicate grammatical concepts or to express emotions. For example, the particles 了 **le**, 着 **zhe**, 过 **guo** are attached to verbs to indicate, respectively, whether the actions denoted are completed, in progress or past experiences.

4.5 Word Classes
Following are brief explanations of the basic terms in Chinese grammar used in this dictionary. (A word of warning: it is a rather complicated matter to define grammatical terms accurately. Here we will be content with some very general but useful ideas.)

ADJECTIVE	a describing word, a word that describes people, things or actions, typically used before a noun.
ADVERB	a word that modifies a verb, an adjective or another adverb.
CONJUNCTION	a word used to link two words, phrases or sentences, indicating certain relationships between them.
IDIOM	a set phrase, the meaning of which cannot be readily derived from its components.
INTERJECTION	a word that expresses strong emotions.
MEASURE WORD	a word that connects a numeral to a noun. Measure words are a special feature of Chinese; a list of measure words is included in the front matter.
MODAL VERB	a word used before a verb to indicate necessity, possibility, willingness, etc.
NOUN	a naming word, a word that names people, animals, plants, things, ideas, etc.
NUMERAL	a word that represents a number, typically used with a noun.

ONOMATOPOEIA	a word that imitates the sounds of a thing or an action.
PARTICLE	a word used with another word, phrase, or sentence to indicate certain grammatical meanings or to express strong emotions.
PREPOSITION	a word used before a noun or pronoun to indicate time, place, direction, manner, reason of an action, etc.
PRONOUN	a word that is used in the place of a noun, a verb, an adjective, etc.
VERB	an action word, a word that indicates what somebody does or feels.

5   CULTURAL AND USAGE NOTES

As a dictionary for learners rather than a mere wordlist, this dictionary goes out of its way to give essential information on cultural context, pronunciation, grammar and usage of words. For example:

lǐwù 礼物 [modif: 礼 gift + 物 thing] ɴ gift, present (件 **jiàn**)

...

> NOTE: Chinese modesty requires that you belittle your present, describing it as 一件小礼物 yí jiàn xiǎo lǐwù *a small/insignificant gift.* Upon receiving a present, it is bad manners to open it immediately. The recipient is first supposed to say 不用不用 **búyòng búyòng** *You didn't have to* and then express thanks for the gift, describing it as 这么好的礼物 Zhème hǎo de lǐwù *such a nice gift,* e.g. ■ 谢谢你送给我这么好的礼物。Xièxie nǐ sònggei wǒ zhème hǎo de lǐwù. *Thank you for giving me such a nice gift.*

There are hundreds of such notes in the dictionary.

6   HOW TO LOOK UP A WORD IN THE DICTIONARY

6.1   By Pinyin Romanization

This dictionary arranges headwords alphabetically according to *pinyin.* So if you know how a word is pronounced, you can find it easily, just the way you will look up an English word in an English dictionary.

6.2   By Radical

Very often, however, you do not know the pronunciation of a word when you come across it in reading. In that case you can find it either by its radical or the number of its strokes.

Radicals (部首 **bùshǒu**) are certain component parts of characters that have been used in Chinese dictionary-making for nearly 2,000 years. Characters sharing a radical are grouped together under the heading of that radical. To find a character in a dictionary, follow these steps:

(i)   In the **List of Radicals**, look up the character's radical according to the number of strokes in the radical. This gives a Radical Index number.

(ii) Turn to the number in the **Radical Index**

(iii) Locate the character according to the number of remaining strokes needed to write the character (i.e. number of total strokes minus radical strokes = remaining strokes). You will find the pinyin by the character.

For example, to find 活:

(i)   The radical group of 活 is 氵 , which has three strokes. In the **List of Radicals**, look up 氵 in the section marked "3 strokes":

      3 strokes
      氵 33

(ii) Turn to number 33 in the **Radical Index**.

(iii) As there are nine strokes in 活, and the radical has three strokes, six strokes remain to complete the character 活 (9 – 3 = 6). Look in the section "6 strokes" and locate 活:

      6 strokes
      活 **huó**

(iv) Turn to **huó** in the dictionary:
      huó 活 …

6.3   By Number of Strokes

Unfortunately, looking for a character by its radical is not an entirely satisfactory method as learners may not always know which part of the character is the radical. Therefore, this dictionary includes a **Stroke Index** to aid the learner further. Simply look for the character according to the number of its strokes, and then locate the character by its first stroke.

For example, to find 活:

(i)   There are nine strokes in 活. Go to the section of nine strokes.

      9 strokes

(ii)   As the first stroke of 活 is " 、", locate 活 under " 、".

、

…

活 **huó**

(iii) Turn to **huó** in the dictionary.
       huó 活…

6.4 By English Meaning

To find out the Chinese equivalent or near-equivalent of an English
word, use the English-Chinese Word Finder, which is practically
a handy English-Chinese dictionary. Chinese equivalents or near-
equivalents of over 4,000 English words are listed alphabetically in the
Finder.

For example, to find out what *airport* is in Chinese, turn to "A" in the
Finder and locate *airport* in the list of words beginning with "A":

   airport **fēijī chǎng** 飞机场 *31*, **jīchǎng** 机场 *49*

The entry for 飞机场 **fēijī chǎng** is found on page 31 and the entry for
机场 **jīchǎng**, on page 49.

It is my firm belief that learners of Chinese will find this dictionary a
valuable learning aid.

List 1
Meaningful Character Components

Most of Chinese characters are made up of two or more component parts. "Signific graphs" (义符 **yìfú**) are components that suggest the meaning of characters. Hence, learning the meaning of these component parts will deepen your understanding of characters you know, and help you guess the meaning of unfamiliar characters. The following is a list of such meaningful character components.

冫 = freezing, ice (e.g. 冰 **bīng**, 冷 **lěng**, 寒 **hán**)

讠, 言 = word (e.g. 语 **yǔ**, 词 **cí**)

八 = dividing (e.g. 分 **fēn**, 半 **bàn**)

亻, 人 = man, person (e.g. 他 **tā**, 信 **xìn**)

刂, 刀 = knife (e.g. 利 **lì**, 剩 **shèng**)

力 = muscle, strength (e.g. 男 **nán**, 办 **bàn**)

阝 (on the left) = mound, steps (e.g. 院 **yuàn**, 附 **fù**)

阝 (on the right) = city, region (e.g. 部 **bù**, 邮 **yóu**)

氵, 水 = water (e.g. 河 **hé**, 海 **hǎi**)

忄, 心 = the heart, emotions (e.g. 情 **qíng**, 怕 **pà**)

宀 = roof, house (e.g. 家 **jiā**, 室 **shì**)

广 = roof, hut (e.g. 庭 **tíng**, 店 **diàn**)

门 = door, gate (e.g. 闻 **wén**, 间 **jiān**)

土 = earth (e.g. 场 **chǎng**, 城 **chéng**)

女 = woman (e.g. 妇 **fù**, 妈 **mā**)

饣, 食 = food (e.g. 饭 **fàn**, 饱 **bǎo**)

口 = the mouth, speech, eating (e.g. 问 **wèn**, 吃 **chī**)

囗 = boundary (e.g. 围 **wéi**, 园 **yuán**)

子, 孑 = child (e.g. 孩 **hái**, 学 **xué**)

艹 = plant, vegetation (e.g. 草 **cǎo**, 菜 **cài**)

纟 = silk, texture (e.g. 组 **zǔ**, 纸 **zhǐ**)

辶 = walking (e.g. 道 **dào**, 过 **guò**)

彳 = path, walking (e.g. 行 **xíng**, 往 **wǎng**)

巾 = cloth (e.g. 布 **bù**, 带 **dài**)

马 = horse (e.g. 骑 **qí**)

扌, 手, 攵 = the hand, action (e.g. 拿 **ná**, 擦 **cā**)

灬, 火 = fire, heat (e.g. 烧 **shāo**, 热 **rè**)

礻, 示 = spirit (e.g. 神 **shén**, 祖 **zǔ**)

户 = door, window (e.g. 房 **fáng**)

父 = father (e.g. 爸 **bà**)

日 = the sun (e.g. 晴 **qíng**, 暖 **nuǎn**)

月 = the moon (e.g. 阴 **yīn**, 明 **míng**)

月, 肉 = flesh, human organ (e.g. 脸 **liǎn**, 脚 **jiǎo**)

贝 = shell, treasure (e.g. 贵 **guì**)

止 = toe (e.g. 步 **bù**)

木 = tree, timber (e.g. 树 **shù**, 板 **bǎn**)

王, 玉 = jade (e.g. 理 **lǐ**, 球 **qiú**)

见 = seeing (e.g. 视 **shì**, 现 **xiàn**)

气 = vapor (e.g. 汽 **qì**)

车 = vehicle (e.g. 辆 **liàng**)

疒 = disease, ailment (e.g. 病 **bìng**, 疼 **téng**)

立 = standing (e.g. 站 **zhàn**, 位 **wèi**)

穴 = cave, hole (e.g. 空 **kōng**, 窗 **chuāng**)

衤 , 衣 = clothing (e.g. 裤 **kù**, 袜 **wà**)

钅 , 金 = metal (e.g. 银 **yín**, 钱 **qián**)

石 = stone, rock (e.g. 碗 **wǎn**, 磁 **cí**)

目 = the eye (e.g. 眼 **yǎn**, 睡 **shuì**)

田 = farm, field (e.g. 界 **jiè**, 里 **lǐ**)

禾 = seedling, crop (e.g. 种 **zhǒng**, 秋 **qiū**)

鸟 = bird (e.g. 鸡 **jī**)

米 = rice (e.g. 糖 **táng**, 精 **jīng**)

竹 , 竹 = bamboo (e.g. 筷 **kuài**, 笔 **bǐ**)

舌 = the tongue (e.g. 话 **huà**, 活 **huó**)

舟 = boat (e.g. 船 **chuán**)

酉 = fermentation (e.g. 酒 **jiǔ**)

走 = walking (e.g. 起 **qǐ**)

⻊ , 足 = the foot (e.g. 跳 **tiào**, 踢 **tī**)

List 2
Measure Words

Measure words are a special feature of Chinese. A particular measure word, or set of measure words, occurs with each noun whenever one is speaking of numbers. The measure word may function like a collective noun (like a pride [of lions] or a school [of fish]) or may be related to the shape of the object. Noun phrases using measure words often have the structure "number + measure word + noun," e.g.

- 一把刀 **yì bǎ dāo** *a knife*
- 两道难题 **liǎng dào nántí** *two difficult questions*

Some measure words occur with verbs, and may be related to the frequency or duration of the action. For verbs, the expression may have the structure "verb + number + measure word," e.g.

- 看了三遍 **kànle sān biàn** *read three times*
- 去过两次 **qùguo liǎng cì** *have been ... twice*

bǎ 把 for objects with handles; a handful

bān 班 class (in school)

bèi 倍 fold, time

běn 本 for books

bǐ 笔 for a sum of money

biàn 遍 times, indicating the frequency of an action done in its complete duration from the beginning to the end

cè 册 volume (books)

céng 层 story, floor

chǎng 场 for movies, sport events

chǐ 尺 a traditional Chinese unit of length (equal to 1/3 meter)

cì 次 time, expressing frequency of an act

cùn 寸 a traditional Chinese unit of length (equal to 1/30 meter)

dào 道 for questions in a school exercise, examination, etc.; for things in the shape of a line

dī 滴 drop (of liquid)

diǎn 点 o'clock

dù 度 degree (of temperature, longitude, latitude, etc.)

duàn 段 section of something long

dùn 顿 for meals

duǒ 朵 for flowers

fēn 分 Chinese currency (1 分 **fēn** = 0.1 角 **jiǎo** = 0.01 元 **yuán**), cent

fèn 份 for a set of things or newspapers, documents, etc.

fēng 封 for letters

fú 幅 for pictures, posters, maps, etc.

gè 个 the most commonly used measure word for nouns that do not take special measure words, or in default of any other measure word

gēn 根 for long, thin things

gōngchǐ 公尺 meter (formal)

gōngjīn 公斤 kilogram

gōnglǐ 公里 kilometer

háng 行 used with nouns that are formed in lines; line, row, queue

hù 户 used with nouns denoting households and families

huí 回 number of times

jiā 家 for families or businesses

jià 架 for machines, aircraft

jiān 间 for rooms

jiàn 件 for things, affairs, clothes or furniture

jiǎo 角 Chinese currency (0.1 **yuan** or 10 **fen**), ten cents, a dime

jié 节 a period of time

jīn 斤 *jin*, unit of weight equivalent to half a kilogram

jù 句 for sentences

kē 棵 for trees

kè 克 gram

kè 刻 quarter of an hour

kǒu 口 for members of a family

kuài 块 for things that can be broken into lumps or chunks; for money; *yuan*, dollar

lǐ 里 a Chinese unit of length, equivalent to 0.5 kilometer

lì 粒 for rice, pearls

liǎng 两 a traditional Chinese unit of weight, equivalent to 50 grams; ounce

liàng 辆 for vehicles

liè 列 for trains

máo 毛 a Chinese money unit, colloquialism for 角 **jiǎo** (= 0.1 元

yuán or 10 分 **fēn**)

mén 门 for school subjects, languages, etc.

mǐ 米 meter (colloquial)

miàn 面 for flat objects

miǎo 秒 second (of time)

míng 名 for people, especially for those with a specific position or occupation

mǔ 亩 a traditional Chinese unit of area, especially in farming (equal to $1/15$ hectare or 667 square meters)

pái 排 for things arranged in a row

pī 批 for a batch of goods, and for things/people arriving at the same time

pǐ 匹 for horses

piān 篇 for a piece of writing

piàn 片 for a thin and flat piece, slice

píng 瓶 a bottle of

qún 群 a crowd/group of

shēn 身 for clothes

shǒu 首 for songs and poems

shuāng 双 a pair of (shoes, chopsticks, etc.)

suì 岁 year (of age)

suǒ 所 for houses, or institutions housed in a building

tái 台 for machines, big instruments, etc.

tàng 趟 for trips

tào 套 a set of

tiáo 条 for things with a long, narrow shape

tóu 头 for cattle or sheep

wèi 位 a polite measure word for people

xià 下 used with certain verbs to indicate the number of times the action is done

xiàng 项 item, component

xiē 些 some, a few, a little

yè 页 for pages (of a book)

yīngchǐ 英尺 foot (as a measurement of length)

yīngcùn 英寸 inch

yuán 元 the basic unit of Chinese currency (1 元 **yuán** = 10 角 **jiǎo** /毛 **máo** = 100 分 **fēn**), dollar

zhāng 张 for paper, beds, tables, desks

zhèn 阵 for an action or event that lasts for some time

zhī 支 for stick-like things

zhī 只 for animals, utensils, or objects

zhǒng 种 kind, sort

zuò 座 for large and solid objects, such as a large building

List of Radicals

1 stroke

丶 1
一 2
乙 3
亅 4
丿 5

2 strokes

亠 6
冫 7
讠 8
 9
二 10
十 11
厂 12
匚 13
卜 14
刂 15
冖 16
冂 17
勹 18
刀 19
力 20
八 21
亻 22
人 23
儿 24
几 25
又 26
凵 27
厶 28
 29

阝 30
阝(on left) 31
阝(on right) 32

3 strokes

氵 33
忄 34
小 35
宀 36
丬 37
广 38
门 39
辶 40
工 41
干 42
土 43
士 44
上 45
艹 46
廾 47
大 48
寸 49
扌 50
口 51
囗 52
巾 53
山 54
彳 55
彡 56
夕 57
夂 58
犭 59

60
彐 61
尸 62
已 63
己 64
巳 65
弓 66
女 67
子 68
纟 69
马 70

4 strokes

灬 71
文 72
方 73
心 74
户 75
斗 76
王, 玉 77
木 78
犬 79
歹 80
瓦 81
车 82
比 83
日 84
曰 85
贝 86
见 87
父 88
攵 89

牛 90
手 91
毛 92
气 93
片 94
斤 95
爪 96
月 97
欠 98
风 99
殳 100
火 101
礻 102
戈 103
水 104
止 105

5 strokes

石 106
业 107
目 108
田 109
皿 110
四 111
钅 112
矢 113
禾 114
白 115
用 116
母 117
鸟 118
疒 119

立 120
穴 121
衤 122
示 123
去 124
疋 125
皮 126

6 strokes

老 127
耳 128
西 129
页 130
虫 131
缶 132
舌 133
竹 134
自 135
舟 136
衣 137
亦 138
羊 139
米 140
耒 141
艮 142
羽 143
糸 144

7 strokes

走 145
里 146
足 147

身 148
豸 149
角 150
言 151
辛 152
束 153
非 154
酉 155
豆 156

8 strokes

佳 157
青 158
鱼 159
雨 160
齿 161

9 strokes

革 162
是 163
食 164
音 165

10 strokes

鬼 166

11 strokes

麻 167

12 strokes

黑 168

Radical Index

All characters are listed here under their radical plus the number of additional strokes needed to write them.

1 丶

1–5 strokes

半	bàn
为	wéi/wèi
义	yì
永	yǒng
之	zhī
主	zhǔ

6–11 strokes

登	dēng
举	jǔ

2 一

1–3 strokes

一	yī/yí/yì
不	bú/bù
才	cái
长	cháng/zhǎng
丰	fēng
互	hù
开	kāi
亏	kuī
了	le/liǎo
七	qī
三	sān
天	tiān
万	wàn
无	wú
五	wǔ
下	xià
牙	yá
尤	yóu
于	yú
与	yǔ
丈	zhàng
专	zhuān

4–6 strokes

东	dōng
而	ér
更	gèng
击	jī
夹	jiā
来	lái
丽	lì
两	liǎng
龙	lóng
平	píng
求	qiú
世	shì
亚	yà
严	yán
再	zài
至	zhì

7–12 strokes

表	biǎo
哥	gē
面	miàn
丧	sāng
甚	shèn
事	shì
肃	sù
昼	zhòu

3 乙

乙	yǐ

1–7 strokes

承	chéng
丑	chǒu
飞	fēi
买	mǎi
民	mín

4 丨

3–6 strokes

旧	jiù
且	qiě
申	shēn
师	shī
史	shǐ
中	zhōng

7–12 strokes

鉴	jiàn
临	lín

5 丿

1–5 strokes

长	cháng
川	chuān
乏	fá
瓜	guā
乎	hū
及	jí
九	jiǔ
久	jiǔ
乐	lè/yuè
年	nián
农	nóng
升	shēng
生	shēng
失	shī
书	shū
丸	wán
习	xí
乡	xiāng
向	xiàng
血	xiě/xuè
也	yě

6–13 strokes

囱	cōng
乖	guāi
乳	rǔ
鼠	shǔ
舞	wǔ

6 亠

1–7 strokes

哀	āi
变	biàn
产	chǎn
充	chōng
交	jiāo
京	jīng
亮	liàng
六	liù
亩	mǔ
市	shì
亭	tíng
亡	wáng
享	xiǎng
夜	yè
亦	yì

8–15 strokes

帝	dì
高	gāo
豪	háo
就	jiù
离	lí
率	lǜ
商	shāng
赢	yíng

7 冫

冰	bīng
冲	chōng
次	cì
凑	còu
冻	dòng
减	jiǎn
净	jìng
决	jué
冷	lěng
凉	liáng
凝	níng
捎	shāo
准	zhǔn

8 讠

2–6 strokes

诚	chéng
词	cí
诞	dàn
订	dìng
讽	fěng
该	gāi
话	huà
计	jì
记	jì
讲	jiǎng
论	lùn
评	píng
让	ràng
认	rèn
设	shè
诗	shī
识	shí
试	shì
诉	sù
讨	tǎo
详	xiáng
许	xǔ
询	xún
训	xùn
议	yì
译	yì
诈	zhà
诊	zhěn
证	zhèng

7–12 strokes

调	diào/tiáo
谍	dié
读	dú
谎	huǎng
谨	jǐn
课	kè
谜	mí
谬	miù
谋	móu
谦	qiān
请	qǐng
谁	shéi/shuí
说	shuō
诵	sòng
谈	tán
谓	wèi
误	wù
谢	xiè
语	yǔ
谊	yì

9 二

二	èr
互	hù

10 十

十	shí

1–11 strokes

毕	bì
博	bó
华	huá
克	kè
卖	mài
南	nán
千	qiān
升	shēng
午	wǔ
协	xié
罩	zhào
真	zhēn
支	zhī
直	zhí

11 厂

厂	chǎng

2–10 strokes

厕	cè
厨	chú
盾	dùn
后	hòu
厚	hòu
厘	lí
历	lì
厉	lì
厅	tīng
压	yā
原	yuán

12 匚

巨	jù
匹	pǐ
区	qū
卧	wò
医	yī

13 匕

北	běi
些	xiē

14 卜

卡	kǎ
上	shàng
占	zhàn

15 刂

3–5 strokes

别	bié
创	chuàng
刚	gāng
划	huá/huà
利	lì
列	liè
判	pàn
删	shān
刑	xíng
则	zé

6–10 strokes

刺	cì
到	dào
刮	guā
剂	jì
剧	jù
刻	kè
剖	pōu
剩	shèng
刷	shuā
削	xuē
制	zhì

16 冖

冠	guàn
军	jūn
写	xiě

17 冂

册	cè
内	nèi
肉	ròu
同	tóng
网	wǎng

周	zhōu

18 勹

匆	cōng
句	jù
勺	sháo
勿	wù

19 刀

刀	dāo

2–6 strokes

矛	máo
切	qiē/qiè
色	sè
兔	tù
危	wēi
召	zhào
争	zhēng

7–13 strokes

象	xiàng
豫	yù

20 力

力	lì

2–5 strokes

办	bàn
动	dòng
加	jiā
劲	jìn
励	lì
劣	liè
男	nán
努	nǔ
劝	quàn
务	wù
助	zhù

6–11 strokes

舅	jiù
勉	miǎn
勤	qín
勇	yǒng

21 八

八	bā

2–5 strokes

兵	bīng
并	bìng
弟	dì
兑	duì
分	fēn
公	gōng
共	gòng
谷	gǔ
关	guān
兰	lán
兴	xīng/xìng

6–13 strokes

曾	céng
单	dān
兼	jiān
具	jù
其	qí
前	qián
首	shǒu
兽	shòu

22 亻

1–5 strokes

伴	bàn
保	bǎo
伯	bó
传	chuán
伺	cì
代	dài
但	dàn
低	dī
份	fèn
佛	fó
伏	fú
估	gū
何	hé
化	huà
伙	huǒ

价	jià
件	jiàn
仅	jǐn
们	men
你	nǐ
仁	rén
任	rèn
仍	réng
伤	shāng
伸	shēn
什	shén
似	shì/sì
他	tā
体	tǐ
伟	wěi
位	wèi
仙	xiān
休	xiū
仪	yí
亿	yì
佣	yōng
优	yōu
仗	zhàng
住	zhù
仔	zǐ
作	zuò

6–9 strokes

便	biàn/pián
倍	bèi
促	cù
倒	dǎo/dào
俄	é
供	gōng
候	hòu
佳	jiā
假	jiǎ/jià
俭	jiǎn
健	jiàn
借	jiè
俱	jù
倦	juàn

倔	jué
俊	jùn
例	lì
俩	liǎ
侣	lǚ
偶	ǒu
佩	pèi
偏	piān
侨	qiáo
侵	qīn
使	shǐ
停	tíng
偷	tōu
信	xìn
修	xiū
依	yī
债	zhài
侦	zhēn
值	zhí
侄	zhí
做	zuò

10–14 strokes

傲	ào
傍	bàng
储	chǔ
傅	fù
僻	pì
儒	rǔ
傻	shǎ
像	xiàng

23 人

人	rén
入	rù

1–10 strokes

从	cóng
个	gè
会	huì/kuài
介	jiè
今	jīn
金	jīn

令	lìng			阻	zǔ	泳	yǒng
命	mìng	**27 凵**		**7–11 strokes**		油	yóu
禽	qín	出	chū	隘	ài	汁	zhī
伞	sǎn	画	huà	除	chú	治	zhì
舍	shè/shě			隔	gé	注	zhù
以	yǐ	**28 厶**		陪	péi	**6–8 strokes**	
众	zhòng	参	cān	随	suí	测	cè
		么	me	陶	táo	淡	dàn
24 儿		能	néng	险	xiǎn	洞	dòng
儿	ér	台	tái	陷	xiàn	浮	fú
光	guāng	县	xiàn	院	yuàn	海	hǎi
先	xiān	云	yún			洪	hóng
兄	xiōng	允	yǔn	**32 阝 (on right)**		混	hùn
元	yuán			部	bù	活	huó
		29 廴		都	dōu/dū	济	jì
25 几		建	jiàn	邻	lín	渐	jiàn
虎	hǔ	延	yán	那	nà/nèi	浇	jiāo
几	jǐ/jǐ			邮	yóu	洁	jié
凭	píng	**30 卩**				酒	jiǔ
秃	tū	即	jí	**33 氵**		浪	làng
		却	què	**2–5 strokes**		浏	liú
26 又		危	wēi	波	bō	流	liú
又	yòu	卫	wèi	沉	chén	浓	nóng
1–12 strokes		卸	xiè	池	chí	派	pài
叉	chā	印	yìn	法	fǎ	清	qīng
叠	dié			沟	gōu	洒	sǎ
对	duì	**31 阝 (on left)**		汉	Hàn	涉	shè
发	fā	**2–6 strokes**		河	hé	深	shēn
反	fǎn	阿	ā	汇	huì	淘	táo
艰	jiān	陈	chén	江	jiāng	添	tiān
聚	jù	队	duì	泪	lèi	涂	tú
难	nán	防	fáng	没	méi	洗	xǐ
叛	pàn	附	fù	沐	mù	消	xiāo
敲	qiāo	际	jì	泥	ní	洋	yáng
圣	shèng	降	jiàng	泊	pō	涌	yǒng
受	shòu	阶	jiē	泼	pō	渔	yú
叔	shū	陆	lù	汽	qì	浴	yù
双	shuāng	陌	mò	浅	qiǎn	涨	zhǎng
叙	xù	限	xiàn	沙	shā	洲	zhōu
友	yǒu	阳	yáng	汤	tāng	**9–10 strokes**	
		阴	yīn	污	wū	滨	bīn
		阵	zhèn				

滚	gǔn	惜	xī
湖	hú	性	xìng
滑	huá	忆	yì
渴	kě	忧	yōu
滤	lǜ	**9–13 strokes**	
满	mǎn	懂	dǒng
漠	mò	憾	hàn
湿	shī	慌	huāng
湾	wān	愧	kuì
温	wēn	懒	lǎn
游	yóu	慢	màn
滋	zī	愉	yú
11–17 strokes			
澳	ào	**35 小**	
潮	cháo	小	xiǎo
滴	dī	**1–7 strokes**	
灌	guàn	尝	cháng
激	jī	常	cháng
漏	lòu	尘	chén
漂	piào	当	dāng/dàng
演	yǎn	党	dǎng
澡	zǎo	恭	gōng
		辉	huī
34 忄		慕	mù
1–8 strokes		杀	shā
惭	cán	少	shǎo/shào
怪	guài	余	yú
惯	guàn		
恨	hèn	**36 宀**	
怀	huái	**2–5 strokes**	
恢	huī	安	ān
惊	jīng	宝	bǎo
惧	jù	定	dìng
快	kuài	官	guān
怜	lián	牢	láo
忙	máng	宁	níng/nìng
怕	pà	实	shí
恰	qià	守	shǒu
悄	qiāo	它	tā
情	qíng	完	wán
惋	wǎn		

灾	zāi	庞	páng	这	zhè/zhèi			声	shēng	薪	xīn

灾	zāi	庞	páng	这	zhè/zhèi

灾 zāi
宅 zhái
宗 zōng
6–11 strokes
宾 bīn
察 chá
宫 gōng
富 fù
害 hài
寒 hán
寂 jì
寄 jì
家 jiā
客 kè
宽 kuān
容 róng
塞 sāi
赛 sài
室 shì
宿 sù
宣 xuān
宴 yàn

37 爿
将 jiāng
状 zhuàng

38 广
广 guǎng
3–11 strokes
床 chuáng
底 dǐ
店 diàn
度 dù
府 fǔ
腐 fǔ
废 fèi
康 kāng
库 kù
廉 lián
庙 miào

庞 páng
庆 qìng
庭 tíng
席 xí
应 yìng/yīng
庸 yōng
座 zuò

39 门
门 mén
2–10 strokes
闭 bì
间 jiān
阔 kuò
闷 mēn
闹 nào
闪 shǎn
闻 wén
问 wèn
闲 xián
阅 yuè

40 辶
2–5 strokes
边 biān
迟 chí
达 dá
返 fǎn
过 guò
还 hái/huán
近 jìn
进 jìn
连 lián
迫 pò
述 shù
违 wéi
巡 xún
迅 xùn
迎 yíng
远 yuàn
运 yùn

这 zhè/zhèi
6–9 strokes
遍 biàn
逮 dài
道 dào
递 dì
逛 guàng
逻 luó
迷 mí
适 shì
逝 shì
送 sòng
速 sù
逃 táo
通 tōng
透 tòu
途 tú
退 tuì
选 xuǎn
造 zào
逐 zhú
追 zhuī
10–13 strokes
避 bì
邀 yāo
遥 yáo
遗 yí
遇 yù
遭 zāo
遵 zūn

41 工
工 gōng
功 gōng
攻 gōng
巩 gǒng
巧 qiǎo
项 xiàng
左 zuǒ

42 干
干 gān/gàn
旱 hàn

43 土
土 tǔ
1–7 strokes
场 chǎng
城 chéng
地 de/dì
坏 huài
圾 jī
坚 jiān
均 jūn
块 kuài
垄 lǒng
寺 sì
坛 tán
坦 tǎn
型 xíng
幸 xìng
在 zài
址 zhǐ
坐 zuò
8–17 strokes
壁 bì
堵 dǔ
基 jī
培 péi
墙 qiáng
壤 rǎng
塑 sù
堂 táng
填 tián
增 zēng

44 士
鼓 gǔ
壶 hú
嘉 jiā
壳 ké/qiào

声 shēng
喜 xǐ

45 上
上 shàng

46 艹
1–7 strokes
草 cǎo
茶 chá
范 fàn
花 huā
荒 huāng
荤 hūn
获 huò
荐 jiàn
节 jié
茎 jīng
苦 kǔ
劳 láo
茂 mào
苗 miáo
芽 yá
药 yào
艺 yì
荧 yíng
8–15 strokes
蔼 ǎi
薄 báo
菜 cài
藏 cáng
葱 cōng
黄 huáng
蕉 jiāo
菌 jūn
蓝 lán
萝 luó
落 luò
蒙 mēng
苹 píng
蔬 shū

薪 xīn
营 yíng
蕴 yùn
著 zhù

47 廾
弄 nòng
弃 qì

48 大
奥 ào
大 dà
奋 fèn
夫 fū
奖 jiǎng
夸 kuā
类 lèi
奇 qí
太 tài
套 tào
天 tiān
头 tóu
奏 zòu

49 寸
寸 cùn
夺 duó
封 fēng
耐 nài
辱 rǔ
寿 shòu
寻 xún
尊 zūn

50 扌
1–5 strokes
拔 bá
把 bǎ
扮 bàn
抱 bào
报 bào

拆 chāi	措 cuò	摊 tān	吓 xià
抄 chāo	挡 dǎng	提 tí	呀 yā/ya
抽 chōu	掉 diào	握 wò	叶 yè
打 dǎ	挂 guà	摇 yáo	右 yòu
担 dān	换 huàn	援 yuán	只 zhī/zhǐ
抖 dǒu	挤 jǐ	摘 zhāi	**6–8 strokes**
扶 fú	捡 jiǎn	撞 zhuàng	唉 āi
拐 guǎi	接 jiē		唱 chàng
护 hù	捷 jié	**51 口**	哈 hā
技 jì	据 jù		咳 ké
拒 jù	捐 juān	口 kǒu	哪 nǎ
扩 kuò	控 kòng	**2–5 strokes**	嗯 ng
拉 lā	掠 lüè	啊 ā	品 pǐn
拦 lán	描 miáo	哎 āi	啤 pí
抹 mǒ	挠 náo	吧 ba	售 shòu
拧 níng	排 pái	吵 chǎo	唾 tuò
拍 pāi	拼 pīn	吃 chī	唯 wéi
披 pī	损 sǔn	吹 chuī	响 xiǎng
批 pī	掏 tāo	否 fǒu	哑 yǎ
抢 qiǎng	挑 tiāo/tiǎo	咐 fù	咽 yàn
扔 rēng	挺 tǐng	告 gào	咬 yǎo
揉 róu	推 tuī	古 gǔ	咱 zán
扫 sǎo	振 zhèn	含 hán	哲 zhé
抬 tái	挣 zhèng	号 hào	咨 zī
投 tóu	指 zhǐ	合 hé	**9–17 strokes**
推 tuī	捉 zhuō	呼 hū	喊 hǎn
托 tuō	**9–16 strokes**	吉 jí	喝 hē
拖 tuō	搬 bān	叫 jiào	嚼 jiáo/jué
押 yā	摆 bǎi	可 kě	噢 ō
扬 yáng	播 bō	另 lìng	喷 pēn
抑 yì	擦 cā	吗 ma	嗓 sǎng
拥 yōng	操 cāo	名 míng	善 shàn
择 zé	插 chā	呢 ne	嗽 sòu
招 zhāo	搞 gǎo	呕 ǒu	喂 wèi
找 zhǎo	揭 jiē	呻 shēn	喧 xuān
挣 zhèng	撇 piē	司 sī	噪 zào
执 zhí	撒 sā	听 tīng	嘱 zhǔ
抓 zhuā	摄 shè	吐 tǔ/tù	嘴 zuǐ
6–8 strokes	摔 shuāi	吞 tūn	
按 àn	撕 sī	味 wèi	**52 囗**
持 chí	搜 sōu	吻 wěn	固 gù

国 guó	律 lù	
回 huí	徒 tú	
困 kùn	往 wǎng	
圈 quān	微 wēi	
图 tú	征 zhēng	
团 tuán		
围 wéi	**56 彡**	
因 yīn	彩 cǎi	
园 yuán	形 xíng	
圆 yuán	影 yǐng	

53 巾	**57 夕**
巾 jīn	**2–8 strokes**
1–12 strokes	多 duō
帮 bāng	够 gòu
布 bù	梦 mèng
带 dài	外 wài
帆 fān	
幅 fú	**58 夂**
帽 mào	备 bèi
帖 tiě	处 chǔ/chù
希 xī	冬 dōng
	复 fù
54 山	各 gè
山 shān	麦 mài
3–8 strokes	条 tiáo
岸 àn	夏 xià
岛 dǎo	
密 mì	**59 犭**
岁 suì	**2–6 strokes**
幽 yōu	独 dú
屿 yǔ	犯 fàn
岳 yuè	狗 gǒu
	狠 hěn
55 彳	狡 jiǎo
待 dāi/dài	狂 kuáng
德 dé	狮 shī
得 dé/děi/de	犹 yóu
行 háng/xíng	狱 yù
很 hěn	**7–9 strokes**
街 jiē	猜 cāi

猴	hóu			姿	zī	缓	huǎn	患	huàn

猴 hóu

65 已

包 bāo
导 dǎo
异 yì

66 弓

弹 dàn/tán
疆 jiāng
强 qiáng
弱 ruò
弯 wān
引 yǐn
张 zhāng
粥 zhōu

67 女

女 nǚ
2–5 strokes
妒 dù
妇 fù
姑 gū
好 hào/ hǎo
姐 jiě
妈 mā
妹 mèi
妙 miào
奶 nǎi
妻 qī
如 rú
始 shǐ
她 tā
姓 xìng
姻 yīn
6–11 strokes
婚 hūn
嫁 jià
媒 méi
嫩 nèn
娘 niáng
娶 qǔ
娱 yú

姿 zī

68 子

子 zǐ/zi
1–6 strokes
存 cún
孤 gū
孩 hái
孙 sūn
孝 xiào
学 xué
孕 yùn
字 zì

69 纟

1–5 strokes
纯 chún
纺 fǎng
纷 fēn
红 hóng
幻 huàn
级 jí
纪 jì
经 jīng
练 liàn
纳 nà
绍 shào
绅 shēn
丝 sī
纹 wén
细 xì
线 xiàn
幼 yòu
约 yuē
织 zhī
纸 zhǐ
终 zhōng
组 zǔ
6–9 strokes
编 biān
给 gěi

缓 huǎn
继 jì
绩 jì
结 jiē/jié
绝 jué
绿 lǜ
绕 rào
绒 róng
绳 shéng
统 tǒng
维 wéi
绪 xù
续 xù
综 zōng
10–13 strokes
缠 chán
缝 fèng
缚 fù
缩 suō

70 马

马 mǎ
3–11 strokes
驳 bó
驾 jià
骄 jiāo
骂 mà
骗 piàn
骑 qí
驱 qū

71 灬

点 diǎn
烈 liè
然 rán
热 rè
熟 shú
熊 xióng
熏 xūn
照 zhào
煮 zhǔ

72 文

文 wén

73 方

方 fāng
4–10 strokes
放 fàng
旅 lǚ
旁 páng
旗 qí
施 shī
族 zú

74 心

心 xīn
1–6 strokes
必 bì
恶 è
恩 ēn
忽 hū
急 jí
忌 jì
恳 kěn
恐 kǒng
恋 liàn
虑 lù
念 niàn
忍 rěn
恕 shù
思 sī
态 tài
忘 wàng
息 xī
要 yào
怨 yuàn
志 zhì
总 zǒng
7–11 strokes
悲 bēi
愁 chóu
感 gǎn

患 huàn
惠 huì
慧 huì
惑 huò
您 nín
慰 wèi
悉 xī
想 xiǎng
意 yì
悠 yōu
愿 yuàn

75 户

户 hù
3–8 strokes
扁 biǎn
房 fáng
启 qǐ
扇 shàn

76 斗

斗 dòu
斜 xié

77 王, 玉

王 wáng
1–8 strokes
斑 bān
班 bān
玻 bō
环 huán
理 lǐ
琴 qín
球 qiú
全 quán
现 xiàn
玉 yù
珍 zhēn
琢 zuó

狼 láng
猎 liè
猫 māo
猪 zhū

60 饣

饱 bǎo
饼 bǐng
饿 è
馆 guǎn
饭 fàn
饺 jiǎo
馒 mán
饮 yǐn

61 彐

归 guī
录 lù

62 尸

1–5 strokes
层 céng
尺 chǐ
届 jiè
尽 jìn/jǐn
居 jū
局 jú
屁 pì
尾 wěi
6–12 strokes
履 lǚ
属 shǔ
屋 wū
展 zhǎn

63 已

已 yǐ

64 己

己 jǐ

78 木

木　mù

1–4 strokes

板　bǎn
杯　bēi
本　běn
材　cái
村　cūn
朵　duǒ
杆　gān/gǎn
构　gòu
柜　guì
果　guǒ
机　jī
极　jí
李　lǐ
林　lín
末　mò
枪　qiāng
权　quán
松　sōng
术　shù
未　wèi
杂　zá
枕　zhěn
枝　zhī

5–7 strokes

标　biāo
查　chá
格　gé
根　gēn
核　hé
架　jià
检　jiǎn
枯　kū
梨　lí
梁　liáng
某　mǒu
柔　róu
桥　qiáo
桑　sāng

柿　shì
树　shù
梯　tī
桶　tǒng
校　xiào
相　xiāng
械　xiè
样　yàng
柱　zhù

8–12 strokes

棒　bàng
概　gài
集　jí
椒　jiāo
橘　jú
棵　kē
楼　lóu
棉　mián
模　mó/mú
森　sēn
橡　xiàng
椅　yǐ
榨　zhà
植　zhí

79 犬

哭　kū
献　xiàn

80 歹

殊　shū
死　sǐ
殖　zhí

81 瓦

瓶　píng
瓦　wǎ

82 车

车　chē

2–10 strokes

辈　bèi
辅　fǔ
轨　guǐ
轰　hōng
辆　liàng
轮　lún
轻　qīng
输　shū
转　zhuǎn

83 比

比　bǐ

84 日

晋　jìn
昆　kūn
量　liáng/
　　liàng
冒　mào
普　pǔ
曲　qǔ
易　yì
暂　zàn
者　zhě
智　zhì
最　zuì

85 日

日　rì

1–5 strokes

春　chūn
旦　dàn
昏　hūn
旷　kuàng
明　míng
时　shí
旺　wàng
星　xīng
映　yìng
早　zǎo

昨　zuó

6–11 strokes

暗　àn
晨　chén
景　jǐng
晾　liàng
暖　nuǎn
晴　qíng
晒　shài
暑　shǔ
替　tì
晚　wǎn
晓　xiǎo
晕　yūn

86 贝

贝　bèi

2–6 strokes

败　bài
财　cái
贷　dài
贩　fàn
费　fèi
负　fù
购　gòu
贵　guì
贺　hè
货　huò
贸　mào
贫　pín
贪　tān
贴　tiē
员　yuán
责　zé
账　zhàng
质　zhì

7–12 strokes

赔　péi
赏　shǎng
赞　zàn
赠　zèng

赚　zhuàn
资　zī

87 见

观　guān
规　guī
见　jiàn
觉　jué
览　lǎn

88 父

爸　bà
父　fù
爷　yé

89 攵

2–6 strokes

改　gǎi
故　gù
收　shōu
效　xiào
政　zhèng
致　zhì

7–11 strokes

敷　fū
敢　gǎn
教　jiāo/jiào
敬　jìng
救　jiù
敏　mǐng
散　sàn
数　shǔ/shù

90 牛

牧　mù
牛　niú
特　tè
物　wù

91 手

拜　bài

摩　mó
拿　ná
攀　pān
手　shǒu
掌　zhǎng

92 毛

毫　háo
毛　máo
毯　tǎn

93 气

气　qì
氢　qīng

94 片

版　bǎn
牌　pái
片　piàn

95 斤

断　duàn
斤　jīn
所　suǒ
欣　xīn
新　xīn

96 爪

爱　ài
采　cǎi
爬　pá

97 月

月　yuè

2–5 strokes

背　bēi/bèi
肠　cháng
胆　dǎn
肚　dù
肥　féi

肺	fèi	期	qī	煤	méi	企	qǐ	眠	mián

肺 fèi
肤 fū
服 fú
肝 gān
骨 gǔ
股 gǔ
胡 hú
肌 jī
肩 jiān
肯 kěn
胖 pàng
朋 péng
胜 shèng
胎 tāi
胃 wèi
有 yǒu
育 yù
胀 zhàng
肿 zhǒng
6–7 strokes
脖 bó
脆 cuì
胳 gē
胶 jiāo
脚 jiǎo
朗 lǎng
脸 liǎn
脑 nǎo
脱 tuō
望 wàng
胸 xiōng
脏 zāng/zàng
8–13 strokes
臂 bì
膊 bó
朝 cháo/zhāo
腹 fù
膏 gāo
腻 nì
膨 péng
脾 pí

期 qī
腔 qiāng
腮 sāi
腿 tuǐ
腥 xīng
腰 yāo
98 欠
欠 qiàn
2–10 strokes
歌 gē
欢 huān
欧 ōu
欺 qī
歉 qiàn
软 ruǎn
歇 xiē
欲 yù
99 风
风 fēng
100 殳
段 duàn
殴 ōu
毅 yì
101 火
火 huǒ
2–5 strokes
炒 chǎo
灯 dēng
灰 huī
灸 jiǔ
烂 làn
炼 liàn
灭 miè
炮 pào
炸 zhà
6–14 strokes
烤 kǎo

煤 méi
燃 rán
烧 shāo
烫 tàng
烟 yān
燥 zào
102 衤
福 fú
祸 huò
礼 lǐ
社 shè
神 shén
视 shì
祝 zhù
祖 zǔ
103 戈
裁 cái
成 chéng
戴 dài
或 huò
戒 jiè
戚 qī
式 shì
威 wēi
我 wǒ
戏 xì
咸 xián
战 zhàn
104 水
泉 quán
水 shuǐ
泰 tài
105 止
止 zhǐ
1–11 strokes
步 bù
此 cǐ

企 qǐ
歪 wāi
武 wǔ
整 zhěng
正 zhèng
106 石
石 shí
3–6 strokes
础 chǔ
硅 guī
矿 kuàng
码 mǎ
破 pò
硕 shuò
研 yán
砖 zhuān
7–11 strokes
碍 ài
碧 bì
磁 cí
碟 dié
磨 mó
碰 pèng
确 què
碎 suì
碳 tàn
碗 wǎn
硬 yìng
107 业
显 xiǎn
虚 xū
业 yè
108 目
目 mù
1–7 strokes
看 kàn
盲 máng
眉 méi

眠 mián
盼 pàn
省 shěng
睡 shuì
眼 yǎn
睁 zhēng
8–13 strokes
睹 dǔ
睛 jīng
瞒 mán
瞧 qiáo
瞎 xiā
瞻 zhān
109 田
畜 chù
电 diàn
甲 jiǎ
界 jiè
留 liú
略 lüè
田 tián
由 yóu
畜 xù
110 皿
盖 gài
盒 hé
盘 pán
盆 pén
盛 shèng
盐 yán
益 yì
111 罒
罚 fá
四 sì
置 zhì

112 钅
1–5 strokes
钓 diào
钉 dīng
钢 gāng
钩 gōu
铃 líng
铅 qiān
钱 qián
铁 tiě
钥 yào
针 zhēn
钟 zhōng
6–17 strokes
错 cuò
锻 duàn
锋 fēng
锅 guō
键 jiàn
镜 jìng
锐 ruì
锁 suǒ
铜 tóng
销 xiāo
银 yín
镇 zhèn
铸 zhù
113 矢
矮 ǎi
短 duǎn
知 zhī
114 禾
税 shuì
2–6 strokes
称 chèn/chēng/chéng
乘 chéng
和 hé
积 jī

季 jì
科 kē
秘 mì
秒 miǎo
秋 qiū
私 sī
香 xiāng
秀 xiù
秩 zhì
种 zhǒng/zhòng
租 zū

7-10 strokes
程 chéng
稻 dào
稿 gǎo
稼 jià
稍 shāo
税 shuì
稳 wěn
稀 xī
移 yí

115 白
白 bái
百 bǎi
的 de
皂 zào

116 用
甩 shuǎi
用 yòng

117 母
毒 dú
每 měi
母 mǔ

118 鸟
鹅 é
鸡 jī

鸟 niǎo
鸦 yā
鸭 yā

119 疒
2-5 strokes
病 bìng
灯 dēng
疯 fēng
疾 jí
疗 liáo
疲 pí
疼 téng
症 zhèng

6-12 strokes
癌 ái
瘤 liú
瘦 shòu
痛 tòng
痒 yǎng

120 立
立 lì
4-9 strokes
竭 jié
竞 jìng
竟 jìng
亲 qīn
童 tóng
站 zhàn

121 穴
穿 chuān
窗 chuāng
究 jiū
空 kōng/kòng
帘 lián
窃 qiè
穷 qióng
突 tū

窄 zhǎi

122 衤
被 bèi
补 bǔ
衬 chèn
初 chū
袱 fú
裤 kù
袍 páo
裙 qún
衫 shān
袜 wà
袖 xiù

123 示
禁 jìn
票 piào
示 shì

124 去
丢 diū
去 qù

125 疋
楚 chǔ
疑 yí

126 皮
皮 pí

127 老
考 kǎo
老 lǎo

128 耳
聪 cōng
耽 dān
耳 ěr
联 lián

聊 liáo
聘 pìn
取 qǔ
职 zhí

129 西
西 xī

130 页
页 yè
2-5 strokes
颁 bān
顶 dǐng
顿 dùn
顾 gù
颈 jǐng
领 lǐng
顺 shùn
颂 sòng
须 xū
预 yù

7-13 strokes
额 é
颗 kē
颜 yán

131 虫
虫 chóng
3-6 strokes
蛋 dàn
虹 hóng
蚂 mǎ
蛮 mán
蛇 shé
虽 suī
蛙 wā
蚊 wén

7-15 strokes
蝶 dié
蜂 fēng
蝴 hú

蜡 là
蜜 mì
蝇 yíng

132 缶
罐 guàn
缺 quē

133 舌
辞 cí
敌 dí
乱 luàn
舌 shé
舒 shū
甜 tián

134 竹
竹 zhú
4-6 strokes
笨 bèn
笔 bǐ
策 cè
答 dā/dá
等 děng
第 dì
符 fú
筋 jīn
笼 lóng
笑 xiào
筑 zhù

7-14 strokes
管 guǎn
籍 jí
简 jiǎn
筷 kuài
篮 lán
篇 piān
签 qiān
算 suàn
箱 xiāng

135 自
鼻 bí
臭 chòu
自 zì

136 舟
舱 cāng
船 chuán
航 háng
艇 tǐng

137 衣
袋 dài
裹 guǒ
衣 yī
装 zhuāng

138 亦
赤 chì

139 羊
差 chā/chà/chāi
美 měi
群 qún
羡 xiàn
羊 yáng
养 yǎng
着 zháo/zhe

140 米
粗 cū
粉 fěn
糕 gāo
糊 hú
精 jīng
米 mǐ
粮 liáng
料 liào
糖 táng

糟 zāo	赶 gǎn	躬 gōng	**154 非**	**159 鱼**	**163 是**
	起 qǐ	射 shè	非 fēi	鲜 xiān	是 shì
141 耒	趣 qù	身 shēn	靠 kào	鱼 yú	匙 shi
耕 gēng	趟 tàng	躺 tǎng			题 tí
	越 yuè		**155 酉**	**160 雨**	
142 艮	走 zǒu	**149 豸**	酱 jiàng	雹 báo	**164 食**
既 jì		貌 mào	酷 kù	雷 léi	餐 cān
良 liáng	**146 里**		酿 niàng	零 líng	食 shí
	重 chóng/	**150 角**	配 pèi	露 lù	
143 羽	zhòng	触 chù	酸 suān	霉 méi	**165 音**
翅 chì	里 lǐ	角 jiǎo/jué	醒 xǐng	霜 shuāng	音 yīn
翻 fān	野 yě	解 jiě	醉 zuì	雾 wù	
羽 yǔ				需 xū	**166 鬼**
	147 足	**151 言**	**156 豆**	雪 xuě	鬼 guǐ
144 糸	跌 diē	警 jǐng	豆 dòu	雨 yǔ	魅 mèi
繁 fán	蹲 dūn	言 yán		震 zhèn	
系 jì/xì	跟 gēn		**157 隹**		**167 麻**
紧 jǐn	距 jù	**152 辛**	焦 jiāo	**161 齿**	麻 má
累 lèi	路 lù	辨 biàn	雄 xióng	齿 chǐ	
索 suǒ	跑 pǎo	辩 biàn	雅 yǎ	龄 líng	**168 黑**
紫 zǐ	踢 tī	辣 là			黑 hēi
	跳 tiào	辛 xīn	**158 青**	**162 革**	墨 mò
145 走	跃 yuè		静 jìng	鞭 biān	默 mò
超 chāo	足 zú	**153 赖**	青 qīng	革 gé	
趁 chèn		赖 lài		鞋 xié	
赴 fù	**148 身**				
	躲 duǒ				

Stroke Index

This index lists all characters in this dictionary according to the number of strokes used to write them. Characters with the same number of strokes are grouped together according to the first stroke used. These groups are listed in the following order:

1. 一 (including ╱ ╲)   4. 丶 (including ╱ ╲)
2. 丨 (including 丨 丿)   5. 乛 (including 乛 乛 乛 乛 乙 乀)
3. 丿 (including 丿 一 丁)   6. ㄴ (including ㄴ ㄴ ㄑ ㄴ ㄣ)

Within each group, characters are arranged alphabetically according to *pinyin*.

1 stroke		3 Strokes				4 Strokes					
一		**一**		勺	sháo	车	chē	长	cháng/zhǎng	仍	réng
一	yī/yí/yì	才	cái	夕	xī	丰	fēng			什	shén
乛		寸	cùn	义	yì	夫	fū	见	jiàn	升	shēng
乙	yǐ	大	dà	亿	yì	互	hù	内	nèi	手	shǒu
		干	gān/gàn	**丶**		开	kāi	日	rì	午	wǔ
2 strokes		工	gōng	广	guǎng	历	lì	少	shǎo/shào	勿	wù
一		亏	kuī	门	mén	木	mù	水	shuǐ	月	yuè
厂	chǎng	三	sān	亡	wáng	匹	pǐ	同	tóng	**丶**	
二	èr	土	tǔ	之	zhī	切	qiē/qiè	止	zhǐ	订	dìng
七	qī	万	wàn	**乛**		区	qū	中	zhōng	斗	dòu
十	shí	下	xià	叉	chā	太	tài	**丿**		方	fāng
丿		于	yú	飞	fēi	天	tiān	从	cóng	户	hù
八	bā	丈	zhàng	马	mǎ	厅	tīng	乏	fá	火	huǒ
儿	ér	**丨**		卫	wèi	瓦	wǎ	反	fǎn	计	jì
几	jǐ/jī	巾	jīn	习	xí	王	wáng	分	fèn	六	liù
九	jiǔ	口	kǒu	也	yě	无	wú	风	fēng	认	rèn
人	rén	上	shàng	已	yǐ	五	wǔ	父	fù	为	wéi/wèi
入	rù	小	xiǎo	子	zǐ/zi	牙	yá	公	gōng	文	wén
乛		**丿**		**ㄴ**		艺	yì	化	huà	心	xīn
刀	dāo	川	chuān	女	nǚ	尤	yóu	介	jiè	忆	yì
己	jǐ	凡	fán	山	shān	友	yǒu	今	jīn	**乛**	
了	le/liǎo	个	gè	乡	xiāng	元	yuán	斤	jīn	办	bàn
力	lì	及	jí			云	yún	仅	jǐn	尺	chǐ
又	yòu	久	jiǔ	**4 Strokes**		支	zhī	牛	niú	丑	chǒu
		么	me	**一**		专	zhuān	片	piàn	队	duì
		千	qiān	不	bú/bù	**丨**		气	qì	劝	quàn
						贝	bèi	欠	qiàn	书	shū

双 shuāng
引 yǐn

乚
比 bǐ
幻 huàn
以 yǐ
与 yǔ
允 yǔn

5 Strokes

一
本 bēn
布 bù
打 dǎ
东 dōng
功 gōng
古 gǔ
击 jī
节 jié
可 kě
龙 lóng
灭 miè
末 mò
平 píng
巧 qiǎo
去 qù
扔 rēng
石 shí
示 shì
世 shì
术 shù
未 wèi
右 yòu
玉 yù
正 zhèng
左 zuǒ

丨
北 běi
旦 dàn
电 diàn
归 guī
号 hào
甲 jiǎ
叫 jiào
旧 jiù
卡 kǎ
另 lìng
目 mù
且 qiě
申 shēn
史 shǐ
帅 shuài
四 sì
田 tián
兄 xiōng
业 yè
叶 yè
由 yóu
占 zhàn
只 zhī/zhǐ

丿
白 bái
包 bāo
册 cè
处 chǔ/chù
匆 cōng
代 dài
冬 dōng
犯 fàn
付 fù
瓜 guā
乎 hū
句 jù
乐 lè/yuè
令 lìng
们 men
鸟 niǎo
生 shēng
失 shī
甩 shuǎi
他 tā
外 wài
务 wù
仙 xiān
仪 yí
印 yìn
用 yòng
孕 yùn
仗 zhàng
仔 zǐ

丶
半 bàn
必 bì
汉 hàn
汇 huì
记 jì
兰 lán
礼 lǐ
立 lì
宁 níng/nìng
让 ràng
闪 shǎn
市 shì
它 tā
讨 tǎo
头 tóu
写 xiě
训 xùn
议 yì
永 yǒng
汁 zhī
主 zhǔ

乛
边 biān
对 duì
加 jiā
矛 máo
民 mín
皮 pí
圣 shèng
司 sī
召 zhào

乚
出 chū
发 fā
母 mǔ
奶 nǎi
丝 sī
台 tái
幼 yòu

6 Strokes

一
百 bǎi
场 chǎng
成 chéng
存 cún
地 dé/dì
动 dòng
夺 duó
而 ér
耳 ěr
巩 gǒng
共 gòng
轨 guǐ
过 guò
划 huá/huà
灰 huī
机 jī
圾 jī
吉 jí
夹 jiā
考 kǎo
夸 kuā
扩 kuò
老 lǎo
列 liè
权 quán
扫 sǎo
式 shì
死 sǐ
寺 sì
托 tuō
西 xī
协 xié
刑 xíng
亚 yà
扬 yáng
页 yè
有 yǒu
再 zài
在 zài
至 zhì

丨
尘 chén
吃 chī
虫 chóng
此 cǐ
当 dāng/dàng
帆 fān
刚 gāng
光 guāng
回 huí
劣 liè
吗 ma
曲 qǔ
肉 ròu
师 shī
吐 tǔ/tù
团 tuán
网 wǎng
吸 xī
吓 xià
因 yīn
屿 yǔ
早 zǎo
则 zé
执 zhí

丿
传 chuán
创 chuàng
丢 diū
多 duō
朵 duǒ
份 fèn
伏 fú
各 gè
行 háng/xíng
合 hé
后 hòu
华 huá
会 huì/kuài
伙 huǒ
肌 jī
价 jià
件 jiàn
名 míng
年 nián
企 qǐ
全 quán
任 rèn
伞 sǎn
色 sè
杀 shā
伤 shāng
舌 shé
似 shì/sì
伟 wěi
先 xiān
向 xiàng
血 xiě/xuè
休 xiū
延 yán
爷 yé
优 yōu
杂 zá
争 zhēng
众 zhòng
舟 zhōu
竹 zhú
自 zì

丶
安 ān
闭 bì
冰 bīng
并 bìng
产 chǎn
池 chí
充 chōng

驳	bó	**8 Strokes**		妻	qī	果	guǒ	侣	lǚ	店	diàn
层	céng	一		其	qí	呼	hū	命	mìng	法	fǎ
陈	chén	拔	bá	奇	qí	虎	hǔ	牧	mù	房	fáng
迟	chí	板	bǎn	枪	qiāng	具	jù	念	niàn	放	fàng
附	fù	抱	bào	青	qīng	昆	kūn	爬	pá	废	fèi
改	gǎi	杯	bēi	取	qǔ	明	míng	佩	pèi	府	fǔ
返	fǎn	奔	bēn	软	ruǎn	呢	ne	朋	péng	该	gāi
还	hái/huán	表	biǎo	事	shì	叔	shū	贫	pín	怪	guài
鸡	jī	厕	cè	抬	tái	帖	tiě	凭	píng	官	guān
即	jí	拆	chāi	态	tài	图	tú	侨	qiáo	河	hé
际	jì	抽	chōu	坦	tǎn	旺	wàng	乳	rǔ	话	huà
忌	jì	刺	cì	拖	tuō	味	wèi	舍	shě/shè	剂	jì
进	jìn	担	dān	卧	wò	些	xiē	使	shǐ	肩	jiān
近	jìn	到	dào	武	wǔ	易	yì	受	shòu	京	jīng
局	jú	顶	dīng	现	xiàn	账	zhàng	所	suǒ	净	jìng
连	lián	范	fàn	型	xíng	丿		贪	tān	刻	kè
陆	lù	奋	fèn	幸	xìng	爸	bà	兔	tù	空	kōng/kòng
屁	pì	构	gòu	押	yā	版	bǎn	往	wǎng	泪	lèi
驱	qū	拐	guǎi	拥	yōng	饱	bǎo	物	wù	怜	lián
忍	rěn	规	guī	雨	yǔ	备	bèi	欣	xīn	帘	lián
违	wéi	柜	guì	择	zé	采	cǎi	依	yī	盲	máng
尾	wěi	轰	hōng	责	zé	待	dāi	鱼	yú	庙	miào
远	yuán	画	huà	斩	zhǎn	的	de	岳	yuè	闹	nào
运	yùn	环	huán	招	zhāo	钓	diào	胀	zhàng	泥	ní
迎	yíng	或	huò	者	zhě	肥	féi	侦	zhēn	怕	pà
张	zhāng	茎	jīng	枕	zhěn	肺	fèi	征	zhēng	庞	páng
这	zhè/zhèi	苦	kǔ	枝	zhī	肤	fū	知	zhī	泊	pō
阻	zǔ	矿	kuàng	直	zhí	服	fú	制	zhì	浅	qiǎn
乚		拉	lā	转	zhuǎn	供	gōng	质	zhì	衫	shān
纯	chún	拦	lán	丨		狗	gǒu	肿	zhǒng	诗	shī
妒	dù	林	lín	啊	ā	股	gǔ	周	zhōu	实	shí
纷	fēn	垄	lǒng	哎	āi	刮	guā	丶		视	shì
钢	gāng	轮	lún	岸	àn	乖	guāi	宝	bǎo	试	shì
妙	miào	卖	mài	败	bài	和	hé	变	biàn	详	xiáng
纳	nà	茂	mào	齿	chǐ	忽	hū	波	bō	享	xiǎng
努	nǔ	苗	miáo	贩	fàn	昏	hūn	炒	chǎo	性	xìng
纹	wén	抹	mǒ	非	fēi	货	huò	衬	chèn	学	xué
纸	zhǐ	拧	níng	附	fù	季	jì	诚	chéng	询	xún
		殴	ōu	购	gòu	佳	jiā	单	dān	夜	yè
		拍	pāi	固	gù	金	jīn	底	dǐ	泳	yǒng
		披	pī	国	guó	例	lì				

油	yóu
育	yù
治	zhì
注	zhù
宗	zōng
丶	
承	chéng
孤	gū
驾	jià
艰	jiān
建	jiàn
降	jiàng
届	jiè
居	jū
录	lù
陌	mò
迫	pò
述	shù
刷	shuā
肃	sù
限	xiàn
降	xiáng
乚	
参	cān
姑	gū
姐	jiě
经	jīng
练	liàn
妹	mèi
绍	shào
绅	shēn
始	shǐ
细	xì
姓	xìng
织	zhī
终	zhōng
组	zǔ

9 Strokes

一

按	àn
帮	bāng
标	biāo
玻	bō
草	cǎo
茶	chá
查	chá
城	chéng
持	chí
春	chūn
带	dài
毒	dú
封	fēng
赴	fù
革	gé
故	gù
挂	guà
厚	hòu
胡	hú
荤	hūn
挤	jǐ
荐	jiàn
枯	kū
厘	lí
茫	máng
面	miàn
某	mǒu
耐	nài
南	nán
挠	náo
拼	pīn
轻	qīng
甚	shèn
柿	shì
树	shù
挑	tiāo/tiǎo
挺	tǐng
歪	wāi
威	wēi

咸	xián
相	xiàng
项	xiàng
鸦	yā
研	yán
药	yào
要	yào
珍	zhēn
挣	zhèng
政	zhèng
指	zhǐ
砖	zhuān
柱	zhù
奏	zòu
丨	
背	bēi/bèi
尝	cháng
点	diǎn
罚	fá
骨	gǔ
贵	guì
哈	hā
虹	hóng
将	jiāng
奖	jiǎng
界	jiè
咳	ké
览	lǎn
临	lín
骂	mà
冒	mào
哪	nǎ
盼	pàn
品	pǐn
省	shěng
是	shì
思	sī
虽	suī
贴	tiē
胃	wèi
显	xiǎn

响	xiǎng
削	xuē
星	xīng
哑	yǎ
咽	yàn
咬	yǎo
映	yìng
战	zhàn
昨	zuó
丿	
拜	bài
保	bǎo
便	biàn/pián
饼	bǐng
重	chóng/zhòng
促	cù
待	dài
胆	dǎn
独	dú
段	duàn
盾	dùn
俄	é
复	fù
钩	gōu
鬼	guǐ
很	hěn
狠	hěn
急	jí
俭	jiǎn
狡	jiǎo
俊	jùn
看	kàn
科	kē
俩	liǎ
律	lǜ
贸	mào
勉	miǎn

秒	miǎo
胖	pàng
盆	pén
氢	qīng
秋	qiū
泉	quán
缺	quē
饶	ráo
胜	shèng
狮	shī
食	shí
顺	shùn
胎	tāi
香	xiāng
卸	xiè
信	xìn
修	xiū
须	xū
叙	xù
钥	yào
盈	yíng
狱	yù
怨	yuàn
钟	zhōng
种	zhǒng/zhòng
丶	
哀	āi
扁	biǎn
测	cè
差	chā/chà/chāi
穿	chuān
洞	dòng
度	dù
疯	fēng
宫	gōng
冠	guàn
恨	hèn
恒	héng
洪	hóng

活	huó
济	jì
浇	jiāo
洁	jié
举	jǔ
觉	jué
客	kè
烂	làn
类	lèi
炼	liàn
亮	liàng
浏	liú
美	měi
浓	nóng
派	pài
叛	pàn
炮	pào
恰	qià
前	qián
窃	qiè
亲	qīn
洒	sǎ
神	shén
施	shī
室	shì
首	shǒu
说	shuō
诵	sòng
汤	tāng
庭	tíng
亭	tíng
突	tū
弯	wān
闻	wén
误	wù
洗	xǐ
宣	xuān
炫	xuàn
洋	yáng
养	yǎng
音	yīn

语	yǔ	**10 Strokes**		样	yàng	胶	jiāo	害	hài	谊	yì	
炸	zhà	一		原	yuán	借	jiè	疾	jí	涌	yǒng	
洲	zhōu	班	bān	哲	zhé	俱	jù	家	jiā	浴	yù	
祝	zhù	翅	chì	振	zhèn	倦	juàn	兼	jiān	阅	yuè	
咨	zī	础	chǔ	真	zhēn	偏	jué	竞	jìng	窄	zhǎi	
姿	zī	耽	dān	致	zhì	狼	láng	酒	jiǔ	站	zhàn	
总	zǒng	捣	dǎo	捉	zhuō	铃	líng	烤	kǎo	涨	zhǎng	
祖	zǔ	都	dōu/dū			留	liú	课	kè	症	zhèng	
丨		顿	dùn	丨		秘	mì	宽	kuān	准	zhǔn	
除	chú	恶	è	唉	āi	拿	ná	朗	lǎng	资	zī	
费	fèi	赶	gǎn	党	dǎng	脑	nǎo	浪	làng	座	zuò	
孩	hái	哥	gē	恩	ēn	铅	qiān	离	lí	丨		
贺	hè	格	gé	紧	jǐn	钱	qián	恋	liàn	递	dì	
既	jì	根	gēn	哭	kū	射	shè	凉	liáng	逛	guàng	
架	jià	恭	gōng	虑	lù	颂	sòng	料	liào	剧	jù	
骄	jiāo	顾	gù	眠	mián	特	tè	流	liú	恳	kěn	
眉	méi	核	hé	晒	shài	铁	tiě	旅	lǚ	难	nán	
迷	mí	壶	hú	蚊	wén	徒	tú	旁	páng	陪	péi	
柔	róu	换	huàn	晓	xiǎo	涂	tú	袍	páo	弱	ruò	
适	shì	获	huò	鸭	yā	息	xī	疲	pí	桑	sāng	
送	sòng	捡	jiǎn	圆	yuán	笑	xiào	瓶	píng	逝	shì	
逃	táo	晋	jìn	晕	yūn	胸	xiōng	剖	pōu	速	sù	
退	tuì	捐	juān	丿		脏	zāng/zàng	悄	qiāo	陶	táo	
屋	wū	恐	kǒng	爱	ài	丨		请	qǐng	通	tōng	
险	xiǎn	烈	liè	颁	bān	债	zhài	容	róng	透	tòu	
选	xuǎn	配	pèi	倍	bèi	值	zhí	扇	shàn	途	tú	
勇	yǒng	破	pò	笔	bǐ	秩	zhì	烧	shāo	预	yù	
院	yuàn	起	qǐ	舱	cāng	租	zū	涉	shè	造	zào	
愿	yuàn	桥	qiáo	称	chèn/chēng	丶		谁	shéi/shuí	展	zhǎn	
昼	zhòu	热	rè		chēng	被	bèi	谈	tán	逐	zhú	
追	zhuī	辱	rǔ	乘	chéng	宾	bīn	烫	tàng	丨		
乚		丧	sāng	臭	chòu	病	bìng	疼	téng	继	jì	
给	gěi	殊	shū	脆	cuì	部	bù	袜	wà	能	néng	
结	jiē/jié	损	sǔn	倒	dǎo/dào	调	diào/	席	xí	娘	niáng	
绝	jué	索	suǒ	敌	dí		tiáo	消	xiāo	娱	yú	
绕	rào	泰	tài	饿	è	读	dú	效	xiào			
绒	róng	套	tào	胳	gē	烦	fán	袖	xiù	**11 Strokes**		
统	tǒng	桶	tǒng	躬	gōng	粉	fěn	畜	xù	一		
姻	yīn	夏	xià	航	háng	浮	fú	烟	yān	菜	cài	
幽	yōu	校	xiào	候	hòu	高	gāo	宴	yàn	盛	chéng	
		盐	yán	积	jī	海	hǎi	益	yì	措	cuò	

掉	diào	晨	chén	偶	ǒu	谜	mí	**12 Strokes**		植	zhí
堵	dǔ	患	huàn	盘	pán	密	mì	一		殖	zhí
辅	fǔ	距	jù	偏	piān	谋	móu	斑	bān	煮	zhǔ
副	fù	累	lèi	售	shòu	清	qīng	棒	bàng	琢	zuó
硅	guī	略	lüè	甜	tián	情	qíng	博	bó	丨	
黄	huáng	啤	pí	停	tíng	商	shāng	裁	cái	悲	bēi
基	jī	圈	quān	铜	tóng	深	shēn	插	chā	辈	bèi
检	jiǎn	蛇	shé	偷	tōu	兽	shòu	超	chāo	幅	fú
教	jiāo/jiào	匙	shi	脱	tuō	率	lǜ	朝	cháo/	喊	hǎn
接	jiē	堂	táng	悉	xī	宿	sù		zhāo	喝	hē
捷	jié	唾	tuò	象	xiàng	淘	táo	趁	chèn	黑	hēi
救	jiù	晚	wǎn	斜	xié	添	tiān	厨	chú	辉	huī
据	jù	唯	wéi	移	yí	望	wàng	葱	cōng	景	jǐng
菌	jūn	虚	xū	银	yín	谓	wèi	搓	cuō	量	liáng/
控	kòng	眼	yǎn	悠	yōu	惜	xī	惠	huì		liàng
理	lǐ	野	yě	猪	zhū	旋	xuán	惑	huò	亮	liàng
辆	liàng	跃	yuè	做	zuò	痒	yǎng	椒	jiāo	暗	mào
聊	liáo	静	zhēng			渔	yú	揭	jiē	帽	
掠	lüè			丶		欲	yù	敬	jìng	跑	pǎo
萝	luó	丿		惭	cán	着	zháo/zhe	棵	kē	赔	péi
梦	mèng	笨	bèn	凑	còu	族	zú	联	lián	喷	pēn
描	miáo	脖	bó	粗	cū			落	luò	晴	qíng
排	pái	猜	cāi	淡	dàn	乛		棉	mián	赏	shǎng
培	péi	彩	cǎi	断	duàn	逮	dài	欺	qī	蛙	wā
票	piào	船	chuán	袱	fú	蛋	dàn	期	qī	喂	wèi
苹	píng	袋	dài	盖	gài	弹	dàn/tán	翘	qiào	喧	xuān
戚	qī	得	dé/děi/de	惯	guàn	敢	gǎn	琴	qín	掌	zhǎng
球	qiú	第	dì	毫	háo	颈	jǐng	确	què	装	zhuāng
盛	shèng	符	fú	谎	huǎng	逻	luó	揉	róu	紫	zǐ
硕	shuò	够	gòu	混	hùn	骑	qí	散	sàn	最	zuì
梯	tī	馆	guǎn	祸	huò	随	suí	森	sēn		
推	tuī	盒	hé	寂	jì			搜	sōu	丿	
械	xiè	假	jiǎ/jià	寄	jì	乚		提	tí	奥	ào
雪	xuě	脚	jiǎo	剪	jiǎn	婚	hūn	替	tì	傲	ào
营	yíng	梨	lí	减	jiǎn	绩	jì	握	wò	傍	bàng
暂	zàn	脸	liǎn	渐	jiàn	绿	lǜ	喜	xǐ	策	cè
职	zhí	猎	liè	惊	jīng	绳	shéng	雄	xióng	程	chéng
著	zhù	领	lǐng	惧	jù	维	wéi	椅	yǐ	储	chǔ
丨		笼	lóng	康	kāng	绪	xù	硬	yìng	答	dā/dá
常	cháng	毛	máo	梁	liáng	续	xù	援	yuán	等	děng
唱	chàng	您	nín	淋	lín	综	zōng	越	yuè	短	duǎn
				麻	má					鹅	é
										锋	fēng

A

ā 阿 PREF (used to address certain relatives or friends to convey sentiment of intimacy)

阿爸 **ābà** daddy / 阿婆 **āpó** (maternal) granny

Ālābówén 阿拉伯文 N the Arabic language (especially the writing)

Ālābóyǔ 阿拉伯语 N the Arabic language

āyí 阿姨 N mother's sister

> NOTE: (1) 阿姨 **āyí** is a form of address used by a child for a woman about his/her mother's age. It is also common to put a family name before 阿姨 **āyí**, e.g. 张阿姨 **Zhāng āyí**. (2) 阿姨 **āyí** is also used by adults and children for domestic helpers and female nursery staff.

ā 啊 I INTERJ (used to express strong emotions such as surprise, admiration, regret, etc.) oh, ah II PARTICLE (attached to a sentence to express strong emotions such as surprise, admiration, regret, etc.)

āi 哀 V & N grieve; grief, sorrow

āi 哎 INTERJ (used to attract attention or express surprise) ▪ 哎，你还在玩电子游戏？ **Āi, nǐ hái zài wán diànzǐ yóuxì?** *Oh, you're still playing computer games?*

āiyā 哎呀 INTERJ (used to express surprise or annoyance) ▪ 哎呀，我说了半天，你怎么还不明白？ **Āiyā, wǒ shuō le bàntiān, nǐ zěnme hái bù míngbai?** *Goodness, I've been explaining for ages; how come you still don't see the point?*

āiyō 哎哟 INTERJ (used to express pain or pity)

āi 唉 INTERJ 1 (as a sigh) alas ▪ 唉，孩子又病了。 **Āi, háizi yòu bìng le.** *Alas, the child is sick again.* 2 (as a response) yes, right

ái 癌 N cancer

肺癌 **fèi'ái** lung cancer / 胃癌 **wèi'ái** stomach cancer

áizhèng 癌症 N cancer

得了癌症 **déle áizhèng** have contracted cancer

ǎi 蔼 TRAD 藹 ADJ friendly, amiable

ǎi 矮 ADJ (of a person or plant) of short stature; short (ANTONYM 高 **gāo**)

ǎixiǎo 矮小 ADJ short and small, undersized

ài 隘 ADJ narrow

ài 爱 TRAD 愛 V 1 love 2 like, be fond of

àihào 爱好 [comp: 爱 love + 好 like, be fond of] V & N like, be interested in, have as a hobby; hobby, interest

àihù 爱护 [comp: 爱 love + 护 protect] V care for and protect, cherish

àiqíng 爱情 [comp: 爱 love + 情 feeling, affection] N romantic love

àirén 爱人 [modif: 爱 love + 人 person] N husband or wife

> NOTE: 爱人 **àirén** as *husband* or *wife* is only used in Mainland China as a colloquialism. On formal occasions 丈夫 **zhàngfu** (husband) and 妻子 **qīzi** (wife) are used instead. Now there is a decreasing tendency to use 爱人 **àirén** in China. In its place 先生 **xiānsheng** and 太太 **tàitai** are used to refer to *husband* and *wife*, a long established practice in Taiwan, Hong Kong and overseas Chinese communities. For example: ▪ 你先生近来忙吗？ **Nǐ xiānsheng jìnlái máng ma?** *Is your husband busy these days?* ▪ 我太太要我下班回家的路上买些菜。 **Wǒ tàitai yào wǒ xiàbān huíjiā de lù shang mǎi xiē cài.** *My wife wants me to buy some vegetables on my way home after work.*

àixī 爱惜 V cherish, value highly

爱惜自己的名誉 **àixī zìjǐ de míngyù** treasure one's reputation

àixīn 爱心 [modif: 爱 love + 心 the heart] N love, compassion

ài 碍 TRAD 礙 V hinder

ān 安 ADJ peaceful, safe

ānjìng 安静 [comp: 安 peace + 静 quiet] ADJ quiet, peaceful, serene

ān jū lè yè 安居乐业 IDIOM live and work in peace and contentment

ānpái 安排 [comp: 安 to settle, to arrange + 排 to arrange, to put in order] v arrange, make arrangements; plan

ānquán 安全 [comp: 安 peace + 全 complete, all-around] ADJ & N safe, secure; security, safety

ānwèi 安慰 [comp: 安 make peace + 慰 comfort] v comfort, console

ānxīn 安心 [v+obj: 安 make peace + 心 the heart] ADJ relaxed and content

ānzhuāng 安装 [modif: 安 safely + 装 to install] v install, fix
安装空调设备 **ānzhuāng kōngtiáo shèbèi** install an air-conditioner

àn 岸 N bank or shore (of a river, lake, or sea) ■ 河的两岸是一个个小村子。**Hé de liǎng àn shì yí gège xiǎo cūnzi.** *The river is flanked by small villages.*
海岸 **hǎi àn** coast / 上岸 **shàng àn** go ashore

àn 按 PREP according to, in accordance with

ànshí 按时 [v+obj: 按 according to + 时 time] ADV according to a fixed time, on time

ànzhào 按照 PREP according to, in accordance with (same as 按 **àn**)

àn 暗 ADJ dark, dim

ào 奥 ADJ deep, profound

ào 傲 ADJ arrogant (See jiāo'ào 骄傲.)

ào 澳 N deep waters

Àodàlìyà 澳大利亚 N Australia

B

bā 八 NUM eight ■ 八八六十四。**Bā bā liùshísì.** *Eight times eight is sixty-four.*

bá 拔 v pull out, pull up

bǎ 把 [1] MEASURE WORD 1 (for objects with handles)
一把刀 **yì bǎ dāo** a knife
2 a handful of
一把米 **yì bǎ mǐ** a handful of rice

bǎ 把 [2] PREP (used before a noun or pronoun to indicate it is the object of the sentence) ■ 我可以把车停在这里吗? **Wǒ kěyǐ bǎ chē tíng zài zhèli ma?** *May I park my car here?*

bǎwò 把握 I N being certain and assured, confidence II v seize (an opportunity)

bǎxì 把戏 N 1 acrobatics, juggery 2 trick, swindle

bà 爸 N dad, daddy, papa

bàba 爸爸 N daddy, papa

ba 吧 PARTICLE 1 (used to make a suggestion) ■ 我们一块儿去吃中饭吧。**Wǒmen yíkuàir qù chī zhōngfàn ba.** *Let's go and have lunch together.*
2 (used to indicate supposition) ■ 你是新加坡来的张先生吧? **Nǐ shì Xīnjiāpō lái de Zhāng xiānsheng ba?** *Aren't you Mr Zhang from Singapore?*

bái 白 I ADJ white

NOTE: In Chinese tradition, white symbolizes death and is the color for funerals.

II ADV in vain, without any result

báicài 白菜 [modif: 白 white + 菜 vegetable] N cabbage (棵 **kē**)

báikāishuǐ 白开水 N plain boiled water

báirén 白人 N white man/woman, white people, Caucasian

báitiān 白天 [modif: 白 white + 天 day] N daytime

bǎi 百 NUM hundred
三百元 **sān bǎi yuán** three hundred yuan/dollars

NOTE: 百 **bǎi** may have the abstract sense of a *great deal of* and *a multitude of*. This sense can be found in many expressions, e.g. 百闻不如一见 **Bǎi wén bùrú yí jiàn**, which literally means "A hundred sounds are not as good as one sight" and may be translated as "Seeing is believing." Another example is 百忙 **bǎi máng**, meaning *very busy*. For example: ▪ 你百忙中来看我，太好了。**Nǐ bǎi máng zhōng lái kàn wǒ, tài hǎo le.** *It's very kind of you to come to see me when you're so busy.*

bǎifēnbǐ 百分比 N percentage
bǎifēndiǎn 百分点 N one percentage
bǎirìké 百日咳 N whooping cough
bǎixìng 百姓 N common people, ordinary people
老百姓 **lǎobǎixìng** common people, ordinary people
bǎi 摆 TRAD 擺 V put, place, arrange
bài 败 TRAD 敗 V be defeated (ANTONYM 胜 **shèng**)
bài 拜 V do obeisance, pay respect to
bān 班 N 1 class (in school) 2 shift (in a workplace)
加班 **jiābān** work overtime / 上班 **shàngbān** go to work / 下班 **xiàbān** leave work
bānzhǎng 班长 [modif: 班 class, squad + 长 leader] N leader (of a class in school, a squad in the army, etc.)
bān 搬 V move (heavy objects)
搬不动 **bān bu dòng** cannot move/cannot be moved / 搬得动 **bān de dòng** can move/can be moved
bānjiā 搬家 V & N move (house); house moving
bǎn 版 N printing plate
bǎn 板 N board (See **hēibǎn** 黑板.)
bàn 办 TRAD 辦 V handle, manage
bànfǎ 办法 [modif: 办 handle, manage + 法 method] N way of doing things, method
想办法 **xiǎng bànfǎ** think up a plan/

find a way of doing things / 有办法 **yǒu bànfǎ** have a way with …, be resourceful / 没有办法 **méiyǒu bànfǎ** there's nothing we can do
bàngōng 办公 [comp: 办 handle + 公 public, public office] V work (as a white-collar worker, usually in an office)
办公时间 **bàngōng shíjiān** office hours, working hours / 办公大楼 **bàngōng dàlóu** office building
bàngōngshì 办公室 N office
bànlǐ 办理 [comp: 办 handle, manage + 理 manage, run] V deal with, go through
bàn 半 MEASURE WORD half
bàntiān 半天 [modif: 半 half + 天 day] N 1 half a day 2 a period of time felt to be very long, a very long time
bànyè 半夜 [modif: 半 half + 夜 night] N midnight, at midnight
bàn 伴 N companion
同伴 **tóngbàn** companion, mate
bàn 扮 V disguise as
bāng 帮 TRAD 幫 V help, assist

NOTE: 帮 **bāng**, 帮忙 **bāngmáng** and 帮助 **bāngzhù** are synonyms. Their differences are: (1) 帮忙 **bāngmáng** is a verb that takes no object, while 帮 **bāng** and 帮助 **bāngzhù** are usually followed by an object. (2) As verbs, 帮 **bāng** and 帮助 **bāngzhù** are interchangeable, but 帮 **bāng** is more colloquial than 帮助 **bāngzhù**. (3) 帮助 **bāngzhù** can also be used as a noun.

bāngmáng 帮忙 V help, help out

NOTE: See note on 帮 **bāng**.

bāngzhù 帮助 [comp: 帮 help + 助 assist] V & N help, assist; help, assistance

NOTE: See note on 帮 **bāng**.

bǎng 膀 N upper arm (See **chìbǎng** 翅膀.)
bàng 傍 V be close to
bàngwǎn 傍晚 [modif: 傍 towards,

close to + 晚 evening] N towards evening, at dusk

bàng 棒[1] N stick, club (根 **gēn**) 铁棒 **tiěbàng** iron bar

bàng 棒[2] ADJ strong, very good

bāo 包 V & N wrap up; parcel, bag 书包 **shūbāo** schoolbag / 邮包 **yóubāo** mailbag, parcel for posting

bāoguǒ 包裹 N parcel, package

bāohán 包含 [comp: 包 wrap up + 含 contain] V contain, have as ingredients

bāokuò 包括 [comp: 包 embrace + 括 include] V include, embrace

bāozi 包子 [suffix: 包 bun + 子 nominal suffix] N steamed bun with filling

báo 薄 ADJ thin, flimsy (ANTONYM 厚 **hòu**) ■ 天冷了, 这条被子太薄, 要换一条厚一点儿的。**Tiān lěng le, zhè tiáo bèizi tài báo, yào huàn yì tiáo hòu yìdiǎnr de.** *It's getting cold. This blanket is too thin. You need a thicker one.*

bǎo 宝 TRAD 寶 N treasure

bǎobèi 宝贝 [comp: 宝 treasure + 贝 shellfish] N treasured object, treasure 小宝贝 **xiǎo bǎobèi** (endearment for children) darling, dear

bǎoguì 宝贵 [comp: 宝 precious + 贵 valuable] ADJ valuable, precious

bǎo 保 V conserve, protect

bǎo'ān 保安 N security guard

bǎochí 保持 [comp: 保 conserve + 持 maintain] V keep, maintain

bǎocún 保存 [comp: 保 conserve + 存 keep] V keep, save, conserve

bǎohù 保护 [comp: 保 conserve + 护 protect] V protect, safeguard, conserve

bǎoliú 保留 [comp: 保 conserve + 留 retain] V retain, reserve

bǎoxiǎn 保险 [comp: 保 protect + 险 risk] I ADJ safe, risk-free II V & N insure; insurance 保险单 **bǎoxiǎndān** insurance policy / 保险费 **bǎoxiǎnfèi** insurance premium /

保险公司 **bǎoxiǎn gōngsī** insurance company

bǎozhèng 保证 [comp: 保 protect + 证 evidence] V & N guarantee, pledge, warrant 产品保证书 **chǎnpǐn bǎozhèng shū** (product) quality guarantee

bǎo 饱 TRAD 飽 ADJ having eaten one's fill, full (ANTONYM 饿 **è**) 吃得饱 **chī de bǎo** have enough to eat / 吃不饱 **chī bu bǎo** not have enough to eat (→ not have enough food)

NOTE: It is customary for a Chinese host to ask a guest who seems to have finished the meal: 您吃饱了吗? **Nín chī bǎo le ma?** *Have you had (← eaten) enough?* The guest is expected to reply: 吃饱了。多谢。您慢慢吃。**Chī bǎo le. Duō xiè. Nín mànman chī.** Yes, *I have. Thank you. Please take your time to eat.*

bào 报 TRAD 報 V & N report, respond; newspaper

bàodào 报到 V report for duty, register

bàodào 报道 V & N report (news), cover; news story

bàogào 报告 V & N report, make known; report

bàomíng 报名 V enter one's name, sign up, apply for (a place in school)

bàoshè 报社 [modif: 报 newspaper + 社 association] N newspaper office

bàozhǐ 报纸 [modif: 报 reporting + 纸 paper] N newspaper (张 **zhāng**, 份 **fèn**)

NOTE: In colloquial Chinese, 报 **bào** is often used instead of 报纸 **bàozhǐ**, e.g.: 你看得懂中文报吗? **Nǐ kàndedǒng Zhōngwén bào ma?** *Can you understand Chinese newspapers*?

bào 抱 V hold ... in arms, embrace, hug

bàoqiàn 抱歉 ADJ apologetic, sorry, regretful

bàoyuàn 抱怨 v complain, grumble

bào 雹 N hail, hailstone

bēi 杯 N cup, mug, glass (只 zhī)

bēizi 杯子 [suffix: 杯 cup + 子 nominal suffix] N cup, mug, glass (只 zhī)
茶杯 chábēi teacup / 酒杯 jiǔbēi wine glass / 一杯茶/酒 yì bēi chá/jiǔ a cup of tea/a glass of wine

NOTE: 杯 **bēi** may denote either cup, mug, or glass. 杯 **bēi** is seldom used alone. It is usually suffixed with 子 zi: 杯子 **bēizi**, or combined with 茶 **chá** or 酒 **jiǔ**: 茶杯 **chábēi**, 酒杯 **jiǔbēi**.

bēi 背 TRAD 揹 v carry... on the back

bēidài 背带 N straps, braces, suspenders

bēi 悲 ADJ grieved

bēiguān 悲观 [comp: 悲 grieved, sad + 观 view] ADJ pessimistic (ANTONYM 乐观 lèguān)

bēitòng 悲痛 [comp: 悲 grieved, sad + 痛 agony] ADJ deeply grieved, agonized, with deep sorrow

běi 北 N north, northern

běibian 北边 [modif: 北 north + 边 side] N north side, to the north, in the north

běifāng 北方 [modif: 北 north + 方 region] N northern region

běijīng 北京 N Beijing (Peking) (the capital of the People's Republic of China)

běimiàn 北面 N Same as 北边 běibian

bèi 备 TRAD 備 v prepare

bèi 背 I N back (of the body)
背痛 bèitòng backache / 手背 shǒubèi the back of the hand
II v turn away, leave

bèibāo 背包 N backpack

bèijǐng 背景 N background
家庭背景 jiātíng bèijǐng family background

bèi 贝 TRAD 貝 N shellfish

bèiké 贝壳 N shell (of shellfish)

bèi 狈 N a kind of wolf with short forelegs

bèi 被 PREP by (introducing the doer of an action) ■ 花瓶被小明打破了。 Huāpíng bèi Xiǎo Míng dǎ pò le. *The vase was broken by Xiao Ming.*

bèizi 被子 N quilt, blanket (条 tiáo)

bèi 倍 MEASURE WORD -fold, times

bèi 辈 TRAD 輩 N people of the same generation (See zhǎngbèi 长辈.)

běn 本[1] N capital, principal
赔本 péi běn lose one's capital in investments or other business dealings

běn 本[2] MEASURE WORD (for books, magazines, etc.)
一本书 yì běn shū a book

běn 本[3] ADJ this one, one's own

NOTE: 本 **běn** in the sense of *this one* is only used on formal occasions. ■ 本店春节照常营业。 **Běn diàn chūnjié zhàocháng yíngyè.** *This store will do business as usual during the Spring Festival.* (→ *We'll be open during the Chinese New Year.*)

běndì 本地 [modif: 本 this + 地 place] N this locality

běnkē 本科 N undergraduate course
本科生 běnkēshēng an undergraduate

běnlái 本来 ADV originally, at first

běnlǐng 本领 N skill, ability, capability

běnzhe 本着 PREP in accordance with, based on

běnzhì 本质 [comp: 本 origin + 质 nature] N innate character, true nature

běnzi 本子 [suffix: 本 a book + 子 nominal suffix] N notebook (本 běn)

bèn 笨 ADJ dumb, stupid

bí 鼻 N Same as 鼻子 bízi

bízi 鼻子 N the nose

bǐ 比 I PREP (introducing the object that is compared with the subject of a sentence), than ■ 今天比昨天冷得多。 **Jīntiān bǐ zuótiān lěng de duō.** *Today is much colder than yesterday.*

bǐjiào 比较 I v compare
和… 比较 **hé... bǐjiào** compare… with
II ADV comparatively, relatively, to some
degree
bǐlì 比例 N ratio, percentage
bǐrú 比如 CONJ for example

NOTE: In spoken Chinese you can also
use 比如说 **bǐrúshuō.**

bǐsài 比赛 [comp: 比 compare + 赛
compete] v & N compete, have a match;
match, game, competition
参加比赛 **cānjiā bǐsài** participate in a
game (or sports event) / 和/跟…比赛
hé/gēn...bǐsài have a match/race with
/ 看比赛 **kàn bǐsài** watch a game (or
sports event)
bǐ 笔¹ TRAD 筆 N writing instrument, pen,
pencil (支 **zhī**)
画笔 **huàbǐ** paintbrush (for art) / 毛笔
máobǐ Chinese writing brush
bǐ 笔² TRAD 筆 MEASURE WORD (for a sum of
money or debt)
bǐjì 笔记 N notes (taken in class or while
reading)
记笔记 **jì bǐjì** take notes (in class, at a
lecture, etc.) / 做笔记 **zuò bǐjì** make
notes (while reading)
bǐjìběn diànnǎo 笔记本电脑 N
notebook computer, laptop
bǐcǐ 彼此 [comp: 彼 that + 此 this] PRON
each other
bì 币 TRAD 幣 N currency (See **huòbì** 货币.)
bì 必 ADV inevitably
bìdìng 必定 v be bound to, be sure to,
must
bìrán 必然 ADJ inevitable, bound to
bìxū 必须 [comp: 必 must + 须 need,
have to] MODAL V must, have to, have
got to
bìyào 必要 [comp: 必 must + 要
require] ADJ necessary, requisite,
indispensable
bì 闭 TRAD 閉 v close, shut up

bìmù 闭幕 [v+obj: 闭 close + 幕
curtain] v the curtain falls, (of a
theatrical performance, an event, etc.)
close
闭幕式 **bìmù shì** closing ceremony
bì zuǐ 闭嘴 v shut your mouth, shut
up, say no more ▪ 她愤怒地喊："闭
嘴！" **Tā fènnù de hǎn: "Bì zuǐ!"** *She
shouted angrily, "Shut up!"*

NOTE: 闭嘴！ **Bìzuǐ!** *Shut your mouth!* is a
very impolite expression to tell people to
stop talking. You can also say: 闭上你的
嘴！ **Bì shang nǐ de zuǐ!** *Shut your mouth!*

bì 碧 ADJ bluish green
bìyù 碧玉 N green jade
bì 臂 N the arm
手臂 **shǒubì** the arm
bì 毕 TRAD 畢 v finish
bìjìng 毕竟 ADV after all, anyway
bìyè 毕业 [v+obj: 毕 finish + 业 course
of study] v graduate from school
bì 避 v evade, avoid
bìmiǎn 避免 [comp: 避 evade + 免 be
free from] v avoid, avert
bì 壁 N wall (See **gébì** 隔壁.)
biān 边 TRAD 邊 N side, border

NOTE: The most frequent use of 边 **biān** is
to form "compound location nouns": 东边
dōngbian *east side*, 南边 **nánbian** *south
side*, 西边 **xībian** *west side*, 北边 **běibian**
north side, 里边 **lǐbian** *inside*, 外边 **wàibian**
outside. 边 **biān** in such cases is often
pronounced in the neutral tone.

biān ⋯ biān 边 ⋯ 边 CONJ (used with
verbs to indicate simultaneous actions)
▪ 他们边走边谈，不一会儿就到市中心
了。 **Tāmen biān zǒu biān tán, bùyíhuìr
jiù dào shì zhōngxīn le.** *They chatted
while walking, and soon reached the city
center.*
biān 编 TRAD 編 v compile, edit,
compose
biānjí 编辑 [comp: 编 compile,

compose + 辑 compile] **v & n** edit,
compile; editor

biān 鞭 n whip
鞭子 **biānzi** whip (条 **tiáo**)

biānpào 鞭炮 n firecracker
放鞭炮 **fàng biānpào** set off
firecrackers

biǎn 扁 adj flat

biàn 变 trad 變 **v** change, become
different, transform

biànchéng 变成 [v+compl: 变 change +
成 into] **v** change into, turn into

biànhuà 变化 [comp: 变 change + 化
transform] **v & n** transform, change;
transformation, change

NOTE: As a verb 变化 **biànhuà** is interchangeable with 变 **biàn**, 变化 **biànhuà**
being a little more formal than 变 **biàn**.

biàn 便 adj convenient

biànlì 便利 [comp: 便 convenient + 利
benefit] **adj** convenient, easy

biàn 遍 measure word (used to indicate
the frequency of an action done in its
complete duration from the beginning
to the end) ▪ 上个月我看了三个电影，
其中一个看了两遍。**Shàng ge yuè wǒ
kànle sān ge diànyǐng, qízhōng yí ge
kànle liǎng biàn.** *I saw three movies last
month, one of which I saw twice.*

biàn 辩 trad 辯 **v** argue

biànlùn 辩论 [comp: 辩 argue + 论
discuss] **v & n** debate (场 **chǎng**)
举行一场辩论 **jǔxíng yì chǎng biànlùn**
hold a debate

biàn 辨 v distinguish, recognize

biāo 标 trad 標 **v** mark

biāodiǎn 标点 [comp: 标 mark + 点
point] **n** punctuation mark

biāozhì 标志 [comp: 标 mark + 志
record] **n** sign, mark
社会地位的标志 **shèhuì dìwèi de biāozhì**
status symbol

biāozhǔn 标准 [comp: 标 standard + 准

accuracy] **n & adj** standard, criterion; up
to standard, perfect
达到标准 **dádào biāozhǔn** reach the
standard

biǎo 表[1] **trad** 錶 **n** wrist watch, watch
(块 **kuài**, 只 **zhī**)
戴表 **dài biǎo** wear a watch / 男表 **nán
biǎo** men's watch / 女表 **nǔbiǎo** ladies'
watch

biǎo 表[2] **n** form, diagram, table
乘法表 **chéngfǎbiǎo** multiplication table

biǎogé 表格 n form (张 **zhāng**, 份 **fèn**)

biǎo 表[3] **v** express one's feelings

biǎodá 表达 [comp: 表 express + 达
reach] **v** express (thoughts or emotions)

biǎomiàn 表面 [modif: 表 surface + 面
face] **n** surface

biǎomíng 表明 [v+compl: 表 express +
明 clear] **v** make clear, demonstrate

biǎoqíng 表情 [modif: 表 surface + 情
feelings] **n** facial expression
一副严肃的表情 **yífù yánsù de biǎoqíng**
with a serious expression

biǎoshì 表示 [comp: 表 show, express +
示 indicate] **v** express, show, manifest

biǎoxiàn 表现 [comp: 表 show, express
+ 现 display] **v** display, show

biǎoyǎn 表演 [comp: 表 show + 演
act] **v & n** put on (a show), perform,
demonstrate; performance, show

biǎoyáng 表扬 [comp: 表 display +
扬 raise, make known] **v & n** praise,
commend (**antonym** 批评 **pīpíng**); praise,
commendation

bié 别 adv don't

NOTE: 别 **bié** is a contraction of 不要
búyào in an imperative sentence. It is used
colloquially only.

biéde 别的 pron other, anotherr

biérén 别人 [modif: 别 other + 人
person, people] **pron** other people,
others

bīn 宾 trad 賓 **n** guest

bīnguǎn 宾馆 [modif: 宾 guest + 馆 house] N guesthouse, hotel

bīn 滨 TRAD 濱 N waterside

bīng 冰 N ice

bīngjīlíng 冰激凌 N ice cream

bīngqílín 冰淇淋 Same as 冰激凌 bīngjīlíng

bīngxiāng 冰箱 [modif: 冰 ice + 箱 box] N refrigerator, freezer
电冰箱 diàn bīngxiāng refrigerator

bīng 兵 N soldier
当兵 dāng bīng be a soldier, serve in the armed forces

bǐng 饼 TRAD 餅 N cake

bǐnggān 饼干 [modif: 饼 cake + 干 dried food] N cookie(s), biscuit(s) (片 piàn, 包 bāo)

bìng 并 TRAD 並 I ADV (used before a negative word for emphasis) ■ 事情并不象你想象的那么简单。 Shìqíng bìng bú xiàng nǐ xiǎngxiàng de nàme jiǎndān. *Things are not at all as simple as you imagine.* II CONJ Same as 并且 bìngqiě. Used only in written Chinese.

NOTE: 并 bìng is used to emphasize the negation. It is not grammatically essential; without 并 bìng the sentences still stand. The following is perfectly acceptable: ■ 事情不象你想象的那么简单。 Shìqíng bú xiàng nǐ xiǎngxiàng de nàme jiǎndān. *Things are not as simple as you imagine.*

bìngcún 并存 V exist side by side, co-exist

bìngqiě 并且 CONJ moreover, what's more, and

bìng 病 V & N fall ill, be ill; illness, disease
生病 shēng bìng fall ill

bìng jià 病假 N sick leave
请病假 qǐng bìngjià ask for/apply for sick leave

bìngdú 病毒 [modif: 病 disease + 毒 poison] N virus
电脑病毒 diànnǎo bìngdú computer virus

bìngfáng 病房 [modif: 病 sickness + 房 room] N (hospital) ward
重病房 zhòngbìngfáng intensive care ward

bìngrén 病人 [modif: 病 sick + 人 person] N patient
住院病人 zhùyuàn bìngrén inpatient

bō 波 N ripple, wave

bōdòng 波动 V fluctuate (like a wave)
情绪波动 qíngxù bōdòng constantly changing moods

bōlàng 波浪 [comp: 波 ripple + 浪 wave] N wave

bō 玻 N as in 玻璃 bōli

bōli 玻璃 N glass
玻璃窗 bōli chuāng glass window, window

bō 播 V sow

bōfàng 播放 [comp: 播 sow + 放 release] V broadcast (radio or TV programmes)

bó 伯 N Same as 伯父 bófù

bófù 伯父 N father's elder brother

NOTE: 伯父 bófù is also a form of address for men older than your father but not old enough to be your grandfather. The colloquialism for 伯父 bófù is 伯伯 bóbo.

bómǔ 伯母 N father's elder brother's wife

NOTE: 伯母 bómǔ is also a form of address for women older than your mother but not old enough to be your grandmother. It is generally used by well-educated urban Chinese.

bó 脖 N neck

bózi 脖子 [suffix: 脖 neck + 子 nominal suffix] N neck

bó 博 ADJ abundant, extensive

bókè 博客 V & N write and post a blog; web log, blog, blogger

bóshì 博士 [modif: 博 erudite + 士 scholar] N doctor, Ph.D.
博士生 bóshìshēng Ph.D. candidate /

博士生导师 **bóshìshēng dǎoshī** Ph.D. supervisor / 博士后 **bóshìhòu** post-doctorate / 博士学位 **bóshì xuéwèi** Ph.D. degree

bówùguǎn 博物馆 [modif: 博物 natural science + 馆 building] N museum 历史博物馆 **lìshǐ bówùguǎn** historical museum

bó 膊 N arm (See **gēbo** 胳膊.)

bó 驳 TRAD 駁 V refute, retort

bǔ 补 TRAD 補 V mend, patch

bǔchōng 补充 [comp: 补 supplement + 充 fill up] V supplement, add

bǔkè 补课 [v+obj: 补 make up+ 课 lessons] V make up for missed lessons

bù 不 ADV no, not ■ 今天不冷。**Jīntiān bù lěng.** *It's not cold today.*

> NOTE: When followed by a syllable in the fourth (falling) tone, 不 undergoes tone change from the normal fourth tone to the second (rising) tone, e.g. 不对 **búduì**, 不是 **búshì**.

> NOTE: See note on 别 **bié**.

bù'ān 不安 [modif: 不 not + 安 peace, peaceful] ADJ upset, disturbed

búbì 不必 [modif: 不 not + 必 necessary] ADV need not, not have to, unnecessarily

búcuò 不错 [modif: 不 not + 错 wrong] ADJ 1 not wrong; quite right 2 not bad, quite good

búdà 不大 ADV not very, not much

búdàn ··· érqiě 不但 ··· 而且 CONJ not only ... but also ... ■ 这家饭店的菜不但好吃，而且好看。**Zhè jiā fàndiàn de cài búdàn hǎochī, érqiě hǎokàn.** *The dishes in this restaurant are not only delicious but also beautiful.*

bùdébù 不得不 ADV have to, have no choice but

bùdéliǎo 不得了 ADJ 1 horrible, extremely serious 2 extremely (used after an adjective and introduced by 得 de) ■ 昨天热得不得了。**Zuótiān rè de** *bùdéliǎo. It was extremely hot yesterday.*

búduàn 不断 [modif: 不 not + 断 interrupt] ADV without interruption, continuously, incessantly

bùguǎn 不管 CONJ no matter (what, who, how, etc.) ■ 不管他多么忙，他总是每天给妈妈发一份电子邮件。**Bùguǎn tā duōme máng, tā zǒngshì měi tiān gěi māma fā yí fèn diànzǐ yóujiàn.** *No matter how busy he is, he always sends his mother a daily e-mail.*

búguò 不过 CONJ Same as 但是 **dànshì**. Used colloquially.

bù hǎo yìsi 不好意思 IDIOM I'm embarrassed (polite phrase used when you are offering an apology, giving a gift, or receiving a gift or other acts of kindness)

bú jiàndé 不见得 ADV not necessarily, unlikely

bùjǐn 不仅 CONJ Same as 不但 **búdàn**. Often used in writing.

bùjiǔ 不久 N not long afterwards, near future, soon

búkèqi 不客气 [modif: 不 not + 客气 polite, standing on ceremony] you're welcome, not at all ■ "谢谢你！" "不客气。" **"Xièxie nǐ!" "Búkèqi."** *"Thank you!" "You're welcome."*

búlì 不利 ADJ unfavorable, disadvantageous

búlùn 不论 CONJ Same as 不管 **bùguǎn**. Used more in writing.

búnàifán 不耐烦 ADJ impatient

bùrán 不然 CONJ otherwise, or

> NOTE: To be more emphatic, you can use 不然的话 **bùrán de huà** instead of 不然 **bùrán**.

bùrú 不如 V be not as good as, be not as ... as

bùshǎo 不少 [modif: 不 not + 少 few, little] ADJ quite a few

bùtíng 不停 [modif: 不 not + 停 stop] ADV without let-up, incessantly

bùtóng 不同 ADJ not the same, different ···和/跟···不同 ... hé/gēn...bùtóng ... is/ are different from ...

bùxíng 不行 v 1 will not do, be not allowed 2 be no good (at something), be poor in

búxìng 不幸 [modif: 不 not + 幸 fortunate] ADJ unfortunate

bùxǔ 不许 v not allow, must not

búyào 不要 ADV (used in an imperative sentence or as advice) do not

búyàojǐn 不要紧 ADJ unimportant, doesn't matter

búyòng 不用 ADV no need, there's no need, don't have to

bùzú 不足 [modif: 不 not + 足 sufficient] ADJ inadequate, insufficient

bù 布 N cotton or linen cloth (块 kuài, 片 piàn)

bù 步 N step, pace

bùzhòu 步骤 N procedure, steps

bù 部 N part, unit

bùduì 部队 N troops, the army

bùfen 部分 [comp: 部 part + 分 division] N portion, part 大部分 dà bùfen most of ..., the majority of ...

bùmén 部门 [comp: 部 department + 门 gate, door] N department, branch

bùzhǎng 部长 [modif: 部 ministry + 长 chief, the person in charge] N (government) minister

C

cā 擦 v clean or erase by wiping or rubbing

cāi 猜 v guess, speculate

cái 才[^1] TRAD 纔 ADV 1 (before a verb) a short time ago, just 2 (used before a word of time or quantity to indicate that the speaker feels the time is too early,

too short or the quantity is too little), only, as early as, as few/little as ▪ 这本书才十块钱，太便宜了。**Zhè ben shū cái shí kuài qián, tài piányi le.** *This book is only ten dollars. It's really cheap.* 3 (used after a word of time to indicate that the speaker feels the time is too late or there is too much delay), as late as ▪ 这个小孩三岁才会走。**Zhè ge xiǎo hái sānsuì cái huì zǒu.** *This child learned to walk as late as three years old.*

cái 才[^2] N talent, remarkable ability

cái 财 TRAD 財 N wealth, property

cáichǎn 财产 [comp: 财 property, fortune + 产 property] N property, belongings

cái 材 N material

cáiliào 材料 N 1 materials, e.g. steel, timber, plastic 2 data (for a thesis, a report, etc.)

cái 裁 v 1 cut into parts, cut down 2 judge, decide

cáipàn 裁判 [comp: 裁 arbitrate + 判 judge] I v 1 (in law) adjudicate, judge 2 (in sports) act as referee or umpire II N 1 adjudication, decision made by the court 2 referee, umpire (位 wèi, 名 míng) 当裁判 dāng cáipàn act as a referee / 裁判员 cáipànyuán Same as 裁判 cáipàn II 2

cǎi 采 TRAD 採 v pick, pluck

cǎifǎng 采访 [comp: 采 gather + 访 visit] v (of mass media) interview

cǎiqǔ 采取 [comp: 采 pick + 取 take] v adopt (a policy, a measure, an attitude, etc.)

cǎiyòng 采用 [comp: 采 pick + 用 use] v use, employ

cǎi 彩 ADJ colorful

cǎihóng 彩虹 [modif: 彩 multi-colored + 虹 rainbow] N rainbow

cǎisè 彩色 [modif: 彩 multi-colored + 色 color] ADJ multi-colored 彩色电视机 cǎisè diànshìjī color TV set

cài 菜 N 1 vegetables
种菜 **zhòng cài** grow vegetables / 买菜
mǎi cài buy non-staple food, do grocery
shopping
2 cooked dish ∎ 请别客气，多吃点
菜! **Qǐng bié kèqi, duō chī diǎn cài!**
Please don't be too polite. Eat more food!
点菜 **diǎn cài** order a dish (in a restaurant)
càidān 菜单 N menu
cān 参 TRAD 參 V call, enter
cānguān 参观 [comp: 参 call + 观
watch, see] V visit (a place)
cānjiā 参加 [v+comp: 参 enter + 加 add]
V 1 join 2 participate, attend
cānkǎo 参考 V consult, refer to
仅供参考 **jǐn gōng cānkǎo** For reference
only
cānkǎoshū 参考书 N reference book(s)
cānyú 参与 V participate, involve
cān 餐 N meal
cāntīng 餐厅 [modif: 餐 meal + 厅 hall]
N restaurant
cán 惭 TRAD 慚 N shame
cánkuì 惭愧 [comp: 惭 shame + 愧
sense of guilt] ADJ be ashamed
cāng 舱 TRAD 艙 N cabin (in a ship or an
airplane)
经济舱 **jīngjì cāng** economy class
(cabin) / 商务舱 **shāngwù cāng** business
class (cabin) / 头等舱 **tóuděng cāng** first
class (cabin)
cáng 藏 V hide, conceal
cāo 操 N drill, exercise
cāochǎng 操场 [modif: 操 drill, exercise
+ 场 ground] N sports ground, playground
(在) 操场上 **(zài) cāochǎng shang** on the
sports ground
cāoxīn 操心 [v+obj: 操 exercise + 心 the
heart] V deeply concern, be at pains
cǎo 草 N grass, weed (棵 **kē**)
cǎodì 草地 [modif: 草 grass + 地 land]
N lawn
cǎoyuán 草原 [modif: 草 grass + 原 flat
land] N grassland, steppe, pasture

cè 册 MEASURE WORD (used for books)
volume
两千册图书 **liǎngqiān cè túshū** two
thousand [volumes of] books
cè 厕 TRADE 廁 N toilet
cèsuǒ 厕所 N toilet
公共厕所 **gōnggòng cèsuǒ** public toilet
/ 男厕所 **nán cèsuǒ** men's toilet / 女厕所
nǚcèsuǒ women's toilet

> NOTE: See note on 洗手间 **xǐshǒujiān** (in 洗
> **xǐ**).

cè 测 TRAD 測 V measure, gauge
cèyàn 测验 [comp: 测 measure + 验
test] V & N test (in a school), do exam;
examination
cè 策 N plan
cèlüè 策略 [comp: 策 plan + 略 strategy]
N tactics
有策略的 **yǒu cèlüè de** tactful
céng 层 TRAD 層 MEASURE WORD story,
level, floor

> NOTE: See note on 楼 **lóu**.

céng 曾 ADV Same as 曾经 **céngjīng**.
Used more in writing.
céngjīng 曾经 ADV once, formerly
chā 叉 N fork
chāzi 叉子 N fork (把 **bǎ**)
chā 差 N difference, discrepancy
chājù 差距 [comp: 差 difference + 距
distance] N gap, disparity
贫富差距 **pín-fù chājù** the gap between
the rich and poor
chā 插 V insert, stick in
chāzuò 插座 N (electric) socket
chá 茶 N tea
红茶 **hóngchá** black tea / 绿茶 **lǜchá**
green tea / 喝茶 **hē chá** drink tea
chábēi 茶杯 N teacup
cháhú 茶壶 N teapot
chá 查 V check, look up
chá cídiǎn 查词典 V look up words in a
dictionary

cházhǎo 查找 v & n search; searching

chá 察 v examine, look over closely (See guānchá 观察.)

chà 差 I v be short of, lack in II ADJ poor, not up to standard

chàbuduō 差不多 ADJ 1 more or less the same 2 almost

chàdiǎnr 差点儿 ADV almost, nearly

chāi 拆 v take apart, demolish

chāi 差 n errand (See chūchāi 出差.)

chán 缠 TRAD 纏 v 1 wind, twine 2 pester, bother ■ 这孩子总缠着我，要我跟他玩。Zhè háizi zǒng chánzhe wǒ, yào wǒ gēn tā wán. *This child keeps pestering me to play with him.*

chǎn 产 TRAD 產 v produce

chǎnliàng 产量 [modif: 产 product + 量 quantity] n (production) output, yield

chǎnpǐn 产品 [modif: 产 production + 品 goods] n product, produce

chǎnshēng 产生 [comp: 产 produce + 生 grow] v produce, give rise to, lead to

cháng 尝 TRAD 嘗 v taste, experiencee

cháng 长 TRAD 長 ADJ long, lengthy (ANTONYM 短 duǎn)

Chángchéng 长城 n the Great Wall (a historic landmark in Northern China)

Chángjiāng 长江 n the Yangtze River (China's longest river)

chángpǎo 长跑 n long-distance running

chángqī 长期 [modif: 长 long + 期 period] n a long period of time

chángtú 长途 [modif: 长 long + 途 way] n long distance
长途电话 **chángtú diànhuà** long-distance telephone call / 国际长途电话 **guójì chángtú diànhuà** international telephone call / 长途汽车 **chángtú qìchē** long-distance bus, coach

cháng 肠 TRAD 腸 n intestine (See xiāngcháng 香肠.)

cháng 常 ADV often
常常 **chángcháng** often / 不常 **bù cháng** not often, seldom

NOTE: Colloquially, 常常 **chángcháng** is often used instead of 常 **cháng**.

chángnián 常年 ADV all the year round, year in and year out

chángshí 常识 [modif: 常 common + 识 knowledge] n 1 common sense 2 basic knowledge

chángwù 常务 ADJ in charge of day-to-day business
常务副市长 **chángwù fù shìzhǎng** executive vice-mayor

chǎng 厂 TRAD 廠 n factory (See gōngchǎng 工厂.)

chǎng 场 TRAD 場 I n ground, field
操场 **cāochǎng** sports ground, playground / 体育场 **tǐyùchǎng** stadium / 飞机场 **fēijīchǎng** airport / 市场 **shìchǎng** market
II MEASURE WORD (for movies, sport events, etc.) ■ 一场球赛 **yì chǎng qiúsài** *a ball game, a ball match*

chàng 唱 v sing

chànggē 唱歌 [v+obj: 唱 sing + 歌 song] v sing songs, sing

chāo 抄 v copy by hand

chāoxiě 抄写 v Same as 抄 chāo

chāo 超 v go beyond, exceed

chāoguò 超过 v 1 overtake 2 exceed

chāojí 超级 [modif: 超 exceed + 级 grade] ADJ super

chāojí gōnglù 超级公路 n superhighway, motorway

chāo(jí) shì(chǎng) 超(级)市(场) n supermarket (家 jiā)

cháo 朝¹ v & PREP face; towards, to

cháo 朝² n dynasty
唐朝 **Táng cháo** the Tang Dynasty

cháo 潮 ADJ wet

cháoshī 潮湿 [comp: 潮 wet + 湿 damp] ADJ damp, humid

chǎo 吵 v 1 quarrel 2 make a big noise, be noisy

chǎojià 吵架 v & n quarrel

chǎo 炒 v 1 stir fry, sauté 2 sensationalize, create a commotion
炒股票 **chǎo gǔpiào** speculate on the stock exchange

chē 车 TRAD 車 N vehicle, traffic (辆 **liàng**)
开车 **kāi chē** drive an automobile / 骑车 **qí chē** ride a bicycle / 停车场 **tíngchēchǎng** car park, parking lot / 学车 **xué chē** learn to drive / 修车 **xiū chē** repair a car/bicycle / 修车行 **xiū chē háng** motor vehicle repair and servicing shop

chējiān 车间 N workshop (in a factory)

chēkù 车库 [modif: 车 vehicle + 库 storeroom] N garage

chē pái 车牌 N (vehicle) license plate
车牌号 **chē pái hào** (vehicle) license plate number

chēxiāng 车厢 N carriage (in a train)

chēzhàn 车站 [modif: 车 vehicle + 站 station] N bus stop, coach station, railway station
长途汽车站 **chángtú qìchē zhàn** coach station / 出租汽车站 **chūzū qìchē zhàn** taxi stand / 火车站 **huǒchē zhàn** railway station

chén 陈 TRAD 陳 I N a common family name II ADJ old, stale III v display

chén 晨 N early morning (See **zǎochén** 早晨.)

chén 沉 I v sink II ADJ 1 deep, profound 2 heavy

chénmò 沉默 [comp: 沉 deep + 默 silent] ADJ silent, reticent

chéntòng 沉痛 [modif: 沉 heavy + 痛 agonized] ADJ deeply grieved, in deep sorrow

chén 尘 TRAD 塵 N dust (See **huīchén** 灰尘.)

chèn 衬 TRAD 襯 N lining, underwear

chènshān 衬衫 N shirt (件 **jiàn**)

chènyī 衬衣 N shirt or similar underwear (件 **jiàn**)

chèn 趁 PREP taking advantage of, while, when

chèn 称 TRAD 稱 v match, suit

chènxīn 称心 [v+obj: 称 suit + 心 one's heart] ADJ very much to one's liking, find … satisfactory

chēng 称 TRAD 稱 v 1 call, be known as, address … as 2 weigh

chēnghu 称呼 [comp: 称 call, name + 呼 call] v & N call, address; form of address

chēngzàn 称赞 [comp: 称 praise + 赞 praise] v compliment, praise

chéng 成 v become, turn into

chéngfèn 成分 [comp: 成 percentage + 分 element] N component part, ingredient (种 **zhǒng**)

chénggōng 成功 [v+obj: 成 accomplish + 功 merit, feat] I v succeed ■ 祝你成功! **Zhù nǐ chénggōng!** *I wish you success!* II ADJ successful

chéngguǒ 成果 [comp: 成 achievement + 果 fruit, good result] N positive result, achievement (项 **xiàng**)

chéngjì 成绩 [comp: 成 achievement + 绩 result] N achievement, examination result
取得成绩 **qǔdé chéngjì** make achievement, get (positive, good) results

chéngjiù 成就 [comp: 成 achievement + 就 achievement] N great achievement (项 **xiàng**)

chénglì 成立 [comp: 成 accomplish + 立 establish] v establish, set up

chéngmíng 成名 v become famous

chéngrén 成人 N adult
成人教育 **chéngrén jiàoyù** adult education / 成人电影 **chéngrén diànyǐng** adult movie

chéngshú 成熟 [comp: 成 accomplish + 熟 mature] v & ADJ mature, ripen; mature, ripe

chéngwéi 成为 [comp: 成 become + 为 be] v become

chéngyǔ 成语 N idiom, idiomatic expression, set phrase

chéngyuán 成员 N member (of a family or group)

chéngzhǎng 成长 [comp: 成 become + 长 grow] v grow up

chéng 诚 TRAD 誠 ADJ sincere

chéngkěn 诚恳 [comp: 诚 sincere + 恳 sincere] ADJ sincere

chéngshí 诚实 [comp: 诚 sincere + 实 true] ADJ honest, sincere

chéng 城 N city, town (座 zuò)
进城 jìn chéng go to town, go to the city center

chéngbǎo 城堡 N castle, citadel (座 zuò)

chénglǐ 城里 N in town, downtown

chéngshì 城市 [comp: 城 city wall, city + 市 market] N city, urban area (as opposed to rural area) (座 zuò) (ANTONYM 农村 nóngcūn)

chéngwài 城外 N out of town, suburban area

chéng 盛 v fill, ladle

chéngfàn 盛饭 v fill (a bowl/plate) with rice

chéng 承 v support, undertake, assume

chéngdān 承担 [comp: 承 bear + 担 responsibility] v take responsibility for, undertake

chéngrèn 承认 v 1 acknowledge, recognize 2 admit (mistakes, errors, etc.)

chéngshòu 承受 v endure, bear
承受力 chéngshòu lì endurance

chéng 程 N regulation, procedure

chéngdù 程度 N level, degree

chéngxù 程序 [comp: 程 regulation + 序 order] N 1 procedure
会议程序 huìyì chéngxù agenda of a meeting
2 computer programming 计算机程序 jìsuànjī chéngxù computer program / 应用程序 yìngyòng chéngxù app, application (program)

chéng 乘[1] v use (a means of transport), travel (by car, train, plane, etc.) ▪ 你打算乘火车，还是乘飞机到北京去? **Nǐ** dǎsuàn chéng huǒchē, háishì chéng fēijī qù Běijīng? *Do you plan to go to Beijing by train or by plane?*

chéng 乘[2] v multiply ▪ 二乘三等于六。 **Èr chéng sān děngyú liù.** *Two multiplied by three is six. (2 x 3=6)*

chéngzuò 乘坐 v Same as 乘[1] **chéng**

chī 吃 v eat, take (food or medicine)

chījīng 吃惊 v be shocked, be startled, be alarmed
大吃一惊 dà chī yì jīng greatly shocked, have the fright of one's life

chīkuī 吃亏 [v+obj: 吃 eat + 亏 loss] v suffer losses, be at a disadvantage

chí 迟 TRAD 遲 ADJ late

chídào 迟到 [modif: 迟 late + 到 arrive] v come late, be late (for work, school, etc.)

chízǎo 迟早 [comp: 迟 late + 早 early] ADV sooner or later, eventually

chí 持 v persevere

chíxù 持续 [comp: 持 persevere + 续 continue] ADJ continue, sustain, persist
可持续发展 kě chíxù fāzhǎn sustainable development

chí 池 N pool, pond
游泳池 yóuyǒngchí swimming pool

chítáng 池塘 [comp: 池 pool + 塘 pond] N pond

chí 驰 TRAD 馳 v gallop

chǐ 尺 I N ruler (把 bǎ) II MEASURE WORD a traditional Chinese unit of length (equal to 1/3 meter)
公尺 gōngchǐ meter / 英尺 yīngchǐ foot (as a measurement of length)

chǐcùn 尺寸 N size, measurements

chǐmǎ 尺码 N size (of shoes, shirts, ready-made clothing, etc.)

chǐ 齿 TRAD 齒 N tooth, teeth

chì 翅 N wing

chìbǎng 翅膀 N wing (of a bird)

chōng 充 ADJ sufficient, full

chōngdiànqì 充电器 N (battery) charger

chōngfèn 充分 ADJ abundant, ample, adequate

chōngmǎn 充满 [comp: 充 filled + 满 full] ADJ full of, filled with

chōng 冲 TRAD 衝 V 1 clash 2 charge, rush, dash

chóng 虫 TRAD 蟲 N insect, worm

chóngzi 虫子 [suffix: 虫 insect + 子 nominal suffix] N insect, worm (只 zhī).

chóng 重 ADV again, once again

chóngfù 重复 [comp: 重 once again + 复 repeat] V repeat

chóngxīn 重新 [comp: 重 once again + 新 renew] ADV Same as 重 **chóng**

Chóngyáng Jié 重阳节 N the Double Ninth Festival (the 9th day of the 9th lunar month)

chōu 抽 V take out (from in-between)

chōukòng 抽空 V manage to find time (to do something)

chōuti 抽屉 N drawer

chōuxiàng 抽象 ADJ abstract

chōuyān 抽烟 [v+obj: 抽 suck + 烟 smoke] V smoke a cigarette (cigar), smoke

chóu 愁 V worry ▪ 你别愁，大伙儿会帮助你的。 Nǐ bié chóu, dàhuǒr huì bāngzhù nǐ de. *Don't worry. We'll all help you.*

发愁 fā chóu worry over

chǒu 丑 TRAD 醜 ADJ ugly

chòu 臭 ADJ smelly, stinking (ANTONYM 香 **xiāng**)

chū 出 V emerge from, get out of 出来 chūlai come out ▪ 请你出来一下。 Qǐng nǐ chūlai yíxià. *Would you please step out for a while?* 出去 chūqu go out ▪ 请你出去一下。 Qǐng nǐ chūqu yíxià. *Please go out for a while. (→ Please leave us for a while.)*

chūbǎn 出版 V publish

chūchāi 出差 V be on a business trip, leave town on business

chūfā 出发 [comp: 出 depart + 发 discharge] V set off (on a journey), start (a journey)

chūguó 出国 V go abroad, go overseas

chūkǒu 出口 [v+obj: 出 leave + 口 mouth, port] I V export (ANTONYM 进口 jìnkǒu) II N exit 出口公司 chūkǒu gōngsī export company / 出口贸易 chūkǒu màoyì export business in foreign trade

chūsè 出色 ADJ outstanding, remarkable

chūshēng 出生 [comp: 出 come out + 生 be born] V be born 出生地 chūshēng dì place of birth / 出生日期 chūshēng rìqī date of birth / 出生证 chūshēng zhèng birth certificate

chūshì 出示 V take out to show, produce

chūxí 出席 V attend (a meeting, a court trial, etc.)

chūxiàn 出现 [comp: 出 emerge + 现 appear] V come into view, appear, emerge

chū yángxiàng 出洋相 V make a laughing stock of oneself, be held up for mockery

chūyuàn 出院 V be discharged from hospital ▪ 医生，我什么时候可以出院？ Yīshēng, wǒ shénme shíhou kěyǐ chūyuán? *When can I be discharged, doctor?*

chūzū 出租 [comp: 出 out + 租 rent] V have … for hire, rent

chūzūchē 出租车 N taxi (辆 liàng)

NOTE: The slang expression 打的 dǎdī, which means *to call a taxi* or *to travel by taxi*, is very popular in everyday Chinese.

chū 初 I N beginning 月初 yuèchū at the beginning of a month / 年初 niánchū at the beginning of a year II ADJ at the beginning, for the first time III PREF (used for the first ten days of a lunar month), the first 初一 chū yī the first day (of a lunar month) / 五月初八 wǔyuè chū bā the eighth day of the fifth lunar month / 年初一 / 大年初一 nián chū yī / dà nián chū yī the first day of the first lunar

month (Chinese New Year's Day)

chūjí 初级 [modif: 初 initial + 级 grade] **ADJ** elementary, initial

初级中学 **chūjí zhōngxué** / 初中 **chūzhōng** junior high school

chú 除 v get rid of

除草 **chú cǎo** to weed / 除虫 **chú chóng** kill insects, insecticide

chúfēi 除非 **CONJ** unless, only if

chúle … (yǐwài) 除了 … (以外) **PREP** except, besides

NOTE: (1) While *except* and *besides* are two distinct words in English, 除了… 以外, **chúle … yǐwài** may mean either *except* or *besides*. (2) 以外 **yǐwài** may be omitted, i.e. 除了…以外 **chúle … (yǐwài)** and 除了… **chúle** are the same.

chúxī 除夕 **N** Chinese New Year's Eve

NOTE: In colloquial Chinese, the Chinese New Year's Eve is called 大年夜 **dàniányè**. The dinner on the Chinese New Year's Eve is 年夜饭 **niányèfàn**.

chú 厨 TRAD 廚 **N** kitchen

chúfáng 厨房 [modif: 厨 kitchen + 房 room] **N** kitchen

chǔ 处 TRAD 處 v handle, deal with

chǔlǐ 处理 v handle, deal with

chǔ 储 TRAD 儲 v store

chǔxù 储蓄 [comp: 储 store + 蓄 save up] v save (money), deposit (money) 活期储蓄 **huóqī chǔxù** checking account

chǔ 础 TRAD 礎 **N** plinth (See jīchǔ 基础.)

chǔ 楚 adj clear, neat (See qīngchu 清楚.)

chù 处 TRAD 處 **N** 1 place, location 2 a government department (bigger than a section 科 and smaller than a bureau 局)

chù 触 TRAD 觸 v touch (See jiēchù 接触.)

chù 畜 **N** (domestic) animal, beast

chùsheng 畜生 **N** animal (used as a verbal abuse)

chuān 穿 v 1 wear (clothes or shoes), be dressed in 2 put on (clothes or shoes)

chuānzhe 穿着 v be dressed in

chuānzhuó 穿着 **N** dress, the way of dressing, attire ■ 他很讲究穿着。 **Tā hěn jiǎngjiu chuānzhuó.** *He pays a great deal of attention to his clothes.*

chuán 船 **N** boat, ship

坐船 **zuòchuán** travel by boat/ship / 划船 **huáchuán** row a boat

chuán 传 TRAD 傳 v 1 pass (something) on 2 spread (news, rumor)

chuánbō 传播 [comp: 传 spread + 播 sow] v propagate, disseminate

chuánshuō 传说 **N** legend, folktale

chuántǒng 传统 **N** tradition, heritage

chuánzhēn 传真 [v+obj: 传 transmit + 真 true] **N** fax

chuāng 窗 **N** window

chuānghu 窗户 [comp: 窗 window + 户 door] **N** window

打开窗户 **dǎkāi chuānghu** open a window / 关上窗户 **guānshang chuānghu** close a window

chuānglián 窗帘 **N** (window) curtain

chuáng 床 **N** bed (张 zhāng)

单人床 **dānrén chuáng** single bed / 双人床 **shuāngrén chuáng** double bed

chuángdān 床单 **N** bedsheet (条 tiáo)

chuàng 创 TRAD 創 v create

chuàngzào 创造 [comp: 创 create + 造 build, make] v create

chuàngzàoxìng 创造性 **N** creativity

chuàngzuò 创作 [comp: 创 create + 作 make] **V & N** create (works of art and literature); work of art or literature

chuī 吹 v blow, puff

chūn 春 **N** spring

chūnjié 春节 [modif: 春 spring + 节 festival] **N** the Spring Festival (the Chinese New Year)

chūntiān 春天 [modif: 春 spring + 天 days] **N** spring

chún 纯 TRAD 純 **ADJ** pure

chúnjié 纯洁 **ADJ** pure, clean-minded, unselfish

cí 词 TRAD 詞 **N** word

cídiǎn 词典 N dictionary (本 **běn**)

cíhuì 词汇 N vocabulary, lexicon

cíyǔ 词语 [comp: 词 word + 语 speech] N word, phrase, wording

cí 磁 N magnetism

cíkǎ 磁卡 [modif: 磁 magnetic + 卡 card] N magnetic card (for making telephone calls, etc.)

cípán 磁盘 [modif: 磁 magnetic + 盘 disc] N magnetic disc

cí 辞 TRAD 辭 V take leave

cízhí 辞职 [v+obj: 辞 take leave + 职 position] V resign

cí 雌 ADJ female (of animals) (ANTONYM 雄 **xióng**)

cǐ 此 PRON 1 this ▪ 此路不通。**Cǐ lù bù tōng.** *This road is blocked. (→ No through road.)* 此时此地 **cǐshí cǐdì** here and now 2 here ▪ 会议到此结束。**Huìyì dào cǐ jiéshù.** *The meeting ends here/at this point. (→ This is the end of the meeting.)*

cǐhòu 此后 CONJ after this, ever after

cǐkè 此刻 N this moment

cǐshí 此时 N right now

cǐwài 此外 CONJ besides, apart from (that), as well

cì 次¹ MEASURE WORD time (expressing frequency of an act) ▪ 我去过他家两次。**Wǒ qùguo tā jiā liǎng cì.** *I've been to his home twice.*

cì 次² ADJ inferior

cìpǐn 次品 [modif: 次 inferior + 品 article, product] N substandard product

cìyào 次要 ADJ next in importance, of secondary importance

cì 伺 V wait on

cìhou 伺候 V wait on, serve

cì 刺 V & N prick; thorn

cìjī 刺激 [comp: 刺 prick + 激 excite] V & N 1 irritate; irritation 2 stimulate, give incentive to; stimulation, incentive

cōng 囱 N chimney (See **yāncōng** 烟囱.)

cōng 聪 TRAD 聰 ADJ acute hearing

cōngmíng 聪明 [comp: 聪 acute sense of hearing + 明 keen sense of eyesight] ADJ clever, bright, intelligent

cōng 匆 ADJ hurriedly

cōngcōng 匆匆 ADJ hurriedly, in a rush

cōngmáng 匆忙 [comp: 匆 hurriedly + 忙 busy] ADJ in a hurry, in haste

cōng 葱 N onion, scallion 大葱 **dàcōng** green Chinese onion / 小葱 **xiǎocōng** spring onion / 洋葱 **yángcōng** onion

cóng 从 TRAD 從 PREP following, from 从···出发 **cóng...chūfā** set out from …

cóngbù 从不 ADV never

cóngcǐ 从此 CONJ since then, from then on

cóng ··· dào ··· 从 ··· 到 ··· PREP from … to …, from … till … 从早到晚 **cóng-zǎo-dào-wǎn** from morning till night, long hours in a day / 从古到今 **cóng-gǔ-dào-jīn** from remote past till now in history

cóng'ér 从而 CONJ thus, thereby

cónglái 从来 ADV always, ever 从来不 **cónglái bù** never

cóng ··· qǐ 从 ··· 起 PREP starting from …

cóngqián 从前 I N past time, past, in the past II ADV once upon a time (used in story-telling)

cóngróng 从容 ADJ unhurried, leisurely

còu 凑 V put together, pool 凑钱 **còu qián** pool money

còuqiǎo 凑巧 ADJ luckily, as luck would have it

cū 粗 ADJ thick (ANTONYM 细 **xì**)

cūxīn 粗心 [modif: 粗 thick + 心 the heart] ADJ careless (ANTONYM 细心 **xìxīn**)

cù 促 V urge

cùjìn 促进 [v+obj: 促 promote + 进 progress] V promote, advance

cuì 脆 ADJ crisp (See **gāncuì** 干脆.)

cuìruò 脆弱 [comp: 脆 crispy + 弱 weak] ADJ fragile, frail

cūn 村 N village

cūnzi 村子 [suffix: 村 village + 子 nominal suffix] **n** village (座 **zuò**)

cún 存 v store, keep

cúnzài 存在 v exist

cùn 寸 MEASURE WORD a traditional Chinese unit of length (equal to ¹/₃₀ meter)
英寸 **yīngcùn** inch

cuò 错 TRAD 錯 ADJ wrong, mistaken (**ANTONYM** 对 **duì**)
错字 **cuòzì** a wrong character

cuòwù 错误 [comp: 错 wrong + 误 miss] **n & ADJ** mistake, error; wrong, mistaken
犯错误 **fàn cuòwù** make a mistake / 纠正错误 **jiūzhèng cuòwù** correct a mistake

cuò 措 v arrange, handle

cuòshī 措施 n measure, step

D

dā 答 v Same as 答 **dá**

dāying 答应 [comp: 答 reply + 应 respond] **v 1** answer, reply **2** promise

dá 达 TRAD 達 v reach, attain

dádào 达到 [comp: 达 reach + 到 reach] **v** reach, achieve

dá 答 v answer, reply ∎ 这个问题我不会答。**Zhège wèntí wǒ bú huì dá.** *I can't answer this question.*

dá'àn 答案 [modif: 答 answer + 案 file] **n** answer (to a list of questions)

dǎ 打 v 1 strike, hit **2** play (certain ball games)
打篮球 **dǎ lánqiú** play basketball **3** send, dispatch
打电话 **dǎ diànhuà** make a telephone call

NOTE: While its basic meaning is *strike, hit*, **dǎ 打** forms many semi-idioms with the words following it, and has multiple meanings in everyday Chinese.

dǎban 打扮 v dress up, make up

dǎchà 打岔 v interrupt (somebody's talk), cut in

dǎ chē 打车 v call a taxi

dǎdǎo 打倒 [v+compl: 打 strike + 倒 down] **v** strike down, overthrow, down with ...

dǎ dī 打的 v Same as 打车 **dǎ chē**

dǎgōng 打工 v work (especially as a manual laborer)

dǎ jiāodao 打交道 v to have dealings with, negotiate with
和各式各样的人打交道 **hé gèshìgèyàng de rén dǎjiāodào** deal with all kinds of people

dǎ kǎ 打卡 v punch a card, record presence at work by punching a time clock

dǎ kēshui 打瞌睡 v doze, doze off
打一会儿瞌睡 **dǎ yíhuìr kēshuì** have a doze-off

dǎ pēnti 打喷嚏 v sneeze

dǎpò 打破 v break
打破花瓶 **dǎpò huāpíng** break a vase / 打破世界纪录 **dǎpò shìjiè jìlù** break a world record

dǎ qiú 打球 v play baseball/basketball/ volleyball, etc.

dǎrǎo 打扰 v disturb, interrupt

NOTE: When you call on someone, especially at their home, you can say 打扰你们了 **Dǎrǎo nǐmen le** as a polite expression. You can use **dǎjiǎo 打搅** instead of **dǎrǎo 打扰**, with exactly the same meaning.

dǎsǎo 打扫 v clean up

dǎsuàn 打算 [comp: 打 act + 算 calculate] **v** plan, intend

dǎtīng 打听 v inquire, ask

dǎyìnjī 打印机 n printer

dǎ zhāohu 打招呼 v 1 greet, say hello to **2** let know, notify

dǎzhé 打折 v give a discount

dǎzhēn 打针 v give (or get) an injection

dǎzì 打字 v type

dà 大 ADJ big, large (ANTONYM 小 xiǎo)

dàdǎn 大胆 [modif: 大 big + 胆 gall bladder] ADJ bold, courageous

NOTE: The ancient Chinese believed that the gall bladder was the organ of courage—if one had a big gall bladder it meant that the person was endowed with courage and daring, and if one was timid it was because he had a small gall bladder. Therefore, 他胆子很大 Tā dǎnzi hěn dà and 他很大胆 Tā hěn dàdǎn mean *He is bold*; 他胆子很小 Tā dǎnzi hěn xiǎo and 他很胆小 Tā hěn dǎnxiǎo mean *He is timid*.

dàduō 大多 [modif: 大 big + 多 many] ADV for the most part, mostly

dàduōshù 大多数 [modif: 大 big + 多数 majority] N great majority, overwhelming majority

dàfang 大方 ADJ 1 generous, liberal
出手大方 chūshǒu dàfang spend money freely, very generous
2 elegant and natural
式样大方 shìyàng dàfang elegant style

dàgài 大概 I ADJ general, more or less
大概的意思 dàgài de yìsi the general idea
II ADV probably

dàhuì 大会 [modif: 大 big + 会 meeting] N assembly, congress, rally

dàjiā 大家 PRON all, everybody
我们大家 wǒmen dàjiā all of us /
你们大家 nǐmen dàjiā all of you /
他们大家 tāmen dàjiā all of them

dàjiē 大街 [modif: 大 big + 街 street] N main street
逛大街 guàng dàjiē take a stroll in the streets, do window-shopping

dàliàng 大量 ADJ a large amount of, a large number of

dàlù 大陆 [modif: 大 big + 陆 land] N continent, mainland

dàmǐ 大米 [modif: 大 big + 米 rice] N rice

dàpī 大批 [modif: 大 big + 批 batch] ADJ a large quantity of, lots of

dàren 大人 [modif: 大 big + 人 person] N adult, grown-up (ANTONYM 小孩儿 xiǎoháir)

dà rénwù 大人物 N great personage, big shot, very important person (VIP)

dàshà 大厦 N big, imposing building (座 zuò)

dàshēng 大声 [modif: 大 big + 声 sound, voice] ADJ in a loud voice

dàshǐ 大使 N ambassador
中国驻美国大使 Zhōngguó zhù Měiguó dàshǐ Chinese ambassador to the US

dàshǐguǎn 大使馆 [modif: 大 big + 使 envoy + 馆 house] N embassy

dàshì 大事 N matter of importance

dàxiàng 大象 N elephant (头 tóu)

dàxiǎo 大小 [comp: 大 big + 小 small] N size

NOTE: 大 dà and 小 xiǎo are opposites. Put together, 大小 dàxiǎo means *size*. There are other Chinese nouns made up of antonyms, e.g. 高矮 gāo'ǎi *height*, 长短 chángduǎn *length*, 好坏 hǎohuài *quality*.

dàxíng 大型 [modif: 大 big + 型 model] ADJ large-scale, large-sized

dàxué 大学 [modif: 大 big + 学 school] N university, institution of higher education (座 zuò, 所 suǒ)
考大学 kǎo dàxué sit for the university entrance examination / 考上大学 kǎo shàng dàxué pass the university entrance examination / 上大学 shàng dàxué go to university, study in a university

Dàyángzhōu 大洋洲 [modif: 大 big + 洋 ocean + 洲 continent] N Oceania

dàyī 大衣 [modif: 大 big + 衣 clothes, coat] N overcoat

dàyuē 大约 ADV approximately, about, nearly

dāi 待 V stay (used colloquially)

dàifu 大夫 N Same as 医生 yīshēng, used more as a colloquialism (位 wèi)

dài 代[1] v take the place of, perform on behalf of
代课老师 **dàikè lǎoshī** substitute teacher / 代校长 **dài xiàozhǎng** acting principal / 代部长 **dài bùzhǎng** acting minister
dài 代[2] N 1 generation 2 dynasty

NOTE: The major Chinese dynasties are 秦 **Qín**, 汉 **Hàn**, 唐 **Táng**, 宋 **Sòng**, 元 **Yuán**, 明 **Míng**, 清 **Qīng**.

dàibiǎo 代表 [comp: 代 substitute + 表 manifest] v & N represent, indicate; representative
dàitì 代替 v substitute for, replace, instead of
dài 贷 TRAD 貸 v loan
dàikuǎn 贷款 [modif: 贷 loan + 款 fund] v & N loan money to, borrow money from; loan
贷款给一家小企业 **dàikuǎn gěi yìjiā xiǎo qǐyè** loan money to a small business / 向银行贷款 **xiàng yínháng dàikuǎn** ask the bank for a loan / 无息贷款 **wúxīdàikuǎn** interest-free loan
dài 带 TRAD 帶 v bring, take
带来/带 ⋯ 来 **dàilai/dài ... lái** bring … / 带去/带 ⋯ 去 **dàiqu/dài ... qù** take…
■ ...你不知道图书馆在哪儿？我带你去。**Nǐ bù zhīdào túshūguǎn zài nǎr? Wǒ dài nǐ qù.** *You don't know where the library is? I'll take you there.*
dài 待 v treat, deal with
dàiyù 待遇 N 1 treatment 2 remuneration
dài 袋 N sack, bag
口袋 **kǒudài** pocket

NOTE: 袋 **dài** is seldom used alone. It is either used with the nominal suffix 子 **zi** to form 袋子 **dài zi**, or with another noun to form a compound word, e.g. 口袋 **kǒudài** (pocket).

dài 戴 v wear, put on
戴手套儿 **dài shǒutàor** wear gloves / 戴眼镜 **dài yǎnjìng** wear spectacles

dài 逮 v catch
dàibǔ 逮捕 [comp: 逮 arrest + 捕 capture] v arrest, take into custody
dān 单 TRAD 單 ADJ single, separate
dānchún 单纯 [comp: 单 single + 纯 pure] ADJ simple-minded, ingenuous
dāncí 单词 [modif: 单 single + 词 word] N (a single) word
dāndiào 单调 [modif: 单 single + 调 tone] ADJ monotonous
dāndú 单独 [comp: 单 single + 独 alone] ADJ alone, on one's own
dānqīn jiātíng 单亲家庭 N single-parent family
dānrén chuáng 单人床 N single bed
dānrén fángjiān 单人房间 N (hotel) room for a single person
dānshù 单数 N odd number
dānwèi 单位 N work unit, e.g. a factory, a school, a government department
dānyuán 单元 N unit (in an apartment house), apartment, flat
dān 担 TRAD 擔 v carry on the shoulder, take on
dānrèn 担任 [comp: 担 shoulder + 任 act as] v assume the office of, act in the capacity of
dānxīn 担心 v worry, feel anxious
dān 耽 v delay
dānwù 耽误 [comp: 耽 delay + 误 miss] v delay
dǎn 胆 TRAD 膽 N 1 gall bladder 2 courage

NOTE: Ancient Chinese believed that the gall bladder determined one's courage and bravery — the bigger the gall bladder, the more courage. See note on 大胆 **dàdǎn**.

dǎndà 胆大 ADJ brave, bold
dǎnliàng 胆量 [modif: 胆 courage + 量 amount] N courage, guts
试试他的胆量 **shìshi tāde dǎnliàng** test his courage, see how brave he is
dǎnxiǎo 胆小 ADJ timid, cowardly

dǎnxiǎo guǐ 胆小鬼 N coward
dǎnzi 胆子 N courage
　胆子大 **dǎnzidà** Same as 胆大 **dǎndà** /
　胆子小 **dǎnxiǎo** Same as 胆小 **dǎnxiǎo**
dàn 旦 N dawn, morning (See **yuándàn**
　元旦.)
dàn 但 CONJ Same as 但是 **dànshì**. Used
　in writing.
dànshì 但是 CONJ but, yet
dàn 淡 ADJ 1 not salty, tasteless, bland
　2 weak (of tea, coffee) (ANTONYM 浓
　nóng)
dàn 蛋 N egg (especially chicken egg)
dàngāo 蛋糕 [modif: 蛋 egg + 糕 cake]
　N (western-style) cake
dàn 弹 TRAD 彈 N bullet
dāng 当¹ TRAD 當 PREP at the time of,
　when
dāng 当² TRAD 當 V work as, serve as
dāng … de shíhou 当 … 的时候 CONJ
　when ... ■ 当我在工作的时候，不希望
　别人来打扰我。**Dāng wǒ zài gōngzuò
　de shíhou, bù xīwàng biérén lái dǎrǎo
　wǒ.** *When I am working, I don't want to
　be disturbed.*

NOTE: 当 **dāng** may be omitted, especially
colloquially, e.g. 我在工作的时候，不希
望别人来打扰我。**Wǒ zài gōngzuò de
shíhou, bù xīwàng biérén lái dárǎo wǒ.**

dāngdì 当地 N at the place in question,
　local
　当地人 **dāngdì rén** a local / 当地时间
　dāngdì shíjiān local time
dāngjú 当局 N the authorities
dāngnián 当年 N in those years, then
dāngrán 当然 ADJ of course, that goes
　without saying
dāngshí 当时 N at that time, then
dāngxīn 当心 V be cautious, take care
dǎng 党 TRAD 黨 N political party

NOTE: 党 **dǎng** in China usually refers to
中国共产党 **Zhōngguó Gòngchǎn Dǎng**
the Chinese Communist Party.

dǎngyuán 党员 [modif: 党 party + 员
　member] N party member
dǎng 挡 TRAD 擋 V block, keep off
dàng 当 TRAD 當 V treat as, regard as,
　take for
dàngzuò 当做 V treat as, regard as
dāo 刀 N knife (把 **bǎ**)
　铅笔刀 **qiānbǐ dāo** pencil sharpener /
　水果刀 **shuǐguǒ dāo** penknife
dāozi 刀子 [suffix: 刀 knife + 子
　nominal suffix] N Same as 刀 **dāo**
dǎo 导 TRAD 導 V lead, guide
dǎoyǎn 导演 [modif: 导 guiding +
　演 acting] V & N direct (a film or play);
　director (of films or plays)
　名导演 **míng dǎoyǎn** famous director
dǎoyóu 导游 [modif: 导 guide + 游
　tourism] N tourist guide
dǎozhì 导致 V lead to, cause
dǎo 岛 TRAD 島 N island
dǎoyǔ 岛屿 [comp: 岛 island + 屿 small
　island] N island, islet
dǎo 倒 V fall, topple
dǎoméi 倒霉 V have bad luck, be out of
　luck
dào 到 V arrive, come to; up to
dàochù 到处 ADV everywhere
dàodá 到达 [comp: 到 get to + 达 reach]
　V arrive, reach
dàodǐ 到底 [v+obj: 到 get to + 底
　bottom] ADV in the end, finally, after all
dào 倒¹ V 1 put upside down 2 pour
　(water), make (tea)
dào 倒² ADV contrary to what may be
　expected (used before a verb or an
　adjective to indicate an unexpected
　action or state) ■ 弟弟倒比哥哥高。
　Dìdi dào bǐ gēge gāo. *The younger
　brother is unexpectedly taller than his
　elder brother.*
dào 道¹ N way, path
dàodé 道德 [modif: 道 the way +
　德 virtue] N moral, ethics
　讲道德 **jiǎng dàodé** pay attention to

ethics / 不道德 **bú dàodé** immoral, unethic

dàolǐ 道理 [comp: 道 way, principle + 理 pattern, reason] **N** reason, basis 讲道理 **jiǎng dàolǐ** (of a person) reasonable / 有道理 **yǒu dàolǐ** reasonable, true

NOTE: 道 **dào** and 理 **lǐ** are two important concepts in Chinese thought. The original meaning of 道 **dào** is *path, way*. By extension it denotes the fundamental principle of the universe. 理 **lǐ** originally meant *the grain of a piece of jade* and came to mean *the underlying logic of things*.

dàolù 道路 [comp: 道 way + 路 road] **N** road, path

dào 道[2] **V** Same as 说 **shuō**, used only in old-fashioned writing

dàoqiàn 道歉 [v+obj: 道 say + 歉 apology] **V & N** apologize, say sorry; apology

dào 道[3] **MEASURE WORD 1** (for things in the shape of a line) 一道光线 **yí dào guāngxiàn** a ray of sunshine **2** (for questions in school exercises, examinations, etc.) 两道难题 **liǎng dào nántí** two difficult questions

dào 稻 **N** rice, paddy

dàogǔ 稻谷 **N** seeds of rice with husk on

dé 得 **V** get, obtain

dédào 得到 **V** succeed in getting/ obtaining

NOTE: The verb 得 **dé** is seldom used alone. It is often followed by 到 **dào**, grammatically a complement, to mean *get* or *obtain*.

déyì 得意 **ADJ** complacent, deeply pleased with oneself 得意忘形 **déyì wàng xíng** be dizzy with success / 得意洋洋 **déyì yángyáng** show extreme self-complacency; be elated

dé 德 **TRAD** 德 **N** virtue, morality (See 品德 **pǐndé**, 道德 **dàodé**)

Déguó 德国 **N** Germany

Déwén 德文 **N** the German language (especially the writing)

Déyǔ 德语 **N** the German language

de 的 **PARTICLE** (attached to a word or phrase to indicate that it is an attribute. 的 **de** is normally followed by a noun.) 我的电脑 **wǒ de diànnǎo** my computer / 最新型的电脑 **zuì xīnxíng de diànnǎo** the latest model computer / 学校刚买来的电脑 **xuéxiào gāng mǎilai de diànnǎo** the computer that the school just bought

NOTE: 的, 得, 地 have different functions and are three distinct words. However, as they are pronounced the same **(de)** in everyday speech, some Chinese speakers do not distinguish them.

··· **de huà** ··· 的话 **CONJ** if

de 得 **PARTICLE** (introducing a word, phrase or clause to indicate that it is a complement. 得 **de** is normally preceded by a verb or an adjective.) 来得很早 **lái de hěn zǎo** come early / 说得大家都笑了起来 **shuō de dàjiā dōu xiàole qǐlái** talk in such a way that everybody starts laughing / 贵得很 **guì de hěn** very expensive

NOTE: See note on 的 **de**.

de 地 **PARTICLE** (attached to a word or phrase to indicate that it is an adverbial. 地 **de** is normally followed by a verb or an adjective.) 慢慢地说 **mànman de shuō** speak slowly / 愉快地旅行 **yúkuài de lǚxíng** travel pleasantly

NOTE: See note on 的 **de**.

děi 得 **MODAL V** have to, have got to

dēng 灯 **TRAD** 燈 **N** lamp, lighting 电灯 **diàndēng** light, electric light / 关灯 **guān dēng** turn off the light / 开灯 **kāi**

dēng turn on the light / 灯光 **dēngguāng**
dēng fluorescent lamp / 台灯 **táidēng** desk lamp
dēng 登 v publish (in a newspaper, a journal, etc.)
dēngjīpái 登机牌 N boarding card
dēngjì 登记 v register, check in
děng 等[1] v wait, wait for
děngdài 等待 [comp: 等 wait + 待 await, anticipate] v wait (usually used in writing)
děng yíxià 等一下 wait a minute
děng 等[2] N grade, rank, class
děngyú 等于 v be equal to, equal ■ 一加二等于三。**Yī jiā èr děngyú sān.** *One plus two equals three.*
děng 等[3] PARTICLE 1 and so on and so forth, et cetera 2 (used at the end of an enumeration)
dī 低 ADJ & V low (ANTONYM 高 **gāo**); lower
dī 滴 MEASURE WORD drop (used with liquids)
díquè 的确 ADV really, truly
dí 敌 TRAD 敵 N enemy, foe
dírén 敌人 [modif: 敌 enemy + 人 person, people] N enemy, those who are hostile
dǐ 底 N base, bottom
dǐxia 底下 [comp: 底 bottom + 下 under] N underneath, under
dì 地 N earth, ground
dìbù 地步 N 1 extent 2 (poor) condition
dìdào 地道 [modif: 地 ground + 道 way] N tunnel, underpass (条 **tiáo**)
dìdiǎn 地点 [comp: 地 place + 点 point] N the place of an event or activity, venue
dìfang 地方 [comp: 地 earth + 方 place] N 1 place, location, area (个 **gè**) 2 part of, aspect ■ 这本书我有些地方不大明白。**Zhè běn shū wǒ yǒuxie dìfang búdà míngbai.** *I'm not quite clear about parts of the book.*

NOTE: 地方 **dìfang** is a word of wide application. It has both concrete, specific senses and abstract, general senses, as in the following examples: ■ 医生: 你什么地方不舒服? **Yīshēng: Nǐ shénme dìfang bù shūfu?** *Doctor: What spot ails you? (→ What's wrong with you?)* ■ 照顾不到的地方，请多多原谅。 **Zhàogù búdào de dìfang, qǐng duōduō yuánliàng.** *If there's anything not well attended to, please accept my sincere apology.*

dìlǐ 地理 N geography
国家地理学会 **Guójiā Dìlǐ Xuéhuì** National Geographic Society / 地理学 **dìlǐxué** geography / 地理学家 **dìlǐxué jiā** geographer
dìmiàn 地面 N the earth's surface
dìqiú 地球 [modif: 地 ground + 球 ball] N the Earth, the globe
dìqū 地区 [modif: 地 place + 区 region] N region, area
dìtǎn 地毯 [modif: 地 ground + 毯 blanket] N carpet (张 **zhāng**)
dìtiě 地铁 N underground railway, subway
dìtú 地图 N map (张 **zhāng**)
dìtúcè 地图册 N atlas
dìwèi 地位 [comp: 地 place + 位 seat] N status, position
dìxià 地下 [modif: 地 ground + 下 under] N underground
地下商场 **dìxià shāngchǎng** underground shopping center / 地下铁路 (地铁) **dìxià tiělù (dìtiě)** underground railway, subway / 地下停车场 **dìxià tíngchēchǎng** parking garage, underground car park
dìzhèn 地震 [modif: 地 earth + 震 quake] N earthquake, seism (场 **cháng**)
dìzhǐ 地址 N address
dì 弟 N younger brother
dìdi 弟弟 N younger brother
dì 递 TRAD 遞 v hand over, pass on
快递 **kuàidì** fast delivery (of mail) / 快递服务 **kuài dì fúwù** fast delivery service
dì 第 PREF (used before a number to form an ordinal numeral)
第一 **dì-yī** the first / 第一天 **dì-yī tiān** the first day / 第十 **dì-shí** the tenth /

第十课 **dì-shí kè** the tenth lesson, Lesson 10

diǎn 点¹ TRAD 點 N **1** drop, point, dot
墨点 **mò diǎn** ink stain / 水点 **shuǐ diǎn** water stain
2 (indicating decimal)
三点四 **sān diǎn sì** 3.4 (three point four)

diǎn 点² TRAD 點 V drip, put a dot, touch

diǎn 点³ TRAD 點 MEASURE WORD a little, a bit
有(一)点儿… **yǒu (yì) diǎnr…** a bit…, a little… (used before nouns and adjectives)
■ 我有一点儿累，想休息一会儿。**Wǒ yǒu yìdiǎnr lèi, xiǎng xiūxi yíhuìr.** *I'm a bit tired. I want to take a little break.*

diǎnxīn 点心 N snack, light refreshments

diǎnzhōng 点钟 N o'clock ■ "现在几点钟?" "三点钟。" **"Xiànzài jǐ diǎnzhōng?" "Sān diǎnzhōng."** *"What time is it?" "Three o'clock."*

NOTE: In colloquial Chinese 点钟 **diǎn-zhōng** can be shortened to 点 **diǎn**, e.g.: ■ "现在几点?" "三点。" **"Xiànzài jǐ diǎn?" "Sān diǎn."** *"What time is it?" "Three o'clock."*

diàn 电 TRAD 電 N electricity, power; electronics
停电 **tíng diàn** power outage

diànbào 电报 [modif: 电 electric + 报 report] N telegram, cable (份 **fèn**)

diànchē 电车 [modif: 电 electricity + 车 vehicle] N trolley bus, streetcar (辆 **liàng**)

diànchí 电池 [comp: 电 electricity + 池 pool] N battery, electrical cell (节 **jié**)
可充电电池 **kě chōngdiàn diànchí** rechargeable battery

diàndēng 电灯 [modif: 电 electricity + 灯 lamp] N electric light (个 **gè**)
开电灯 **kāi diàndēng** turn on the light / 关电灯 **guān diàndēng** turn off the light

diànhuà 电话 [modif: 电 electricity + 话 speech] N telephone, telephone call (个 **gè**)
打电话 **dǎ diànhuà** use the telephone, be on the phone / 给 … 打电话 **gěi …**

… on the telephone,
听电话 **tīng diànhuà** answer a telephone call

diànnǎo 电脑 [modif: 电 electricity + 脑 brain] N computer (台 **tái**)

diànshàn 电扇 [modif: 电 electricity + 扇 fan] N electric fan

diànshì 电视 [modif: 电 electricity + 视 view] N television
看电视 **kàn diànshì** watch TV / 电视机 **diànshì jī** TV set / 电视台 **diànshì tái** TV station

diàntái 电台 [modif: 电 electricity + 台 station] N radio station

diàntī 电梯 [modif: 电 electricity + 梯 stairs] N elevator, lift
乘电梯 **chéng diàntī** go up/down by elevator

diànyǐng 电影 [modif: 电 electricity + 影 shadow] N film, movie (场 **chǎng**, 个 **gè**)
看电影 **kàn diànyǐng** see a film, go to the movies / 电影票 **diànyǐng piào** film ticket

diànyǐngyuàn 电影院 [modif: 电 影 film, movie + 院 place (for certain activities)] N cinema, cinema complex, movie theater (座 **zuò**)

diànzǐ 电子 [suffix: 电 electricity, electron + 子 nominal suffix] N electron
电子工业 **diànzǐ gōngyè** electronics industry / 电子贺卡 **diànzǐ hèkǎ** e-card / 电子游戏 **diànzǐ yóuxì** electronic game

diànzǐ yóujiàn 电子邮件 N e-mail
收到电子邮件 **shōu dào diànzǐ yóujiàn** receive e-mails / 发电子邮件 **fā diànzǐ yóujiàn** send e-mails

diàn 店 N Same as 商店 **shāngdiàn**

diào 掉 V fall, drop

NOTE: 掉 **diào** is often used after a verb, as a complement to mean "finish [doing…]," e.g. 吃掉 **chīdiao** eat up ■ 水果都吃掉了。**Shuǐguǒ dōu chīdiao le.** *The fruit is all eaten up.*

diào 钓 TRAD 釣 v angle ▪ 你钓到几条
鱼? **Nǐ diàodao jǐ tiáo yú?** *How many fish
have you caught [with hook and line]?*

diào 调 TRAD 調 v 1 exchange, swap
2 transfer

diàochá 调查 V & N investigate;
investigation

dié 叠 v lap, overlap

dié 碟 N disc (See **guāngdié** 光碟.)

dié 蝶 N butterfly (See **húdié** 蝴蝶.)

dīng 钉 TRAD 釘 N nail

dīngzi 钉子 N nail

dǐng 顶 TRAD 頂 I N top (of the head),
peak, summit
山顶 **shāndǐng** peak / 头顶 **tóudǐng**
crown of the head / 屋顶 **wūdǐng** roof
II v carry on the head, hit with the head

dìng 订 TRAD 訂 v book
订房间 **dìng fángjiān** reserve a hotel
or motel room / 订票 **dìng piào** book a
ticket / 订座 **dìng zuò** book a table (at a
restaurant), book a seat (in a theater)

diū 丢 v lose, throw away ▪ 我的表丢了。
Wǒ de biǎo diū le. *I've lost my watch.*

dōng 东 TRAD 東 N east; eastern

dōngbēi 东北 [comp: 东 east + 北
north] N northeast, the Northeast

NOTE: 东北 **dōngběi** as a specific geograph-
ical term refers to the northeastern part of
China, which used to be known in the West
as Manchuria.

dōngbian 东边 N the east side, to the
east, in the east

Dōngfāng 东方 [modif: 东 east + 方
direction, part] N the East, the Orient
东方文化 **Dōngfāng wénhuà** the cultures
of the East

dōngmiàn 东面 N Same as 东边 **dōngbian**

dōngnán 东南 [comp: 东 east + 南
south] N southeast

dōngxi 东西 N 1 thing, things (个 **gè**,
件 **jiàn**, 种 **zhǒng**) ▪ 这些东西都是小
明的。**Zhèxiē dōngxi dōu shì Xiǎo Míng**

de. *All these things are Xiao Ming's.* 2 a
person or animal (used affectionately or
disapprovingly in colloquial Chinese)
▪ 这小东西真可爱。**Zhè xiǎo dōngxi
zhēn kě'ài.** *What a cute little thing.
(referring to a baby or kitten).*

NOTE: 东西 **dōngxi**, which literally means
east and west, is an extremely common
"all-purpose" noun that can denote
any object or objects in Chinese. More
examples: ▪ 妈妈出去买东西了。**Māma
chūqu mǎi dōngxi le.** *Mother's gone
shopping.* ▪ 我想喝点儿东西。**Wǒ xiǎng
hē diǎnr dōngxi.** *I'd like to have a drink.*

dōng 冬 N winter

dōngtiān 冬天 [modif: 冬 winter +
天 days] N winter

dǒng 懂 v comprehend, understand
读懂 **dúdǒng** read and understand / 看懂
kàndǒng see (or read) and understand /
听懂 **tīngdǒng** listen and understand

dòng 动 TRAD 動 v move

dònggōng 动工 v begin construction

dònghuà piàn 动画片 N animated
cartoon, cartoons (部 **bù**)

dòngrén 动人 [modif: 动 moving +
人 people] ADJ moving, touching

dòngwù 动物 [modif: 动 moving +
物 object] N animal (只 **zhī**)

dòngwùxué 动物学 N zoology

dòngwùyuán 动物园 N zoo

dòngzuò 动作 [comp: 动 act + 作 do] N
movement (of the body)

dòng 冻 TRAD 凍 v freeze
冻肉 **dòngròu** frozen meat / 肉冻
ròudòng jellied meat / 水果冻 **shuǐguǒ
dòng** fruit jelly

dòng 洞 N hole, cave, cavity

dòngxué 洞穴 N cave (for hiding),
cavern

dōu 都 ADV all, both, every and each,
without exception ▪ 我每天都跑步。
Wǒ měi tiān dōu pǎobù. *I jog every day.*
▪ 我所有的朋友都来了。**Wǒ suǒyǒu de**

péngyou dōu lái le. *All my friends have come.*

NOTE: When words like 每天 **měi tiān** (every day), 每个 **měi ge** (every one), 大家 **dàjiā** (everybody) or 所有的 **suǒyǒu de** (all) are used, they usually occur with the adverb 都 **dōu.**

dǒu 抖 v tremble, shiver (See **fādǒu** 发抖.)

dòu 斗 TRAD 鬥 v fight

dòu 豆 N bean, pea

dòufu 豆腐 [modif: 豆 soybean + 腐 curd] N bean curd, tofu

dū 都 N capital city, metropolis

dūshì 都市 N metropolis, big city

dú 独 TRAD 獨 ADJ solitary, alone

dúlì 独立 [modif: 独 solitary + 立 stand] v be independent ■ 孩子大了都想独立，父母不用太担心。**Háizi dàle dōu xiǎng dúlì, fùmǔ búyòng tài dānxīn.** *When children grow up, they all want to be independent. Parents should not be too worried.*

dútè 独特 [comp: 独 solitary + 特 unique] ADJ unique, distinctive 独特的风格 **dú tè de fēnggé** unique style

dú 读 TRAD 讀 v 1 read, read aloud 2 attend (a school), study (in a school) 读小学/中学/大学 **dú xiǎoxué/ zhōngxué/dàxué** attend a primary school/high school/university

NOTE: (1) In colloquial Chinese, 读 **dú** may be replaced by 看 **kàn** when used in the sense of "read," e.g. 看书 **kàn shū**, 看报 **kàn bào**. (2) When used in the sense of "attend (school)" or "study (in a school)" 读 **dú** may be replaced by 念 **niàn** to become 念小学/中学/大学 **niàn xiǎoxué/zhōngxué/dàxué**, which is more colloquial.

dúshū 读书 [v+obj: 读 read + 书 book] v read, study

dúzhě 读者 [suffix: 读 read + 者 nominal suffix] N reader

dú 毒 N poison, toxin

毒蛇 **dúshé** poisonous snake / 蛇毒 **shé dú** venom of a snake / 有毒 **yǒudú** poisonous

dǔ 堵 v block up, stop up

dǔchē 堵车 N traffic jam

dù 肚 N stomach

dùzi 肚子 [suffix: 肚 stomach + 子 nominal suffix] N abdomen, stomach, belly

dù 度 I N limit, extent II MEASURE WORD degree (of temperature, longitude, latitude, etc.) ■ 今天最高气温是二十五度。**Jīntiān zuì gāo qìwēn shì èrshíwǔ dù.** *The highest temperature today is 25 degrees.*

dùguò 度过 v spend (a period of time)

dù 妒 v be jealous

dùjì 妒忌 v be jealous, envy

duǎn 短 ADJ (of length, time) short (ANTONYM 长 **cháng**)

duǎnqī 短期 [modif: 短 short + 期 period] N short-term

duǎnxìn 短信 [modif: 短 short + 信 letter] N text message (by cell phone), text

duàn 段 MEASURE WORD section (of something long) 一段路 **yí duàn lù** a section of a road/ street, part of a journey / 一段时间 **yí duàn shíjiān** a period of time / 一段经历 **yí duàn jīnglì** an experience (in life)

duàn 断 TRAD 斷 v break, snap, break off, cut off 断电 **duàn diàn** cut off electricity / 断水 **duàn shuǐ** cut off water supply

duàn duàn xù xù 断断续续 ADJ intermittent, sporadic, off and on

duàn nǎi 断奶 v wean (a child)

duàn 锻 TRAD 鍛 v forge, shape metal

duànliàn 锻炼 [comp: 锻 shape metal + 炼 smelt] v undergo physical training, do physical exercises

duì 对[1] TRAD 對 v 1 treat, deal with 2 Same as 对于 **duìyú**

duì 对[2] TRAD 對 ADJ correct, true (ANTONYM 错 cuò) ▪ 你说得很对。 **Nǐ shuō de hěn duì.** *You spoke correctly. (→ You're right.)*

NOTE: 对不对 **duì bu duì** is used at the end of a sentence to form a question, e.g. ▪ 你是英国人，对不对? **Nǐ shì Yīngguórén, duì bu duì?** *You're from the UK, aren't you?*

duì 对[3] TRAD 對 MEASURE WORD pair, two (matching people or things)
一对花瓶 **yí duì huāpíng** two matching vases / 一对夫妻 **yí duì fūqī** a couple (husband and wife)

duìbǐ 对比 [comp: 对 check + 比 compare, contrast] v compare and contrast

duìbuqǐ 对不起 IDIOM I'm sorry, I beg your pardon

NOTE: 对不起 **duìbuqǐ** is a very useful idiomatic expression in colloquial Chinese. It is used when you've done something wrong or caused some inconvenience to others. For more formal occasions, use 请原谅 **qǐng yuánliàng** *please forgive me* or *my apologies.*

duìdài 对待 [comp: 对 deal with + 待 treat] v treat (people), approach (matters)

duìfāng 对方 [modif: 对 the opposite side + 方 side] N the other side, the other party

duìhuà 对话 V & N have a dialogue; dialogue

duìmiàn 对面 N opposite, the opposite side

duìshǒu 对手 [modif: 对 opposite + 手 hand] N opponent
竞争对手 **jìngzhēng duìshǒu** opponent in a competition, rival

duìxiàng 对象 N 1 person or thing to which an action or a feeling is directed, object 2 marriage partner, fiancé(e)
找对象 **zhǎo duìxiàng** look for a marriage partner

duìyú 对于 PREP 1 (introducing the object of an action), regarding 2 (indicating a certain relationship), to, towards

duì 队 TRAD 隊 N team
队员 **duìyuán** member of a team / 篮球队 **lánqiú duì** basketball team / 足球队 **zúqiú duì** soccer team

duìzhǎng 队长 [modif: 队 team + 长 chief] N team leader

duì 兑 v exchange, convert

duìhuàn 兑换 [comp: 兑 convert + 换 exchange] v (of currency) exchange, convert
兑换率 **duìhuànlǜ** exchange rate

dūn 吨 TRAD 噸 MEASURE WORD ton

dūn 蹲 v squat

dùn 盾 N shield (See **máodùn** 矛盾.)

dùn 顿 TRAD 頓 MEASURE WORD (for meals) ▪ 我们一天吃三顿饭: 早饭、午饭、晚饭。 **Wǒmen yì tiān chī sān dùn fàn: zǎofàn, wǔfàn, wǎnfàn.** *We have three meals a day: breakfast, lunch and supper (or dinner).*

duō 多 I ADJ many, much, more (ANTONYM 少 shǎo) II ADV 1 how ...! ▪ 要是我能去北京学中文，多好啊! **Yàoshì wǒ néng qù Běijīng xué Zhōngwén, duō hǎo a!** *How nice it would be if I could go to Beijing to study Chinese!* 2 how ...? ▪ 老先生，您多大了? **Lǎo xiānsheng, nín duō dà le?** *How old are you, sir? (to an elderly man)*

duōkuī 多亏 ADV luckily, fortunately

duōme 多么 ADV Same as **duō** 多 II 1

duōshǎo 多少 [comp: 多 many, much + 少 few, little] PRON how many, how much
多少钱... **duōshǎo qián** ... How much is ...? / 没有多少 **méiyǒu duōshǎo** not many, not much

NOTE: See note on 几 **jǐ**.

duōshù 多数 [modif: 多 many + 数 number] N majority

duōyú 多余 [comp: 多 more + 余 spare] **ADJ** surplus

duó 夺 TRAD 奪 **V** take by force, win

duǒ 朵 MEASURE WORD (for flowers)
■ 送给你一朵花。**Sòng gěi nǐ yì duǒ huā.** *Here's a flower for you.*

duǒ 躲 V hide (oneself)

duǒbì 躲避 [comp: 躲 hide + 避 avoid] **V** hide, avoid, keep away from
躲避债主 **duǒbì zhàizhǔ** hide from the creditor

duǒcáng 躲藏 [comp: 躲 hide + 藏 hide] **V** go into hiding

E

é 额 TRAD 額 **N** the forehead
额头 **étóu** the forehead

é 俄 N (a shortened form of) Russia or Russian

Éguó 俄国 N Russia, the state of Russia

Éluósī 俄罗斯 N Russia
俄罗斯人 **Éluósī rén** a Russian person, the Russian people

Éwén 俄文 [comp: 俄 Russian + 文 writing] **N** the Russian language (especially the writing)

Éyǔ 俄语 [comp: 俄 Russia + 语 speech] **N** the Russian language

é 鹅 TRAD 鵝 **N** goose (只 **zhī**)
天鹅 **tiān'é** swan

è 饿 TRAD 餓 **ADJ** hungry, famished (ANTONYM 饱 **bǎo**)

è 恶 TRAD 惡 **ADJ** bad, evil, wicked (ANTONYM 善 **shàn**) ■ 人性是善，还是恶? **Rénxìng shì shàn, háishi è?** *Is human nature good or bad?*

èdú 恶毒 [comp: 恶 evil + 毒 poisonous] **ADJ** vicious, malicious

èliè 恶劣 [comp: 恶 bad + 劣 inferior] **ADJ** very bad, abominable

ēn 恩 N kindness, grace

ér 儿 TRAD 兒 **N** child, son

értóng 儿童 [comp: 儿 child + 童 child] **N** child, children
儿童时代 **értóng shídài** childhood

érzi 儿子 [suffix: 儿 son + 子 nominal suffix] **N** son (个 **gè**)

ér 而 CONJ (indicating a contrast) but, yet, on the other hand ■ 学而不用，等于没学。**Xué ér bú yòng, děngyú méi xué.** *If you learn skills but do not use them, it is tantamount to not having learnt them at all.*

érqiě 而且 CONJ moreover, what's more
不但 …, 而且 … **búdàn ..., érqiě ...** not only …, but also … ■ 我爸爸不但会开车，而且会修车。**Wǒ bàba búdàn huì kāi chē, érqiě huì xiū chē.** *My daddy can not only drive but also fix cars.* ■ 这个电脑游戏不但小孩爱玩，而且大人也爱玩。**Zhège diànnǎo yóuxì búdàn xiǎohái ài wán, érqiě dàren yě ài wán.** *Not only children but also grown-ups like to play this electronic game.*

ěr 耳 N the ear

ěrduo 耳朵 N the ear (只 **zhī**)

ěrhuán 耳环 N earrings (付 **fù**)
戴耳环 **dài ěrhuán** wear earrings

èr 二 NUMERAL second, two ■ 二千二百二十二 **èrqiān èrbǎi èrshí'èr** *two thousand, two hundred and twenty-two*

NOTE: See note on 两 **liǎng**.

F

fā 发 TRAD 發 **V 1** send out, release **2** develop (into a state)
发传真 **fā chuánzhēn** send a fax / 发电子邮件 **fā diànzǐ yóujiàn** send an e-mail message / 发（手机）短信 **fā (shǒujī) duǎnxin** send a text message (by cell phone)

fābiǎo 发表 [comp: 发 release + 表 express] v publicize, make known, publish

fāchóu 发愁 [v+obj:发 develop + 愁 worry] v get worried, fret

fāchū 发出 [comp: 发 release + 出 out] v 1 produce, emit, give off 2 send out

fādá 发达 ADJ developed, well-developed

fādǒu 发抖 v tremble, shiver, shake

fāhuī 发挥 v allow display, give free rein to

fāhuǒ 发火 [v+obj: 发 release + 火 fire] v lose one's temper, flare up

fāmíng 发明 v & n invent; invention (项 xiàng)

fāpiào 发票 n receipt (张 zhāng)

fāshāo 发烧 [v+obj: 发 develop + 烧 burning, fever] v run a fever

fāshēng 发生 [comp: 发 develop + 生 grow] v take place, happen, occur

fāxiàn 发现 [comp: 发 develop + 现 show] v discover, find, find out

fāyán 发言 [v+obj: 发 release + 言 words] v & n speak (at a meeting), make a speech; speech, talk

fāyánrén 发言人 n spokesperson

fāyīn 发音 [v+obj: 发 send out + 音 sound] n pronunciation

fāzhǎn 发展 [comp: 发 develop + 展 unfold] v develop, expand, grow 发展中国家 fāzhǎnzhōng guójiā developing country

fá 乏 v lack (See quēfá 缺乏.)

fá 罚 TRAD 罰 v punish, penalize 罚款单 fákuǎndān fine notice / 缴罚款 jiāo fákuǎn pay a fine

fǎ 法 n method, law

Fǎguó 法国 [modif: 法 France + 国 state, country] n France

fǎlǜ 法律 [comp: 法 law + 律 rule] n law 违反法律 wéifǎn fǎlǜ violate the law / 修改法律 xiūgǎi fǎlǜ amend a law

Fǎwén 法文 [comp: 法 France + 文 writing] n the French language (especially the writing)

Fǎyǔ 法语 [comp: 法 France + 语 speech] n the French language

fǎyuàn 法院 [modif: 法 law + 院 house] n law court, court 高级人民法院 gāojí rénmín fǎyuàn Supreme People's Court / 中级人民法院 zhōngjí rénmín fǎyuàn Intermediate People's Court

fān 翻 v turn, turn over

fānyì 翻译 v & n translate, interpret; translator, interpreter 把 … 翻译成 … bǎ ... fānyì chéng ... translate … into … ◼ 你能不能把这封信翻译成中文? Nǐ néng bu néng bǎ zhè fēng xìn fānyì chéng Zhōngwén? *Can you translate this letter into Chinese?* 当翻译 dāng fānyì to work as a translator (or interpreter)

fān 帆 n sail

fānchuán 帆船 n sailboat (艘 sōu)

fán 烦 TRAD 煩 ADJ annoyed

fánmèn 烦闷 [comp: 烦 annoyed + 闷 stuffy] ADJ worried and unhappy

fánnǎo 烦恼 [comp: 烦 annoyed + 恼 angry] ADJ annoyed and angry, vexed

fán 繁 ADJ numerous, abundant

fánróng 繁荣 [comp: 繁 abundant + 荣 flourishing] ADJ prosperous, thriving

fántǐ zì 繁体字 [modif: 繁 complicated + 体 style + 字 character] n the original complicated form of a Chinese character, traditional character, e.g. 門 for 门.

NOTE: As 繁体字 literally means *complicated style character*, some people don't like the negative implication, and prefer to use the term 正体字 zhèngtǐ zì *orthographic characters* or 传统字 chuántǒng zì *traditional characters*. 繁体字 are used in Taiwan, Hong Kong and overseas Chinese communities.

fǎn 反 ADJ reverse, opposite (ANTONYM 正 zhèng) ◼ 请看反面。Qǐng kàn fǎnmiàn. *Please read the reverse side.*

fǎnduì 反对 [modif: 反 opposing + 对 deal with] v oppose, object (ANTONYM 同意 **tóngyì**)

反对意见 **fǎnduì yìjiàn** opposing opinion / 反对党 **fǎnduì dǎng** the Opposition [party]

fǎn'ér 反而 ADV contrary to expectations, instead

fǎnfù 反复 [comp: 反 reverse + 复 duplicate] ADV repeatedly, over and over again

fǎnyìng 反应 [comp: 反 opposite + 应 reply, respond] N response, reaction

fǎnyìng 反映 v 1 reflect, mirror 2 report, make known, convey

fǎnzheng 反正 [comp: 反 reverse + 正 front] ADV anyway, at any rate ▪ 你同意也好，不同意也好，我反正决定这么办了。 **Nǐ tóngyì yěhǎo, bùtóngyì yěhǎo, wǒ fǎnzheng juédìng zhème bàn le.** *Whether you approve or not, I have decided to do it anyway.*

fǎn 返 v return (See **wǎngfǎn** 往返.)

fàn 犯 v violate, offend

fàn fǎ 犯法 v violate the law

fàn guī 犯规 v foul (in sports), break a rule

fàn zuì 犯罪 v commit a crime, break the law

犯罪分子 **fàn zuì fènzi** a criminal

fàn 饭 TRAD 飯 N 1 cooked rice ▪ 他是南方人，爱吃米饭，不爱吃馒头和面条儿。 **Tā shì nánfāngrén, ài chī mǐfàn, bú ài chī mántou hé miàntiáor.** *He is a Southerner. He loves rice and doesn't like steamed buns or noodles.* 2 meal (顿 **dùn**) ▪ 我请你吃饭。 **Wǒ qǐng nǐ chīfàn.** *I'll treat you to a meal.*

fàndiàn 饭店 [modif: 饭 meal + 店 shop, store] N 1 restaurant (家 **jiā**) 2 hotel (家 **jiā**)

NOTE: The original meaning of *fàndiàn* is *restaurant*, but it is also used to denote *a hotel*. For example, 北京饭店 **Běijīng**

fàndiàn may mean Beijing Restaurant or Beijing Hotel.

fànwǎn 饭碗 N rice bowl; way of making a living, job

fàn 范 TRAD 範 N 1 model 2 border

fànwéi 范围 [comp: 范 border + 围 boundary] N scope, range, limits

fàn 贩 TRAD 販 v buy to resell

fāng 方 ADJ square

fāng'àn 方案 [comp: 方 method + 案 file] N plan, program (for a major project)

fāngbiàn 方便 ADJ convenient, handy (ANTONYM 麻烦 **máfan**)

NOTE: A euphemism for "going to the toilet" is 方便一下 **fāngbiàn yíxià**, e.g. ▪ 我要方便一下。 **Wǒ yào fāngbiàn yíxià.** *I'm going to use the restroom.*

fāngbiàn miàn 方便面 N instant noodles

fāngfǎ 方法 [comp: 方 method, way of doing things + 法 method] N method, way, means

fāngmiàn 方面 [comp: 方 side + 面 face, surface] N side, aspect

fāngshì 方式 [comp: 方 method + 式 manner] N manner, way

生活方式 **shēnghuó fāngshì** way of life, lifestyle

fāngxiàng 方向 N direction, orientation

fáng 防 v prevent, guard against

防火 **fánghuǒ** fire prevention / 防病 **fángbìng** disease prevention / 防盗 **fángdào** anti-burglary measures

fáng'ài 妨碍 [comp: 妨 prevent + 碍 hinder] v hinder, hamper, disturb

fáng 房 N 1 house, home

草房 **cǎofáng** thatched cottage / 楼房 **lóufáng** house of two or more levels / 平房 **píngfáng** single-story house, bungalow

2 room (间 **jiān**)

病房 **bìngfáng** sick room, ward / 客房 **kèfáng** guest room

fángdōng 房东 N landlord, landlady

fángjiān 房间 [comp: 房 room, home + 间 space] N room (间 **jiān**)

fángzi 房子 [suffix: 房 house + 子 nominal suffix] N house, housing

fǎngfú 仿佛 V be like, be alike

fǎng 访 TRAD 訪 V visit

fǎngwèn 访问 [comp: 访 visit + 问 ask, ask after] V visit, interview

fàng 放 V put, place, put in

fàngjià 放假 [v+obj: 放 release + 假 holiday] V be on holiday, have the day off

fàngqì 放弃 [comp: 放 release + 弃 abandon] V abandon, give up

fàngsōng 放松 [comp: 放 release + 松 loose] V relax, rest and relax

fàngxīn 放心 [v+obj: 放 set in place + 心 the heart] V set one's mind at ease, be at ease (ANTONYM 担心 **dānxīn**)

fēi 飞 TRAD 飛 V fly, flutter

fēijī 飞机 [modif: 飞 flying + 机 machine] N aircraft, airplane
坐/乘飞机 **zuò/chéng fēijī** travel by plane / 飞机票 **fēijī piào** air ticket / 飞机场 **fēijī chǎng** airport / 开飞机 **kāi fēijī** pilot a plane

fēi 非 ADV not, do not

fēi … bùkě 非 … 不可 ADV have no choice but to …, simply must … ∎ 我今天非写完这个报告不可。**Wǒ jīntiān fēi xiěwán zhège bàogào bùkě.** *I simply must finish writing this report today.*

NOTE: 非…不 … **fēi … bùkě** is used to emphasize the verb after 非 **fēi**. 不可 **bùkě** may be omitted, e.g. 我今天非写完这个报告。**Wǒ jīntiān fēi xiěwán zhège bàogào.** *I simply must finish writing this report today.*

fēicháng 非常 [modif: 非 not + 常 usual] ADV unusually, very

Fēizhōu 非洲 [modif: 非 Africa + 洲 continent] N Africa

féi 肥 ADJ fat, fattened

NOTE: 肥 **féi** is normally used to describe animals. It is insulting to use it to describe humans.

féiliào 肥料 [modif: 肥 fat, fatten + 料 material] N fertilizer
有机肥料 **yǒujī féiliào** organic fertilizer

féizào 肥皂 N soap (块 **kuài**)
肥皂粉 **féizàofěn** detergent powder

fèi 肺 N the lungs ∎ 吸烟伤害肺。**Xīyān shānghài fèi.** *Smoking harms the lungs.*

fèi 费 TRAD 費 1 N fee, charge
机场费 **jīchǎng fèi** airport tax / 交费 **jiāo fèi** pay fees, a charge, etc. / 水电费 **shuǐdiàn fèi** water and electricity bill / 学费 **xué fèi** tuition fee
2 V cost, spend ∎ 他费了很多钱才把车修好。**Tā fèi le hěn duō qián cái bǎ chē xiūhǎo.** *Only after spending a small fortune did he get his car repaired.*

fèiyòng 费用 N expense, cost
生活费用 **shēnghuó fèiyòng** living expenses, cost of living / 办公费用 **bàngōng fèiyòng** administration cost, overheads

fèi 废 TRAD 廢 ADJ useless

fèihuà 废话 [modif: 废 useless + 话 words] N nonsense, rubbish

fèipǐn 废品 [modif: 废 useless + 品 article] N junk, reject, useless product
废品回收 **fèipǐn huíshōu** collecting junk, waste recycling

fèiqì 废气 N waste gas
减少废气排放 **jiǎnshǎo fèiqì páifàng** reduce waste gas emission

fèiwù 废物 [modif: 废 useless + 物 object] N 1 waste material 2 good-for-nothing

fēn 分 I V divide II N 1 point, mark 2 minute ∎ 现在是十点二十分。**Xiànzài shì shí diǎn èrshí fēn.** *It's ten twenty now.*
III MEASURE WORD (Chinese currency; 1 分 **fēn** = 0.1 角 **jiǎo** = 0.01 元 **yuán**), cent

fēnbié 分别 V 1 part with, be separated

from **2** distinguish, differentiate

fēnbù 分布 v & n be distributed (over an area); distribution

fēnpèi 分配 [comp: 分 divide + 配 ration] v & n distribute, allocate; distribution, allocation

fēnshù 分数 n number recorded when grading, mark, grade

fēnxī 分析 [comp: 分 divide + 析 analyze] v & n analyze; analysis

... **fēnzhī** ... ... 分之 ... NUMERAL (indicating fraction)
三分之二 **sān fēnzhī èr** two thirds (⅔) / 百分之七十 **bǎi fēnzhī qīshí** seventy percent (70%)

fēnzhōng 分钟 n minute (of an hour)

fēn 纷 TRAD 紛 ADJ numerous, varied

fēnfēn 纷纷 ADJ one after another, numerous and disorderly

fěn 粉 n powder

fěnbǐ 粉笔 [modif: 粉 powder + 笔 pen] n chalk (支 zhī)

fèn 份 MEASURE WORD (for a set of things or newspapers, documents, etc.)
一份礼物 **yí fèn lǐwù** a present / 一份报告 **yí fèn bàogào** a report

fèn 奋 TRAD 奮 v exert oneself

fèndòu 奋斗 [modif: 奋 exert oneself + 斗 fight] v fight, struggle, strive

fèn 愤 TRAD 憤 n anger

fènnù 愤怒 [comp: 愤 angry + 怒 enraged] ADJ enraged, angry

fēng 丰 TRAD 豐 ADJ abundant

fēngfù 丰富 [comp: 丰 abundance + 富 wealth] ADJ abundant, rich, plenty

fēng 风 TRAD 風 n wind, draft

fēnggé 风格 n style (of doing things)
管理风格 **guǎnlǐ fēnggé** managerial style / 建筑风格 **jiànzhù fēnggé** architectural style

fēngguāng 风光 n scenery, sight

fēngjǐng 风景 n landscape, scenery

fēnglì 风力 [modif: 风 wind + 力 force] n wind force, wind power

fēngsú 风俗 n custom, social customs

fēngxiǎn 风险 n risk
冒风险 **mào fēngxiǎn** run a risk, take a chance, risk-taking

fēngxiàng 风向 n wind direction

fēng 疯 TRAD 瘋 ADJ insane, crazy
■ 你疯啦? **Nǐ fēng la?** Are you crazy?

fēngkuáng 疯狂 [comp: 疯 insane + 狂 mad] ADJ insane, frenzied

fēng 封 I MEASURE WORD (for letters) II v close, seal up

fēng 蜂 n wasp (See mìfēng 蜜蜂.)

fēng 锋 TRAD 鋒 n sharp point of a knife

fěng 讽 TRAD 諷 v satirize

fěngcì 讽刺 [comp: 讽 mock + 刺 prick] v & n satirize, ridicule, mock; satire

fèng 缝 n seam, chink, slit

fó 佛 n Buddha

fójiào 佛教 n Buddhism

fǒu 否 v negate

fǒudìng 否定 v negate, deny (ANTONYM 肯定 kěndìng)

fǒurèn 否认 v deny, repudiate (ANTONYM 承认 chéngrèn)

fǒuzé 否则 CONJ otherwise, or

fū 夫 n man

fūqī 夫妻 [comp: 夫 husband + 妻 wife] n husband and wife
夫妻关系 **fūqī guānxi** marital relationship

fū 肤 TRAD 膚 n skin (See pífū 皮肤.)

fū 敷 v apply
敷药 **fū yào** apply medicine (to a wound)

fú 服 I v obey II n clothes

fúcóng 服从 [comp: 服 obey + 从 follow] v obey, submit to

fúwù 服务 [comp: 服 obey + 务 work] v serve, work for
为 … 服务 **wèi … fúwù** serve …, work for …

fúwù qì 服务器 n server (for computers)

fúwù yè 服务业 n service industry

fúwù yuán 服务员 [suffix: 服务 serve + 员 person] n attendant, waiter/waitress

fúzhuāng 服装 N clothes, garments, apparel
服装商店 **fúzhuāngshāngdiàn** clothes store

fú 扶 v support with the hand
扶着老人过马路 **fúzhe lǎorén guò mǎlù** help an old person walk across the street

fú 浮 v float

fú 幅 MEASURE WORD (for pictures, posters, maps, etc.)
一幅中国画 **yì fú Zhōngguó huà** a Chinese painting

fú 福 N blessing, happiness

fú 伏 v bend over, lean on

fú 袱 N cloth-wrapper

fú 符 v be in accord

fúhé 符合 [comp: 符 conform to + 合 accord with] v conform to, accord with

fǔ 府 N government office (See **zhèngfǔ** 政府.)

fǔ 腐 ADJ rotten

fǔ 辅 TRAD 輔 N assistance, supplement

fǔdǎo 辅导 v coach, tutor
辅导课 **fǔdǎo kè** tutorial class, tutorial / 辅导老师 **fǔdǎo lǎoshī** tutor, teaching assistant

fù 父 N father

fùqin 父亲 [modif: 父 father + 亲 parent] N father

NOTE: 爸爸 **bàba** and 父亲 **fùqin** denote the same person. While 爸爸 **bàba** is colloquial, like "daddy," 父亲 **fùqin** is formal, equivalent to "father." When referring to another person's father, 父亲 **fùqin** is preferred. As a form of address to your own father, only 爸爸 **bàba** is normally used.

fù 付 I v pay, hand over (a sum) II MEASURE WORD (for pairs or sets of things—earrings, gloves, etc)

fùchù 付出 [v+compl: 付 pay + 出 out] v pay out, contribute

fùkuǎn 付款 [v+obj: 付 pay + 款 fund] N & v pay a sum of money, make a payment

fù 负 TRAD 負 v carry on the back

fùzé 负责 [v+obj: 负 carry on back + 责 responsibility] v be responsible, be in charge

fùzérén 负责人 N the person in charge

fù zérèn 负责任 Same as 负责 **fùzé**

fù 妇 TRAD 婦 N woman

fùnǚ 妇女 [comp: 妇 woman + 女 woman] N woman, womankind

fù 附 v 1 be close to 2 attach, add

fùjìn 附近 [comp: 附 close to + 近 close by] N the area nearby, neighborhood

fù 咐 v instruct (See **zhǔfu** 嘱咐.)

fù 复 TRAD 復 v & N repeat; compound

fùshù 复述 [modif: 复 repeat + 述 narrate] v retell, repeat

fùxí 复习 [modif: 复 repeat + 习 study] v review (one's lesson)

fùyìn 复印 v make a photocopy of, photocopy

fùyìnjī 复印机 N photocopier

fùyìnjiàn 复印件 N a photocopy

fùzá 复杂 [comp: 复 multiple + 杂 miscellaneous] ADJ complicated, complex (ANTONYM 简单 **jiǎndān**)

fùzhì 复制 [modif: 复 double + 制 make] v copy, clone

fù 腹 N abdomen, belly

fù 副 I MEASURE WORD (for objects in pairs or sets) pair, set
一副手套 **yí fù shǒutào** a pair of gloves / 一副眼镜 **yí fù yǎnjìng** a pair of spectacles
II ADJ deputy, vice-…
副校长 **fù xiàozhǎng** deputy principal

fù zuòyòng 副作用 N side effect

fù 富 ADJ rich, wealthy (ANTONYM 穷 **qióng**)

NOTE: In everyday Chinese, 富 **fù** is not used as much as 有钱 **yǒuqián** to mean *rich*.

fù 傅 N teacher, advisor (See **shīfu** 师傅.)

fù 缚 TRAD 縛 v tie up

fù 赴 v go to, attend

G

gāi 该[1] TRAD 該 I MODAL V should, ought to II V be somebody's turn to do something ■ 今天该你洗碗。Jīntiān gāi nǐ xǐ wǎn. *It's your turn to wash dishes today.*

gāi 该[2] TRAD 該 PRON that, the said, the abovementioned

gǎi 改 V alter, change, correct

gǎibiàn 改变 [comp: 改 alter + 变 change] V & N transform, change, alter; transformation, change, alteration

gǎigé 改革 [comp: 改 change + 革 remove] V & N reform

gǎiháng 改行 V change one's profession (or trade)

gǎijìn 改进 [v+comp: 改 change + 进 progress] V & N make ... more advanced/sophisticated, improve; improvement (项 xiàng)

gǎiqī 改期 V change a scheduled time, change the date (of an event)

gǎishàn 改善 [v+comp: 改 change + 善 good] V & N make ... better/more favorable, ameliorate; improvement, amelioration

gǎizào 改造 [comp: 改 change + 造 build up] V & N remold, rebuild; remolding, rebuilding

gǎizhèng 改正 [v+comp: 改 change + 正 correct] V put ... right, rectify

gài 盖[1] TRAD 蓋 V build

gài 盖[2] TRAD 蓋 N cover, lid, top 锅盖 guōgài pot lid / 盖子 gàizi cover, lid

gài 概 ADV totally

gàikuò 概括 [comp: 概 total + 括 include] V summarize, generalize

gàiniàn 概念 [modif: 概 total + 念 idea] N concept, notion

gān 干 TRAD 乾 ADJ dry

gānbēi 干杯 [v+obj: 干 to dry + 杯 cup] V drink a toast, "Bottoms up!" ■ 为我

们的友谊，干杯！Wèi wǒmen de yǒuyì, gānbēi! *To our friendship!*

gāncuì 干脆 [comp: 干 dry + 脆 crisp] ADJ decisive, not hesitant, straight to the point

gānjing 干净 [comp: 干 dry + 净 clean] ADJ clean (ANTONYM 脏 zāng)

gānzào 干燥 [comp: 干 dry + 燥 arid] ADJ dry, arid

gān 杆 N pole

gān 肝 N the liver

gānxīn 甘心 V do something willingly

gǎn 赶 TRAD 趕 V 1 catch up with 2 rush for, try to catch 赶得上 gǎn de shàng can catch up / 赶不上 gǎn bu shàng cannot catch up / 赶上 gǎn shàng succeed in catching up / 没赶上 méi gǎn shàng fail to catch up

gǎnjǐn 赶紧 ADV hasten (to do something)

gǎnkuài 赶快 ADV Same as 赶紧 gǎnjǐn

gǎn 敢 MODAL V dare ■ 这么多人，我不敢讲话。Zhè me duō rén, wǒ bù gǎn jiǎnghuà. *There're so many people here; I don't dare to speak.*

gǎn 感 V feel

gǎndào 感到 [v+comp: 感 feel + 到 arrive (as a complement)] V feel

gǎndòng 感动 [comp: 感 feel + 动 move] V move, touch emotionally

gǎnjī 感激 [comp: 感 feel + 激 excite] V feel deeply grateful

gǎnjué 感觉 [comp: 感 feel + 觉 be conscious of] V & N feel; feeling, impression

gǎnmào 感冒 V & N catch a cold; cold, flu

gǎnqíng 感情 [comp: 感 feeling + 情 emotion, affection] N 1 feelings, emotion 2 affection, love

gǎnshòu 感受 N impression or lesson learned from personal experiences

gǎnxiǎng 感想 [comp: 感 feeling + 想 thoughts] N impressions, reflections, thoughts

gǎnxiè 感谢 [v+obj: 感 feel + 谢 grateful] v be grateful, thank

gǎn xìngqù 感兴趣 v be interested (in) 对…感兴趣 **duì … gǎn xìngqù** be interested in …

gǎn 杆 TRAD 桿 N shaft

gàn 干 TRAD 幹 v do, work

gànbù 干部 N cadre, official (位 **wèi**)

NOTE: 干部 **gànbù** is a communist party term, denoting *party (or government) officials.* It is not commonly used today. In its stead, 官员 **guānyuán** is the word for *government officials.*

gàn huór 干活儿 v work (especially manually)

gāng 刚 TRAD 剛 ADV just, barely

gāngcái 刚才 [comp: 刚 just + 才 only] N a short while ago, just

gānggāng 刚刚 ADV Same as 刚 **gāng**, but more emphatic.

gāng 钢 TRAD 鋼 N steel

gāngbǐ 钢笔 [modif: 钢 steel + 笔 pen] N fountain pen (支 **zhī**)

gāngtiě 钢铁 [comp: 钢 steel + 铁 iron] N iron and steel, steel.

gāo 高 ADJ tall, high (ANTONYMS 矮 **ǎi**, 低 **dī**)

gāodà 高大 ADJ tall and big (ANTONYM 矮小 **ǎixiǎo**)

gāodàng 高档 [modif: 高 high + 档 grade] ADJ top grade, high quality 高档家具 **gāodàng jiājù** fine furniture

gāodù 高度 [comp: 高 high + 度 degree] I N altitude, height II ADJ with a high degree 高度赞扬 **gāodù zànyáng** praise highly

gāojí 高级 [modif: 高 advanced, senior + 级 grade] ADJ advanced, high-level 高级中学 (高中) **gāojí zhōngxué (gāozhōng)** senior high school

gāokǎo 高考 N abbreviation for 高等院校入学考试 **gāoděng yuànxiào rùxué kǎoshì** Entrance Examination for Institutions of Higher Education

gāosù 高速 [modif: 高 high + 速 speed] ADJ of high speed 高速公路 **gāosù gōnglù** superhighway, motorway / 高速铁路 **gāosù tiělù** high speed railroad

gāoxìng 高兴 [comp: 高 high + 兴 excited] ADJ joyful, delighted, glad, willing

gāoyuán 高原 [modif: 高 high + 原 plain] N highland, plateau

gāo 膏 N paste, ointment (See **yágāo** 牙膏.)

gāo 糕 N cake

gāodiǎn 糕点 N cakes and pastries

gǎo 搞 v 1 do, be engaged in, carry on ■ "你父亲搞什么工作？" "他搞软件设计。" **"Nǐ fùqin gǎo shénme gōngzuò?" "Tā gǎo ruǎnjiàn shèjì."** *"What does your father do?" "He's engaged in software design."* 2 get hold of, fetch

gǎo guǐ 搞鬼 v play tricks, get up to mischief

gǎo 稿 N draft (of an essay, a painting, etc.) 初稿 **chūgǎo** initial draft

gǎozi 稿子 N draft, sketch, manuscript 打稿子 **dǎgǎozi** draw up a draft

gào 告 v 1 tell, inform 2 sue, bring a legal action against ■ 有人告他偷东西。**Yǒurén gào tā tōu dōngxi.** *He was sued for theft.*

gàobié 告别 v bid farewell to, part with

gàosu 告诉 [comp: 告 tell + 诉 inform] v tell, inform

gē 哥 N elder brother

gēge 哥哥 N elder brother, older brother

gē 胳 N arm

gēbo 胳膊 N the arm (只 **zhī**)

gē 歌 N song

gēcí 歌词 N words of a song

gēshǒu 歌手 N (professional) singer

gé 革 v expel

gémìng 革命 N revolution (场 **chǎng**)

gé 格 N pattern, standard

géwài 格外 ADV exceptionally, unusually

gé 隔 v separate, partition

gébì 隔壁 N next door

gè 个 TRAD 個 MEASURE WORD (the most commonly used measure word, used in default of any other measure word; normally pronounced in the neutral tone)

一个人 **yí ge rén** a person / 两个苹果 **liǎng ge píngguǒ** two apples / 三个工厂 **sān ge gōngchǎng** three factories

gèbié 个别 ADJ 1 very few, exceptional

个别现象 **gèbié xiànxiàng** an isolated case

2 individual, one-to-one

gèrén 个人 [modif: 个 individual + 人 person] N individual, personal (ANTONYM 集体 jítǐ)

gèxìng 个性 [modif: 个 personal + 性 nature] N personality

gèzi 个子 N height and size (of a person), build

gè 各 PRON each, every ∎ 各人的事，各人自己负责。**Gè rén de shì, gè rén zìjǐ fùzé.** *Everyone should be responsible for his own affairs.*

各种 **gè zhǒng** all kinds of

gèzì 各自 PRON by oneself

gěi 给 TRAD 給 I v give, provide II PREP for, to

gēn 根 I N root II MEASURE WORD (for long, thin things)

一根筷子 **yì gēn kuàizi** a chopstick

gēnběn 根本 [comp: 根 root + 本 root] N & ADJ essence, what is fundamental; essential, fundamental, basic

gēnjù 根据 I v do according to, on the basis of II N grounds, basis

gēn 跟 I v follow II PREP with ∎ 老师："请大家跟我念。" **Lǎoshī: "Qǐng dàjiā gēn wǒ niàn."** *Teacher: "Read after me, please."*

跟上 **gēnshàng** catch up with, keep abreast with / 跟 … 一起 **gēn ... yìqǐ** together with ... ∎ 跟爸爸一起去看足球

赛 **gēn bàba yìqǐ qù kàn zúqiú sài** *I watch soccer games together with my father*

gèng 更 ADV still more, even more

gèngjiā 更加 ADV Same as 更 **gèng**

gōng 工 N work

gōngchǎng 工厂 [modif: 工 work + 厂 factory] N factory, works (座 **zuò**, 家 **jiā**)

办工厂 **bàn gōngchǎng** run a factory / 建工厂 **jiàn gōngchǎng** build a factory / 开工厂 **kāi gōngchǎng** set up a factory

gōngchéng 工程 [modif: 工 work + 程 course] N project, construction work, engineering

土木工程 **tǔmù gōngchéng** civil engineering / 水利工程 **shuǐlì gōngchéng** water conservancy project

gōngchéngshī 工程师 [modif: 工程 engineering + 师 master] N engineer (位 **wèi**)

总工程师 **zǒng gōngchéngshī** chief engineer

gōngfu 工夫 N 1 time 2 efforts

gōnghuì 工会 [modif: 工 workers + 会 association] N labor union, trade union

gōngjù 工具 [modif: 工 work + 具 implement] N tool, implement

gōngrén 工人 [modif: 工 work + 人 person] N workman, worker

gōngyè 工业 [modif: 工 work + 业 industry] N (manufacturing) industry

gōngzī 工资 [modif: 工 work + 资 fund] N wages, salary

gōngzuò 工作 [comp: 工 work + 作 do] v & N work; work, job (件 **jiàn**)

gōng 公¹ ADJ male (of certain animals) (ANTONYM 母 **mǔ**)

gōng 公² ADJ 1 public (ANTONYM 私 **sī**) ∎ 天下为公。**Tiānxià wéi gōng.** *The world is for public interests.* (→ *The world is for the people.*) 2 open 3 fair

gōngbù 公布 v make a public announcement, publish

gōngchǐ 公尺 [modif: 公 metric + 尺

a traditional Chinese measurement of length] MEASURE WORD meter

gōngfèi 公费 [modif: 公 public + 费 expenditure] N public expense, at public expense
公费医疗 **gōngfèi yīliáo** public medical system

gōngfēn 公分 [modif: 公 metric + 分 a traditional Chinese measurement of length] MEASURE WORD centimeter

gōnggòng 公共 [comp: 公 public + 共 shared] ADJ public, communal

gōnggòng qìchē 公共汽车 N bus

gōnggòng guānxi 公共关系 N public relations

gōngjīn 公斤 [modif: 公 metric + 斤 a traditional Chinese measurement of weight] MEASURE WORD kilogram

gōngkāi 公开 [comp: 公 public + 开 open] ADJ & V open, public (ANTONYM 秘密 mìmì); make public, reveal

gōnglǐ 公里 [modif: 公 metric + 里 a traditional Chinese measurement of distance] kilometer

gōnglù 公路 [modif: 公 public + 路 road] N public road, highway (条 tiáo)
高速公路 **gāosù gōnglù** motorway, expressway

gōngpíng 公平 [comp: 公 fair + 平 equal] ADJ fair, impartial
买卖公平 **mǎimài gōngpíng** fair trade

gōngpó 公婆 N husband's parents

gōngsī 公司 N commercial firm, company, corporation
总公司 **zǒng gōngsī** company head-quarters / 分公司 **fēn gōngsī** branch of a company

gōngyòng diànhuà 公用电话 [modif: 公用 public use + 电话 telephone] N public telephone, payphone

gōngyù 公寓 N apartment house, housing complex
一套公寓 **yítào gōngyù** a flat, a unit of housing / 一幢公寓 **yízhuàng gōngyù** an

apartment house, a housing complex

gōngyuán 公元 N of the Christian/common era, AD (ANNO DOMINI)
公元前 **gōngyuán qián** BC/BCE

gōngyuán 公园 [modif: 公 public + 园 garden] N public garden, park (座 zuò)

gōngzhǔ 公主 N princess (位 wèi)

gōng 功 N skill

gōngfu 功夫 N 1 Same as 工夫 **gōngfu** 2 martial arts
练功夫 **liàn gōngfu** practice martial arts

gōngfu piàn 功夫片 N martial arts film

gōngkè 功课 N schoolwork, homework

gōngnéng 功能 N function
功能键 **gōngnéng jiàn** function key(s)

gōng 恭 ADJ deferential

gōngxǐ 恭喜 V & N congratulate; congratulation
恭喜发财 **gōngxǐ fācái** Happy new year and may you prosper! (greeting on Chinese New Year's Day)

gōng 攻 V attack

gōng 供 V supply, provide ▪ 供大于求。**Gōng dà yú qiú.** *Supply exceeds demand.*

gōng 宫 TRAD 宫 N palace
皇宫 **huánggōng** royal palace (for an emperor) / 王宫 **wánggōng** royal palace (for a king)

gōng 躬 V bow (bend the head or body)

gǒng 巩 TRAD 鞏 V consolidate

gòng 共 ADV 1 altogether, in total 2 jointly, together (used only in writing)

gòngchǎndǎng 共产党 [modif: 共 to share + 产 property + 党 party] N communist party
中国共产党 **Zhōngguó Gòngchǎndǎng** the Chinese Communist Party

gònghéguó 共和国 N republic

Gòngqīngtuán 共青团 N abbreviation for 中国共产主义青年团 **Zhōngguó Gòngchǎn zhǔyì Qīngniántuán** the Chinese Communist Youth League

gòngshí 共识 [modif: 共 shared + 识 understanding] N common

understanding, consensus
达成共识 **dáchéng gòngshí** achieve common understanding, reach a consensus
gòngtóng 共同 [comp: 共 together + 同 shared] ADJ common, shared
gòngxiàn 贡献 [comp: 贡 tribute + 献 offer] V contribute, dedicate
为…作出贡献 **wèi ... zuòchu gòngxiàn** make a contribution to ...
gōu 沟 TRAD 溝 N ditch, trench (条 **tiáo**)
gōutōng 沟通 V link up, connect
沟通意见 **gōutōng yìjiàn** exchange ideas
gōu 钩 TRAD 鉤 N hook
gǒu 狗 N dog (只 **zhī**, 条 **tiáo**)
母狗 **mǔ gǒu** bitch / 小狗 **xiǎo gǒu** puppy
gòu 构 TRAD 構 V construct, form
gòuchéng 构成 V make up, form, constitute
gòuzào 构造 N structure
gòu 购 TRAD 購 V purchase, buy
gòumǎi 购买 [comp: 购 purchase + 买 buy] V purchase
购买采矿设备 **gòumǎi cǎi kuàng shèbèi** purchase mining equipment / 购买力 **gòumǎilì** purchasing power
gòuwù 购物 [v+obj: 购 buy + 物 things] V & N shop; shopping
购物单 **gòuwù dān** shopping list
gòu 够 TRAD 夠 ADJ enough, sufficient ■ 够了，够了，谢谢你！ **Gòu le, gòu le, xièxie nǐ!** *That's enough. Thank you!*
gū 孤 ADJ lonely
gū'ér 孤儿 [modif: 孤 lonely + 儿 child] N orphan
孤儿院 **gū'éryuàn** orphanage
gūlì 孤立 [modif: 孤 lonely + 立 stand] ADJ isolated, without support or sympathy
gū 估 V estimate
gūjì 估计 [comp: 估 estimate + 计 calculate] V & N estimate, reckon, size up; estimate, approximate calculation, appraisal

gū 姑 N aunt, woman
gūgu 姑姑 N one's father's sister, aunt
gūniang 姑娘 N unmarried young woman, girl, lass
小姑娘 **xiǎo gūniang** little girl / 大姑娘 **dàgūniang** young woman (usually unmarried), lass
gǔ 古 ADJ ancient ■ 中国是一个文明古国，有很多古建筑。 **Zhōngguó shì yí ge wénmíng gǔguó, yǒu hěnduō gǔ jiànzhù.** *China is a country of ancient civilization and boasts a large number of ancient buildings.*
gǔdài 古代 [modif: 古 ancient + 代 generation, time] N ancient times, antiquity
gǔdiǎn 古典 ADJ classic, classical
古典音乐 **gǔdiǎn yīnyuè** classical music
gǔjì 古迹 [modif: 古 ancient + 迹 footprints] N historic site, place of historic interest
gǔlǎo 古老 [comp: 古 ancient + 老 old] ADJ ancient, time-honored
gǔ 鼓 N drum
gǔlì 鼓励 V encourage
物质鼓励 **wùzhì gǔlì** material incentive / 精神鼓励 **jīngshén gǔlì** moral incentive, moral encouragement
gǔwǔ 鼓舞 [comp: 鼓 drum up + 舞 dance] V inspire, fire up ... with enthusiasm, hearten
gǔzhǎng 鼓掌 [v+obj: 鼓 drum + 掌 palm] V clap one's hands, applaud
gǔ 骨 N bone
gǔtou 骨头 N bone (根 **gēn**) ■ 他扔给小狗一根骨头。 **Tā rēng gěi xiǎogǒu yì gēn gǔtou.** *He threw the puppy a bone.*
gǔ 股 N share
gǔpiào 股票 [modif: 股 share + 票 ticket] N share, stock
gǔ 谷¹ TRAD 穀 N cereal, grain (See **dàogǔ** 稻谷.)
gǔ 谷² N valley
山谷 **shāngǔ** mountain valley, ravine

gù 固 ADJ & V secure, solid; secure, consolidate

gùdìng 固定 [comp: 固 secure + 定 fix] V fix, make immovable
固定资产 gùdìng zīchǎn fixed assets / 固执己见 gù zhí jǐ jiàn stubbornly stick to one's opinions; pigheaded

gù 故 ADJ old, former

gùshi 故事 [modif: 故 old, past + 事 happening, event] N story, tale
讲故事 jiǎng gùshi tell a story / 听故事 tīng gùshi listen to a story

gùxiāng 故乡 [modif: 故 former years + 乡 village, homeland] N native place, hometown, home village

gùyì 故意 [modif: 故 on purpose + 意 intention] ADJ deliberate, intentional, on purpose

gù 顾 TRAD 顧 V attend to, care for

gùkè 顾客 N customer, client (位 wèi).

guā 瓜 N melon, gourd (See huángguā 黄瓜, xīguā 西瓜.)

guā 刮 V (of a wind) blow

guā fēng 刮风 V (of wind) blow, be windy

guà 挂 TRAD 掛 V hang up, put up

guàhào 挂号 V register (at a hospital)
挂号费 guàhào fèi registration fee, doctor's consultation fee / 挂号处 guàhào chù registration office

NOTE: In China if you are sick, you go to a hospital where doctors work in their specialist departments, e.g. internal medicine, gynecology and dermatology. 挂号 guàhào means to tell a receptionist which department you want to go to and pay the consultation fee. Dentistry is usually one of the departments and a dentist is generally considered just another doctor.

guāi 乖 ADJ (of children) be good, be well-behaved
乖孩子 guāi háizi a well-behaved child

guǎi 拐 V turn, make a turn

guǎiwān 拐弯 V turn a corner

guài 怪[1] ADJ strange, odd, queer

guài 怪[2] V blame

guàibudé 怪不得 ADV no wonder, so that's why

guān 关 TRAD 關 V close, shut; turn off, switch off; clock
把电灯/电视机/录音机/机器关掉 bǎ diàndēng/diànshì jī/lùyīn jī/jīqì guāndiào turn off the lights/TV/recorder/machine / 把门/窗关上 bǎ mén/chuāng guānshang close the door/window

guānbì 关闭 [comp: 关 close + 闭 close] V close down, shut down
关闭机场 guānbì jīchǎng shut down the airport

guānjiàn 关键 [comp: 关 pass + 键 key] N what is crucial or critical

guānxi 关系 [comp: 关 related + 系 connected] I N connection, relation II V affect, have bearing on

guānxīn 关心 [v + obj: 关 connected + 心 the heart] V be concerned about, care for

guānyú 关于 PREP about, on ■ 我很久没有听到关于他的消息了。Wǒ hěn jiǔ méiyǒu tīngdào guānyú tā de xiāoxi le. *I haven't heard about him for a long time.*

guān 观 TRAD 觀 V look at, observe

guānchá 观察 [comp: 观 see + 察 examine] V observe, watch
观察员 guāncháyuán observer (at a conference, especially an international conference)

guāndiǎn 观点 [modif: 观 observe + 点 point] N viewpoint, view

guānniàn 观念 N concept, sense
是非观念 shìfēi guānniàn the sense of what is right and what is wrong

guānzhòng 观众 [modif: 观 watch + 众 crowd] N audience (in a theater, of TV, etc.), spectator

guān 官 N (government) official

NOTE: 官 **guān** is a colloquial word. For more formal occasions, use 官员 **guānyuán**.

guānyuán 官员 [suffix: 官 official + 员 nominal suffix] N official, officer, mandarin (位 **wèi**)
负责官员 **fùzé guānyuán** (the) official in charge

NOTE: See note on 干部 **gànbù**.

guǎn 管 V be in charge, take care (of) ■ 别管我! **Bié guǎn wǒ!** *Leave me alone!*

guǎndào 管道 [comp: 管 pipe + 道 path] N pipeline, conduit

guǎnlǐ 管理 [comp: 管 be in charge + 理 put in order] V & N manage, administer; management, administration
商业管理 **shāngyè guǎnlǐ** business administration

guǎn 馆 TRAD 館 N building (for a specific purpose)
饭馆 **fànguǎn** restaurant / 馆子 **guǎnzi** restaurant [colloquial] / 体育馆 **tǐyùguǎn** gymnasium / 图书馆 **túshūguǎn** library

guàn 冠 N the best

guànjūn 冠军 N champion, championship

guàn 惯 TRAD 惯 ADJ accustomed to

guàn 灌 V fill (water, air), pour

guàngài 灌溉 V & N irrigate; irrigation

guàn 罐 N tin, jar

guàntou 罐头 [suffix: 罐 tin, can + 头 nominal suffix] N can, tin
罐头食品 **guàntou shípǐn** canned food

guāng 光[1] N light ■ 发光的不一定是金子。**Fā guāng de bù yídìng shì jīnzi.** *All that glitters is not gold.*
灯光 **dēngguāng** lamplight / 阳光 **yángguāng** sunlight / 月光 **yuèguāng** moonlight

guāngdié 光碟 [modif: 光 light, laser + 碟 disc] Same as 光盘 **guāngpán**

guānghuá 光滑 [comp: 光 smooth + 滑 smooth] ADJ smooth, glossy

guānglín 光临 V (a polite expression) be present, come ■ 欢迎光临! **Huānyíng guānglín!** *You're cordially welcome! We welcome you.*

guāngmíng 光明 [comp: 光 light + 明 bright] ADJ light, bright, promising

guāngpán 光盘 N compact disc (CD)
刻录光盘 **kèlùguāngpán** burn a CD

guāngróng 光荣 [comp: 光 light + 荣 glory] ADJ glorious, honorable

guāng 光[2] ADV only, sole ■ 光有钱就能幸福吗? **Guāng yǒu qián jiù néng xìngfú ma?** *Can money alone make you happy?*

guǎng 广 TRAD 廣 ADJ extensive, wide

guǎngbō 广播 [modif: 广 extensive, wide + 播 sow, spread] I V broadcast II N broadcasting
广播电台 **guǎngbō diàntái** radio station / 广播公司 **guǎngbō gōngsī** broadcasting company

guǎngchǎng 广场 [modif: 广 broad + 场 ground] N square, plaza

guǎngdà 广大 [comp: 广 broad + 大 big] ADJ vast, extensive

guǎngfàn 广泛 [comp: 广 broad + 泛 extensive] ADJ widespread, wide-ranging, extensive

guǎnggào 广告 [modif: 广 broad + 告 inform] N advertisement, (TV) commercial

guàng 逛 V stroll, take a random walk
逛公园 **guàng gōngyuán** stroll in the park / 逛街 **guàng jiē** stroll around the streets, do window shopping

guī 规 TRAD 規 N regulation, rule

guīdìng 规定 [comp: 规 stipulate + 定 decide] V & N stipulate, regulate, specify; stipulation, regulation, provision,

guīju 规矩 [comp: 规 compass + 矩 ruler] I N rule, established practice
老规矩 **lǎoguīju** well-established practice II ADJ well behaved, behaving within the norm

guīlǜ 规律 [comp: 规 regulation + 律 law] N law, regular pattern

guīmó 规模 N scale, scope, dimension

guīzé 规则 N rule, law, regulation
交通规则 **jiāotōng guīzé** traffic regulations / 游戏规则 **yóuxì guīzé** rules of a game

guī 归 TRAD 歸 V return, go back to

guīnà 归纳 V & N sum up, induce; summing-up, induction
归纳法 **guīnàfǎ** inductive method

guī 硅 N silicium, silicon (Si)
硅谷 **guīgǔ** Silicon Valley

guǐ 鬼 N ghost, phantom
鬼故事 **guǐ gùshi** ghost story / 鬼屋 **guǐ wū** haunted house

guǐ 轨 TRAD 軌 N rail
出轨 **chūguǐ** (of a train) derail

guǐdào 轨道 N track; orbit
上了轨道 **shàng le guǐdào** settle into normal routine

guì 贵 TRAD 貴 ADJ expensive, of great value (ANTONYM 便宜 **piányi**)

guìxìng 贵姓 [modif: 贵 valuable + 姓 family name] IDIOM your family name

NOTE: (1) While 贵姓 **guìxìng** is the polite form when asking about somebody's family name, the polite way to ask somebody's given name is: 请问，您大名是…? **Qǐngwèn, nín dàmíng shì…?** *And your (honorific) name is* …大名 literally means *big name*. The answer to this question is 我叫 XX。**Wǒ jiào XX.** *I am* … (2) The word 贵 **guì** in the sense of *valuable* is added to certain nouns to mean *your…*, e.g. 贵姓 **guìxìng** *your family name*, 贵国 **guìguó** *your country*, 贵校 **guìxiào** *your school*. They are only used in formal and polite contexts.

guì 柜 TRAD 櫃 N cupboard, cabinet
书柜 **shūguì** bookcase

guìtái 柜台 N counter, bar

guìzi 柜子 N cupboard, cabinet

gǔn 滚 V roll

NOTE: 滚 **gǔn** is used to tell somebody "get out of here" or "beat it," e.g. ■ 滚! 滚出

去! **Gǔn! Gǔn chūqu!** *Get lost! Get out of here!* ■ 滚开! **Gǔn kāi!** *Beat it!* These are highly offensive.

guō 锅 TRAD 鍋 N pot, pan, wok

guó 国 TRAD 國 N country, state, nation
德国 **Déguó** Germany / 俄国 **Éguó** Russia / 法国 **Fǎguó** France / 美国 **Měiguó** the United States of America / 英国 **Yīngguó** the United Kingdom

guójí 国籍 N nationality, citizenship
加入加拿大国籍 **jiārù Jiānádà guójí** obtain Canadian citizenship, be naturalized as a Canadian citizen

guójì 国际 ADJ concerning two or more nations, international
国际法 **guójì fǎ** international law / 国际会议 **guójì huìyì** international conference

guójiā 国家 [comp: 国 country + 家 family] N country, state, nation

NOTE: It is significant that the Chinese word meaning *country* — 国家 **guójiā** — is composed of the word 国 **guó** (country) and the word 家 **jiā** (family). In traditional Chinese thought, China was one big family and the country was ruled as such, with the emperor as the patriarch.

Guómíndǎng 国民党 N the Kuomintang (KMT, the political party which ruled China before 1949 and is now a major party in Taiwan.)

Guóqìngjié 国庆节 [modif: 国 nation + 庆 celebration + 节 festival] N National Day (October 1 in the People's Republic of China)

guówáng 国王 [modif: 国 country + 王 king] N king, monarch (位 **wèi**)

guǒ 果 N fruit

guǒrán 果然 ADV sure enough, as expected

guǒshí 果实 N fruit, fruits

guǒzhī 果汁 N fruit juice

guǒ 裹 V wrap, bind (See **bāoguǒ** 包裹.)

guò 过[1] TRAD 過 v 1 pass, cross
过来 **guòlai** come over, come across
(towards the speaker) ▪ 公共汽车开过
来了。**Gōnggòng qìchē kāi guòlai le.**
A bus is coming over.
过去 **guòqu** go over, go across (away
from the speaker) ▪ 街上车太多，很
难过去。**Jiē shang chē tài duō, hěn nán
guòqu.** *Traffic in the street is too heavy.
It's very difficult to go across.*
2 spend (time), live (a life), observe
(a festival)
过日子 **guò rìzi** live a life / 过年 **guò
nián** observe New Year's Day / 过节
guò jié observe a festival
guòchéng 过程 N process, course
guòdù 过渡 [comp: 过 cross + 渡 ferry]
N transition
guòlǜ 过滤 v filter
guònián 过年 v observe the (Chinese)
New Year's Day
guòqī 过期 [v+obj: 过 pass + 期 period]
ADJ invalid after the expiry date, past the
sell-by date
guòqù 过去 [comp: 过 pass + 去 gone] N
(something) in the past
guò 过[2] TRAD 過 ADJ excess, excessive
guòfèn 过分 [v+obj: 过 pass + 分 limit]
ADJ excessive, going too far
过分的要求 **guòfèn de yāoqiú** excess
demands
guòmǐn 过敏 [modif: 过 excessive + 敏
sensitive] ADJ over-sensitive, allergic
▪ 我对这种药过敏。**Wǒ duì zhè
zhong yào guòmǐn.** *I'm allergic to this
medicine.*
guòyú 过于 ADV too, excessively
guo 过[3] TRAD 過 PARTICLE (used after a
verb or adjective to emphasize a past
experience) ▪ "你去过中国没有？"
"去过。" **"Nǐ qùguo Zhōngguó
méiyǒu?" "Qùguo."** *"Have you been to
China?" "Yes, I have."*

H

hā 哈 ONOMATOPOEIA (sound of loud
laughter)
hāhā 哈哈 ONOMATOPOEIA (representing
loud laughter)
hái 还 TRAD 還 ADV still, yet ▪ 时间还早，
我想看一会儿书再睡。**Shíjiān hái zǎo,
wǒ xiǎng kàn yíhuìr shū zài shuì.** *It's still
early. I want to do a little reading before
going to bed.*
háishì 还是[1] ADV still, as before ▪ 老师
说了两遍，我还是不大懂。**Lǎoshī shuō
le liǎng biàn, wǒ háishì bú dà dǒng.** *The
teacher has explained twice, but I still
don't quite understand.*
háishì 还是[2] CONJ or ▪ 你喝茶还是喝
咖啡？**Nǐ hē chá háishì hē kāfēi?** *Would
you like tea or coffee?*
hái 孩 N child
háizi 孩子 [suffix: 孩 child + 子 nominal
suffix] N child, children
男孩子 **nán háizi** boy, son / 女孩子 **nǚ
háizi** girl, daughter
hǎi 海 N sea or big lake
hǎigǎng 海港 N seaport
hǎiguān 海关 [modif: 海 sea + 关 pass]
N customs, customs house
海关检查 **hǎiguān jiǎnchá** customs
inspection, customs examination /
海关手续 **hǎiguān shǒuxù** customs
formalities / 海关人员 **hǎiguān rényuán**
customs officer
hǎixiān 海鲜 N seafood
海鲜馆 **hǎixiān guǎn** seafood restaurant
hǎiyáng 海洋 [comp: 海 sea + 洋 ocean]
N sea, ocean, seas and oceans
海洋生物 **hǎiyáng shēngwù** sea life /
海洋权 **hǎiyáng quán** maritime rights
hài 害 v harm, cause harm to
有害 **yǒuhài** harmful
hàichóng 害虫 N pest (insect)
hàichu 害处 [modif: 害 harmful + 处

place] N harm (ANTONYM 好处 hǎochu)

hàipà 害怕 v fear, be fearful

hàixiū 害羞 ADJ be bashful, be shy

hán 含 v hold in the mouth, contain, have … as ingredients

hánhu 含糊 ADJ vague, ambiguous

hán 寒 ADJ cold

hánjià 寒假 [modif: 寒 cold + 假 holiday] N winter vacation, winter holiday

hánlěng 寒冷 [comp: 寒 freezing + 冷 cold] ADJ freezing cold

hǎn 喊 v shout, cry out, yell

hàn 汗 N sweat, perspiration
出汗 chūhàn sweat, perspire

Hàn 汉 TRAD 漢 N the Han people

Hànyǔ 汉语 [modif: 汉 the Han people + 语 speech] N the language of the Han people, the Chinese language

NOTE: In Chinese there are a number of words denoting the Chinese language. 汉语 Hànyǔ literally means the language of the Han Chinese people, in contrast with the languages of the non-Han peoples in China. 汉语 Hànyǔ is therefore the accurate, scientific term for the language. However, the most popular term for the Chinese language is 中文 Zhōngwén. In Singapore and other Southeast Asian countries, the standard Chinese language is often referred to as 华语 Huáyǔ in contrast to the various Chinese dialects spoken there. Also see note on 普通话 Pǔtōnghuà.

Hànzì 汉字 [modif: 汉 the Han people + 字 word, character] N Chinese character

hàn 旱 ADJ dry spell, drought

hàn 憾 N regret

háng 行 MEASURE WORD line, row, queue (used with nouns that are formed in lines)

hángqíng 行情 N price quotations

hángyè 行业 [comp: 行 line, occupation + 业 industry] N trade and profession, industry
各行各业 gèháng gèyè every trade and profession

háng 航 v navigate

hángbān 航班 N flight, flight number
飞往广州的航班 fēiwǎng Guǎngzhōu de hángbān a flight to Guangzhou

hángkōng 航空 N aviation
航空公司 hángkōng gōngsī aviation company, airline / 航空学校 hángkōng xuéxiào aviation school

háo 毫 N fine long hair

háo bù 毫不 ADV not in the least, not at all

NOTE: 毫不 háo bù is an adverb used before an adjective of two or more syllables. For example, you can say 毫不奇怪 háo bù qíguài *not at all strange*, but you cannot say 毫不怪 háo bú guài.

háo 豪 ADJ bold and unrestrained

háohuá 豪华 [comp: 豪 bold and unrestrained + 华 brilliant] ADJ luxurious, sumptuous

hǎo 好[1] ADJ good, all right (ANTONYMS 坏 huài, 差 chà) ■ 他总是愿意帮助学生，他是个好老师。Tā zǒngshì yuànyì bāngzhù xuésheng, tā shì ge hǎo lǎoshī. *He is always ready to help his students. He is a good teacher.* ■ 你中文说得很好。Nǐ Zhōngwén shuō de hěn hǎo. *You speak Chinese very well.*

hǎochu 好处 N benefit; being beneficial (ANTONYMS 坏处 huàichu, 害处 hàichu)
对 … 有好处 duì … yǒu hǎochu be beneficial to

hǎoxīn 好心 ADJ kind-hearted, with good intention
好心人 hǎoxīn rén a kind-hearted person.

hǎo 好[2] ADV very, very much ■ 你这件新衣服好漂亮！Nǐ zhè jiàn xīn yīfu hǎo piàoliang! *Your new dress is very pretty indeed!*

hǎochī 好吃 ADJ delicious, palatable

hǎo duō 好多 ADJ a good many, many, much

hǎohǎor 好好儿 ADJ normal, nothing wrong

hǎojiǔ 好久 ADV a long time

hǎokàn 好看 ADJ 1 pleasant to the eye, good-looking, pretty (ANTONYM 难看 nánkàn) 2 (of a book, movie, etc.) interesting, absorbing

hǎo róngyì 好容易 ADV with great difficulty

hǎotīng 好听 ADJ pleasant to the ear, melodious (ANTONYM 难听 nántīng)

hǎowánr 好玩儿 ADJ great fun ■ 这个游戏很好玩儿。 Zhège yóuxì hěn hǎowánr. *This game is great fun.*

hǎoxiàng 好像 v be like, be similar to

hǎoxiē 好些 ADJ a good many, a large number of, lots of

NOTE: 好些 hǎoxiē is a colloquial word, only used in casual, familiar styles.

hào 好 v be fond of, love

hào chī 好吃 v be fond of eating, be gluttonous

hào kè 好客 [v+obj: 好 be fond of + 客 guest] ADJ hospitable
热情好客 rèqíng hàokè warm and hospitable

hào qí 好奇 ADJ curious

hào sè 好色 ADJ oversexed, lewd

hào xué 好学 ADJ fond of learning, thirsty for knowledge

hào 号 TRAD 號 N 1 order of sequence ■ 小王住在三号楼五号房间。 Xiǎo Wáng zhù zài sān hào lóu, wǔ hào fángjiān. *Xiao Wang lives in Building 3, Room 5.* 2 date of month ■ "今天几号？" "今天二十号，九月二十号。" "Jīntiān jǐ hào?" "Jīntiān èrshí hào, Jiǔyuè èrshí hào." *"What is the date today?" "It's the 20th, September 20th."*

NOTE: See note on 日 rì.

hàomǎ 号码 [comp: 号 order of sequence + 码 size] N 1 serial number
手机号码 shǒujī hàomǎ cell phone number
2 size (of clothing, shoes, etc.)

■ "你穿多大号码的衬衫？" "我穿四十码。" "Nǐ chuān duō dà hàomǎ de chènshān?" "Wǒ chuān sìshí mǎ." *"What size shirt do you wear?" "Size 40."*

hē 喝 v drink

NOTE: 喝 hē (drink) and 渴 kě (thirsty) look similar. Be careful not to confuse the two characters.

hé 合 v close, shut

héfǎ 合法 [v+obj: 合 conform to + 法 the law] ADJ legal, legitimate

hégé 合格 [v+obj: 合 conform to + 格 standard] ADJ qualified, up to standard

héhu 合乎 v conform with, correspond to

hélǐ 合理 [v+obj: 合 conform to + 理 reason] ADJ conforming to reason, reasonable, logical

héshēn 合身 v (of clothes) have the proper size and shape for a figure, fit well

héshì 合适 [comp: 合 harmony + 适 fit] ADJ suitable, appropriate, right

hétóng 合同 N contract, agreement (份 FÈN)
签订合同 qiāndìng hétóng sign a contract

héyǐng 合影 N group photo (张 zhāng)

hézuò 合作 [modif: 合 jointly + 作 operate] V & N cooperate; cooperation

hé 何 PRON which, what

hébì 何必 ADV there is no need, why

hékuàng 何况 CONJ 1 what's more, moreover 2 let alone

hé 河 N river

hé 和[1] ADJ 1 gentle, mild, harmonious 2 peaceful

hépíng 和平 N peace

hé 和[2] I CONJ and
我和你 wǒ hé nǐ you and I
II PREP with
hé ... yìqǐ 和…一起 together with…

hé 盒 N box

hézi 盒子 [suffix: 盒 box + 子 nominal suffix] N box, case (只 zhī)

hé 核 N kernel, core, nucleus

hédiànzhàn 核电站 N nuclear power plant

héwǔqì 核武器 N nuclear weapon

héxīn 核心 [comp: 核 core + 心 the heart] N core, kernel

hè 贺 TRAD 賀 V congratulate

hèkǎ 贺卡 [modif: 贺 greeting + 卡 card] N greeting card (张 zhāng)
电子贺卡 diànzǐ hèkǎ e-card / 圣诞贺卡 Shèngdàn hèkǎ Christmas card / 生日贺卡 shēngrì hèkǎ birthday card / 新年贺卡 Xīnnián hèkǎ New Year's Day card

hēi 黑 ADJ black, dark

hēi'àn 黑暗 [comp: 黑 black, dark + 暗 dim] ADJ dark (ANTONYM 光明 guāngmíng)

hēibǎn 黑板 N blackboard

hēikè 黑客 N hacker

hěn 很 ADV very

NOTE: When used as predicates, Chinese adjectives normally require an adverb. For example, 我高兴 Wǒ gāoxìng sounds unnatural, while 我很高兴 Wǒ hěn gāoxìng (I'm [very] happy); 我不高兴 Wǒ bù gāoxìng (I'm not happy); or 我非常高兴 Wǒ fēicháng gāoxìng (I'm very happy) are normal sentences. The adverb 很 hěn is often used as a default adverb before an adjective. In such cases the meaning of 很 hěn is very weak.

hěn 狠 ADJ 1 cruel, relentless
心毒手狠 xīndú shǒuhěn with a vicious mind and cruel means
2 severe, stern
狠狠地批评 hěnhěnde pīpíng criticize severely

hěndú 狠毒 [comp: 狠 cruel + 毒 poisonous] ADJ cruel and vicious

hèn 恨 V hate, be angry with (ANTONYM 爱 ài)

hènbude 恨不得 ADV how ... wish to
■ 他恨不得马上回家过年。 Hā hènbude mǎshàng huíjiā guònián. *How he wished*

he could go home right now for the Spring Festival.

NOTE: We use 恨不得 to express a wish that is very strong but cannot be fulfilled. If we say 他恨不得马上回家过年。 Tā hènbude mǎshàng huíjiā guònián, it means it is quite impossible for him to go back home right now.

héng 恒 ADJ permanent

hōng 轰 TRAD 轟 V rumble, explode

hōngzhà 轰炸 V drop bombs, attack with bombs

hóng 洪 ADJ big

hóngshuǐ 洪水 N flood

hóng 红 TRAD 紅 ADJ red

hóngbāo 红包 a red envelope (containing money), bribe or gift for children on Chinese New Year's Day

hóngchá 红茶 [modif: 红 red + 茶 tea] N black tea

hónglǜdēng 红绿灯 N traffic lights, stoplights

hóng 虹 N rainbow (See cǎihóng 彩虹.)

hóu 猴 N monkey

hóuzi 猴子 [suffix: 猴 monkey + 子 nominal suffix] N monkey (只 zhī)

hòu 后 TRAD 後 N back, rear (ANTONYMS 前 qián, 先 xiān)
后门 hòumén (the) back door

hòubèi 后背 N the back (of the body)

hòubian 后边 [modif: 后 back, rear + 边 side] N back, rear (ANTONYM 前边 qiánbian)

hòuguǒ 后果 [modif: 后 later + 果 result] N consequences, (bad) results

hòuhuǐ 后悔 [modif: 后 afterwards + 悔 regret, repent] V regret, feel sorry (for having done something)

hòulái 后来 [modif: 后 late + 来 come] N afterwards, later on

hòumiàn 后面 N Same as 后边 hòubian

hòunián 后年 [modif: 后 late + 年 year] N the year after next

hòutiān 后天 [modif: 后 late + 天 day] N

the day after tomorrow

hòu 厚 ADJ thick (ANTONYM 薄 **báo**)

hū 乎 PARTICLE (added to another word to express strong emotions) (See jīhū 几乎, sìhū 似乎.)

hū 呼 v exhale

hūxī 呼吸 [comp: 呼 exhale + 吸 inhale] v breathe, inhale and exhale

hūyù 呼吁 v appeal, call on

hū 忽 ADV suddenly

hūrán 忽然 ADV suddenly

hūshì 忽视 v overlook, negelect

hú 胡 ADJ reckless, wantonly

húluàn 胡乱 ADV rashly, carelessly

húshuō 胡说 [modif: 胡 foreign + 说 talking] V & N talk nonsense; nonsense

hú shuō bā dào 胡说八道 IDIOM pure nonsense, drivel

hú 壶 TRAD 壺 N kettle (把 **bǎ**)

水壶 **shuǐhú** kettle

hú 糊 v paste

hútu 糊涂 [comp: 糊 muddled + 涂 mire] ADJ muddle-headed, muddled, confused

hú 蝴 as in 蝴蝶 **húdié**

húdié 蝴蝶 N butterfly

hú 湖 N lake

湖边 **húbiān** lakeside

hǔ 虎 N tiger (See lǎohǔ 老虎.)

hù 互 ADJ reciprocal

hùliánwǎng 互联网 [modif: 互 each other + 联 link + 网 net] N the Internet, the World Wide Web

hùxiāng 互相 ADV each other, one another

hù 户 MEASURE WORD (used with nouns denoting households and families)

hù 护 TRAD 護 v protect

hùshi 护士 N (hospital) nurse

NOTE: In China nurses are almost exclusively women. To address a nurse politely, use 护士小姐 **hùshì xiǎojiě**, e.g. ▪ 护士小姐，我还需要吃这个药吗？ **Hùshì**

xiǎojiě, wǒ hái xūyào chī zhè ge yào ma? *Nurse, do I still need to take this medicine?* or you can put her family name before 护士 **hùshì**, e.g. 张护士 **Zhāng hùshì**, 李护士 **Lǐ hùshì**.

hùzhào 护照 N passport

huā 花[1] N flower (朵 **duǒ**)

种花 **zhòng huā** plant flowers, do gardening

huāpíng 花瓶 N vase

huār 花儿 ADJ full of colors, mottled, loud

huāshēng 花生 N peanut

花生酱 **huāshēngjiàng** peanut butter

huāyuán 花园 [modif: 花 flower + 园 garden] N garden (座 **zuò**)

huā 花[2] v 1 spend ▪ 去年我花了两百元买书。**Qùnián wǒ huāle liǎngbǎi yuán mǎi shū.** *Last year I spent 200 yuan on books.* 2 cost (money) ▪ 这次旅行花了我三千块钱。**Zhè cì lǚxíng huāle wǒ sānqiān kuài qián.** *This trip cost me 3,000 yuan.* 3 take (time) ▪ 写这篇文章花了我整整两天。**Xiě zhè piān wénzhāng huāle wǒ zhěngzhěng liǎng tiān.** *It took me two full days to write this essay.*

NOTE: In writing, the character 化 **huā** can be used instead of 花 **huā** as a verb meaning *spend, cost*, etc.

huá 华 TRAD 華 I N China

华人 **Huárén** foreign citizen of Chinese descent, ethnic Chinese

II ADJ magnificent, gorgeous

Huáyì 华裔 N person of Chinese descent

huá 划 TRAD 劃 v scratch or scrape with a sharp object

huá 滑 ADJ slippery

huábīng 滑冰 V & N skate; ice-skating

huáxuě 滑雪 V & N ski; skiing

huà 化 v melt, thaw

huàgōng 化工 N shortened form of 化学工业 **huàxué gōngyè** (chemical

industry) / 化工厂 **huàgōngchǎng** chemical plant

huàxué 化学 [modif: 化 change, transform + 学 study] N chemistry 化学工业 **huàxué gōngyè** chemical industry

huàyàn 化验 [modif: 化 chemical + 验 test] N chemical test, laboratory test 化验报告 **huàyàn bàogào** laboratory test report / 化验单 **huàyàndān** laboratory test application (a form signed by a doctor for the patient to have a test done in a laboratory) / 化验室 **huàyànshì** laboratory / 化验员 **huàyànyuán** laboratory assistant, laboratory technician

huà 画 TRAD 畫 V draw, paint 铅笔画 **qiānbǐ huà** pencil drawing / 水彩画 **shuǐcǎi huà** watercolor (painting) / 油画 **yóuhuà** oil painting

huàbào 画报 [modif: 画 picture + 报 paper] N illustrated magazine, pictorial (份 **fèn**, 本 **běn**)

huàjiā 画家 [suffix: 画 paint + 家 nominal suffix denoting an expert] N painter, artist (位 **wèi**)

huàr 画儿 N picture, drawing (张 **zhāng**, 幅 **fú**)

huà 话 TRAD 話 N speech, what is said, words (句 **jù**)

huàtí 话题 [modif: 话 speech + 题 theme] N topic of conversation, subject of a talk, theme

huái 怀 N TRAD 懷 bosom

huáiniàn 怀念 [comp: 怀 miss + 念 think of] V cherish the memory of, think of tenderly

huáiyí 怀疑 [v+obj: 怀 harbor + 疑 doubt] V disbelieve, doubt, suspect

NOTE: 怀疑 **huáiyí** has two seemingly contradictory meanings – *disbelieve and think something is likely*, but the context will make the meaning clear.

huáiyùn 怀孕 V be pregnant

huài 坏 TRAD 壞 I ADJ bad (ANTONYM 好 **hǎo**) II V break down, be out of order

huàichu 坏处 [modif: 坏 bad + 处 place] N negative effect, disadvantage (ANTONYM 好处 **hǎochu**)

NOTE: 坏处 **huàichu** and 害处 **hàichu** both refer to the undesirable effects of an action or actions. 坏处 **huàichu** connotes general negativity while 害处 **hàichu** emphasizes the harm that results.

huān 欢 TRAD 歡 ADJ joyful

huānsòng 欢送 [modif: 欢 joyfully + 送 send off] V send off (people) 欢送会 **huānsònghuì** a send-off party (e.g. a farewell tea party)

huānyíng 欢迎 [modif: 欢 joyfully + 迎 meet] V welcome ■ 热烈欢迎您! **Rèliè huānyíng nín!** *A warm welcome to you!*

huán 还 TRAD 還 V return, pay back ■ 有借有还，再借不难。 **Yǒu jiè yǒu huán, zài jiè bù nán.** *Return what you borrowed, and it won't be difficult to borrow again.*

huán 环 TRAD 環 N circle

huánjìng 环境 [comp: 环 surroundings + 境 boundary, area] N environment, surroundings, ecology

huǎn 缓 TRAD 緩 ADJ leisurely

huǎnjiě 缓解 V alleviate, relieve

huàn 换 TRAD 換 V change, replace

huàn 患 V suffer (from a disease)

huàn 幻 ADJ illusionary

huànxiǎng 幻想 [modif: 幻 illusionary + 想 think] V & N fantasize, have an illusion; fantasy, illusion

huāng 慌 V be flustered, panic 慌了手脚 **huāngle shǒu jiǎo** be so flustered as to not know what to do

huāngmáng 慌忙 ADJ hurried and confused, in a great rush

huāngzhāng 慌张 ADJ in frantic haste, flustered, flurried

huáng 黄 TRAD 黃 ADJ yellow

huángguā 黄瓜 N cucumber (根 **gēn**)

Huánghé 黄河 N the Yellow River

huángjīn 黄金 N 1 gold 2 something that is precious
黄金地段 **huángjīn dìduàn** golden section (of property)

huángsè 黄色 N & ADJ 1 yellow
2 pornography; pornographic
黄色电影 **huángsè diànyǐng** pornographic movie / 黄色杂志 **huángsè zázhì** pornographic magazine

huángyóu 黄油 N butter

huǎng 谎 TRAD 謊 N lie, falsehood

huǎngyán 谎言 N lie, falsehood

huī 灰 I N ash, lime II ADJ gray

huīchén 灰尘 N dust

huīxīn 灰心 ADJ disheartened, discouraged

huī 恢 ADJ extensive, vast

huīfù 恢复 V recover, restore

huī 辉 TRAD 輝 N splendor

huīhuáng 辉煌 [comp: 辉 splendid + 煌 bright] ADJ brilliant, splendid

huí 回[1] V return (to a place), go back
回来 **huílai** return to a place (coming towards the speaker) ■ 妈, 我回来了!
Mā, wǒ huílai le! *Mom, I'm home!*
回去 **huíqu** return to a place (away from the speaker)

huídá 回答 [comp: 回 reply + 答 answer] V reply, answer

huíguó 回国 V return to one's home country

huítóu 回头 ADV later ■ 回头再说。
Huítóu zài shuō. *I'll talk to you later.*

NOTE: 回头 **huítóu** is a colloquialism, used only in very informal styles.

huíxìn 回信 [modif: 回 reply + 信 message] V & N write back, write in reply; letter in reply

huíyì 回忆 V & N recall, recollect; recollection, memory

huí 回[2] MEASURE WORD number of times (of doing something)

huì 会[1] TRAD 會 MODAL V 1 know how to, can 2 probably, will ■ 我看夜里会下雨。
Wǒ kàn yèlǐ huì xiàyǔ. *I think it will rain tonight.*

huì 会[2] TRAD 會 N meeting, conference
大会 **dàhuì** an assembly, a rally / 开会 **kāi huì** have a meeting

huìchǎng 会场 [modif: 会 meeting, conference + 场 venue] N venue for a meeting, conference, assembly or rally

huìhuà 会话 V & N talk, hold a conversation; conversation

huìjiàn 会见 [comp: 会 meet + 见 see] V (formal) meet, receive

huìkè 会客 [v+obj: 会 meet + 客 guest] V receive visitors

huìtán 会谈 [comp: 会 meet + 谈 talk] V (formal) talk

huìyì 会议 [comp: 会 meet + 议 discuss] N meeting, conference
参加会议 **cānjiā huìyì** participate in a meeting or conference / 出席会议 **chūxí huìyì** attend a meeting or conference / 举行会议 **jǔxíng huìyì** hold a meeting or conference / 取消会议 **qǔxiāo huìyì** cancel a meeting or conference / 召开会议 **zhàokāi huìyì** convene a meeting or conference

huì 汇 TRAD 匯 V 1 converge, gather 2 remit

huìkuǎn 汇款 [v+obj: 汇 remit + 款 money] V & N remit money, send remittance; remittance

huìlǜ 汇率 N (currency) exchange rate

huì 慧 ADJ intelligent (See **zhìhui** 智慧.)

huì 惠 N kindness, favor

hūn 荤 TRAD 葷 N meat food (animal, fowl, fish meat) (ANTONYM 素 **sù**)

hūncài 荤菜 N meat dish (animal, fowl, fish meat) (ANTONYM 素菜 **sùcài**)

hūn 昏 V faint

hūnmí 昏迷 [comp: 昏 faint + 迷 coma] V fall into a coma

hūn 婚 v marry

hūnlǐ 婚礼 N wedding ceremony

hūnyīn 婚姻 [comp: 婚 marriage + 姻 marriage] N marriage

huó 活 v be alive

huódòng 活动 [comp: 活 alive + 动 move] V & N do physical exercise, move about; activity, purposeful action
参加活动 cānjiā huódòng participate in an activity

huópo 活泼 ADJ lively, vivacious

huór 活儿 N work, job
干活儿 gàn huór work, do a job

NOTE: 活儿 **huór** and 干活儿 **gàn huór** are very colloquial, and usually refer to manual work.

huóyuè 活跃 [comp: 活 alive + 跃 leap, jump] ADJ active, brisk

huǒ 火 N fire
着火 zháo huǒ catch fire, be caught on fire ■ 着火了！着火了！Zháo huǒ le! Zháo huǒ le! *Fire! Fire!*

huǒchái 火柴 [modif: 火 fire + 柴 wood] N match (根 gēn, 盒 hé)
划火柴 huá huǒchái strike a match / 火柴盒 huǒchái hé a matchbox

huǒchē 火车 [modif: 火 fire + 车 vehicle] N train (辆 liàng, 列 liè)
火车站 huǒchē zhàn railway station / 火车票 huǒchē piào train ticket / 火车时刻表 huǒchē shíkè biǎo railway timetable

huǒshān 火山 [modif: 火 fire + 山 mountain] N volcano (座 zuò)
火山爆发 huǒshān bàofā the eruption of a volcano / 活火山 huó huǒshān active volcano / 死火山 sǐ huǒshān dormant volcano

huǒzāi 火灾 [modif: 火 fire + 灾 disaster] N fire disaster, fire (场 cháng)

huǒ 伙 TRAD 夥 N partner

huǒbàn 伙伴 [comp: 伙 partner + 伴 companion] N partner, mate

huǒshí 伙食 N meals (provided by a school, a factory, etc.)

huò 或 CONJ Same as 或者 **huòzhě**. Used more in writing.

huòxǔ 或许 ADV perhaps, maybe

huòzhě 或者 CONJ or ■ 你们去北京，可以乘飞机，或者坐高铁。Nǐmen qù Běijīng, kěyǐ chéng fēijī, huòzhě zuò gāotiě. *You may fly to Beijing, or go by the high speed train.*

huò 货 TRAD 貨 N goods

huòbì 货币 N currency
货币贬值 huòbì biǎnzhí currency devaluation / 货币升值 huòbì shēngzhí currency appreciation

huò 获 TRAD 獲 v gain, win

huòdé 获得 [comp: 获 gain, win + 得 get] v win, obtain, get

huò 惑 v be puzzled

huò 祸 TRAD 禍 N disaster
车祸 chēhuò car accident, traffic accident

J

jī 几 TRAD 幾 ADV nearly

jīhū 几乎 ADV almost, nearly, practically

jī 机 TRAD 機 N machine

jīchǎng 机场 [modif: 机 airplane + 场 ground, field] N airport, airfield
机场安全检查 jīchǎng ānquán jiǎnchá airport security check / 机场费 jīchǎng fèi airport tax

jīchuáng 机床 N machine tool (台 tái)

jīguān 机关 N government office, state organ

jīhuì 机会 [comp: 机 situation, opportunity + 会 by chance] N opportunity, chance
放弃机会 fàngqì jīhuì give up an opportunity / 抓住机会 zhuāzhù jīhuì grasp an opportunity

jīqì 机器 [comp: 机 device, machine + 器

utensil] N machine, machinery (台 **tái**) 使用机器 **shǐyòng jīqì** operate a machine / 修理机器 **xiūlǐ jīqì** repair a machine / 机器人 **jīqì rén** automation, robot

jītǐ 机体 N organism

jīzhì 机智 N & ADJ wit; sharp-witted

jī 鸡 TRAD 雞 N chicken, hen, rooster (只 **zhī**)

公鸡 **gōngjī** rooster / 母鸡 **mǔjī** hen / 小鸡 **xiǎojī** chick

NOTE: 鸡 **jī** may denote either *a hen, a rooster* or *chick*, though they may be specified by 公鸡 **gōngjī** *cock*, 母鸡 **mǔjī** *hen* and 小鸡 **xiǎojī** *chicken*. As food, it is always 鸡 **jī**.

jīdàn 鸡蛋 [modif: 鸡 hen + 蛋 egg] N hen's egg (只 **zhī**, 个 **gè**)

jī 肌 N muscle

jīròu 肌肉 [comp: 肌 muscle + 肉 flesh] N muscle

jī 圾 N garbage (See **lājī** 垃圾.)

jī 积 TRAD 積 V accumulate

jījí 积极 ADJ (ANTONYM 消极 **xiāojí**) 1 enthusiastic, active, energetic 2 positive 3 proactive

jījíxìng 积极性 N initiative, enthusiasm, zeal

jīlěi 积累 [comp: 积 accumulate + 累 pile up] V accumulate, build up

jī 基 N (earthen) foundation

jīběn 基本 [comp: 基 (earthen) foundation + 本 root] ADJ fundamental, basic

基本上 **jīběn shang** basically, on the whole

jīchǔ 基础 [comp: 基 foundation + 础 plinth, base] N foundation, base, basis

jīdì 基地 [modif: 基 base + 地 place] N base

jījīn 基金 [modif: 基 foundation + 金 money] N stock of money (for special purposes), fund, foundation

教育基金 **jiàoyù jījīn** education fund

jīyīn 基因 [comp: 基 base + 因 cause] N gene

基因工程 **jīyīn gōngchéng** genetic engineering

jī 激 V arouse, excite

jīdòng 激动 [comp: 激 arouse emotion + 动 move] ADJ exciting, stirring, moving, excited

jīfā 激发 [comp: 激 excite + 发 release] V arouse, stir up

激发爱国主义 **jīfā àiguózhǔyì** arouse patriotism

jīliè 激烈 [comp: 激 exciting + 烈 fierce] ADJ fierce, intense

jī 击 TRAD 擊 V beat, hit, strike

拳击 **quánjī** boxing

jīshù 奇数 N odd number

jí 及 CONJ and, with

jígé 及格 [comp: 及 reach + 格 grade] V pass (a test, an examination, etc.)

jíshí 及时 [v+obj: 及 reach + 时 time] ADJ 1 timely, at the proper time 2 immediately, without delay

jí 级 TRAD 級 N 1 grade, rank ■ 他是一级教师。**Tā shì yī-jí jiàoshī.** *He is a first-class teacher.* 2 school grade

一年级 **yī-niánjí** Grade One, first year of study / 一年级学生 **yī-niánjí xuésheng** grade one student, first-year student

jí 极 TRAD 極 ADV extremely, highly ■ 今天天气极好。**Jīntiān tiānqì jí hǎo.** *The weather is extremely good today.*

jíle 极了 ADV extremely, very ■ 这两天我忙极了。**Zhè liǎng tiān wǒ máng jíle.** *I'm extremely busy these days.*

NOTE: 极了 **jíle** is used after adjectives or some verbs to mean *extremely ...* or *very ...* For example: ■ 高兴极了 **gāoxìng jíle** *very happy, delighted.*

jíqí 极其 ADV extremely, highly

jí 即 V be, mean

非此即彼 **fēi cǐ jí bǐ** If it is not this one, it must be that one.

jíshǐ 即使 CONJ even if, even though
■ 他即使非常忙，也要抽工夫学中文。
Tā jíshǐ fēicháng máng, yě yào chōu gōngfu xué Zhōngwén. *Even though he is very busy, he will try and find time to learn Chinese.*

jí 籍 N 1 registration 2 membership
国籍 **guójí** nationality / 会籍 **huìjí** membership of an association

jíguàn 籍贯 N place of one's birth or origin

jí 急 ADJ 1 anxious, worried, impatient 2 urgent, worrying

jímáng 急忙 [comp: 急 hurried + 忙 hastened] ADJ hurried, hastily

jíxìng 急性 ADJ acute (disease) (ANTONYM 慢性 **mànxìng**)

jíxìngzi 急性子 N an impatient or impetuous person, a quick-tempered person

jízhěn 急诊 N medical emergency
急诊室 **jízhěnshì** emergency room

jí 疾 N disease

jíbìng 疾病 [comp: 疾 disease + 病 illness] N disease, illness

jí 吉 ADJ lucky, fortunate

jíxiáng 吉祥 [comp: 吉 lucky + 祥 auspicious] ADJ lucky, auspicious

jíxiángwù 吉祥物 [modif: 吉祥 lucky + 物 thing] N mascot

jí 集 V gather

jíhé 集合 [comp: 集 assemble + 合 combine] V gather together, assemble

jítǐ 集体 [modif: 集 collective + 体 body] N collective (ANTONYM 个人 **gèrén**)

jízhōng 集中 V & ADJ concentrate, focus; concentrated, focused

jídù 嫉妒 V envy, be jealous, hate

jǐ 几 TRAD 幾 PRON 1 several, some ■ 我上星期买了几本书。**Wǒ shàng xīngqī mǎi le jǐ běn shū.** *I bought several books last week.* 2 how many ■ 你上星期买了几本书？**Nǐ shàng xīngqī mǎi le jǐ běn shū?** *How many books did you buy last week?*

NOTE: When 几 **jǐ** is used in a question to mean *how many*, it is presumed that the answer will be a number less than ten. Otherwise 多少 **duōshǎo** should be used instead. Compare: ■ 你有几个哥哥？**Nǐ yǒu jǐ ge gēge?** *How many elder brothers do you have?* ■ 你们学校有多少学生？**Nǐmen xuéxiào yǒu duōshǎo xuésheng?** *How many students are there in your school?*

jǐ 己 PRON self (See zìjǐ 自己.)

jǐ 挤 TRAD 擠 I V squeeze, press II ADJ crowded, packed

jì 计 TRAD 計 V plan

jìhuà 计划 [comp: 计 plan + 划 plan] V & N plan, program, project
制定计划 **zhìdìng jìhuà** draw up a plan / 执行计划 **zhíxíng jìhuà** implement a plan

jìsuàn 计算 [comp: 计 calculate + 算 calculate] V compute, count, calculate

jìsuànjī 计算机 Same as 电脑 **diànnǎo**. Used as a more formal term.

jì 记 TRAD 記 V 1 remember, recall 2 bear in mind
记得 **jìdé** can remember, can recall / 记不得 **jì bu dé** cannot remember, cannot recall / 记住 **jìzhù** learn by heart, bear in mind

jìlù 记录 [comp: 记 record + 录 record] V & N record, register
会议记录 **huìyì jìlù** minutes (of a meeting)

jìyì 记忆 [comp: 记 remember + 忆 recall] V & N remember, memorize; memory

jìzhě 记者 [suffix: 记 record + 者 nominal suffix] N news reporter, correspondent, 新闻记者 **xīnwén jìzhě** journalist, news reporter

jì 纪[1] TRAD 紀 N discipline

jìlǜ 纪律 [comp: 纪 discipline + 律 rule] N discipline (条 **tiáo**)

jì 纪[2] TRAD 紀 V record, memory

jìniàn 纪念 [comp: 纪 record + 念 remember] V & N commemorate; commemoration

jì 寂 ADJ lonely

jìjìng 寂静 [comp: 寂 lonely + 静 silent] ADJ peaceful and quiet, still

jìmò 寂寞 ADJ lonely

jì 技 N skill

jìnéng 技能 N technical ability

jìshù 技术 [comp: 技 skill + 术 craft] N technique, technology, skill
技术工人 jìshù gōngrén skilled worker

jìshùyuán 技术员 [modif: 技术 technique, technology + 员 person] N technician (位 wèi)

jì 际 TRAD 際 N boundary, border (See **guójì** 国际, **shíjì** 实际.)

jì 季 N season

jìjié 季节 [comp: 季 season + 节 solar term] N season

jì 系 V fasten, tie
系领带 jì lǐngdài knot a necktie, tie a tie

jì 济 TRAD 濟 V aid (See **jīngjì** 经济.)

jì 剂 TRAD 劑 N a pharmaceutical and other chemical preparation

jìliàng 剂量 N dosage

jì 既 CONJ 1 both ... and ...
既 ⋯ 又 jì ... yòu ... both ... and ... / 既 ⋯ 也 jì ... yě ... both ... and ...
■ 她既要上班，又要管孩子。Tā jì yào shàngbān, yòu yào guǎn háizi. *She has to both work and care for the children.*
2 Same as 既然 jìrán. Used more in writing.

jìrán 既然 CONJ now that, since, as

jì 绩 TRAD 績 N accomplishment (See **chéngjì** 成绩.)

jì 继 TRAD 繼 V continue

jìxù 继续 [comp: 继 continue + 续 keep on] V continue, go on

jì 寄 V send by mail, post ■ 请你马上把这些书寄给王先生。Qǐng nǐ mǎshàng bǎ zhèxiē shū jìgei Wáng xiānsheng. *Please post these books to Mr Wang immediately.*

jì 忌 V avoid, shun

忌酒 jìjiǔ avoid wine, refrain from drinking wines

jìdu 忌妒 Same as 嫉妒 jídù

jiā 加 V add, plus ■ 一加二等于三。Yì jiā èr děngyú sān. *One plus two equals three.*

jiābān 加班 [modif: 加 add + 班 shift] V work overtime
加班费 jiābān fèi overtime pay

jiāgōng 加工 [v+obj: 加 add + 工 work] V process (unfinished products)
来料加工 láiliào jiāgōng processing of supplied materials / 食品加工 shípǐn jiāgōng food processing

Jiānádà 加拿大 N Canada

jiāqiáng 加强 [comp: 加 add + 强 strong] V strengthen, reinforce

jiāyóu 加油 V 1 add fuel, fuel up 2 make extra efforts
加油干 jiāyóugàn double one's efforts, put more efforts into work

NOTE: 加油 jiāyóu is the colloquial expression used to cheer on a sportsperson or a sporting team in competition, equivalent to *Come on!*, or *Go! Go!*

jiāyóuzhàn 加油站 N gas station, service station

jiā 嘉 ADJ good, fine

jiābīn 嘉宾 N honored guest

jiā 佳 ADJ good, fine, beautiful

jiājié 佳节 N joyous festival

jiā 夹 V pinch, squeeze, wedge between, sandwich

jiākè 夹克 N same as 夹克衫 jiākèshān
皮夹克 píjiākè leather jacket

jiākèshān 夹克衫 N jacket (件 jiàn)

jiāzi 夹子 N tongs, clip
衣服夹子 yīfu jiāzi clothes pin

jiā 家 I N 1 family, household 2 home
II MEASURE WORD (for families or businesses)
四家人家 sì jiā rénjiā four families / 一家商店 yì jiā shāngdiàn a store / 两家工厂 liǎng jiā gōngchǎng two factories

III SUFFIX (denoting an accomplished expert)

画家 **huàjiā** painter, artist / 科学家 **kēxuéjiā** scientist

jiājù 家具 [modif: 家 home + 具 implements] N furniture (套 **tào**, 件 **jiàn**)

jiātíng 家庭 [comp: 家 home, family + 庭 courtyard] N family, household (个 **gè**)

NOTE: 家 jiā has more meanings than 家庭 jiātíng. While 家庭 jiātíng means only *family*, 家 jiā may mean *family, household* or *home*.

jiāwù 家务 [modif: 家 family, home + 务 work, duty] N household chores, housework (件 **jiàn**)

jiāxiāng 家乡 [modif: 家 home + 乡 village] N hometown, home village

jiǎ 假 ADJ false, untrue, fake (ANTONYM 真 **zhēn**)

jiǎhuà 假话 N lie, falsehood

jiǎhuò 假货 N fake (goods), forgery

jiǎrú 假如 CONJ supposing, if

jiǎshè 假设 V suppose, assume

jiǎshǐ 假使 CONJ if, in case

jiǎtuǐ 假腿 N artificial leg

jiǎyá 假牙 N false tooth, dentures

jiǎzhuāng 假装 [comp: 假 false + 装 disguise] V pretend, feign

jiǎ 甲¹ N first

jiǎ 甲² N shell, nail

指甲 **zhǐjia** finger nail

jià 价 TRAD 價 N price

jiàgé 价格 N price

jiàqián 价钱 [comp: 价 price + 钱 money] N price

jiàzhí 价值 [comp: 价 price + 值 worth] N value, worth

jiàzhíguān 价值观 N values

核心价值观 **héxīn jiàzhíguān** core values

jià 驾 TRAD 駕 V drive, pilot

jiàshǐ 驾驶 V drive, pilot

驾驶轮船 **jiàshǐ lúnchuán** pilot a ship / 驾驶飞机 **jiàshǐ fēijī** pilot a plane /

驾驶汽车 **jiàshǐ qìchē** drive an automobile

jiàshǐyuán 驾驶员 [suffix: 驾驶 drive, pilot + 员 nominal suffix] N driver, pilot

jià 架 MEASURE WORD (used for machines, aircraft, etc.)

一架客机 **yí jià kèjī** a passenger plane

jià 嫁 V (of a woman) marry

jià 稼 V sow (grain seeds)

jià 假 N leave of absence, holiday, vacation

jiàqī 假期 [modif: 假 holiday + 期 period] N holiday, holiday period, leave

jiàtiáo 假条 [comp: 假 leave + 条 slip] N an application for leave, a leave form

病假条 **bìngjiàtiáo** an application for sick leave, a doctor's certificate of illness, a medical certificate

jiān 坚 TRAD 堅 ADJ hard, firm

jiānchí 坚持 [modif: 坚 firm, firmly + 持 hold] V uphold, persist (in)

jiānjué 坚决 [comp: 坚 solid + 决 determined] ADJ resolute, determined

jiānqiáng 坚强 [comp: 坚 solid+ 强 strong] ADJ strong, staunch

性格坚强 **xìnggé jiānqiáng** strong character

jiān 间 TRAD 間 I MEASURE WORD (for rooms)

一间教室 **yì jiān jiàoshì** a classroom / 两间办公室 **liǎng jiān bàngōngshì** two offices

II N room (for a special purpose)

洗澡间 **xǐzǎo jiān** bathroom / 手术间 **shǒushù jiān** operating room, surgical room

jiān 肩 N the shoulder

jiānbǎng 肩膀 N shoulder

jiān 艰 TRAD 艱 ADJ difficult

jiānjù 艰巨 [comp: 艰 difficult + 巨 gigantic] ADJ (of a big and important task) very difficult, strenuous

jiānkǔ 艰苦 [comp: 艰 difficult + 苦 bitter, harsh] ADJ difficult, hard, tough

jiān 兼 V act concurrently, double as

jiānzhí 兼职 v & n (hold) concurrent post, (do) part-time job

jiǎn 剪 v cut (with scissors), shear

jiǎndāo 剪刀 n scissors, shears (把 bǎ)

jiǎn 减 v subtract, deduct ▪ 三百六十七减二百八十六是多少？ **Sānbǎiliùshíqī jiǎn èrbǎibāshíliù shì duōshǎo?** *How much is 367 minus 286?*
减数 jiǎnshù subtrahend (e.g. 286 in the example) / 被减数 bèi jiǎnshù minuend (e.g. 367 in the example)

jiǎnféi 减肥 v reduce weight

jiǎnqīng 减轻 [v+compl: 减 subtract + 轻 light] v lighten, alleviate

jiǎnshǎo 减少 [v+compl: 减 subtract + 少 few, little] v make fewer, make less, reduce

jiǎn 检 TRAD 檢 v examine

jiǎnchá 检查 [comp: 检 examine + 查 inspect, check] v examine, inspect, check

jiǎnxiū 检修 [comp: 检 examine + 修 repair] v examine and repair (a machine), maintain
大检修 dàjiǎnxiū overhaul / 汽车检修工 qìchē jiǎnxiū gōng car mechanic

jiǎnyàn 检验 [comp: 检 examine + 验 test] v & n examine, test; examination, testing
质量检验 zhíliàng jiǎnyàn quality control

jiǎn 捡 TRAD 撿 v pick up
把垃圾捡起来 bǎ lājī jiǎn qǐlai pick up the litter

jiǎn 俭 TRAD 儉 ADJ thrifty, frugal

jiǎn pǔ 俭朴 ADJ thrifty and simple
生活俭朴 shénghuó jiǎn pǔ lead a thrifty and simple life

jiǎn 简 TRAD 簡 ADJ simple, simplified, brief

jiǎndān 简单 [comp: 简 simple + 单 single] ADJ simple and convenient, handy (ANTONYM 复杂 fùzá)

jiǎnlì 简历 [modif: 简 simple + 历 history] résumé, curriculum vitae

jiǎntǐzì 简体字 [modif: 简 simple + 体 style + 字 character] n simplified Chinese character

NOTE: See note on 繁体字 fántǐzì.

jiǎnzhí 简直 ADV simply, virtually
简直叫人不敢相信 jiǎnzhí jiào rén bùgǎn xiāngxìn simply unbelievable

jiàn 件 MEASURE WORD (for things, affairs, clothes or furniture)
一件东西 yí jiàn dōngxi a thing, something ▪ 我有一件东西忘在机场了。 **Wǒ yǒu yí jiàn dōngxi wàng zài jīchǎng le.** *I've [inadvertently] left something in the airport.*
一件事情 yí jiàn shìqing a matter ▪ 我有几件事情要跟你说。 **Wǒ yǒu jǐ jiàn shìqing yào gēn nǐ shuō.** *I've something to discuss with you.*
一件衣服 yí jiàn yīfu a piece of clothing (e.g. a jacket, dress)

jiàn 见 TRAD 見 v see, perceive

jiànmiàn 见面 [v+obj: 见 see + 面 face] v meet, see (a person)

jiànshi 见识 n knowledge, experience

jiàn 建 v build, construct

jiànlì 建立 [comp: 建 found + 立 establish] v 1 establish, set up 2 Same as 建 jiàn

jiànshè 建设 [comp: 建 build + 设 install] v build, construct

jiànyì 建议 v & n suggest, propose; suggestion, proposal

jiànzhù 建筑 [comp: 建 build + 筑 build] v & n build, erect; building, edifice (座 zuò)

jiànzhùxué 建筑学 n (the discipline of) architecture

jiànzhùshī 建筑师 n architect

jiàn 荐 TRAD 薦 v recommend (See tuījiàn 推荐.)

jiàn 健 ADJ strong

jiànkāng 健康 [comp: 健 energetic + 康 good health] n & ADJ health; healthy, in good health

jiànshēn 健身 [v+obj: 健 invigorate + 身 the body] v do physical exercises, have a work-out
健身房 **jiànshēnfáng** gymnasium, health club

jiàn 键 TRAD 鍵 N key

jiànpán 键盘 N keyboard

jiàn 渐 TRAD 漸 ADV Same as 渐渐 **jiànjiàn**

jiànjiàn 渐渐 ADV gradually, by and by

jiāng 江 N river (条 **tiáo**)

NOTE: The most famous 江 **jiāng** in China is 长江 **Chángjiāng**, the longest river in China. 长江 **Chángjiāng**, which literally means *the long river*, is also known as the Yangtze River.

jiāng 将[1] TRAD 將 PREP Same as 把 **bǎ**. Only used in writing.

jiāng 将[2] TRAD 將 ADV will, shall, be going to, be about to

jiānglái 将来 [modif: 将 shall, will + 来 come] N future

jiāngyào 将要 ADV Same as 将[2] **jiāng** ADV

jiāng 疆 N boundary, border (See **biānjiāng** 边疆.)

jiǎng 讲 TRAD 講 v talk, speak, tell
讲道理 **jiǎng dàolǐ** See **dàolǐ** 道理. / 讲故事 **jiǎng gùshi** See **gùshi** 故事.

jiǎnghuà 讲话 [comp: 讲 speak + 话 speak] N speech, talk

jiǎngjiu 讲究 I v be particular about, pay much attention to II ADJ exquisite, of very high standard
做工讲究 **zuògōng jiǎngjiu** exquisite workmanship

jiǎngzuò 讲座 N lecture, course of lectures
当代中国经济讲座 **dāngdài Zhōngguó jīngjì jiǎngzuò** lecture(s) on Contemporary Chinese Economy

jiǎng 奖 TRAD 獎 V & N award; prize, award
奖杯 **jiǎngbēi** trophy, cup (given as a prize) / 奖金 **jiǎngjīn** prize money, bonus, award

jiǎngxuéjīn 奖学金 [modif: 奖 award + 学 study + 金 gold, money] N scholarship

jiàng 降 v fall, lower (ANTONYM 升 **shēng**) ▪ 一天中气温降了十度。**Yì tiān zhōng qìwēn jiàngle shí dù.** *The temperature fell by ten degrees within a day.*

jiàngdī 降低 [comp: 降 fall + 低 lower] (ANTONYM 升高 **shēnggāo**) v lower, cut, reduce

jiàngluò 降落 v descend, land
降落伞 **jiàngluòsǎn** parachute

jiàng 酱 TRAD 醬 N soy paste

jiàngyóu 酱油 [comp: 酱 soybean + 油 oil, sauce] N soy sauce, sauce, paste

jiāo 交 v hand over, pay (bills, fees)

jiāohuàn 交换 [comp: 交 transfer + 换 exchange] v exchange, swap

jiāojì 交际 V & N make social contacts; social contact, social intercourse, communication

jiāojìfèi 交际费 N entertainment expense

jiāojìhuā 交际花 N social butterfly

jiāojìwǔ 交际舞 N ballroom dancing

jiāoliú 交流 [comp: 交 associate with + 流 flow] v exchange, communicate

jiāoshè 交涉 v negotiate

jiāotōng 交通 [comp: 交 transfer + 通 open, through] N transport, transportation, traffic
交通事故 **jiāotōng shìgù** traffic accident, road accident / 交通警察 **jiāotōng jǐngchá** traffic policeman, traffic police

jiāowǎng 交往 v associate with, be in contact with

jiāoqū 郊区 N suburbs, outskirts (of a city)

jiāo 教 v teach, instruct

jiāoshū 教书 v teach in school, be a teacher

jiāo 骄 TRAD 驕 ADJ conceited

jiāo'ào 骄傲 [comp: 骄 conceited, proud + 傲 arrogant] ADJ proud, conceited, arrogant

jiāo 蕉 N banana (See **xiāngjiāo** 香蕉)

jiāo 椒 N hot spice plant
花椒 **huājiāo** Chinese prickly ash
jiāo 浇 TRAD 澆 V water
浇花 **jiāohuā** water flowers / 浇水
jiāoshuǐ supply water to plants or crops
jiāoguàn 浇灌 V irrigate, water
jiāo 胶 TRAD 膠 N rubber
jiāoshuǐ 胶水 N glue, mucilage
jiáo 嚼 V chew, munch, masticate
jiǎo 角[1] N corner, horn
jiǎo 角[2] N angle
jiǎodù 角度 N angle, point of view
jiǎo 角[3] MEASURE WORD (Chinese currency:
1 角 **jiǎo** = 0.1 元 **yuán** = 10 分 **fēn**) ten
cents, a dime ■ 两角钱 **liǎng jiǎo qián**
two *jiao*; twenty cents ■ 八块九角五
分 **bā kuài jiǔ jiǎo wǔ fēn** *eight* yuan
nine jiao *and five* fen; *eight dollars and
ninety-five cents*

NOTE: In colloquial Chinese 毛 **máo** is often
used instead of 角 **jiǎo**, e.g. 两毛钱 **liǎng
máo qián** two *mao*; twenty cents

jiǎo 饺 TRAD 餃 N Same as 饺子 **jiǎozi**
jiǎozi 饺子 [suffix: 饺 dumpling + 子
nominal suffix] N stuffed dumpling,
jiaozi
包饺子 **bāo jiǎozi** wrap *jiaozi*, make
jiaozi
jiǎo 脚 N foot, feet (只 **zhī**)
jiǎo 狡 ADJ sly, cunning
jiǎohuá 狡猾 [comp: 狡 sly, cunning +
猾 sleek] ADJ cunning, crafty
jiào 叫[1] V call, address, shout, cry out ■
大家都叫他小王。**Dàjiā dōu jiào tā Xiǎo
Wáng.** *Everybody calls him Xiao Wang.*
jiào 叫[2] PREP Same as 被 **bèi**. Used more
in colloquialisms.
jiàozuò 叫做 V be called, be known as,
be referred to as
jiào 教 N teaching
jiàocái 教材 [modif: 教 teaching + 材
material] N teaching material, textbook,
coursebook (份 **fèn**, 本 **běn**)

jiàoliàn 教练 [comp: 教 teach + 练 train]
N (sports) coach
jiàoshī 教师 [modif: 教 teaching +
师 teacher, master] N teacher (位 **wèi**,
名 **míng**)
jiàoshì 教室 [modif: 教 teaching +
室 room] N classroom (间 **jiān**)
教室大楼 **jiàoshì dàlóu** classroom
building
jiàoshòu 教授 [comp: 教 teach +
授 teach] N university professor
jiàoxué 教学 N teaching and studying,
teaching
jiàoxùn 教训 [comp: 教 teach + 训
lecture] I V lecture, talk down to
II N lesson (learnt from mistakes or
experience)
jiàoyù 教育 [modif: 教 teach + 育
nurture] V & N educate, teach; education
jiàoyuán 教员 [modif: 教 teaching + 员
staff] N teacher (in a particular school)
jiē 阶 TRAD 階 N steps, grade
jiēduàn 阶段 [comp: 阶 steps, stair +
段 section) N period, stage
jiējí 阶级 [comp: 阶 steps, stair + 级
grade] N social class
jiē 揭 V take off, reveal
jiēfā 揭发 V expose (wrongdoing), bring
to light
jiēlù 揭露 V uncover, expose
揭露阴谋 **jiēlù yīnmóu** uncover a
conspiracy
jiē 结 TRAD 結 V bear (fruit), form (seeds)
jiēshi 结实 ADJ sturdy, strong, robust
jiē 接 V 1 receive (a letter, a telephone
call) 2 meet and greet (a visitor)
jiēchù 接触 [comp: 接 join + 触 touch]
V get in touch (with), come into contact
with
jiēdài 接待 [comp: 接 receive + 待
entertain] V receive (a visitor)
jiēdào 接到 [v+compl: 接 receive +
到 arrive] V have received
jiējiàn 接见 [comp: 接 receive +

见 see] v receive (somebody), meet (somebody), give an audience

jiējìn 接近 v be close to, be near

jiēshòu 接受 [comp: 接 receive + 受 accept] v accept, take

jiēzhe 接着 conj and immediately, then, at the heels of (a previous action or event)

jiē 街 n street (条 tiáo)
街上 jiē shang on the street / 步行街 bùxíng jiē pedestrian street / 逛大街 guàng dàjiē stroll the streets, do window shopping

jiēdào 街道 [comp: 街 street + 道 way] n street (条 tiáo)

jié 节¹ TRAD 節 n festival, (public) holiday
过节 guò jié observe a festival, celebrate a festival

jié 节² TRAD 節 MEASURE WORD a period of time
一节课 yì jié kè a period of class

jiémù 节目 [comp: 节 section + 目 item] n TV program, item in a theatrical performance
儿童节目 értóng jiémù children's program / 体育节目 tǐyù jiémù sports program / 文艺节目 wényì jiémù theatrical program / 新闻节目 xīnwén jiémù news program (on TV or radio)

jiérì 节日 [modif: 节 festival + 日 day] n festival day, red-letter day

jiéshěng 节省 v economize, cut down on, be frugal with (ANTONYM 浪费 làngfèi)

jiéyuē 节约 v save, practice thrift (ANTONYM 浪费 làngfèi)

jié 竭 v exhaust

jiélì 竭力 [v+obj: 竭 exhaust + 力 strength, power] v do one's utmost, do everything within one's power
竭力满足顾客 jiélì mǎnzú gùkè do all one can to satisfy customers

jié 结 TRAD 結 n knot

jiégòu 结构 n structure, construction, composition

jiéguǒ 结果 [v+obj: 结 bear + 果 fruit]

I n result, outcome, consequence II conj as a result, consequently, finally

jiéhé 结合 [comp: 结 tie + 合 merge] v combine, integrate

jiéhūn 结婚 [v+obj: 结 tie + 婚 marriage] v marry, get married (ANTONYM 离婚 líhūn)

jiélùn 结论 [modif: 结 end + 论 view, treatise] n verdict, conclusion

jiéshù 结束 [comp: 结 tie + 束 knot] v end, finish, wind up, terminate (ANTONYM 开始 kāishǐ)

jiézhàng 结账 v settle accounts, balance the books

jié 洁 ADJ clean

jié 捷 ADJ prompt, nimble, quick (See mǐnjié 敏捷.)

jiě 姐 n Same as 姐姐 jiějie

jiějie 姐姐 n elder sister

jiě 解 v untie, undo

jiědá 解答 [comp: 解 untie + 答 reply] v provide an answer, give an explanation

jiějué 解决 [comp: 解 dissect + 决 finalize] v solve (a problem), settle (an issue)

jiěshì 解释 [comp: 解 untie + 释 clarify] v & n explain, account for; explanation, interpretation

jiè 介 v intervene

jièshào 介绍 [comp: 介 intervene + 绍 connect] v introduce, present, recommend

jièshào rén 介绍人 n 1 matchmaker, go-between 2 sponsor (for membership in a club, a political party, an association etc.)

jiè 届 MEASURE WORD (used for a conference or congress held at regular intervals, for graduating classes)

jiè 界 n realm (See shìjiè 世界.)

jiè 戒 v guard against

jièzhi 戒指 n (finger) ring

jiè 借 v borrow, lend

NOTE: This verb may mean either *borrow* or *lend*, depending on the patterns in which it

occurs: A 借给 B ... **A jiègei B** ... *A lends B* ..., e.g. ■ 他借给我一百元。**Tā jiègei wǒ yìbǎi yuán.** *He lent me one hundred dollars.* A 向 B 借... **A xiàng B jiè...** *A borrows ... from B* ■ 我向他借了一百元。**Wǒ xiàng tā jièle yìbǎi yuán.** *I borrowed one hundred dollars from him.*

jièkǒu 借口 [v+obj: 借 borrow + 口 mouth] **v & n** use as an excuse; excuse, pretext
找借口 **zhǎo jièkǒu** make up an excuse, invent an excuse

jīn 巾 n towel (See **máojīn 毛巾**.)

jīn 今 n this (day or year), now, the present

jīnhòu 今后 n from today, from now on

jīnnián 今年 [modif: 今 now + 年 year] **n** this year

jīntiān 今天 [modif: 今 now + 天 day] **n** today

jīn 斤 measure word *jin* (a traditional Chinese unit of weight equal to half a kilogram)

jīn 金 n gold (两 **liǎng**, ounce)
奖学金 **jiǎngxuéjīn** scholarship / 奖金 **jiǎngjīn** bonus, prize money / 退休金 **tuìxiū jīn** superannuation, pension

jīnqián 金钱 n money, currency

jīnshǔ 金属 n metal ■ 金、银、铜、铁都是金属。**Jīn, yín, tóng, tiě dōu shì jīnshǔ.** *Gold, silver, copper and iron are all metals.*

jīnzi 金子 n gold

jīn 筋 n muscle, tendon, sinew

jīndǒu 筋斗 n somersault
翻筋斗 **fān jīndǒu** turn/do a somersault

jīn pí lì jìn 筋疲力尽 idiom exhausted, dog-tired

jǐn 仅 trad 僅 **adv** only, merely

jǐnjǐn 仅仅 adv Same as 仅 **jǐn**, but more emphatic

jǐn 尽 trad 盡 **v** to the greatest extent

jǐnguǎn 尽管 I adv feel free to, not hesitate **II conj** even though

jǐn kuài 尽快 adv as soon as possible, as fast as possible

jǐnliàng 尽量 adv as far as possible, to the best of one's ability

jǐn 紧 trad 緊 **adj** tight, taut; pressing

jǐnjí 紧急 [comp: 紧 pressing + 急 urgent] **adj** urgent, pressing
紧急任务 **jǐnjí rènwù** urgent task / 紧急状况 **jǐnjí zhuàngkuàng** emergency situation, contingency

jǐnmì 紧密 adj close together, inseparable

jǐnzhāng 紧张 [comp: 紧 tight + 张 tense] **adj** tense, nervous

jǐn 谨 trad 謹 **adj** cautious

jǐnshèn 谨慎 [comp: 谨 cautious + 慎 cautious] **adj** cautious, careful
谨慎驾驶 **jǐnshèn jiàshǐ** drive carefully

jìn 尽 trad 盡 **v** exhaust

jìnlì 尽力 v do all one can, do one's utmost

jìn 进 trad 進 **v** move forward, enter
进去 **jìnqu** go in, go into ■ 他们在开会，请不要进去。**Tāmen zài kāihuì, qǐng bú yào jìnqu.** *They're having a meeting. Please don't go in.*

jìnbù 进步 n & adj progress, progressive (**antonym** 落后 **luòhòu**)

jìnkǒu 进口 [v+obj: 进 enter + 口 the mouth] **v** import, call at a port (**antonym** 出口 **chūkǒu**)

jìnrù 进入 [comp: 进 enter + 入 enter] **v** enter, enter into

jìnxíng 进行 [comp: 进 enter + 行 walk] **v** conduct, carry out

jìnxiū 进修 v do advanced studies, undergo in-service advanced training

jìnyíbù 进一步 [v+obj: 进 advance + 一步 one (more) step] **adv** advancing a step further, further, more deeply

jìn 晋 v go forward, advance

jìnshēng 晋升 [comp: 晋 advance + 升 rise] **v** promote (to a higher position)
晋升为地区经理 **jìnshēng wéi dìqū jīnglǐ** be promoted to area manager

jìn 近 ADJ close to, close by (ANTONYM 远 yuǎn)

离 … 近 lí … jìn be close to ∎ 爸爸的办公室离家很近。Bàba de bàngōngshì lí jiā hěn jìn. *My father's office is close to home.*

jìndài 近代 [modif: 近 close to + 代 generations] N modern times (usually from the year 1840)

jìnshì 近视 N myopia, near-sightedness, short-sightedness

jìn 劲 TRAD 勁 N physical strength, energy, vigor

没劲 méijìn dull, boring, bored

jìn 禁 V forbid

jìnzhǐ 禁止 [comp: 禁 forbid + 止 stop] V forbid, prohibit, ban

jīng 茎 TRAD 莖 N stem or stalk (of a plant)

jīng 经 TRAD 經 V pass through, experience

jīngcháng 经常 [comp: 经 constant + 常 often] ADV often, day-to-day

jīngdiǎn 经典 N classics, classical works

jīngguò 经过 [comp: 经 go through + 过 pass] I V go through, pass II PREP as a result, through, after

jīngjì 经济 [comp: 经 govern + 济 bring relief to] N economy

经济学 jīngjìxué economics / 经济学家 jīngjìxué jiā economist / 市场经济 shìchǎng jīngjì market economy

jīnglǐ 经理 [comp: 经 manage + 理 administrate] N manager (位 wèi)

副经理 fù jīnglǐ deputy manager / 市场经理 shìchǎng jīnglǐ marketing manager / 总经理 zǒng jīnglǐ general manager, chief executive officer (CEO)

jīnglì 经历 V & N experience, undergo; personal experience

jīngshāng 经商 V engage in business, be a businessman

jīngyàn 经验 [comp: 经 go through + 验 test] N experience, lesson (learnt from experiences)

取得经验 qǔdé jīngyàn acquire experience

/ 有经验 yǒu jīngyàn experienced

jīngyíng 经营 V operate (a business)

jīng 惊 TRAD 驚 V be startled

jīnghuāng 惊慌 [comp:惊 be startled + 慌 confused] V be alarmed, be scared, be panic-stricken

惊慌失措 jīnghuāng shīcuò be panic-stricken and at a loss what to do

jīng 睛 N eyeball, the pupil of the eye (See yǎnjing 眼睛.)

jīng 精 ADJ choice

jīngcǎi 精彩 [comp: 精 choice + 彩 colorful, brilliant] ADJ (of a theatrical performance or sports event) brilliant, thrilling, wonderful

jīnglì 精力 [comp: 精 energy + 力 strength] N energy, vigor, stamina

jīngshén 精神 [comp: 精 essence + 神 spirit] N 1 spirit, mind 2 vigor, vitality, stamina

jīngshén bìng 精神病 N mental illness, psychosis

精神病医生 jīngshén bìng yīshēng psychiatrist / 精神病医院 jīngshén bìng yīyuàn mental hospital

jīng 京 N capital city

jīngjù 京剧 [modif: 京 Beijing (Peking) + 剧 opera] N Beijing (Peking) opera

jǐng 景 N view, scenery

jǐngsè 景色 [comp: 景 view + 色 color] N view, scenery

jǐng 警 V warn

jǐngchá 警察 N policeman, police

NOTE: In China the police bureau is called 公安局 gōng'ānjú *Public Security Bureau*, which should be distinguished from 国安局 guó'ānjú *Bureau of National Security*.

jǐngwèi 警卫 V guard and defend (a military installation, a VIP, etc.)

jǐng 颈 TRAD 頸 N neck

头颈 tóujǐng the neck / 长颈鹿 chángjǐnglù giraffe (long-necked-deer)

jìng 净 ADJ clean (See gānjìng 干净.)

jìng 竞 TRAD 競 V compete

jìngzhēng 竞争 [comp: 竞 compete + 争 strive] **v & n** compete; competition

jìng 竟 **ADV** unexpectedly

jìngrán 竟然 **ADV** unexpectedly, contrary to expectation

jìng 敬 **v** respect

jìng'ài 敬爱 [comp: 敬 respect + 爱 love] **v** respect and love

jìngjiǔ 敬酒 **v** propose a toast, toast

jìng 静 **ADJ** quiet, peaceful, silent

jìng 镜 **TRAD** 鏡 **n** mirror

jìngzi 镜子 [suffix: 镜 mirror + 子 nominal suffix] **n** mirror (面 **miàn**)
照镜子 **zhào jìngzi** look at oneself in a mirror

jiū 究 **v** investigate

jiūjìng 究竟 **ADV** Same as 到底 **dàodǐ**

jiǔ 九 **NUMERAL** nine
九千九百九十九 **jiǔqiān jiǔbǎi jiǔshíjiǔ** 9,999

jiǔ 久 **ADJ** for a long time ■ 日久见人心。**Rì jiǔ jiàn rén xīn.** *As time goes on, you will know a person's nature.*

jiǔ 灸 **n** moxibustion (See **zhēnjiǔ 针灸.**)

jiǔ 酒 **n** alcoholic beverage, wine (种 **zhǒng**, 瓶 **píng**)
白酒 **báijiǔ** colorless spirit distilled from grains / 黄酒 **huángjiǔ** yellow rice wine

jiǔbā 酒吧 **n** (wine) bar, pub

jiǔdiàn 酒店 **n 1** wine shop, restaurant **2** hotel

jiǔhuì 酒会 **n** cocktail party, reception

jiù 旧 **TRAD** 舊 **ADJ** (of things) old, past, second-hand (**ANTONYM** 新 **xīn**)

jiù 舅 **n** mother's brother, uncle

jiùfù 舅父 mother's brother, uncle

jiùjiu 舅舅 Same as 舅父 **jiùfù**, used as a form of address

jiùmā 舅妈 Same as 舅母 **jiùmǔ**, used as a form of address

jiùmǔ 舅母 mother's brother's wife, aunt

jiù 救 **v** save, rescue, salvage ■ 他在河中大叫，"救命！救命！" **Tā zài hé zhong dà jiào, "Jiù mìng! Jiù mìng!"** *He cried out in the river, "Help! Help!"*

jiùhù 救护 **v** give first aid, rescue
救护车 **jiùhùchē** ambulance / 救护人员 **jiùhù rényuán** rescue personnel, rescue team

jiùhuǒ 救火 **v** put out a fire, fire fighting
救火车 **jiùhuǒchē** fire engine

jiù 就[1] **PREP** with regard to, concerning ■ 就人口来说，中国是世界上第一大国。**Jiù rénkǒu láishuō, Zhōngguó shì shìjiè shang dì-yī dà guó.** *In terms of population, China is the biggest country in the world.*

jiù 就[2] **ADV** as early as ..., as soon as ... (used before a verb to emphasize that the action takes place very early, very quickly or only for a very short period of time) ■ 他今天早上六点钟就起床了。**Tā jīntiān zǎoshang liù diǎnzhōng jiù qǐchuáng le.** *He got up as early as six o'clock this morning.*
一… 就 … **yī** ... **jiù** ... as soon as ... ■ 妈妈一下班就做晚饭。**Māma yí xiàbān jiù zuò wǎnfàn.** *Mom prepared supper as soon as she got off work.*

jiùshì 就是 **CONJ** even if, even

jū 居 **v** occupy, dwell

jūmín 居民 [modif: 居 occupy + 民 people] **n** resident, inhabitant

jūrán 居然 **ADV** unexpectedly, shockingly

jūzhù 居住 [comp: 居 occupy + 住 live] **v & n** reside; residency

jú 局 **n** office

júzhǎng 局长 [modif: 局 bureau + 长 chief] **n** director/chief of a bureau

jú 橘 **n** tangerine

júzi 橘子 [suffix: 橘 tangerine + 子 nominal suffix] **n** tangerine (只 **zhī**)

NOTE: 橘子 **júzi** can also be written 桔子 **júzi**.

jǔ 举 **TRAD** 舉 **v** hold high, raise, lift

jǔxíng 举行 **v** hold (a meeting, a ceremony)

jù 巨 ADJ gigantic

jùdà 巨大 [comp: 巨 gigantic + 大 big] ADJ huge, gigantic, tremendous

jù 句 MEASURE WORD (for sentences)
一句话 yí jù huà one sentence / 这句话 zhè jù huà this sentence

jùzi 句子 [suffix: 句 sentence + 子 nominal suffix] N sentence (句 jù, 个 gè)

jù 拒 V resist, repel

jùjué 拒绝 V refuse, reject

jù 具 V own, possess

jùbèi 具备 V possess, be provided with

jùtǐ 具体 ADV specific, concrete, particular

jùyǒu 具有 V have, possess, be provided with

jù 俱 ADV together, completely

jùlèbù 俱乐部 [modif: 俱 together + 乐 joy + 部 department] N club

jù 惧 TRAD 懼 V fear

jù 剧 TRAD 劇 N drama

jùchǎng 剧场 [modif: 剧 drama + 场 site] N theater (座 zuò)

jù 据 TRAD 據 PREP according to

jùshuō 据说 V it is said, they say, rumor has it

jù 距 PREP (stretch of distance) from

jùlí 距离 N distance

jù 聚 V assemble, get together

jùhuì 聚会 [comp: 聚 get together + 会 meet] N social gathering, (social) party
举行生日聚会 jǔxíng shēngrì jùhuì throw a birthday party

juān 捐 V donate

juānkuǎn 捐款 [v+obj: 捐 donate + 款 fund] V & N contribute money, make a cash donation; cash donation, financial donation

juānxiàn 捐献 [comp: 捐 donate + 献 offer] V donate (something of considerable value)

juàn 倦 ADJ tired, fed up (See píjuàn 疲倦.)

juàn 绢 TRAD 絹 N silk

jué 决 ADV definitely, under any circumstance (used before a negative word, e.g. 不 bù)

juédìng 决定 [comp: 决 determine + 定 decide] V & N decide, make up one's mind; decision
做决定 zuò juédìng make a decision

juésài 决赛 [modif: 决 decisive + 赛 match] N final game (of a match), final round, finals

juéxīn 决心 [modif: 决 determined + 心 heart] V & N be determined, make up one's mind; determination, resolve

jué 觉 TRAD 覺 V feel

juéde 觉得 V feel, find, think

jué 绝 TRAD 絕 ADJ absolute

juéduì 绝对 ADJ absolute
绝对多数 juéduì duōshù absolute majority

jué 角 N role, part

juésè 角色 N role, part

jué 掘 V dig

jué 嚼 V Same as 嚼 jiáo

> NOTE: jué 嚼 is pronounced as jué only in jǔjué 咀嚼, which is a medical term. In everyday Chinese 嚼 is pronounced as jiáo. See jiáo 嚼.

jūn 军 TRAD 軍 N army, armed forces
中国人民解放军 Zhōngguó Rénmín Jiěfàng Jūn the Chinese People's Liberation Army (PLA) / 海军 hǎijūn navy / 空军 kōngjūn air force / 陆军 lùjūn army

jūnduì 军队 [modif: 军 army + 队 rows of people] N armed forces, troops

jūnhuǒ 军火 N arms and ammunition

jūnrén 军人 N soldier (名 míng)

jūnshì 军事 [modif: 军 army + 事 affair] N military affairs

jūnzhuāng 军装 N army uniform (套 tào)

jūn 均 ADJ equal

jūnyún 均匀 ADJ well distributed, evenly applied

jūn 菌 N fungus, bacterium

jùn 俊 ADJ handsome (See yīngjùn 英俊.)

K

kāfēi 咖啡 N coffee (杯 **bēi**)
冲咖啡 **chōng kāfēi** make (instant) coffee / 煮咖啡 **zhǔ kāfēi** brew coffee

NOTE: 咖啡 **kāfēi** is one of the few trans-literations (音译词 **yīnyìcí**) in Chinese vocabulary, as it represents more or less the sound of "coffee."

kǎ 卡 N card (张 **zhāng**)
贺卡 **hèkǎ** greeting card / 信用卡 **xìnyòng kǎ** credit card / 银行卡 **yínháng kǎ** banking card
kǎchē 卡车 N lorry, truck (辆 **liàng**)

NOTE: The composition of 卡车 **kǎchē** is semi-transliteration (半音译词 **bàn yīnyìcí**): 卡 **kǎ** represents the sound of the English word "car" and 车 **chē** means *vehicle*. Refer to 咖啡 **kāfēi** for an example of transliteration.

kāi 开 TRAD 開 v 1 open, open up (ANTONYM 关 **guān**) ▪ 开开门! Kāikai mén! *Open the door, please!* 2 turn on, switch on (ANTONYM 关 **guān**) ▪ 天黑了，开灯吧。 **Tiān hēi le, kāi dēng ba.** *It's dark. Let's turn on the light.* 3 drive (a vehicle), pilot (a plane) ▪ 我会开汽车，不会开飞机。 **Wǒ huì kāi qìchē, bú huì kāi fēijī.** *I can drive a car, but I can't pilot a plane.*
kāifā 开发 [comp: 开 open + 发 develop] v develop (resources, products, etc.), open up and exploit
kāifàng 开放 [comp: 开 open + 放 release] v open, open up
kāiguān 开关 N switch
kāihuì 开会 [v+obj: 开 open up + 会 meeting] v attend a meeting, hold a meeting
kāikuò 开阔 v open up (land, space, etc.)
kāimén 开门 N open for business
kāimíng 开明 ADJ civilized, enlightened

kāimù 开幕 [v+obj: 开 open + 幕 curtain] v (of a play, a ceremony, conference, etc.) open, start
kāimù shì 开幕式 N opening ceremony
kāishǐ 开始 [comp: 开 open + 始 begin] v & N begin, start, commence (ANTONYM 结束 **jiéshù**); beginning, start
kāishuǐ 开水 N boiled water
kāi wánxiào 开玩笑 v joke, crack a joke, make fun of, kid
跟/和 … 开玩笑 **gēn/hé … kāi wánxiào** joke with …, make fun of …
kāixué 开学 [v+obj: 开 open + 学 school] v start (a school term/semester)
kāiyǎn 开演 [v+obj: 开 open + 演 performance] v start (a performance, a film, etc.)
kāi yèchē 开夜车 burn the midnight oil
kàn 看 v 1 look, see 2 watch (TV, a movie, etc.) 3 read
看电视 **kàn diànshì** watch TV / 看电影 **kàn diànyǐng** watch a film / 看体育比赛 **kàn tǐyù bǐsài** watch a sport event

NOTE: See note on 看见 **kànjiàn**.

kànbìng 看病 [v+obj: 看 see + 病 illness] v go and see a doctor, visit a clinic
kànbuqǐ 看不起 v look down upon, despise
kànfǎ 看法 [modif: 看 view + 法 way, method] N 1 way of looking at things, view 2 negative opinion
kànjiàn 看见 [v+compl: 看 look + 见 see] v see, get sight of
看不见 **kàn bu jiàn** cannot see / 看得见 **kàn de jiàn** can see ▪ "山上的人，你看得见吗？ 看不见。" **"Shān shang de rén, nǐ kàn de jiàn ma?" "Kàn bu jiàn."** *"Can you see the man (or people) on the hill?" "No, I can't."* / 没看见 **méi kànjiàn** fail to see ▪ 我没看见他在图书馆里。 **Wǒ méi kànjiàn tā zài túshūguǎn li.** *I did not see him in the library.*

NOTE: While 看 **kàn** is *to look* or *to look at*, 看见 **kànjiàn** is *to see* or *to catch sight of*. For example: ■ 我朝窗外看，没有看见什么。**Wǒ cháo chuāng wài kàn, méiyǒu kànjiàn shénme.** *I looked out of the window and did not see anything.*

kànlái 看来 ADV it looks as if, it seems as if

kànwàng 看望 [comp: 看 see + 望 look] V call on, pay a visit to

kànyàngzi 看样子 ADV Same as 看来 kànlái

kāng 康 N good health (See **jiànkāng** 健康.)

kǎo 考 V examine, test, quiz
考得好 **kǎo de hǎo** do well in an examination / 考得不好 **kǎo de bù hǎo** do poorly in an examination

kǎolǜ 考虑 V think over carefully, consider, contemplate

kǎoshì 考试 [comp: 考 examine, inquire + 试 test] V & N examine, test; examination, test (次 **cì**)
汉语水平考试 **Hànyǔ Shuǐpíng Kǎoshì** (HSK) Chinese Proficiency Test

kǎo 烤 V bake, roast, toast

kǎo yā 烤鸭 N roast duck

kào 靠 V rely on, depend on
靠得住 **kàodezhù** trustworthy, reliable / 靠不住 **kàobuzhù** untrustworthy, unreliable

kē 科 N classification

kēxué 科学 [modif: 科 classification + 学 study] N science
科学研究 (科研) **kēxué yánjiū (kēyán)** scientific research / 科学院 **kēxué yuàn** academy of sciences / 中国科学院 **Zhōngguó Kēxué Yuàn** Chinese Academy of Sciences

kēxuéjiā 科学家 [modif: 科学 science + 家 nominal suffix] N scientist (位 **wèi**)

kē 棵 MEASURE WORD (for plants)
三棵树 **sān kē shù** three trees / 一棵草 **yì kē cǎo** a blade of grass

kē 颗 MEASURE WORD (for beans, pearls, etc.)

一颗黄豆 **yìkē huángdòu** a soybean

kēlì 颗粒 N 1 pellet 2 grain

ké 咳 V cough

késou 咳嗽 [comp: 咳 cough + 嗽 cough up] V cough
咳嗽药水 **késou yàoshuǐ** cough syrup

késoutáng 咳嗽糖 N cough lozenge

ké 壳 TRAD 殼 N shell (See **bèiké** 贝壳.)

kě 可[1] ADV 1 indeed (used before an adjective for emphasis) ■ 当父母可不容易呢! **Dāng fùmǔ kě bù róngyì ne!** *Being a parent is indeed no easy job!* 2 after all (used before a verb for emphasis) ■ 我可找到你了! **Wǒ kě zhǎodào nǐ le!** *I've found you after all. (after such a long time)* 3 be sure to (used in an imperative sentence for emphasis) ■ 可别忘了给他发一份电子邮件。**Kě bié wàngle gěi tā fā yí fèn diànzǐ yóujiàn!** *Be sure not to forget to send him an e-mail. (→ Be sure to send him an e-mail.)*

NOTE: 可 **kě** is only used colloquially. When using 可 **kě** to emphasize an adjective or a verb, 啦 **la**, 呢 **ne** or 了 **le** is often used at the end of the sentence.

kě 可[2] CONJ Same as 可是 **kěshì**

kě'ài 可爱 ADJ lovable, lovely

kějiàn 可见 CONJ it can be seen, it is thus clear

kěkào 可靠 ADJ reliable, trustworthy

kěkǒukělè 可口可乐 N Coca-Cola (瓶 **píng**)
百事可乐 **bǎishìkělè** Pepsi[-Cola]

NOTE: 可口可乐 **kěkǒukělè** is a transliteration of "Coca-Cola." It can be shortened into 可乐 **kělè**.

kělián 可怜 ADJ pitiful, pitiable

kěnéng 可能 [comp: 可 may + 能 can] I MODAL V may, possible, possibly II N possibility

kěpà 可怕 ADJ fearsome, frightening, terrible, terrifying

kěshì 可是 CONJ Same as 但是 **dànshì**.

kěxī 可惜 ADJ be a pity, be a shame ∎ 真
可惜！**Zhēn kěxī!** *What a shame!*

kěxiào 可笑 ADJ laughable, ridiculous

kěyǐ 可以 MODAL V giving permission,
may, can, be allowed ∎ "我可以走了
吗？" "可以。" **"Wǒ kěyǐ zǒu le ma?"**
"Kěyǐ." *"May I leave now?" "Yes, you
may."*

kě 渴 ADJ thirsty
口渴 **kǒukě** thirsty ∎ 你口渴吗？这里有
水。**Nǐ kǒu kě ma? Zhèli yǒu shuǐ.** *Are
you thirsty? Here's some water.*

NOTE: See note on 喝 **hē**.

kè 克 MEASURE WORD gram
五百克 **wǔbǎi kè** 500 grams

kèfú 克服 V overcome, conquer

kè 刻¹ V carve, engrave, cut

kè 刻² MEASURE WORD quarter of an hour
一刻钟 **yí kè zhōng** a quarter of an hour;
15 minutes / 三点一刻 **sān diǎn yí kè** a
quarter past three

kèkǔ 刻苦 ADJ hardworking, assiduous,
painstaking

kè 客 N guest

kèguān 客观 ADJ 1 objective 2 impartial,
without bias

kèqi 客气 [modif: 客 guest + 气 manner]
ADJ 1 polite, courteous, stand on ceremony 2 modest ∎ 你太客气了。**Nǐ tài
kèqi le.** *You are too modest.*

kèren 客人 N guest, visitor

kètīng 客厅 [modif: 客 guest + 厅 hall]
N living room, sitting room

kè 课 TRAD 課 N lesson, class, lecture
上课 **shàng kè** go to class / 下课 **xià kè**
finish class

kèběn 课本 [modif: 课 lesson + 本
book] N textbook, course book (本 **běn**)

kèchéng 课程 [modif: 课 lesson + 程
course] N course, a program of study

kèwén 课文 [modif: 课 lesson + 文
writing] N text (篇 **piān**)

kěn 肯 MODAL V be willing to, be ready to

kěndìng 肯定 V & ADJ confirm,
acknowledge; affirmative, positive,
definite (ANTONYM 否定 **fǒudìng**)

kěn 恳 TRAD 懇 ADJ sincere

kěnqiè 恳切 ADJ earnest, sincere

kōng 空 ADJ empty, void, hollow

kōngjiān 空间 N space, room

kōngqì 空气 [modif: 空 empty + 气
vapor] N air, atmosphere

kōngqián 空前 ADJ unprecedented

kōngtiáo 空调 N air conditioning
有空调的房间 **yǒu kōngtiáo de fángjiān**
air-conditioned room

kōngtiáojī 空调机 N air conditioner

kōngzhōng 空中 N in the sky, in the air

kǒngbù 恐 V fear

kǒngpà 恐怕 [comp: 恐 fear, dread +
怕 fear] ADV I'm afraid, perhaps

NOTE: 恐怕 **kǒngpà** and 也许 **yěxǔ** may
both mean *perhaps*, but 恐怕 **kǒngpà**
implies that what will perhaps happen is
undesirable.

kòng 控 V control

kòngzhì 控制 V control, command

kòng 空 I V leave empty or blank II N free
time, unoccupied space

kòngxián 空闲 ADJ & N be free, not
occupied; free time, leisure

kǒu 口 I N mouth ∎ 病从口入。**Bìng cóng
kǒu rù.** *Disease enters your body by the
mouth. (→ Bad food causes disease.)*
II MEASURE WORD (for members of a family)
∎ 我家有四口人。**Wǒ jiā yǒu sì kǒu rén.**
There're four people in my family.

kǒuchī 口吃 V stammer, stutter

kǒudài 口袋 N pocket (只 **zhī**)

kǒuhào 口号 N slogan (条 **tiáo**)

kǒuwèi 口味 N 1 flavor or taste of food
2 one's taste ∎ 各人的口味不一样。**Gè
rén de kǒuwèi bù yíyàng.** *Tastes differ.*

kǒuyǔ 口语 [modif: 口 the mouth + 语
speech] N spoken language, speech

kū 哭 V cry, weep, sob (ANTONYM 笑 **xiào**)

kū xiào bu dé 哭笑不得 ɪᴅɪᴏᴍ not know whether to laugh or cry, find something both funny and annoying

kū 枯 ᴀᴅᴊ withered

kūjié 枯竭 ᴀᴅᴊ dry up, exhausted

kǔ 苦 ᴀᴅᴊ **1** (of food) bitter **2** (of life) hard, suffering, miserable
吃苦 **chīkǔ** suffer hardships, endure hardships

kù 裤 ᴛʀᴀᴅ 褲 ɴ trousers

kùzi 裤子 [suffix: 裤 trousers + 子 nominal suffix] ɴ trousers (条 **tiáo**)

kù 酷[1] ᴀᴅᴊ cruel (See **cánkù** 残酷.)

kù 酷[2] ᴀᴅᴊ cool, relaxed and fashionable, attractive

kù 库 ɴ warehouse

kuā 夸 ᴠ **1** exaggerate, boast **2** praise

kuāzhāng 夸张 ᴠ exaggerate

kuài 快 ᴀᴅᴊ quick, fast, speedy (ᴀɴᴛᴏɴʏᴍ 慢 **màn**)

kuàilè 快乐 ᴀᴅᴊ joyful, happy ■ 祝你生日快乐! **Zhù nǐ shēngrì kuàilè!** *Happy birthday!*

kuài 块 ᴛʀᴀᴅ 塊 ᴍᴇᴀsᴜʀᴇ ᴡᴏʀᴅ **1** (for things that can be broken into lumps or chunks)
一块蛋糕 **yí kuài dàngāo** a piece/slice of cake / 两块面包 **liǎng kuài miànbāo** two pieces of bread
2 (for money) *yuan*, dollar (only in spoken Chinese)
三块钱 **sān kuài qián** three *yuan* (or dollars)

NOTE: See note on 元 **yuán**.

kuài 筷 ɴ chopstick

kuàizi 筷子 [suffix: 筷 chopstick + 子 nominal suffix] ɴ chopsticks (双 **shuāng** a pair)

kuài 会 ᴛʀᴀᴅ 會 as in 会计 **kuàijì**

kuàijì 会计 ɴ **1** accounting
会计年度 **kuàijì niándù** fiscal year
2 accountant
会计主任 **kuàijì zhǔrèn** chief accountant

kuān 宽 ᴛʀᴀᴅ 寬 ᴀᴅᴊ wide, broad

kuāndài 宽带 ɴ broadband

kuáng 狂 ᴀᴅᴊ mad, crazy (See **fēngkuáng** 疯狂.)

kuàng 矿 ᴛʀᴀᴅ 礦 ɴ (coal, gold, etc.) mine (座 **zuò**)
金矿 **jīnkuàng** gold mine / 煤矿 **méikuàng** coal mine / 油矿 **méikuàng** oilfield

kuànggōng 矿工 [modif: 矿 mine + 工 worker] ɴ miner

kuàngquánshuǐ 矿泉水 [modif: 矿 mine + 泉 spring + 水 water] ɴ mineral water

kuàng 旷 ᴛʀᴀᴅ 曠 ᴀᴅᴊ free from worries

kuànggōng 旷工 ᴠ absent from work without leave

kuī 亏 ᴛʀᴀᴅ 虧 ᴠ & ɴ lose, be deficient; loss (ᴀɴᴛᴏɴʏᴍ 盈 **yíng**)
转亏为盈 **zhuǎn kuī wéi yíng** turn loss into gain

kuì 愧 ᴀᴅᴊ ashamed (See **cánkuì** 惭愧.)

kūn 昆 as in 昆虫 **kūnchóng**

kūnchóng 昆虫 ɴ insect (只 **zhī**)

kùn 困 ᴠ be stranded, be in a tough spot

kùnnan 困难 [comp: 困 be stranded + 难 difficult] ɴ & ᴀᴅᴊ difficulty; difficult
克服困难 **kèfú kùnnan** overcome difficulty

kuò 扩 ᴛʀᴀᴅ 擴 ᴠ spread out

kuòdà 扩大 ᴠ expand, enlarge

kuò 括 ᴠ include, embrace (See **gàikuò** 概括.)

kuò 阔 ᴛʀᴀᴅ 闊 ᴀᴅᴊ wide

L

lā 拉 ᴠ pull ■ 请你拉这个门，别推这个门。 **Qǐng nǐ lā zhège mén, bié tuī zhège mén.** *Please pull this door; not push it.*

lājī 垃圾 ɴ rubbish, garbage

lājī chǔlǐ 垃圾处理 ɴ rubbish disposal

lājī dài 垃圾袋 N rubbish bag
lājī xiāng 垃圾箱 N rubbish bin
lāsuǒ 拉锁 N zipper, zip fastener
là 辣 ADJ spicy hot, peppery
làjiāo 辣椒 N hot pepper
lái 来¹ TRAD 來 V come, come to; move toward the speaker (ANTONYM 去 qù)
láibují 来不及 V not enough time (to do something)

NOTE: The opposite is 来得及 **láidejí**, e.g. ■ 还来得及吃早饭。**Hái láidejí chī zǎofàn.** *There is still enough time to have breakfast.*

láixìn 来信 [modif: 来 arriving + 信 letter] N letter received, incoming letter
láizì 来自 V come from
lái 来² TRAD 來 NUMERAL approximately, more or less, close to (used after the number 10 or a multiple of 10 to indicate approximation)
十来辆车 **shí lái liàng chē** about ten cars / 五十来个学生 **wǔshí lái ge xuésheng** approximately fifty students
lài 赖 TRAD 賴 V rely on
lán 兰 TRAD 蘭 N orchid
lánhuā 兰花 N orchid
lán 拦 TRAD 攔 V stop, block, hold back
lán 蓝 TRAD 藍 ADJ blue, indigo
lán 篮 TRAD 籃 N basket
lánqiú 篮球 [modif: 篮 basket + 球 ball] N basketball
打篮球 **dǎ lánqiú** play basketball
lánzi 篮子 N basket
lǎn 览 TRAD 覽 V view (See **yóulǎn** 游览, **zhǎnlǎn** 展览 etc.)
lǎn 懒 TRAD 懶 ADJ lazy, indolent
好吃懒做 **hào chī lǎn zuò** like eating but hate working, be gluttonous and lazy
làn 烂 TRAD 爛 V & ADJ go rotten, go bad; rotten
láng 狼 N wolf (只 zhī)
披着羊皮的狼 **pīzhe yángpí de láng** a wolf in sheep's clothing / 一群狼 **yì qún láng** a pack of wolves

lǎng 朗 ADJ loud and clear
lǎngdú 朗读 [modif: 朗 loud and clear + 读 read] V read in a loud and clear voice
làng 浪 N wave, billow, breaker
làngfèi 浪费 V waste, squander
làngmàn 浪漫 ADJ romantic
láo 劳 TRAD 勞 V toil
láodòng 劳动 [comp: 劳 toil + 动 move] V do manual labor
脑力劳动 **nǎolì láodòng** mental work / 体力劳动 **tǐlì láodòng** physical (manual) labor
Láodòng Jié 劳动节 Labor Day (on May 1)
láojià 劳驾 IDIOM May I trouble you to ..., Would you mind (doing ... for me)

NOTE: 劳驾 **láojià** is a Northern dialect expression. 对不起 **duìbuqǐ** is more widely used.

láo 牢 N shortening for **láofáng** 牢房
坐牢 **zuòláo** serve jail term
láofáng 牢房 N prison, jail
lǎo 老 ADJ 1 old, elderly
老朋友 **lǎo péngyou** long-standing friend
2 PREFIX (added to numerals to indicate seniority among siblings)
老大 **lǎo dà** the eldest child / 老二 **lǎo èr** the second child

NOTE: Chinese tradition values and respects old age. Today, people still attach 老 **lǎo** to a family name as a form of address to show respect and friendliness to an older person, e.g. 老李 **Lǎo Lǐ**, 老王 **Lǎo Wáng**. See note on 小 **xiǎo**.

lǎobǎixìng 老百姓 [modif: 老 old + 百 hundred + 姓 family names] N common people, ordinary folk
lǎobǎn 老板 N boss, one in charge
lǎohǔ 老虎 [prefix: 老 nominal prefix + 虎 tiger] N tiger (头 tóu, 只 zhī)
lǎolao 姥姥 N (maternal) granny
lǎopó 老婆 N (vulgarism) wife, old girl
lǎorén 老人 [modif: 老 old + 人 person] N old person, elderly person (位 wèi)

lǎoshī 老师 [modif: 老 aged + 师 teacher, master] **N** teacher (位 **wèi**)

lǎoshi 老是 **ADV** always, constantly

lǎoshi 老实 **ADJ** 1 honest to goodness, faithful 2 simple-minded, naive
老实说 **lǎoshi shuō** to be frank, to tell the truth

lǎoshihuà 老实话 **N** plain truth

lǎoshi rén 老实人 **N** honest person, simple-minded person, gullible person

lǎoshǔ 老鼠 **N** mouse, mice, rat, rats (只 **zhī**)

lǎotàitai 老太太 **N** (a respectful form of address or reference to an old woman) (位 **wèi**)

lǎoxiānsheng 老先生 [modif: 老 old, elderly + 先生 gentleman] **N** (a respectful form of address or reference to an old man) (位 **wèi**)

lè 乐 TRAD 樂 **ADJ** happy

lèguān 乐观 [modif: 乐 happy + 观 view] **ADJ** optimistic (**ANTONYM** 悲观 **bēiguān**)

le 了 **PARTICLE** 1 (used after a verb to indicate the completion of an action) ■ 他吃了晚饭就上网玩游戏。**Tā chīle wǎnfàn jiù shàngwǎng wán yóuxì.** *As soon as he had eaten supper, he went online to play games.* 2 (used at the end of a sentence to indicate the emergence of a new situation) ■ 秋天来了，树叶黄了。**Qiūtiān lái le, shùyè huáng le.** *Autumn has come and leaves have turned yellow.*

léi 雷 **N** thunder
打雷 **dǎ léi** thunder

léiyǔ 雷雨 [comp: 雷 thunder + 雨 rain] **N** thunderstorm

lèi 泪 TRAD 淚 **N** teardrop, tear (See **yǎnlèi** 眼泪.)

lèi 类 TRAD 類 **N** kind, type, category

lèixíng 类型 [comp: 类 category + 型 type] **N** type (种 **zhǒng**)

lèi 累 **ADJ** exhausted, tired

lěng 冷 **ADJ** cold (**ANTONYM** 热 **rè**)

lěngdàn 冷淡 [comp: 冷 cold + 淡 bland] **ADJ** cold, indifferent, apathetic

lěngjìng 冷静 [comp: 冷 cold + 静 quiet] **ADJ** 1 cool-headed, calm, sober 2 unfrequented, desolate

lěngkù 冷酷 **ADJ** unfeeling, cold-blooded

lěngquèjì 冷却剂 **N** coolant, cooler

lí 厘 MEASURE WORD one hundredth

límǐ 厘米 MEASURE WORD one hundredth of a meter, centimeter

lí 离 TRAD 離 **V** depart, leave
离 … 近 **lí … jìn** close to /
离 … 远 **lí … yuǎn** far

líhūn 离婚 [v+obj: 离 separate + 婚 marriage] **V** divorce

líkāi 离开 [comp: 离 leave + 开 away from] **V** depart, leave

lí 梨 **N** pear (只 **zhī**)

Lǐ 李 **N** (a family name)

lǐ 礼 TRAD 禮 **N** rite

lǐbàitiān 礼拜天 [modif: 礼拜 worship + 天 day] **N** Same as 星期天 **Xīngqītiān**. (a rather old-fashioned word)

lǐmào 礼貌 **ADJ** polite, courteous

lǐtáng 礼堂 [modif: 礼 ceremony, ritual + 堂 hall] **N** auditorium, assembly hall (座 **zuò**)

lǐwù 礼物 [modif: 礼 gift + 物 thing] **N** gift, present (件 **jiàn**)
结婚礼物 **jiéhūn lǐwù** wedding present / 生日礼物 **shēngrì lǐwù** birthday present / 新年礼物 **xīnnián lǐwù** New Year present

belittle your present, describing it as 一件小礼物 yí jiàn xiǎo lǐwù *a small/insignificant gift*. Upon receiving a present, it is bad manners to open it immediately. The recipient is first supposed to say 不用不用 búyòng búyòng *You didn't have to* and then express thanks for the gift, describing it as 这么好的礼物 Zhème hǎo de lǐwù *such a nice gift*, e.g. ■ 谢谢你送给我这么好的礼物。Xièxie nǐ sònggei wǒ zhème hǎo de lǐwù. *Thank you for giving me such a nice gift.*

lǐ 里[1] TRAD 裡 N in, inside (ANTONYM 外 wài)

lǐ 里[2] MEASURE WORD a traditional Chinese unit of distance equivalent to half a kilometer

lǐbian 里边 [modif: 里 inner + 边 side] N inside, in (ANTONYM 外边 wàibian)

lǐmiàn 里面 N Same as 里边 lǐbian

lǐ 理 I N pattern, reason II V 1 manage 2 pay attention

lǐcái 理财 V & N manage financial affairs; fund management

lǐfà 理发 [v+obj: 理 tidy up + 发 hair] V have a haircut and shampoo, have one's hair done

lǐfàdiàn 理发店 N barbershop, hair salon

NOTE: Instead of the straightforward word 理发店 lǐfàdiàn, many hair salons now give themselves fanciful names such as 美发厅 měifàtīng.

理发师 lǐfàshī barber, hairdresser, hairstylist

lǐjiě 理解 [comp: 理 reason + 解 understand] V understand, comprehend ■ 我能理解你的心情。Wǒ lǐjiě nǐ de xīnqíng. *I understand how you feel.*

lǐlùn 理论 [comp: 理 reason + 论 theory] N theory, thinking

lǐxiǎng 理想 [comp: 理 reason + 想 thought, wish] N ideal, aspiration 实现理想 shíxiàn lǐxiǎng realize an ideal

lǐyóu 理由 [comp: 理 reason + 由 origin, cause] N reason, justification, ground

lì 力 N strength, force, might, power

lìliàng 力量 N 1 (physical) strength, power 2 efforts, ability

lìqi 力气 V physical strength

lì 历 TRAD 歷 N past experience

lìshǐ 历史 [comp: 历 past experience + 史 recording] N history

lìshǐxuéjiā 历史学家 N historian

lì 立 V stand 坐立不安 zuò lì bù ān IDIOM on pins and needles, on tenterhooks, anxious

lìjí 立即 ADV immediately, promptly, without delay

lìkè 立刻 [comp: 立 immediately + 刻 a brief time] ADV at once, immediately, right away

lì 厉 TRAD 厲 ADJ severe, strict

lìhai 厉害 ADJ severe, formidable, redoubtable

NOTE: 厉害 lìhai may be written as 利害. It is often used with 得 de to indicate a very high degree, e.g. ■ 这两天热得厉害。Zhèliǎngtiān rède lìhai. *These days are terribly hot.* ■ 情人节花儿贵得厉害。Qíngrénjié huār guìde lìhai. *Flowers are terribly expensive on Valentine's Day.*

lì 丽 TRAD 麗 ADJ beautiful (See měilì 美丽.)

lì 励 TRAD 勵 V encourage (See gǔlì 鼓励.)

lì 利 N benefit

lìbì 利弊 [comp: 利 advantage + 弊 disadvantage] N pros and cons

lìlǜ 利率 N interest rate

lìrùn 利润 N profit

lìxī 利息 N interest (on a loan)

lìyì 利益 [comp: 利 benefit + 益 benefit] N benefit, interest

lìyòng 利用 [comp: 利 benefit + 用 use] V make use of, benefit from, exploit

lì 例 N example

lìrú 例如 [comp: 例 example + 如 same as] CONJ for example, such as

lìzi 例子 [suffix: 例 example + 子 nominal suffix] N example (个 gè) 举例子 jǔ lìzi give an example

liǎ 俩 TRAD 倆 NUMERAL two (colloquial

usage for people, objects) ■ 他们俩是
好朋友，经常在一起玩。**Tāmen liǎ shì
hǎo péngyou, jīngcháng zài yìqǐ wán.**
*The two of them are good friends. They
often play together.*

lián 连 TRAD 連 I v connect, join II ADV in
succession, repeated

lián … dōu … 连 … 都 … IDIOM even
■ 连三岁小孩都知道。**Lián sān suì
xiǎohái dōu zhīdào.** *Even a toddler
(← a three-year-old) knows this.*

NOTE: (1) 连… 都 … **lián … dōu …** is an
emphatic expression, stressing the word
after 连 **lián**. (2) 都 **dōu** may be replaced by
也 **yě**, i.e. 连 … 也 … **lián … yě**… is the same
as 连 … 都 … **lián … dōu …**, for example:
■ 连三岁小孩也知道。**Lián sān suì xiǎohái
yě zhīdào.** *Even a toddler knows this.*

liánmáng 连忙 ADV make haste, hasten
without the slightest delay

liánxù 连续 v in succession, in a row

lián 怜 TRAD 憐 v pity (See **kělián** 可怜.)

lián 联 TRAD 聯 v connect

liánhé 联合 [comp: 联 join + 合 merge]
v unite, get together (to do something),
jointly develop their ocean resources.

Liánhéguó 联合国 N the United Nations
Organization

liánxì 联系 [comp: 联 connect + 系
tie, knot] v & N get in touch, contact;
connection, being related

lián 廉 ADJ 1 inexpensive, cheap
2 morally clean

liánjià 廉价 ADJ low-priced, inexpensive
廉价出售 **liánjià chūshòu** sell at a low
price

lián 帘 N curtain (See **chuānglián** 窗帘.)

liǎn 脸 TRAD 臉 N face (张 **zhāng**)
丢脸 **diūliǎn** be disgraced, lose face

liàn 练 TRAD 練 v practice, train, drill

liànxí 练习 [comp: 练 drill, train + 习
practice] v & N exercise, train, drill

liàn 炼 TRAD 煉 v smelt (See **duànliàn** 锻
炼.)

liàn 恋 TRAD 戀 N infatuation

liàn'ài 恋爱 [comp: 恋 infatuate + 爱
love] v & N be in romantic love, be
courting; romantic love
谈恋爱 **tán liàn'ài** in courtship, in love

liáng 良 ADJ good

liánghǎo 良好 [comp: 良 good + 好
good] ADJ good, fine, commendable

liáng 凉 ADJ cool, chilly

liángkuai 凉快 [comp: 凉 cool + 快
pleasant] ADJ pleasantly cool, nice and
cool

liáng 量 v measure, take measurements
■ 你量一量，这个房间有多大。**Nǐ
liáng yi liáng, zhège fángjiān yǒu duō
dà.** *Measure the room; find out how big
it is.*

liáng 粮 TRAD 糧 N grain

liángshí 粮食 [comp: 粮 grain + 食
food] N grain, cereal, staple food

liáng 梁 TRAD 樑 N beam (in structure)
(See **qiáoliáng** 桥梁)

liǎng 两¹ MEASURE WORD (a traditional
Chinese unit of weight equivalent to 50
grams), ounce

liǎng 两² NUMERAL 1 two ■ 两个人 **liǎng
ge rén** *two people* ■ 两本书 **liǎng běn
shū** *two books* 2 (as an approximation)
a couple of, a few ■ 我来说两句话。
Wǒ lái shuō liǎng jù huà. *Let me say a
few words.*

NOTE: Both 两 **liǎng** and 二 **èr** may mean
two, but are used differently. 二 **èr** must be
used in mathematics or when saying the
number 2 in isolation, e.g.: ■ 一、二、
三、四 …**yī, èr, sān, sì** … *1, 2, 3, 4* … ■ 二
加三是五。**Èr jiā sān shì wǔ.** *2 plus 3 is 5.*
Use 两 **liǎng** when referring to *two*
something, e.g.: ■ 两张桌子 **liǎng zhāng
zhuōzi** *two tables* ■ 两个小时 **liǎng ge
xiǎoshí** *two hours.* The ordinal number
second is 第二 **dì-èr**.

liàng 亮 ADJ light, bright, shining

liàng 晾 v dry in the air, air dry

liàng 辆 TRAD 輛 MEASURE WORD (for vehicles)
一辆汽车 **yí liàng qìchē** a car / 两辆自行车 **liǎng liàng zìxíngchē** two bicycles

liàng 量 N quantity (See **chǎnliàng** 产量, **dàliàng** 大量, **lìliàng** 力量, **zhìliàng** 质量, **zhòngliàng** 重量.)

liáo 聊 V chat

liáotiān 聊天 V chat, shoot the bull/breeze

liáo 疗 V treat, cure (See **zhìliáo** 治疗.)

liǎo 了 V finish, be done with

> NOTE: 了 **liǎo**, together with 得 **de** or 不 **bu**, is often used after a verb as a complement to mean *can ...* or *cannot ...* For example:
> ■ 这件事我干得了，那件事我干不了。
> **Zhè jiàn shì wǒ gàn de liǎo, nà jiàn shì wǒ gàn bu liǎo.** *I can do this job, but I can't do that job.*

liǎobuqǐ 了不起 ADJ wonderful, terrific

liǎojiě 了解 [comp: 了 see through + 解 analyze, comprehend] V know, understand, find out

liào 料¹ N material (See **cáiliào** 材料, **sùliào** 塑料, etc.)

liào 料² V anticipate

liè 列 MEASURE WORD (for trains)
一列火车 **yí liè huǒchē** a train (consisting of several carriages)

lièchē 列车 N train
20 次列车 **èrshí cì lièchē** train No 20

lièchē yuán 列车员 N train attendant

liè 烈 ADJ intense (See **jīliè** 激烈, **rèliè** 热烈.)

liè 猎 TRAD 獵 V hunt

lièrén 猎人 N hunter

liè 劣 ADJ inferior, of low quality (See **èliè** 恶劣.)

lín 邻 TRAD 鄰 N neighbor

línjū 邻居 [modif: 邻 neighboring + 居 residents] N neighbor

lín 林 N wood, woods (See **sēnlín** 森林, **shùlín** 树林.)

lín 淋 V drench, pour

línyù 淋浴 N shower (bath)
洗淋浴 **xǐ línyù** take a shower

lín 临 TRAD 臨 V arrive

línshí 临时 ADJ tentative, provisional, temporary

líng 零 NUMERAL zero
一百零二 **yìbǎi líng èr** 102 / 四千零五 **sìqiān líng wǔ** 4005

> NOTE: (1) No matter how many zeros there are between digits, only one 零 **líng** is used. For example, 4005 is 四千零五 **sìqiān líng wǔ**, not 四千零零五 **sìqiān líng líng wǔ**.
> (2) 零 **líng** can also be written as 0, e.g, 一百0五 **yìbǎi líng wǔ** 105.

língjiàn 零件 N part, spare part

língqián 零钱 [modif: 零 parts + 钱 money] N allowance, pocket money, small change

língshí 零食 [modif: 零 parts + 食 food] N between-meal nibbles

língshòu 零售 V retail, sell retail (ANTONYM 批发 **pīfā**)

líng 铃 TRAD 鈴 N bell

líng 龄 TRAD 齡 N age (See **niánlíng** 年龄.)

lǐng 领 TRAD 領 V lead, take

lǐngdài 领带 N necktie, tie (条 **tiáo**)
戴领带 **dài lǐngdài** wear a tie

lǐngdǎo 领导 [comp: 领 lead + 导 guide] V & N lead, exercise leadership; leader, the person in charge, leadership

lǐngshì 领事 N (diplomatic) consul

lǐngshìguǎn 领事馆 N consulate
美国驻上海领事馆 **Měiguó zhù Shànghǎi lǐngshìguǎn** the US consulate in Shanghai

lǐngyù 领域 N 1 territory, domain 2 field (of activity or thinking)

lìng 令 V command, cause (See **mìnglìng** 命令.)

lìng 另 ADJ Same as 另外 **lìngwài**. Used before a monosyllabic verb.

lìngwài 另外 ADJ other, another

liú 流 V flow ■ 河水慢慢地向东流去。

Hé shuǐ mànmàn de xiàng dōng liúqù.
The river flows slowly to the east.

liúchuán 流传 v circulate, spread

liúlèi 流泪 v shed tears

liúlì 流利 ADJ fluent

liúxíng 流行 v be fashionable, be popular
流行歌手 **liúxíng gēshǒu** pop singer /
流行音乐 **liúxíng yīnyuè** pop music

liúxíngbìng 流行病 N epidemic

**liúxíngxìng gǎnmào (liúgǎn) 流行性
感冒 (流感)** N influenza, flu

liú 留 v remain (in the same place), stay
behind, remain, retain

liúxué 留学 [comp: 留 stay + 学 study] v
study abroad

liúxuéshēng 留学生 international
students (especially in a university)

liú 瘤 N tumor (See **zhǒngliú 肿瘤**.)

liú 浏 TRAD 瀏 as in 浏览 **liúlǎn**

liúlǎn 浏览 v browse
浏览器 **liúlǎnqì** (computer) browser

liù 六 NUMERAL six
六十六 **liùshí liù** sixty-six / 六十五岁
liùshí wǔ suì sixty-five years of age

lóng 龙 TRAD 龍 N dragon (条 tiáo)

lóng 笼 TRAD 籠 N cage
笼子 **lóngzi** cage / 鸟笼 **niǎolóng** bird
cage

lǒngzhào 笼罩 v shroud, envelope

lǒng 垄 TRAD 壟 N ridge

lǒngduàn 垄断 N monopoly

lóu 楼 TRAD 樓 N 1 building with two or
more stories (座 zuò) 2 floor (层 céng)
大楼 **dàlóu** a big building (especially
a high-rise building) / 高楼 **gāo lóu**
high-rise

NOTE: In naming floors, the Chinese system
is the same as the American system and
different from the British one, i.e. 一楼
yī-lóu is the American first floor, and the
British ground floor.

lóu fáng 楼房 N multi-storied building
(contrast with 平房 **píngfáng** one-story
building, bungalow)

lóu shang 楼上 N upstairs

lóutī 楼梯 [modif: 楼 floor, story + 梯
steps] N stairs, stairway, staircase

lóu xia 楼下 N downstairs

lòu 漏 v leak

lù 陆 TRAD 陸 N land

lùdì 陆地 N dry land, land

lùxù 陆续 ADV one after another, in
succession

lù 录 TRAD 錄 v record

lùqǔ 录取 v enroll (students), appoint
(job applicants)

lùxiàng 录像 [v+obj: 录 record + 像
image] v record with a video camera or
video recorder

lùxiàngjī 录像机 N video recorder

lùyīn 录音 [v+obj: 录 record + 音 sound]
v make a recording of sounds (e.g. music,
reading)

lùyīnjī 录音机 N audio recorder, sound
recorder

lù 路 N road, path, way (条 tiáo)
马路 **mǎlù** road (in a city)

lùshang 路上 N on one's way (to)

lùxiàn 路线 [modif: 路 road + 线 line] N
route, itinerary

lù 露 v show, reveal

lǚ 旅 v travel

lǚguǎn 旅馆 [modif: 旅 travel + 馆
house] N hotel (座 zuò, 家 jiā)
汽车旅馆 **qìchē lǚguǎn** motel / 五星旅馆
wǔxīng lǚguǎn five-star hotel

lǚkè 旅客 [modif: 旅 traveling + 客
guest] N hotel guest, passenger (of
coach, train, plane, etc.)

lǚtú 旅途 [modif: 旅 travel + 途 journey]
N journey, travel

lǚxíng 旅行 [comp: 旅 travel + 行 walk,
go] v travel, journey, tour
旅行社 **lǚxíngshè** travel agency, travel
service

lǚyóu 旅游 [comp: 旅 travel + 游 play,
holiday] v travel for pleasure, tour, go
sight-seeing

旅游车 **lǚyóuchē** tour bus / 旅游公司 **lǚyóu gōngsī** tourist company / 旅游路线 **lǚyóu lùxiàn** tour itinerary / 旅游团 **lǚyóutuán** tour group / 旅游者 **lǚyóuzhě** tourist, holiday-maker

lǚ 履 N shoe

lǚlì 履历 N résumé

lǚ 侣 N companion

lǜ 虑 V consider, ponder (See **kǎolǜ** 考虑.)

lǜ 滤 V filter (See **guòlǜ** 过滤.)

lǜ 率 N rate (See **xiàolǜ** 效率.)

lǜ 绿 TRAD 綠 ADJ green

lǜdǎng 绿党 N the Green Party

lǜkǎ 绿卡 N green card (permanent residency permit in the USA and some other countries)

lǜ 律 N law

lǜshī 律师 [modif: 律 law + 师 master] N lawyer, solicitor, barrister
律师事务所 **lǜshī shìwùsuǒ** law firm

luàn 乱 TRAD 亂 ADJ 1 disorderly, chaotic (ANTONYM 整齐 **zhěngqí**) 2 at will, random

lüè 略 V capture

lüèwēi 略微 ADV slightly, a little, somewhat

lún 轮 TRAD 輪 N wheel

lúnliú 轮流 V take turns
轮流值班 **lúnliú zhíbān** be on duty by turns

lùn 论 TRAD 論 V discuss

lùnwén 论文 [comp: 论 treatise + 文 essay] N dissertation, thesis, essay (篇 **piān**)

luó 逻 TRAD 邏 V patrol (See **xúnluó** 巡逻.)

luójì 逻辑 N logic
不合逻辑 **bù hé luójì** illogical / 合乎逻辑 **héhu luójì** logical

NOTE: **luójì** 逻辑 is a transliteration from the English word "logic." See note on 咖啡 **kāfēi**.

luósīdīng 螺丝钉 N screw

luó 萝 TRAD 蘿 N trailing plant

luóbo 萝卜 N turnip, radish, carrot (根 **gēn**, 个 **gè**)
白萝卜 **bái luóbo** turnip / 红萝卜 **hóng luóbo** radish / 胡萝卜 **hú luóbo** carrot

luò 落 V fall, drop

luòhòu 落后 ADJ backward, outdated
■ 你这种观点太落后了。**Nǐ zhè zhǒng guāndiǎn tài luòhòu le.** *Your views are outdated.*

M

mā 妈 TRAD 媽 N ma, mama, mom

māma 妈妈 N ma, mama, mother

má 麻[1] N hemp

má 麻[2] ADJ numb

máfan 麻烦 IDIOM I V put somebody to trouble, bother II ADJ troublesome, knotty

NOTE: 麻烦您 **máfan nín** is a polite expression to request somebody's service or to ask a favor. More examples: ■ 麻烦您把盐递给我。**Máfan nín bǎ yán dì gei wǒ.** *Please pass the salt [to me].* ■ 麻烦您查一下他的电话号码。**Máfan nín chá yíxià tā de diànhuà hàomǎ.** *Would you mind finding out his telephone number for me?*

májiàng 麻将 N the game of mahjong, mahjong
打麻将 **dǎmájiàng** play mahjong

mǎ 马 TRAD 馬 N horse (匹 **pǐ**)

mǎhu 马虎 IDIOM sloppy, careless

mǎlù 马路 [modif: 马 horse + 路 road] N street, avenue (条 **tiáo**)
马路上 **mǎlù shang** in the street, on the road / 过马路 **guò mǎlù** walk across a street

mǎ mǎ hū hū 马马虎虎 IDIOM 1 so-so, not too bad, just managing 2 careless, sloppy

mǎshàng 马上 ADV at once, immediately
■ 好，我马上来! **Hǎo, wǒ mǎshàng lái!** *OK, I'm coming!*

mà 骂 TRAD 罵 V curse, swear ■ 你怎么骂人? **Nǐ zěnme mà rén?** *How can you swear at people?*

ma 吗 TRAD 嗎 PARTICLE (used at the end of a sentence to turn it into a yes-or-no question) ▪ 你会说中文吗? **Nǐ huì shuō Zhōngwén ma?** *Do you speak Chinese?*

mǎi 买 TRAD 買 v buy, purchase

mǎimài 买卖 [comp: 买 buy + 卖 sell] N buying and selling, trade, business
做买卖 **zuò mǎimài** do business, be engaged in business

mài 麦 TRAD 麥 N wheat
大麦 **dàmài** barley / 荞麦 **qiáomài** buckwheat / 小麦 **xiǎomài** wheat / 燕麦 **yànmài** oats

màikèfēng 麦克风 N microphone

mài 卖 TRAD 賣 v sell

mán 瞒 v conceal truth from

mán 馒 TRAD 饅 as in 馒头 **mántou**

mántou 馒头 [suffix: 馒 steamed bun + 头 nominal suffix] N steamed bun

mán 蛮 TRAD 蠻 ADJ rough, churlish, crude (See yěmán 野蛮.)

mǎn 满 ADJ full, full to the brim

mǎnyì 满意 [v+obj: 满 make full + 意 wish, desire] ADJ satisfied, satisfactory
对 … 满意 **duì … mǎnyì** be satisfied with

mǎnzú 满足 v meet the needs of, satisfy

màn 慢 ADJ slow, slow down (ANTONYM 快 **kuài**)

mànxìng 慢性 ADJ chronic (disease)

mànxìngzi 慢性子 N slow or indolent person, slow coach

máng 忙 ADJ busy, fully occupied

NOTE: When friends meet in China, a common conversation opener is: 你最近忙吗? **Nǐ zuìjìn máng ma?** *Have you been busy lately?*

máng 盲 ADJ blind

mángrén 盲人 [modif: 盲 blind + 人 person] N blind person
盲人学校 **mángrén xuéxiào** school for the blind

māo 猫 TRAD 貓 N cat (只 **zhī**)

máo 毛[1] N hair
yángmáo 羊毛 wool

máo 毛[2] MEASURE WORD Same as 角[3] **jiǎo** MEASURE WORD. Used colloquially.

máobìng 毛病 N illness

máojīn 毛巾 N towel (条 **tiáo**)

máoxiàn 毛线 N knitting wool, woolen yarn

máoyī 毛衣 [modif: 毛 woolen + 衣 clothing] N woolen sweater, woolen pullover (件 **jiàn**)

máo 矛 N spear

máodùn 矛盾 [comp: 矛 spear + 盾 shield] N & ADJ contradiction, disunity; contradictory, inconsistent
自相矛盾 **zìxiāng máodùn** self-contradictory, inconsistent ▪ 这篇文章前后自相矛盾。**Zhè piān wénzhāng qiánhòu zìxiāng máodùn.** *This article is inconsistent in its argument.*

NOTE: 矛盾 **máodùn** is a colorful word derived from an ancient Chinese fable. A man who sold spears (矛 **máo**) and shields (盾 **dùn**) boasted that his spears were so sharp that they could penetrate any shield, and that his shields were so strong that no spear could ever penetrate them. As there seemed to be a contradiction there, 矛盾 **máodùn** came to mean *inconsistency* or *contradiction*.

mào 冒 v 1 emit, send forth, give off ▪ 开水冒着热气。**Kāishuǐ màozhe rè qì.** *Boiling water gives off steam.* 2 risk 3 make false claims

màopái 冒牌 [v+obj: 冒 falsely claim + 牌 brand] v counterfeit, forge
冒牌货 **màopáihuò** counterfeit, fake, forgery

màoxiǎn 冒险 [v+obj: 冒 risk + 险 danger] v risk, take a risk

mào 帽 N hat, cap

màozi 帽子 [suffix: 帽 hat, cap + 子 nominal suffix] N hat, cap
戴帽子 **dài màozi** put on/wear a hat (or a cap) / 脱帽子 **tuō màozi** take off a hat (or a cap)

mào 贸 TRAD 貿 N transaction

màoyì 贸易 [comp: 贸 transaction + 易 exchange] N trade, exchange
对外贸易 **duìwài màoyì** foreign trade / 国际贸易 **guójì màoyì** international trade / 贸易公司 **màoyì gōngsī** trading company

mào 貌 N appearance (See **lǐmào** 礼貌.)

me 么 TRAD 麼 PARTICLE (used to form certain words) (See **duōme** 多么, **nàme** 那么, **shénme** 什么, **wèishénme** 为什么, **zěnme** 怎么, **zěnmeyàng** 怎么样, **zhème** 这么.)

méi 没 ADJ Same as 没有 **méiyǒu**
没关系 **méi guānxi** (See **guānxi** 关系.) / 没意思 **méi yìsi** (See **yìsi** 意思.)

méishénme 没什么 IDIOM nothing serious, it's nothing, it doesn't matter

méiyòng 没用 ADJ useless ▪ 那本词典太旧，没用了。**Nà běn cí diǎn tài jiù, méi yòng le.** *This dictionary is too old and no longer useful.*

méiyǒu 没有 v 1 do not have 2 there is/ are no 3 did not, have not (indicating negation of past experiences, usually used before a verb or at the end of a question) ▪ 我没有学过这个字。**Wǒ méiyǒu xuéguo zhège zì.** *I haven't learnt this Chinese character.*
还没有 **hái méiyǒu** not yet

NOTE: In spoken Chinese, 没有 **méiyǒu** is often shortened 没 **méi**. However, when 没有 **méiyǒu** is used at the end of a question, as in ▪ 你去过中国没有? **Nǐ qùguo Zhōngguó méiyǒu?** *Have you ever been to China?* it cannot be replaced by 没 **méi**.

méizhé 没辙 v be at a loss what to do, be at one's wit's end

méi 煤 v coal

méikuàng 煤矿 N coal mine

méikuànggōng 煤矿工 N coal miner

méiqì 煤气 N coal gas

méitàn 煤炭 Same as **méi** 煤

méitián 煤田 N coalfield

méi 媒 N matchmaking
做媒 **zuòméi** be a matchmaker

méiren 媒人 N matchmaker

méitǐ 媒体 N medium, media
大众媒体 **dàzhòng méitǐ** mass media

méi 眉 N eyebrow

méimao 眉毛 N eyebrow

méi 霉 N mildew, mold

méijūn 霉菌 N mold (fungi)

měi 每 1 ADV every, each II PRON every, each

NOTE: Usage in Chinese requires that when 每 **měi** is used as a pronoun to mean *every* or *each*, it should be followed by 都 **dōu** *all, without exception*.

měi 美 ADJ beautiful

měiguān 美观 [modif: 美 beautiful + 观 looking] ADJ pleasing to the eye

Měiguó 美国 N USA, America

měihǎo 美好 [comp: 美 beautiful + 好 fine] ADJ (of abstract things) beautiful, bright

měilì 美丽 [comp: 美 beautiful + 丽 beautiful] ADJ beautiful

měishù 美术 [modif: 美 beautiful + 术 craft] N fine arts

měishùguǎn 美术馆 N gallery, art museum

měishùjiā 美术家 N fine arts specialist, artist

Měiyuán 美元 [modif: 美 American + 元 dollar] N US dollar, greenback

Měizhōu 美洲 [modif: 美 America + 洲 continent] N (the continent of) Americas
北美洲 **Běi-Měizhōu** North America / 南美洲 **Nán-Měizhōu** South America / 中美洲 **Zhōng-Měizhōu** Central America

mèi 妹 N younger sister

mèimei 妹妹 N younger sister

mèi 魅 N evil spirit

mèilì 魅力 N charm, enchantment

mēn 闷 TRAD 悶 ADJ stuffy, uncomfortable

mēnrè 闷热 ADJ hot and stifling, muggy, sultry

mén 门[1] TRAD 門 N door, gate (道 **dào**) 门口 **ménkǒu** doorway, by the door, by the gate /大门 **dàmén** gate

mén 门[2] TRAD 門 MEASURE WORD (for school subjects, languages, etc.)

ménzhěn 门诊 N outpatient service (in a hospital)

men 们 TRAD 們 SUFFIX (indicating plural number)

NOTE: As a plural number marker, 们 **men** is only used with nouns denoting people. It is not used when there are words indicating plurality, such as numerals or words like 一些 **yìxiē**, 很多 **hěn duō**. In many cases, the plural number of a personal noun is implicit without the use of 们 **men**. In this example sentence, 们 **men** is not obligatory: 学生都很喜欢这位新老师。**Xuéshēng dōu hěn xǐhuan zhè wèi xīn lǎoshī.** *All the students like this new teacher.* is correct and idiomatic.

mēng 蒙 V 1 cover 2 cheat, deceive

mèng 梦 TRAD 夢 N dream 做梦 **zuòmèng** have a dream

mèngxiǎng 梦想 [comp: 梦 dream + 想 think] V dream of, have a pipe dream

mí 迷 V be lost

mílù 迷路 V lose one's way, get lost

míshī 迷失 V lose (one's way), take a wrong turning

mí 谜 TRAD 謎 N riddle

míyǔ 谜语 N riddle 猜谜语(猜谜) **cāi míyǔ (cāi mí)** guess a riddle

mǐ 米[1] MEASURE WORD meter (colloquial) 一米 **yì mǐ** one meter / 三米半 **sān mǐ bàn** three and a half meters

NOTE: The formal word for *meter* is 公尺 **gōngchǐ**.

mǐ 米[2] N rice, paddy rice (粒 **lì**) 米酒 **mǐjiǔ** rice wine

mǐfàn 米饭 [comp: 米 rice + 饭 meal] N cooked rice (碗 **wǎn**)

NOTE: The staple food for southern Chinese (Chinese living south of the Yangtze River) is 米饭 **mǐfàn**, while northern Chinese mainly eat 面食 **miànshí** (food made of wheat flour), such as 面条儿 **miàntiáor** (noodles) and 馒头 **mántou** (steamed buns).

mì 秘 ADJ secret

mìmì 秘密 [comp: 秘 secret + 密 confidential] N & ADJ secret; secret, confidential 秘密警察 **mìmì jǐngchá** secret police / 秘密文件 **mìmì wénjiàn** classified document

mìshu 秘书 N secretary 私人秘书 **sīrén mìshu** private secretary

mì 密 ADJ 1 close, intimate 2 secret, confidential

mìmǎ 密码 N (computing) password, secret code, cipher code 输入密码 **shūrù mìmǎ** key in the password

mìqiè 密切 [comp: 密 close + 切 intimate] ADJ close, intimate

mì 蜜 N honey

mìfēng 蜜蜂 [modif: 蜜 honey + 蜂 wasp] N bee (只 **zhī**)

mián 棉 N cotton

mián 眠 V sleep

miǎnfèi 免费 [v+obj: 免 do without + 费 fee, payment] ADJ free of charge

miàn 面[1] N face, surface

miànduì 面对 V be faced with 面对一个复杂的问题 **miànduì yí ge fùzá de wèn tí** be faced with a complicated problem

miànjī 面积 N (mathematics) area

miànlín 面临 V be faced with, be up against 面临新的挑战 **miànlín xīn de tiǎozhàn** be up against a new challenge

miànqián 面前 N in the face of, in front of, before

miànzi 面子 n face, honor
爱面子 **ài miànzi** be keen on face-saving / 丢面子 **diū miànzi** lose face / 给… 留面子 **gěi … liú miànzi** save face (for somebody)

miàn 面[2] TRAD 麵 n 1 (面条儿 **miàntiáor**) noodle
方便面 **fāngbiàn miàn** instant noodles
2 wheat flour

miànbāo 面包 [modif: 面 wheat flour + 包 lump] n bread (只 **zhī**, 条 **tiáo**)
一片面包 **yīpiàn miànbāo** a slice of bread

miànbāochē 面包车 [modif: 面包 a loaf of bread + 车 vehicle] n minibus, van (辆 **liàng**)

miànbāo fáng 面包房 n bakery

miànfěn 面粉 n flour

miàntiáor 面条儿 n noodles (碗 **wǎn**)

miàn 面[3] MEASURE WORD (for flat objects)
一面镜子 **yí miàn jìngzi** a mirror / 两面旗子 **liǎng miàn qízi** two flags

miáo 苗 n seedling

miáotiáo 苗条 ADJ slender, slim

miáo 描 v trace, copy

miáoxiě 描写 v describe (in writing)

miǎo 秒 MEASURE WORD (of time) second

miào 妙 ADJ wonderful, excellent, ingenious
不妙 **búmiào** not good, unpromising

miào 庙 TRAD 廟 n temple (座 **zuò**)

miè 灭 TRAD 滅 v extinguish, put out, go out
灭火器 **mièhuǒqì** fire extinguisher

mín 民 n people

mínyòng 民用 ADJ for civil use, civil

mínzú 民族 [comp: 民 people + 族 clan] n ethnic group, nationality (个 **gè**)
少数民族 **shǎoshù mínzú** minority ethnic group

mǐn 敏 ADJ clever, quick-witted

mǐn'gǎn 敏感 ADJ sensitive

míng 名 I n name, (personal) given name II MEASURE WORD (used for people,

especially those with a specific position or occupation)
一名军人 **yì míng jūnrén** a soldier / 两名学生 **liǎng míng xuésheng** two students

míngpái 名牌 n famous brand, name brand

míngpiàn 名片 n name card, visiting card (张 **zhāng**)

míngshèng 名胜 n famous scenic spot

míngshèng gǔjī 名胜古迹 IDIOM famous scenic spots and cultural relics

míngzi 名字 [comp: 名 given name + 字 courtesy name] n name, given name

NOTE: To be exact, 名字 **míngzi** only means *given name*, but informally 名字 **míngzi** may also mean *full name (family name + given name)*. The formal word for *full name* is 姓名 **xìngmíng**. See 姓 **xìng**.

míng 明 ADJ bright

míngbai 明白 [comp: 明 bright + 白 white] I ADJ clear, plain, obvious II v understand, comprehend, see

míngliàng 明亮 [comp: 明 bright + 亮 bright] ADJ bright, well-lit

míngnián 明年 [modif: 明 (in this context) next + 年 year] n next year

NOTE: 明年 **míngnián** is *next year* only in relation to *this year* 今年 **jīnnián**. For the year after another year, we use 第二年 **dì-èr nián** or 下一年 **xià yì nián**. For example: ■ 他们在2012年结婚，第二年生了一个儿子。**Tāmen zài èr-líng-yī-èr nián jiéhūn, dì-èr nián shēngle yí ge érzi.** *They married in 2012 and had a son the following year.* It would be wrong to use 明年 **míngnián** in this example.

míngquè 明确 [comp: 明 clear + 确 definite, specific] ADJ & v definite and explicit; make definite and explicit

míngtiān 明天 [modif: 明 (in this context) next + 天 day] n tomorrow

míngxiǎn 明显 [comp: 明 clear + 显 showing] ADJ obvious, apparent, evident

míngxīng 明星 n movie star, star

体育明星 **tǐyù míngxīng** sports star
mìng 命 N life
mìnglìng 命令 V & N order, command
mìngyùn 命运 [comp: 命 destiny + 运 luck] N fate, destiny
miù 谬 ADJ wrong, false
miùwù 谬误 N error, mistake
mó 模 N mold
mófǎng 模仿 [comp: 模 mould + 仿 simulate] V imitate, ape, be a copycat
móhú 模糊 ADJ fuzzy, blurred
mótè 模特 N a person posing for artists, photographers, fashion designers, etc., model
人体模特 **réntǐ mótè** artistic model / 时装模特 **shízhuāng mótè** fashion model
mó 摩 V rub, scrape
mótuōchē 摩托车 N motorcycle (辆 **liàng**)
mó 磨 V 1 grind
磨刀 **módāo** sharpen a knife
2 waste (time)
磨时间 **móshíjiān** stall, kill time
mǒ 抹 V apply by smearing
mǒshā 抹杀 V totally ignore (a fact), deny
mò 漠 N desert (See **shāmò** 沙漠.)
mò 墨 N ink
mòshuǐ 墨水 [modif: 墨 ink + 水 water] N ink
mò 末 N end (See **zhōumò** 周末.)
mò 默 ADJ silent
mò 陌 N path
mòshēng 陌生 ADJ unfamiliar
mòshēng rén 陌生人 N stranger
móu 谋 TRAD 謀 V plot, plan
móuhài 谋害 V plot for murder
mǒu 某 PRON certain (used to denote an indefinite person or thing, usually in writing)
mú 模 N mold, matrix
múyàng 模样 I N appearance, look II ADV approximately, about
mǔ 母 ADJ 1 maternal, of a mother
2 female (of certain animals) (ANTONYM 公 **gōng**)

mǔqin 母亲 [modif: 母 mother + 亲 parent] N mother
母亲节 **mǔqin jié** Mother's Day
mǔxìng 母性 N maternal instinct, maternity
mǔ 亩 TRAD 畝 MEASURE WORD (a traditional Chinese unit of area, especially in farming; 1 *mu* is equivalent to about 667 square meters)
十亩地 (田) **shí mǔ dì (tián)** 10 *mu* of ground (paddy fields/farmland)
mù 木 N 1 Same as 木头 **mùtou** 2 tree
■ 独木不成林。**Dú mù bù chéng lín.** *A single tree does not make a forest. (→ One swallow doesn't make a summer.)*
mùtou 木头 [suffix: 木 wood + 头 nominal suffix] N wood, timber
mù 沐 V wash one's hair
mù 目 N the eye
mùbiāo 目标 N target, objective, goal
mùdì 目的 N aim, purpose
mùlù 目录 N 1 catalog
产品目录 **chǎnpǐn mùlù** product catalog / 图书目录 **túshū mùlù** library catalog
2 table of contents
mùqián 目前 N at present, at the moment
mù 慕 V admire (See **xiànmù** 羡慕.)
mù 牧 V herd, tend (sheep, cattle, etc.)
mùmín 牧民 N herdsman
mùqū 牧区 N pastureland, pastoral area

N

ná 拿 V hold, carry in hand
拿主意 **ná zhǔyi** make a decision / 拿走 **ná zǒu** take away, remove
nǎ 哪 PRON 1 which ■ 哪辆自行车是你的? **Nǎ liàng zìxíngchē shì nǐ de?** *Which bicycle is yours?* 2 whatever, whichever ■ 下星期我都在家，你哪天来都可以。**Xià xīngqī wǒ dōu zài jiā, nǐ nǎ tiān**

lái dōu kěyǐ. *I'll be home all next week. You may come any day.*

nǎli 哪里 [modif: 哪 which + 里 place] PRON where ▪ 你住在哪里？ **Nǐ zhù zài nǎli?** *Where do you live?*

> NOTE: 哪里哪里 **nǎli nǎli** is an idiomatic expression used as a modest reply to a compliment, e.g. ▪ "你汉字写得真漂亮。" "哪里哪里。" **"Nǐ Hànzì xiě de zhēn piàoliang." "Nǎli, nǎli."** *"You write beautiful Chinese characters." "Thank you."*

nǎpà 哪怕 CONJ even if, even though

> NOTE: 哪怕 **nǎpà** introduces an exaggerated, rather unlikely situation to emphasize the statement of the sentence.

nǎr 哪儿 PRON Same as 哪里 **nǎli**. Used colloquially.

nǎxiē 哪些 PRON the plural form of 哪 **nǎ**, "which ones?"

nà 那 PRON 1 that ▪ 这辆自行车是我的，那辆自行车是我弟弟的。 **Zhè liàng zìxíngchē shì wǒ de, nà liàng zìxíngchē shì wǒ dìdi de.** *This bike is mine. That one is my younger brother's.* 2 Same as 那么 **nàme** II CONJ

nàge 那个 [modif: 那 that + 个 one] PRON that one

nàli 那里 [modif: 那 that + 里 place] PRON there, over there, in that place

> NOTES: (1) 那里 **nàli** is used after a personal noun or pronoun to make it a place word; as a personal noun or pronoun it cannot be used immediately after a preposition. For example, ▪ 我从张小姐听到这个消息。 **Wǒ cóng Zhāng xiǎojiě tīngdào zhège xiāoxi.** is incorrect. 那里 **nàli** must be added after 张小姐 **Zhāng xiǎojiě** (Miss Zhang): ▪ 我从张小姐那里听到这个消息。 **Wǒ cóng Zhāng xiǎojiě nàli tīngdào zhège xiāoxi.** *I learnt the news from Miss Zhang.* In this case 张小姐那里 **Zhāng xiǎojiě nàli** becomes a place word which can occur after the preposition 从 **cóng**.
> (2) Colloquially, 那儿 **nàr** may replace 那里 **nàli**.

nàme 那么 I PRON like that, so ▪ 上海没有北京那么冷。 **Shànghǎi méiyǒu Běijīng nàme lěng.** *Shanghai is not as cold as Beijing.* II CONJ in that case, then

> NOTE: Although 那么 **nàme** as a conjunction is glossed as *in that case, then*, Chinese speakers tend to use it much more than English speakers use "in that case" or "then." In colloquial Chinese 那么 **nàme** is often shortened to 那 **nà**, e.g. ▪ 你不喜欢吃米饭，那吃面包吧。 **Nǐ bù xǐhuan chī mǐfàn, nà chī miànbāo ba.** *You don't like rice; in that case eat bread.*

nàr 那儿 PRON Same as 那里 **nàli**. Used colloquially.

nàxiē 那些 PRON those

nàyàng 那样 PRON Same as 那么 **nàme** I PRON

nà 纳 V pay, offer

nàshuì 纳税 V pay taxes
纳税人 **nàshuìrén** tax-payer

nǎi 奶 N milk

nǎinai 奶奶 N paternal grandmother, granny

> NOTE: The formal word for *paternal grandmother* is 祖母 **zǔmǔ** and that for *maternal grandmother* is 外祖母 **wàizǔmǔ**. While 奶奶 **nǎinai** is the colloquialism for 祖母 **zǔmǔ**, that for 外祖母 **wàizǔmǔ** is 姥姥 **lǎolao**, or 外婆 **wàipó**.

nài 耐 V able to endure

nàifán 耐烦 [v+obj: 耐 tolerate + 烦 irritation] ADJ patient

> NOTE: 耐烦 **nàifán** is only used in its negative form, 不耐烦 **bú nàifán**.

nàixīn 耐心 [modif: 耐 tolerate + 心 heart] ADJ & N patient; patience

nán 男 ADJ (of humans) male (ANTONYM 女 **nǚ**)

nán háizi 男孩子 N boy

nán qīngnián 男青年 N young man

nánrén 男人 N man, men

nánshēng 男生 N male student/pupil

nánzihàn 男子汉 N a true man, true men

nán 南 N south, southern

nánbian 南边 [modif: 南 south + 边 side] N south side, to the south, in the south

nánfāng 南方 N the southern part, the south of a country

nánfāngrén 南方人 N southerner

nánmiàn 南面 N Same as 南边 nánbian

nán 难 TRAD 難 ADJ difficult (ANTONYM 容易 róngyì)

nándào 难道 ADV (used at the beginning of a sentence or before a verb to make it a rhetorical question) ■ 难道你不知道吗? *Nándào nǐ bù zhīdào ma? Didn't you know?*

nánguài 难怪 ADV no wonder

nánguò 难过 ADJ sad, grieved (ANTONYM 高兴 gāoxìng)

> NOTE: 难过 **nánguò** is usually used as a predicate, and seldom as an attribute.

nánkàn 难看 ADJ ugly, not good to look at (ANTONYM 好看 hǎokàn)

nánmiǎn 难免 ADJ hardly avoidable, almost inevitable

nánshòu 难受 ADJ 1 feel ill, uncomfortable 2 feel sorry, feel bad, sad

nántīng 难听 ADJ unpleasant (to the ears), offensive, coarse

náo 挠 TRAD 撓 V 1 gently scratch with one's fingers 挠痒痒 náo yǎngyang scratch an itch 2 obstruct, make trouble

nǎo 脑 TRAD 腦 N brain

nǎodai 脑袋 [modif: 脑 brain + 袋 bag] N Same as 头 tóu. Used only colloquially and in a derogative sense.

nǎozi 脑子 [suffix: 脑 brain + 子 nominal suffix] N brain, mind 动脑子 dòng nǎozi use brains

nào 闹 TRAD 鬧 V make trouble, create a disturbance 闹笑话 nào xiàohua make a fool of oneself, cut a ridiculous figure / 闹脾气 **nào píqi** throw a tantrum

ne 呢 PARTICLE 1 (used at the end of a question to soften the tone of enquiry) ■ 你打算明年做什么呢? *Nǐ dǎsuàn míngnián zuò shénme ne? What do you intend to do next year?* 2 How about…? Where is (are)…? ■ 你们明天出去旅游, 孩子呢? *Nǐmen míngtiān chūqu lǚyóu, háizi ne? You're going on holiday tomorrow. How about the kids?*

nèi 那 Same as 那 nà. Used colloquially.

nèi 内 N inside, within (ANTONYM 外 wài)

nèibù 内部 N interior, inside 内部资料 nèibù zīliào document for internal circulation (e.g. within a government department)

nèicún 内存 N RAM, memory

nèikē 内科 [modif: 内 inside + 科 department] N department of internal medicine (in a hospital)

nèiróng 内容 [modif: 内 inside + 容 contain] N content, substance

nèn 嫩 ADJ young and tender, tender

néng 能 MODAL V can, be able to

> NOTE: See note on 会 huì MODAL V.

nénggàn 能干 ADJ (of people) able, capable, efficient

nénggòu 能够 MODAL V Same as 能 néng

nénglì 能力 [comp: 能 ability + 力 strength] N ability, capacity

néngyuán 能源 [modif: 能 energy + 源 source, resource] N energy sources

ng 嗯 INTERJ (used after a question to reinforce questioning) ■ 你把自行车借给谁了, 嗯? *Nǐ bǎ zìxíngchē jiègei shuí le, ng? Who did you lend your bicycle to, eh?*

ní 泥 N mud

nǐ 你 PRON you (singular)

nǐmen 你们 [suffix: 你 you (singular) + 们 suffix denoting a plural number] PRON you (plural)

nì 腻 ADJ 1 greasy 2 fed up with

nián 年 N year (no measure word required)
今年 **jīnnián** this year / 明年 **míngnián** next year /去年 **qùnián** last year

NOTE: No measure word is used with 年 **nián**, e.g. 一年 **yì nián** (one year), 两年 **liǎng nián** (two years), 三年 **sān nián** (three years).

niándài 年代 [comp: 年 year + 代 age] N a decade of a century

niánjí 年级 [comp: 年 year + 级 grade] N grade (in school)

niánjì 年纪 [comp: 年 year + 纪 number] N age

NOTE: 您多大年纪了? **Nín duōdà niánjì le?** is an appropriate way to ask the age of an elderly person. To ask a young child his/her age, the question should be 你几岁了? **Nǐ jǐ suì le?** For people who are neither children nor elderly, the question to use is 你多大岁数? **Nǐ duō dà suìshu?**

niánlíng 年龄 [comp: 年 year + 龄 age] N age (of a person or other living things)

niánqīng 年轻 [modif: 年 age + 轻 light] ADJ young

niánqīngrén 年轻人 N young person, young people

niàn 念 V 1 read, read aloud 2 study (in a school)

NOTE: See note on 读 **dú**.

niáng 娘 N 1 girl (See gūniang 姑娘.) 2 mother

niàng 酿 V make (wine), brew (beer)
酿酒 **niàngjiǔ** make wine

niǎo 鸟 TRAD 鳥 N bird (只 **zhī**)

nín 您 PRON you (honorific)

NOTE: 您 **nín** is the honorific form of 你 **nǐ**. Use 您 **nín** when respect or deference is called for. Normally, 您 **nín** does not have a plural form. 您们 **nínmen** is absolutely unacceptable in spoken Chinese, and only marginally so in written Chinese. To address more than one person politely, you can say: 您两位 **nín liǎng wèi** (two people), 您三位 **nín sān wèi** (three people), or 您几位 **nín jǐ wèi** (several people).

níng 凝 V freeze, coagulate

níngjié 凝结 [comp: 凝 freeze + 结 coagulate] V (of gas or hot air) becomes liquid, condense

níng 宁 TRAD 寧 ADJ peaceful, tranquil

níngjìng 宁静 ADJ tranquil, quiet

níng 拧 TRAD 擰 V wring, twist
拧毛巾 **níng máojīn** wring a towel

nìng 宁 TRAD 寧 MODAL V would rather
宁死不屈 **nìng sǐ bù qū** would rather die than succumb

nìngkě 宁可 MODAL V would rather ..., would prefer

niú 牛 N cattle, ox, cow, calf, buffalo (头 **tóu**)
公牛 **gōng niú** bull / 黄牛 **huángniú** ox / 奶牛 **nǎiniú** cow / 水牛 **shuǐniú** water buffalo / 小牛 **xiǎo niú** calf

NOTE: In the Chinese context, the ox (黄牛 **huángniú**) and the water buffalo (水牛 **shuǐniú**) are more important than the milk cow (奶牛 **nǎiniú**).

niúnǎi 牛奶 N cow's milk, milk

niúròu 牛肉 N beef
烤牛肉 **kǎo niúròu** roast beef

niúzǎi kù 牛仔裤 N jeans

nóng 农 TRAD 農 N farming

nóngchǎng 农场 [modif: 农 farming + 场 field, ground] N farm

nóngchǎngzhǔ 农场主 N one who owns a farm, farmer

nóngcūn 农村 [modif: 农 farming + 村 village] N farming area, rural area, countryside (ANTONYM 城市 **chéngshì**)

nóngmín 农民 [modif: 农 farming + 民 people] N peasant, farmer

nóngyè 农业 [modif: 农 farming + 业 industry] N agriculture, farming

nóng 浓 TRAD 濃 ADJ (of gas or liquid)

thick, dense (ANTONYM 淡 dàn)
浓雾 **nóng wù** dense fog / 浓咖啡 **nóng kāfēi** strong coffee
nónghòu 浓厚 [comp: 浓 thick + 厚 thick] ADJ 1 (of smoke, cloud, etc.) thick 2 (of atmosphere, interest, etc.) strong, heavy
nòng 弄 v do, manage, get … done
nǔ 努 v work hard
nǔlì 努力 [comp: 努 physical effort + 力 strength] ADJ making great efforts
nǔ 女 ADJ (of humans) female (ANTONYM 男 nán)
nǚ'ér 女儿 N daughter
nǚ qīngnián 女青年 N young woman
nǚrén 女人 [modif: 女 female human + 人 person] N woman, adult woman (ANTONYM 男人 nánrén)
nǚshēng 女生 N female student/pupil
nǚshì 女士 [modif: 女 female human + 士 gentleman, gentlewoman] N (respectful form of address or reference to a woman) Madam, Ms, lady, a woman
nuǎn 暖 ADJ warm
nuǎnhuo 暖和 [comp: 暖 warm + 和 (in this context) mild] ADJ pleasantly warm, mild

O

ō 噢 INTERJ (used to indicate understanding or a promise) ▪ 噢，我明白了。**Ō, wǒ míngbai le.** *Oh, I see.*
Ōu 欧 TRAD 歐 N Europe
Ōuméng 欧盟 N shortening for 欧洲联盟 Ōuzhōu Liánméng, the European Union
Ōuyuán 欧元 [modif: 欧 Europe + 元 dollar] N Euro
Ōuzhōu 欧洲 [modif: 欧 Europe + 洲 continent] N Europe
ǒu 呕 TRAD 嘔 v vomit
ǒu 偶[1] ADV 1 occasionally 2 accidentally

ǒu'ěr 偶尔 ADV occasionally, once in a long while
ǒurán 偶然 ADV accidentally, by chance
ǒu 偶[2] N even number
ǒushù 偶数 N even number (ANTONYM 奇数 jīshù)
ǒu 偶[3] N human figure

P

pá 爬 v crawl, climb
páshān 爬山 V & N climb a hill or mountain; mountaineering
páxíng 爬行 v creep, crawl
páxíng dòngwù 爬行动物 N reptile
pà 怕 v fear, be afraid
pāi 拍 v pat, clap
pāimài 拍卖 v auction, sell at a reduced price
pāishǒu 拍手 v clap, applaud
pāizhào 拍照 v take photos
pái 排 I v 1 arrange in a definite order 2 remove II N row, rank III MEASURE WORD (for things arranged in a row)
　一排椅子 **yì pái yǐzi** a row of chairs
páiduì 排队 v form a line, line up, queue up
páijǐ 排挤 [comp: 排 expel + 挤 squeeze] v elbow out, push aside, squeeze out
páiliè 排列 v arrange, put in order
　按字母顺序排列 **àn zìmǔ shùnxù páiliè** arrange in alphabetical order
páiqiú 排球 [modif: 排 row + 球 ball] N volleyball (只 zhī)
pái 牌[1] N playing cards (张 zhāng, 副 fù)
打牌 **dǎpái** play cards / 发牌 **fāpái** deal cards / 洗牌 **xǐpái** shuffle cards

NOTE: 扑克牌 **pūkèpái** is a more common word for *playing cards* (noun).

pái 牌[2] N brand name, brand
名牌 **míngpái** famous brand, name brand

páizi 牌子 [suffix: 牌 signboard + 子 nominal suffix] **N 1** signboard (块 **kuài**) **2** Same as 牌² **pái**

pài 派¹ **v 1** dispatch **2** assign (a job)

pài 派² **N** faction, school (of thought) 反对派 **fǎnduì pài** the opposing force, opponent

pàichūsuǒ 派出所 **N** police station

pàiduì 派对 **N** (social) party

pān 攀 **v** climb

pāndēng 攀登 [comp: 攀 climb + 登 ascend] **v** climb, scale

pán 盘 TRAD 盤 **N** dish, plate

pánzi 盘子 [suffix: 盘 plate, dish + 子 nominal suffix] **N** plate, dish, tray (只 **zhī**)

pàn 判 **v** judge

pànduàn 判断 [comp: 判 judge + 断 reach a verdict] **v & N** judge, decide; judgment, verdict

pàn 叛 **v** betray, be disloyal to

pànbiàn 叛变 **v** turn traitor, become a turncoat

pànguó 叛国 **v** commit treason

pàn 盼 **v** expect

pànwàng 盼望 [comp: 盼 expect + 望 look forward to] **v** look forward to, long for

páng 庞 TRAD 龐 **ADJ** big

pángdà 庞大 [comp: 庞 big + 大 big] **ADJ** huge, enormous

páng 旁 **N** side 路旁 **lùpáng** by the roadside

pángbiān 旁边 [modif: 旁 aside + 边 side] **N** side, by the side

pángguān 旁观 **v** look on

pángguānzhě qīng 旁观者清 IDIOM The onlooker sees most of the game.

pàng 胖 **ADJ** fat, plump

páo 袍 **N** gown 长袍 **cháng páo** gown, robe (件 **jiàn**)

pǎo 跑 **v** run, run away

pǎobù 跑步 [modif: 跑 run + 步 steps] **v** jog, run (as a physical exercise)

pǎodào 跑道 **N** runway, track (in a sports ground)

pào 炮 **N** cannon, gun (门 **mén**, 座 **zuò**)

pàobīng 炮兵 **N** artillery man

péi 陪 **v** accompany

péi 培 **v** cultivate

péixùn 培训 [comp: 培 cultivate + 训 train] **N** training 培训班 **péixùnbān** training class, training course / 培训生 **péixùnshēng** trainee

péiyǎng 培养 [comp: 培 cultivate + 养 provide for] **v 1** train, develop **2** cultivate, breed

péiyù 培育 [comp: 培 cultivate + 育 nurture] **v** bring up, nurture 培育下一代 **péiyù xià yídài** bring up the next generation, bring up one's children

péi 赔 TRAD 賠 **v** compensate, pay for (damage, loss, etc.)

péicháng 赔偿 [comp: 赔 compensate + 偿 give back] **v & N** compensate for; compensation

pèi 佩 **v** wear

pèifu 佩服 **v** admire

NOTE: You can utter 佩服 **Pèifu** or 佩服! 佩服! **Pèifu! Pèifu!** to express great admiration for a feat or a remarkable achievement, for example: ■ "你五门功课都是一百分？佩服！佩服！" "**Nǐ wǔ mén gōngkè dōu shì yībǎi fēn? Pèifu! Pèifu!**" *"You got full marks for all the five subjects? Wow!"*

pèi 配 **v 1** match, blend **2** be worthy of, deserve 配得上 **pèi de shàng** be worth of, be good enough to be / 配不上 **pèi bu shàng** be not good enough to be, be unworthy of

pèihé 配合 [comp: 配 match + 合 cooperate] **v** cooperate, coordinate ■ 各个部门都要相互配合。**Gè ge bùmén dōu yào xiānghù pèihé.** *All the departments should cooperate with each other.*

pēn 喷 TRAD 噴 **v** sprinkle, spray

pén 盆 **N** basin, pot (个 **gè**)

花盆 **huāpén** flower pot / 洗脸盆 **xǐliǎnpén** washbasin

péng 朋 N companion

péngyou 朋友 [comp: 朋 companion + 友 friend] N friend

男朋友 **nánpéngyou** boyfriend / 女朋友 **nǚpéngyou** girlfriend

péng 膨 V swell

péngzhàng 膨胀 V extend, swell, expand

pèng 碰 V bump into, touch

pèngdao 碰到 V meet unexpectedly, run into

pī 批 MEASURE WORD (for a batch of goods, and for things/people arriving at the same time)

一批新书 **yì pī xīn shū** a batch of new books (published at about the same time) / 两批旅游者 **liǎng pī lǚyóuzhě** two groups of tourists

pīpíng 批评 [comp: 批 criticism + 评 comment] V & N criticize, scold; criticism (ANTONYM 表扬 **biǎoyáng**)

pīzhǔn 批准 [comp: 批 express opinion + 准 approve, permit] V approve, ratify

pī 披 V drape over the shoulder ▪ 他披着大衣，看孩子在雪地里玩。 *Tā pīzhe dàyī, kàn háizi zài xuědì li wán. With an overcoat draped over his shoulders, he watched the children play in the snow.*

pí 皮 N skin, leather

皮衣 **píyī** fur coat

pífū 皮肤 [comp: 皮 skin + 肤 skin] N skin (human)

píxié 皮鞋 N leather shoes (双 **shuāng**)

pí 疲 ADJ fatigued

pífá 乏疲 ADJ tired, weary, exhausted

píláo 疲劳 ADJ fatigued, tired

pí 啤 N beer

píjiǔ 啤酒 N beer (瓶 **píng**, 杯 **bēi**)

pí 脾 N spleen

píqi 脾气 N temper, temperament, disposition

发脾气 **fā píqi** throw a tantrum, lose one's temper

pǐ 匹 MEASURE WORD (for horses)

一匹快马 **yì pǐ kuài mǎ** a fast horse

pì 辟 TRAD 闢 V open up

pì 僻 ADJ remote

pì 屁 N flatulence, fart

放屁 **fàng pì** fart, break wind

piān 偏 ADV must (used to indicate that the action in question is contrary to one's expectation or wishes)

piānchā 偏差 N deviation, error

piān 篇 MEASURE WORD (for a piece of writing)

一篇文章 **yì piān wénzhāng** an article/essay

pián 便 ADJ comfortable

piányi 便宜 ADJ inexpensive, cheap (ANTONYM 贵 **guì**)

piányihuò 便宜货 N cheap goods, bargain

piàn 片 I N thin and flat piece

肉片 **ròupiàn** meat slices

II MEASURE WORD (for thin, flat pieces)

一片面包 **yí piàn miànbāo** a slice of bread

piànmiàn 片面 ADJ one-sided, unilateral (ANTONYM 全面 **quánmiàn**)

piàn 骗 TRAD 騙 V deceive, fool

piànjú 骗局 N hoax, fraud

piànzi 骗子 N swindler, con man

piào 票 N ticket (张 **zhāng**)

电影票 **diànyǐng piào** movie ticket / 飞机票 **fēijī piào** air ticket / 火车票 **huǒchē piào** train ticket / 门票 **ménpiào** admission ticket (to a show, sporting event, etc.) / 汽车票 **qìchē piào** bus/coach ticket

piào 漂 ADJ pretty

piàoliang 漂亮 ADJ handsome, pretty, good-looking

piē 撇 V 1 discard, abandon 2 skim off from the surface of a liquid

pīn 拼 V put together

pīnyīn 拼音 [v+obj: 拼 put together + 音 sound] I V spell, phonetize II N

Romanized Chinese writing, pinyin
拼音文字 **pīnyīn wénzì** phonetic writing
/ 汉语拼音方案 **Hànyǔ Pīnyīn Fāng'àn**
Phonetic System of the Chinese Language
pín 贫 TRAD 貧 **ADJ** poor, lacking
pínfá 贫乏 [comp: 贫 poor + 乏 lacking]
ADJ poor in, short of
资源贫乏 **zīyuán pínfá** poor in natural
resources
pǐn 品 N article
pǐnxíng 品行 [comp: 品 quality + 行
behavior] **N** moral quality and conduct,
behavior
品行不良 **pǐnxíng bùliáng** of poor moral
quality and behave badly
pìn 聘 v appoint to a position, engage
pìnqǐng 聘请 v invite and appoint to a
(professional or managerial) position
pīngpāngqiú 乒乓球 N table tennis,
table tennis ball (只 **zhī**)
píng 平 ADJ flat, level, smooth
píng'ān 平安 [comp: 平 peace + 安
peace] **ADJ** safe and sound
píngbǎn diànnǎo 平板电脑 N tablet
(computer)
píngcháng 平常 [comp: 平 flat + 常
usual] **I ADJ** ordinary, common
II N & ADV ordinary time; usually, normally
píngděng 平等 [modif: 平 flat + 等
grade] **ADJ & N** equal; equality
píngfāng 平方 N square (mathematics)
■ 三平方公尺 **sān píngfāng gōngchǐ** 3
square meters
píngjìng 平静 [comp: 平 peace + 静
quiet] **ADJ** calm, quiet, uneventful
píngjūn 平均 ADJ average
píng 评 TRAD 評 **v** comment
píngjià 评价 [v+obj: 评 appraise + 价
value] **v & N** appraise, evaluate; appraisal,
evaluation
高度评价 **gāodù píngjià** place a high
value on
píng 苹 TRAD 蘋 **N** apple
píngguǒ 苹果 [modif: 苹 apple + 果

fruit] **N** apple (个 **gè**)
píng 瓶 I N bottle **II MEASURE WORD** a bottle of
一瓶啤酒 **yì píng píjiǔ** a bottle of beer /
两瓶可口可乐 **liǎng píng kěkǒukělè** two
bottles of Coca-Cola
píngzi 瓶子 N bottle (个 **gè**)
píng 凭 I N evidence, proof
真凭实据 **zhēnpíng shíjù** hard evidence
II v go by, base on
凭票入场 **píngpiàorùchǎng** admission
by tickets
pō 泊 N lake
pópo 婆婆 N husband's mother
pò 迫 v compel
pòqiè 迫切 ADJ urgent, pressing
pò 破 v & ADJ break, damage, worn-out,
torn, damaged
pòchǎn 破产 v & N go bankrupt;
bankruptcy
pòhuài 破坏 [v+obj: 破 break + 坏 bad]
v vandalize, damage
pōu 剖 v cut open
pútao 葡萄 N grape (颗 **kē**)
pútaojiǔ 葡萄酒 N grape wine, wine
pútaoyuán 葡萄园 N vineyard
pǔ 普 ADJ common
pǔbiàn 普遍 [comp: 普 common
+ 遍 everywhere] **ADJ** widespread,
commonplace
pǔtōng 普通 ADJ common,
commonplace, ordinary
Pǔtōnghuà 普通话 [modif: 普通
common + 话 speech] **N** Standard
Modern Chinese, Mandarin, Putonghua

NOTE: Modern Standard Chinese is known
as 普通话 **Pǔtōnghuà** in China, 国语 **Guóyǔ**
in Taiwan and 华语 **Huáyǔ** in Singapore
and other Southeast Asian countries. They
refer to the same language, though slight
differences do exist among them.

Q

qī 七 NUMERAL seven

七百七十七 **qībǎi qīshíqī** seven hundred and seventy-seven (777)

qī 妻 N wife

qīzi 妻子 [suffix: 妻 wife + 子 nominal suffix] N wife

qī 期 I N fixed time

按期 **àn qī** according to the schedule, on time / 到期 **dàoqī** expire, due / 过期 **guòqī** overdue, expired

II v expect, anticipate

qīdài 期待 v expect, look forward to

qījiān 期间 N during the period of

qī 欺 v cheat, bully

qīpiàn 欺骗 [comp: 欺 cheat + 骗 deceive] v deceive, dupe, cheat

qī 戚 N relative (See **qīnqi** 亲戚.)

qí 其 PRON this, that

qícì 其次 ADV next, second, secondly

qíshí 其实 ADV actually, as a matter of fact, in fact

qítā 其他 PRON other

qíyú 其余 PRON the rest, the remainder

qízhōng 其中 N among them, in it

qí 旗 N flag, banner (面 **miàn**)

旗杆 **qígān** flagstaff, flag pole / 国旗 **guóqí** national flag / 升旗 **shēngqí** hoist a flag

qízi 旗子 [suffix: 旗 flag, banner + 子 nominal suffix] N flag, banner (面 **miàn**)

qí 奇 ADJ strange

qíguài 奇怪 [comp: 奇 strange + 怪 unusual] ADJ strange, unusual, odd

qíjì 奇迹 N miracle, wonder

创造奇迹 **chuàngzào qíjì** perform miracles, work wonders

qímiào 奇妙 ADJ marvelous, intriguing

qí 骑 TRAD 騎 v ride (a horse, bicycle, etc.)

骑自行车 **qí zìxíngchē** ride a bicycle

qí mǎ 骑马 ride a horse

qǐ 企 v hope

qǐyè 企业 N enterprise (家 **jiā**)

国有企业 **guóyǒu qǐyè** state-owned enterprise / 私有企业 **sīyǒu qǐyè** private enterprise

qǐyèjiā 企业家 N entrepreneur

qǐ 启 TRAD 啟 v open

qǐfā 启发 [comp: 启 open + 发 release] V & N enlighten, arouse; enlightenment, inspiration

qǐ 起 v rise, get up

从 … 起 **cóng … qǐ** starting from …

qǐchuáng 起床 v get up (out of bed)

qǐfēi 起飞 v (of a plane) take off

qǐlai 起来 v get up (out of bed), stand up, rise

NOTE: 起来 **qǐlai** is often used after a verb as a complement to express various meanings. Among other meanings, 起来 **qǐlai** may be used after a verb to mean *begin to ...*, e.g. ■ 我们不等爸爸了，吃起来吧。**Wǒmen bù děng bàba le, chī qǐlai ba.** *We're not going to wait for daddy any longer. Let's start eating.*

qǐsù 起诉 v sue, file a lawsuit against

qǐyì 起义 V & N revolt, cause an uprising; uprising

qì 气 TRAD 氣 v be angry, make angry

qìfen 气氛 N atmosphere, ambiance

qìhòu 气候 N climate

qìqiú 气球 N balloon

热气球 **rè qìqiú** hot-air balloon

qìwēn 气温 [modif: 气 atmosphere + 温 temperature] N atmospheric temperature

qìxiàng 气象 N meteorological phenomena, weather

气象预报 **qìxiàng yùbào** weather forecast ■ 你听今天的气象预报了吗？**Nǐ tīng jīntiān de qìxiàng yùbào le ma?** *Have you listened to today's weather forecast?*

qìxiàngtái 气象台 N meteorological observatory

qìxiàngxué 气象学 N meteorology

qì 汽 N vapor, steam

qìchē 汽车 [modif: 汽 vapor + 车 vehicle] N automobile, car (辆 liàng) 开汽车 kāi qìchē drive a car

NOTE: In everyday Chinese, 车 chē is often used instead of 汽车 qìchē to refer to *a car*.

qìshuǐ 汽水 [modif: 汽 vapor + 水 water] N soda water, soft drink, soda, pop (瓶 píng, 杯 bēi)

qìyóu 汽油 N gasoline, gas, petrol

qì 弃 TRAD 棄 V abandon (See fàngqì 放弃.)

qià 恰 ADV just, exactly

qiàqiǎo 恰巧 ADV as luck would have it, fortunately

qiān 千 NUMERAL thousand

qiānwàn 千万 ADV be sure to, must never (used in an imperative sentence for emphasis)

qiān 谦 TRAD 謙 ADJ modest

qiānxū 谦虚 [comp: 谦 modest + 虚 empty] ADJ modest, self-effacing ■ 他对自己的成绩非常谦虚。Tā duì zìjǐ de chéngjì fēicháng qiānxū. *He is very modest about his achievements.*

qiān 签 TRAD 簽 V sign, autograph

qiāndìng 签订 V conclude and sign (a contract, an agreement, etc.)

qiānmíng 签名 [v+obj: 签 sign + 名 name] V & N autograph, sign one's name; autograph, signature 请歌星签名 qǐng gēxīng qiānmíng ask a singer for his/her autograph

qiānshǔ 签署 V sign (a treaty, a contract, etc.)

qiānzhèng 签证 N visa 入境签证 rùjìng qiānzhèng entry visa / 申请签证 shēnqǐng qiānzhèng apply for visa

qiān 铅 TRAD 鉛 N lead

qiānbǐ 铅笔 [modif: 铅 lead + 笔 pen] N pencil (支 zhī)

qiānbǐ dāo 铅笔刀 N pencil sharpener

qiānbǐ hé 铅笔盒 N pencil box

qián 前 N 1 front, in front of (ANTONYM 后 hòu) 2 Same as 以前 yǐqián

NOTE: In everyday Chinese, 前 qián is seldom used alone to mean *front* or *in front of*. Often, it is better to use 前边 qiánbian.

qiánbian 前边 [modif: 前 front + 边 side] N front (ANTONYM 后边 hòubian) ■ 中国人的姓名姓在前边，名在后边。Zhōngguórén de xìngmíng, xìng zài qiánbian, míng zài hòubian. *In a Chinese person's name, the family name comes before the given name.*

qiánjìn 前进 [comp: 前 advance + 进 advance] V advance

qiánmiàn 前面 N Same as 前边 qiánbian

qiánnián 前年 N the year before last

qiántiān 前天 N the day before yesterday

qiántú 前途 [modif: 前 in front + 途 journey] N future, prospects, future prospects

qián 钱 TRAD 錢 N money (笔 bǐ)

qiánbāo 钱包 N wallet, purse

qiǎn 浅 TRAD 淺 ADJ shallow (ANTONYM 深 shēn)

qiàn 欠 V owe, be in debt to

qiàn rénqíng 欠人情 PHR owe a debt of gratitude

qiàn 歉 N apology

qiànyì 歉意 N apology, regret 表达歉意 biǎodá qiànyì offer an apology

qiāng 枪 TRAD 槍 N small arms, gun, pistol (支 zhī, 把 bǎ) 手枪 shǒuqiāng handgun (revolver, pistol)

qiāng 腔 N hollow part of a body, cavity 腹腔 fùqiāng abdominal cavity / 胸腔 xiōngqiāng thoracic cavity

qiáng 强 ADJ strong, powerful (ANTONYM 弱 ruò)

qiángdà 强大 [comp: 强 strong + 大 big] ADJ big and powerful, powerful (ANTONYM 弱小 ruòxiǎo)

qiángdào 强盗 N bandit, robber

qiángdiào 强调 [modif: 强 strong + 调

tone] v emphasize, lay stress on

qiángdù 强度 [modif: 强 strong + 度 degree] N intensity, strength

qiángliè 强烈 [comp: 强 strong + 烈 raging] ADJ strong, intense, violent

qiáng 墙 TRAD 牆 N wall (道 dào)

qiǎng 抢 TRAD 搶 v seize, grab

qiǎngjiù 抢救 v rescue, salvage
抢救病人 qiǎngjiù bìngrén save a patient, give emergency treatment to a patient

qiāo 悄 ADJ quiet

qiāoqiāo 悄悄 ADV quietly, on the quiet

qiāo 敲 v knock, beat, strike

qiáo 桥 TRAD 橋 N bridge (座 zuò)
过桥 guò qiáo cross a bridge

qiáo 侨 TRAD 僑 v live abroad

qiáo 瞧 v Same as 看[1] kàn verb. Used as a colloquialism.

qiǎo 巧 ADJ 1 skillful, clever, ingenious 2 coincidental, ingenious

qiǎokèlì 巧克力 N chocolate (块 kuài)

qiǎomiào 巧妙 [comp: 巧 skilled + 妙 wonderful] ADJ ingenious, very clever

qiào 壳 N shell, crust
地壳 dìqiào the Earth's crust

qiē 切 v cut, slice

qiě 且 CONJ moreover (See érqiě 而且.)

qiè 切 v correspond to, be close to

qiè 窃 TRAD 竊 v steal, pilfer

qiètīng 窃听 v wiretap, bug

qīn 亲 TRAD 親 N blood relation

qīn'ài 亲爱 [comp: 亲 intimate + 爱 love] ADJ dear, beloved, darling

NOTE: Although 亲爱 qīn'ài is glossed as *dear*, the Chinese reserve 亲爱 (的) qīn'ài (de) for the very few people who are really dear and close to their hearts.

qīnqi 亲戚 N relative, relation
走亲戚 zǒu qīnqi visit a relative

qīnqiè 亲切 ADJ cordial

qīnshēn 亲身 ADV Same as 亲自 qīnzì

qīnzì 亲自 ADV by oneself

qín 禽 N fowl, poultry
家禽 jiāqín domestic fowl, poultry

qín 勤 ADJ diligent, hard-working

qínfèng 勤奋 ADJ diligent, applying oneself to

qínkěn 勤恳 ADJ diligent and conscientious

qín 琴 N musical instrument
钢琴 gāngqín piano / 小提琴 xiǎotíqín violin

qīng 青 ADJ green

qīngchūn 青春 [modif: 青 green + 春 spring] N the quality of being young, youth

qīngchūnqī 青春期 N puberty

qīngnián 青年 [modif: 青 green + 年 year] N young person, young people, youth (especially male) (位 wèi, 个 gè)

qīngshàonián 青少年 N adolescents and young people

qīngwā 青蛙 [modif: 青 green + 蛙 frog] N frog (只 zhī)

qīng 清 ADJ 1 clear (water), clean 2 (of matters) clear, easy to understand

qīngchu 清楚 [comp: 清 clear + 楚 clear-cut] ADJ clear (of speech or image), distinct

qīngdàn 清淡 ADJ (of color, smell or taste) light and delicate

qīng 轻 TRAD 輕 ADJ 1 light (of weight) (ANTONYM 重 zhòng) 2 low, soft (of voice) 3 of a low degree

qīng ěr yì jǔ 轻而易举 ADJ extremely easy to do, a piece of cake

qīngsōng 轻松 [comp: 轻 light + 松 loose] ADJ (of a job) easy, not requiring much effort

qīng 氢 N hydrogen (H)

qíng 情 N 1 circumstance, situation 2 emotion, affection

qíngjǐng 情景 [comp: 情 situation + 景 scene] N scene, occasion

qíngkuàng 情况 [comp: 情 circumstance + 况 situation] N situation, circumstance

qíngxù 情绪 [comp: 情 emotion + 绪 mood] **N** mood, feelings

qíng 晴 **ADJ** fine, clear (of weather)

qínglǎng 晴朗 **ADJ** fine (weather), sunny

qǐng 请 **TRAD** 請 **v 1** invite **2** ask, request

NOTE: 请 qǐng is used to start a polite request, equivalent to *Please ...*, e.g.
■ 请您别在这里吸烟。**Qíng nín bié zài zhèli xīyān.** *Please don't smoke here.*
■ 请坐! **Qǐng zuò!** *Sit down, please!*
■ 请喝茶! **Qǐng hē chá.** *Have some tea, please!*

qǐngjià 请假 **v** ask for leave

请病假 **qǐng bìngjià** ask for sick leave

qǐngjiào 请教 [v+obj: 请 ask for + 教 teaching] **v** ask for advice, consult

NOTE: 请教 qǐngjiào is a polite word, used when you want to ask for advice or information, e.g. ■ 我能不能请教您一个问题? **Wǒ néngbunéng qǐng jiào nín yí ge wèntí?** *Could I ask you a question, please?*
■ 请教, 这个汉字是什么意思? **Qǐngjiào, zhège Hànzì shì shénme yìsi?** *Would you please tell me the meaning of this Chinese character?*

qǐngkè 请客 [v+obj: 请 invite + 客 guest] **v 1** invite to dinner, host a dinner party **2** stand treat

qǐngqiú 请求 [comp: 请 request + 求 beseech] **v & N** request, ask for; request

qǐngwèn 请问 **IDIOM** Excuse me, ...

qìng 庆 **TRAD** 慶 **v** celebrate

qìngzhù 庆祝 [comp: 庆 celebrate + 祝 good wishes] **v & N** celebrate; celebration

qióng 穷 **TRAD** 窮 **ADJ** poor, poverty-stricken

qióngrén 穷人 **N** poor person, poor people

qiū 秋 **N** fall, autumn

qiūtiān 秋天 [modif: 秋 autumn + 天 day] **N** fall, autumn

qiú 求 **v** beseech, beg, ask for humbly

qiú 球 **N** ball (只 zhī)

棒球 **bàngqiú** baseball / 比球 **bǐ qiú**

have a (ball game) match / 打球 **dǎ qiú** play basketball, volleyball, etc. / 看球 **kàn qiú** watch a ball game / 篮球 **lánqiú** basketball / 排球 **páiqiú** volleyball / 踢球 **tī qiú** play soccer /足球 **zúqiú** soccer

qiúchǎng 球场 **N** sports ground (especially where ball games are played)

qiúduì 球队 **N** (ball game) team

qiúmí 球迷 **N** (ball game) fan

足球迷 **zúqiú mí** football fan, soccer fan

qū 区 **TRAD** 區 **N** (urban) district

工业区 **gōngyèqū** industrial zone, industrial district / 商业区 **shāngyèqū** commercial area, business district / 住宅区 **zhù zháiqu** residential quarters

qūbié 区别 **v & N** distinguish between, differentiate; difference

qū 驱 **TRAD** 驅 **v** drive

驱车前往 **qūchē qiánwǎng** drive (in a car) to

qǔ 取 **v** fetch, collect

qǔdé 取得 [comp: 取 obtain + 得 get] **v** obtain, achieve

qǔkuǎn 取款 **v** withdraw money

自动取款机 **zìdòng qǔkuǎnjī** ATM

qǔxiāo 取消 **v** cancel

qǔ 娶 **v** (of a man) marry

qǔ 曲 **N** melody, tune

qǔzi 曲子 **N** song, melody

熟悉的曲子 **shúxī de qǔzi** familiar tune

qù 去 **v** leave for, go to (**ANTONYM** 来 **lái**)

NOTE: 到 dào and 到 ··· 去 dào ... qù have the same meaning and are normally interchangeable.

qùnián 去年 [modif: 去 what has gone + 年 year] **N** last year

qùshì 去世 [v+obj: 去 leave + 世 the world] **v** die, pass away ■ 他爸爸去年去世了。**Tā bàba qùnián qùshì le.** *His father passed away last year.*

NOTE: 去世 qùshì must be used when you

want to show respect and/or love to the deceased. For instance, the normal word for *die*, 死 **sǐ**, would be totally inappropriate in the example sentence.

qù 趣 N interest (See **xìngqù** 兴趣, **yǒuqù** 有趣.)

qùwèi 趣味 [comp: 趣 interest + 味 taste] N 1 interest, delight 2 taste 低级趣味 **dījí qùwèi** vulgar taste

quān 圈 N circle, ring

quán 全 ADJ whole, complete 全国 **quánguó** the whole country / 全家 **quánjiā** the whole family / 全世界 **quánshìjiè** the entire world

quánbù 全部 [modif: 全 whole + 部 part] N all, entire, without exception

quánmiàn 全面 [modif: 全 all + 面 side] ADJ all-round, comprehensive

quántǐ 全体 [modif: 全 whole + 体 body] N all, entire, each and every one (of a group of people)

quán 权 TRAD 權 N 1 authority, power 2 right

quánlì 权利 [comp: 权 power + 利 benefit] N right

quánlì 权力 [comp: 权 power + 力 strength] N authority, power

quányì 权益 [comp: 权 power + 益 benefit] N rights and interests

quán 泉 N spring (water) 温泉 **wēnquán** hot spring

quàn 劝 TRAD 勸 V try to talk ... into (or out of) doing something, advise

quē 缺 V lack, be short of 缺人手 **quē rénshǒu** short of hands

quēdiǎn 缺点 [v+obj: 缺 lack + 点 point] N shortcoming, defect

quēfá 缺乏 V be deficient in, lack

quēshǎo 缺少 V be short of, lack

NOTE: 缺乏 **quēfá** and 缺少 **quēshǎo** are synonyms, but 缺乏 **quēfá** has abstract nouns as objects, while 缺少 **quēshǎo** takes as objects nouns denoting concrete persons or things.

què 却 ADV unexpectedly, contrary to what may be normally expected, but, yet ■ 他很有钱，却并不幸福。**Tā hěn yǒuqián, què bìng bù xìngfú.** *He is rich, but he is not happy.*

què 确 TRAD 確 ADJ certain, true, reliable

quèdìng 确定 [comp: 确 true + 定 definite] V confirm, fix, determine

quèrèn 确认 [modif: 确 firmly + 认 acknowledge] V affirm, confirm

quèshí 确实 [comp: 确 true + 实 substantial] ADJ verified to be true, indeed

qún 裙 N skirt

qúnzi 裙子 [suffix: 裙 skirt + 子 nominal suffix] N skirt (条 **tiáo**)

qún 群 MEASURE WORD a crowd of, a group of (for people or animals) 一群狗 **yìqún gǒu** a pack of dogs / 一群鸟 **yìqún niǎo** a flock of birds / 一群牛 **yìqún niú** a herd of cattle / 一群小学生 **yìqún xiǎoxuéshēng** a group of schoolchildren / 一群羊 **yìqún yáng** a flock of sheep

R

rán 然 ADV however

rán'ér 然而 CONJ Same as 但是 **dànshì**. Usually used in writing.

ránhòu 然后 CONJ afterwards, ... and then 先 ... 然后 ... **xiān ... ránhòu ...** first ... and then ...

rán 燃 V burn

ránliào 燃料 [modif: 燃 burn + 料 material, stuff] N fuel

ránshāo 燃烧 [comp: 燃 burn + 烧 burn] V burn

rǎng 壤 N soil (See **tǔrǎng** 土壤.)

ràng 让 TRAD 讓 V 1 let, allow 2 make ■ 他的话让我明白了许多道理。**Tā de huà ràng wǒ míngbaile xǔduō dàolǐ.** *What he said made me understand many things.*

(→ What he said enlightened me.)

rào 绕 TRAD 繞 v make a detour, bypass

rè 热 TRAD 熱 ADJ hot (ANTONYM 冷 lěng)

rè'ài 热爱 [modif: 热 hot + 爱 love] v love ardently, be in deep love with

rèliè 热烈 [comp: 热 hot + 烈 intense] ADJ warm, ardent

rènao 热闹 [comp: 热 hot + 闹 noisy] ADJ noisy and exciting in a pleasant way, boisterous, bustling, lively (of a scene or occasion)

rèqíng 热情 [modif: 热 hot + 情 emotion] ADJ enthusiastic, warm-hearted

rèshuǐpíng 热水瓶 [modfi: 热 hot + 水 water + 瓶 bottle, flask] N thermos, thermos flask (只 zhī)

rèxīn 热心 [modif: 热 hot + 心 heart] ADJ warm-hearted, enthusiastic 对 ··· 热心 duì ... rèxīn be warm-hearted towards, be enthusiastic about

rén 人 N human being, person

réncái 人才 [modif: 人 human + 才 talent] N talented person, person of ability

réngōng 人工 I ADJ artificial, man-made 人工智能 réngōng zhìnéng artificial intelligence
II N manpower, man-day

rénjia 人家 PRON 1 other people 2 he, she, they (used to refer to another person or other people) ▪ 人家不愿意，你别勉强。Rénjia bú yuànyì, nǐ bié miǎnqiáng. *If they aren't willing, don't force them to do it.* 3 I, me (used to refer to oneself, only used among intimate friends or family members)

rénkǒu 人口 [comp: 人 human + 口 mouth] N population (human)

NOTE: It is interesting that the Chinese word for population is made up of 人 rén (human) and 口 kǒu (the mouth). It suggests that feeding people (mouths) has been the primary concern in China.

rénlèi 人类 [modif: 人 human + 类 kind] N humankind, mankind

rénlèi xué 人类学 N anthropology

rénmen 人们 [suffix: 人 person, people + 们 suffix indicating plural number] N people, the public

rénmín 人民 [comp: 人 human beings + 民 the people] N the people (of a country)

Rénmínbì 人民币 [modif: 人民 the people + 币 currency, banknote] N the Chinese currency, Renminbi (RMB)

rénshēng 人生 N (one's entire) life

rénshì 人事 [modif: 人 people + 事 matters] N human resources affairs 人事部门 rénshì bùmén human resources department, personnel department

rénwù 人物 N well-known and important person, figure, personage (位 wèi)

rényuán 人员 [comp: 人 human + 员 staff] N personnel, staff

rénzào 人造 [modif: 人 man + 造 make] ADJ man-made, artificial

rěn 忍 v endure, tolerate, put up with 忍不住 rěn bu zhù be unable to bear, cannot help / 忍得住 rěn de zhù can endure, can bear

rèn 认 TRAD 認 v 1 recognize 2 identify

rènde 认得 v Same as 认识 rènshi

rènshi 认识 [comp: 认 recognize + 识 know] v know, understand

rènwéi 认为 v think, consider (normally followed by a clause)

rènzhēn 认真 [v+compl: 认 consider + 真 real] ADJ earnest, conscientious, serious

rèn 任 CONJ no matter

rènhé 任何 [comp: 任 no matter + 何 what] PRON any, whatever 任何人 rènhé rén anyone, whoever / 任何事 rènhé shì any matter, anything, everything, whatever

rènwù 任务 [comp: 任 mission + 务 work] N assignment, mission

rēng 扔 v throw, toss ▪ 不要乱扔垃圾。 Bú yào luàn rēng lājī. *Do not discard rubbish everywhere. (Don't litter.)*

réng 仍 ADV Same as 仍然 **réngrán**

réngrán 仍然 ADV still, as before

rì 日 N date, day ■ 九月一日 **Jiǔyuè yī rì** *the first of September, September 1*

NOTE: In writing, 日 **rì** is used for dates as shown above. However, in speech it is more common to say 号 **hào**. For example, to say *the twenty-fourth of March* 三月二十四号 **Sānyuè èrshí sì hào** is more natural than 三月二十四日 **Sānyuè èrshi sì rì**.

Rìběn 日本 N Japan

rìcháng 日常 [comp: 日 daily + 常 usual] ADJ daily, routine

rìchéng 日程 [modif: 日 daily + 程 journey] N daily schedule, schedule
议事日程 **yìshì rìchéng** agenda

rìchéngbiǎo 日程表 N timetable (for a schedule), program

rìjì 日记 [modif: 日 daily + 记 record] N diary (本 **běn**, 篇 **piān**)
记日记 **jì rìjì** keep a diary

rìjìběn 日记本 N diary book

rìlì 日历 N calendar (of pages showing dates)

rìqī 日期 [comp: 日 day + 期 fixed time] N date (especially of an event)
过期日期 **guòqī rìqī** sell-by date

Rìwén 日文 [modif: 日 Japanese + 文 writing] N the Japanese language (especially the writing)

rìyè 日夜 N day and night, round the clock

rìyòngpǐn 日用品 [modif: 日 daily + 用 use + 品 article] N daily necessities

Rìyǔ 日语 [modif: 日 Japan + 语 speech] N the Japanese language

Rìyuán 日元 [modif: 日 Japan + 元 dollar] N Japanese currency, yen

rìzi 日子 [suffix: 日 day + 子 nominal suffix] N **1** day, date **2** life, livelihood

róng 容 V tolerate

róngliàng 容量 [modif: 容 accommodating + 量 amount] N the amount that something can hold, capacity, volume

电容量 **diàn róngliàng** electric capacity

róngyì 容易 [comp: 容 tolerant + 易 easy] ADJ **1** easy, not difficult (ANTONYM 难 **nán**) **2** having a tendency to, likely

róng 绒 TRAD 絨 N light hair, down (See **yǔróng** 羽绒.)

róu 柔 ADJ soft, gentle

róuhé 柔和 [comp: 柔 soft + 和 mild] ADJ soft and mild, gentle
柔和的口气 **róuhe de kǒuqì** a gentle and soothing voice

róu 揉 V rub, knead

róumiàn 揉面 V knead dough

ròu 肉 N flesh, meat
鸡肉 **jīròu** chicken meat / 牛肉 **niúròu** beef / 羊肉 **yángròu** mutton / 鱼肉 **yúròu** fish meat / 猪肉 **zhūròu** pork

NOTE: The most popular meat in China is pork. Unspecified, 肉 **ròu** often refers to *pork*.

rú 如 CONJ Same as 如果 **rúguǒ**. Used only in writing.

rúguǒ 如果 CONJ if, in case

NOTE: 如果 **rúguǒ** is usually used with 就 **jiù**.

rúhé 如何 PRON how, what

NOTE: 如何 **rúhé** is one of the few remnants of Classical Chinese still used in Modern Chinese, but it is usually used in writing only. The same is true with 如此 **rúcǐ**, 如今 **rújīn** and 如同 **rútóng**.

rújīn 如今 N today, now

NOTE: See note on 如何 **rúhé**.

rútóng 如同 V be like, as

NOTE: See note on 如何 **rúhé**.

rǔ 儒 N scholar

rǔjiā 儒家 N Confucianism, Confucianists

rǔ 乳 N **1** the breast **2** milk

rǔfáng 乳房 N the breast

rǔzhìpǐn 乳制品 N dairy product

rǔ 辱 V & N insult

rù 入 V enter ■ 病从口入。**Bìng cóng kǒu**

rù. *Disease enters the body by the mouth.* (→ *Bad food causes disease.*)

rùkǒu 入口 N entry, entrance

ruǎn 软 TRAD 軟 ADJ soft, supple (ANTONYM 硬 **yìng**)

ruǎnjiàn 软件 [modif: 软 soft + 件 article] N computer software, software

ruì 锐 TRAD 銳 ADJ sharp

ruò 弱 ADJ weak, feeble (ANTONYM 强 **qiáng**)

S

sā 撒 V cast, spread out
撒渔网 **sā yúwǎng** spread out a fishing net

sǎ 洒 TRAD 灑 V sprinkle, spray

sāi 腮 N cheek

sāi 塞 V fill in, stuff

sāichē 塞车 N Same as 堵车 **dǔchē**

sāizi 塞子 N stopper, plug, cork

sài 赛 TRAD 賽 V compete (See 比赛 **bǐsài**.)

sān 三 NUMERAL three
十三 **shísān** thirteen (13) / 三十 **sānshí** thirty (30)

sānjiǎo 三角 N 1 triangle 2 trigonometry

sǎn 伞 TRAD 傘 N umbrella (把 **bǎ**)

sàn 散 V disperse, distribute

sànbù 散步 [modif: 散 random + 步 step] V take a short leisurely walk, stroll

sāng 丧 TRAD 喪 N funeral
奔丧 **bēnsāng** travel to attend a funeral

sāngshì 丧事 N funeral arrangement, funeral
办丧事 **bànsāngshì** make funeral arrangements, perform a funeral ceremony

sāng 桑 N mulberry

sǎng 嗓 N throat

sǎngzi 嗓子 [suffix: 嗓 throat + 子 nominal suffix] N 1 voice 2 throat

sǎo 扫 TRAD 掃 V sweep

sè 色 N color

sècǎi 色彩 N color, hue
色彩丰富 **sècǎi fēngfù** a riot of color

sèqíng 色情 N sex urge, eroticism
色情狂 **sèqíngkuáng** sex mania, erotomania

sēn 森 N forest

sēnlín 森林 [comp: 森 forest + 林 woods] N forest

shā 杀 TRAD 殺 V kill, slay, put to death

shā 沙 N sand

shāfā 沙发 N upholstered chair, sofa, couch

shāmò 沙漠 [modif: 沙 sand + 漠 desert] N desert

shātān 沙滩 N sandy beach

shāzi 沙子 [suffix: 沙 sand + 子 nominal suffix] N sand, grit (粒 **lì**)

shǎ 傻 ADJ foolish, stupid (ANTONYM 聪明 **cōngmíng**)

shài 晒 TRAD 曬 V dry in the sun, bask
晒太阳 **shài tàiyang** sunbathe

shān 山 N mountain, hill (座 **zuò**)
爬山 **páshān** mountain climbing, mountaineering

shānshuǐ 山水 N landscape
游山玩水 **yóu shān wán shuǐ** IDIOM go sightseeing

shān 衫 N shirt (See 衬衫 **chènshān**.)

shān 删 V delete (words)

shānchú 删除 V delete, remove, cross out

shǎn 闪 N flash

shǎndiàn 闪电 N lightning

shàn 扇 I N fan II V wave a fan

shànzi 扇子 N fan (把 **bǎ**)

shàn 善 ADJ good

shànliáng 善良 [comp: 善 good + 良 good] ADJ kind-hearted, good-hearted

shànyú 善于 V be good at

shāng 伤 TRAD 傷 V & N wound, injure
受伤 **shòushāng** be wounded, be injured

shāngbā 伤疤 N scar

shāngfēng 伤风 N catch a cold, have a cold

shānghài 伤害 [comp: 伤 injure + 害 harm] v harm, hurt

shāngxīn 伤心 [v+obj: 伤 wound + 心 the heart] ADJ heartbreaking, heartbroken

shāng 商 N commerce

shāngchǎng 商场 [modif: 商 commerce + 场 place] N shopping center, mall (家 jiā, 座 zuò)

shāngdiàn 商店 N shop, store (家 jiā) 开商店 kāi shāngdiàn open a shop, keep a shop

shāngliang 商量 [comp: 商 discuss + 量 weigh] v discuss, consult

shāngpǐn 商品 [modif: 商 commerce + 品 article] N commodity (件 jiàn, 种 zhǒng)

shāngwù 商务 N business affairs

shāngyè 商业 [modif: 商 commerce + 业 industry] N commerce, business

shāngyè guǎnlǐ 商业管理 N business administration
商业管理硕士 shāngyè guǎnlǐ shuòshì Master of Business Administration (MBA)

shāngyè qū 商业区 N business district

shǎng 赏 v 1 appreciate (See xīnshǎng 欣赏.) 2 award

shàng 上[1] N 1 on top of, on, above (ANTONYM 下 xià) 2 previous, last
上星期 shàng xīngqī last week / 上一课 shàng yí kè the previous class (lesson)

NOTE: 上 **shàng** is often used after a noun to form words of location. While its basic meaning is *on top*, 上 **shàng** may have various, often semi-idiomatic senses, e.g. 报纸上 **bàozhǐ shang** *in the newspaper* / 地上 **dìshang** *on the ground* / 工作上 **gōngzuò shang** *in work* / 会上 **huì shang** *at the meeting* / 世界上 **shìjiè shang** *in the world* / 手上 **shǒu shang** *in hand, in the hands of*

shàng 上[2] v 1 go upwards, ascend
上来 shànglai come up / 上楼 shàng lóu

go upstairs / 上去 **shàngqu** go up
2 get on (a vehicle), go aboard (a plane, ship)
上车 shàng chē get into a vehicle / 上船 shàng chuán board a ship / 上飞机 shàng fēijī get on the plane
3 attend (school), go to (work)
上班 shàngbān go to work, start work / 上课 shàngkè go to class, teach a class or attend a class / 上学 shàngxué go to school

shàngbian 上边 [modif: 上 top, upper + 边 side] N above, high up (ANTONYM 下边 xiàbian)

shàngdàng 上当 v be fooled, be duped

shàngmiàn 上面 N Same as 上边 shàngbian

shàngwǎng 上网 [v+obj: 上 get on + 网 Internet] v get on the Internet, surf the Internet

shàngwǔ 上午 [modif: 上 upper half + 午 noon] N morning (usually from 8 a.m. to noon) (ANTONYM 下午 xiàwǔ)

NOTE: 上午 **shàngwǔ** does not mean the whole morning. It denotes the part of morning *from about eight or nine o'clock to noon*. The period before eight or nine o'clock is 早晨 **zǎochén** or 早上 **zǎoshang**.

shàngyī 上衣 [modif: 上 upper + 衣 clothing] N upper garment, jacket (件 jiàn)

shàngzài 上载 v upload

shāo 稍 ADV Same as 稍微 shāowēi. Often used in written Chinese.

shāowēi 稍微 [comp: 稍 slight + 微 tiny] ADV slightly, just a little bit

shāo 烧 TRAD 燒 v 1 burn 2 cook, bake 3 run a fever

sháo 勺 N spoon

sháozi 勺子 [suffix: 勺 ladle + 子 nominal suffix] N ladle, spoon (把 bǎ)

shǎo 少 I ADJ 1 small amount, few, little (ANTONYM 多 duō) 2 not often, seldom II v be short, be missing

shǎoshù 少数 [modif: 少 few, little +

数 number] N minority (ANTONYM 多数 duōshù)

shǎoshù mínzú 少数民族 N ethnic minority (non-Han ethnic people in China)

shào 少 ADJ young, early youth

shàonián 少年 [modif: 少 young + 年 age] N young man (from around 10 to 16 years old), adolescent

NOTES: (1) A young woman of around 10 to 16 years old is called 少女 **shàonǚ**. (2) The word 青少年 **qīngshàonián** is often used to mean *young people* collectively.

shào 绍 TRAD 紹 V connect (See jièshào 介绍.)

shé 舌 N tongue

shétou 舌头 [suffix: 舌 the tongue + 头 nominal suffix] N the tongue

shé 蛇 N snake (条 tiáo)

shě 舍 V give up

shěbude 舍不得 V be unwilling to give up, hate to part with

shědé 舍得 V be willing to part with, not grudge

shè 设 TRAD 設 V equip

shèbèi 设备 N equipment, installation

shèjì 设计 [comp: 设 plan + 计 calculate] V & N design

shèshī 设施 N facilities, equipment

shè 社 N association

shèhuì 社会 [comp: 社 god of the earth + 会 gathering] N society
社会上 **shèhuì shang** in society

shèhuìxué 社会学 N sociology

shèhuì zhǔyì 社会主义 N socialism

shèjiāo 社交 N social contact, social life

shèjiāo méitǐ 社交媒体 N social media

shèjiāo wǎngluò 社交网络 N social network

shè 舍 N hut, shed (See sùshè 宿舍.)

shè 摄 TRAD 攝 V absorb, take in

shèqǔ 摄取 V absorb, take in

shèxiàng 摄像 V make a video recording

shèxiàngtóu 摄像头 N webcam

shèyǐng 摄影 [v+obj: 摄 take + 影 shadow] V & N take a picture, shoot a movie, photograph; photography, cinematography

shèyǐngshī 摄影师 N photographer

shè 射 V shoot

shèjī 射击 V shoot, fire

shè 涉 V involve

shèjí 涉及 V involve, touch on, have something to do with

shéi 谁 TRAD 誰 PRON Same as 谁 shuí. Used colloquially.

shēn 申 V explain, state

shēnqǐng 申请 [comp: 申 state + 请 request] V apply for (a visa, a job, a permit, etc.)
申请表 **shēnqǐngbiǎo** application form /
申请人 **shēnqǐngrén** applicant /
申请书 **shēnqǐngshū** letter of application

shēn 伸 V stretch out, extend

shēn 绅 TRAD 紳 as in 绅士 shēnshì

shēnshì 绅士 N gentleman, gentry

shēn 呻 as in 呻吟 shēnyín

shēnyín 呻吟 V groan, moan

shēn 身 I N the human body II MEASURE WORD (for clothes)
一身新衣服 **yì shēn xīn yīfu** a suit of new clothes

shēnbiān 身边 N close by one's side, on one's person

shēncái 身材 N stature, figure
身材苗条 **shēncái miáotiáo** with a slender figure

shēnfen 身分 Same as shēnfen 身份

shēnfen 身份 N social status, identity
身份不明 **shēnfen bùmíng** unknown identity

shēntǐ 身体 [comp: 身 body + 体 physical] N 1 human body 2 health
■ 你要注意身体。**Nǐ yào zhùyì shēntǐ.** *You should pay attention to your health.*

NOTE: Although its original meaning is *the body*, 身体 **shēntǐ** is often used in

colloquial Chinese to mean *health*. Friends often ask about each other's health in greeting: ▪ 你身体好吗? **Nǐ shēntǐ hǎo ma?** *How's your health?* ▪ 你最近身体怎么样? **Nǐ zuìjìn shēntǐ zěnmeyàng?** *How's your health been recently?*

shēn 深 ADJ 1 deep (ANTONYM 浅 **qiǎn**) 2 difficult to understand, profound

shēnhòu 深厚 [comp: 深 deep + 厚 thick] ADJ deep, profound

shēnkè 深刻 [modif: 深 deep + 刻 carve] ADJ incisive, insightful, profound

shēnrù 深入 [modif: 深 deep + 入 enter, penetrate] v enter deeply into

shén 什 PRON what

shénme 什么 PRON what

shénmede 什么的 PRON and so on, and so forth

shén 神 I N god, supernatural being 财神爷 **cáishényé** the God of Wealth, the God of Fortune
II ADJ magical, wondrous

shénhuà 神话 [modif: 神 god + 话 story] N mythology, fairy-tales

shénmì 神秘 [comp: 神 god, supernatural + 秘 secret] ADJ mysterious, mythical

shénqíng 神情 N facial expression, look, air

shénsè 神色 N expression, look

shèn 甚 ADV much, very much

shènzhì 甚至 ADV even, so much so

shēng 升 v rise, go up

shēnggāo 升高 v raise, move up

shēng 生[1] v give birth to, grow

shēng 生[2] ADJ 1 raw, not cooked 2 unripe

shēngbìng 生病 v fall ill, get sick

shēngchǎn 生产 [comp: 生 grow + 产 produce] v produce, manufacture

shēngcí 生词 [modif: 生 unfamiliar + 词 word] N new word (in a language lesson) 记生词 **jì shēngcí** memorize new words

shēngcún 生存 v exist, survive

shēngdòng 生动 [comp: 生 lively + 动 move] ADJ vivid, lively

shēnghuó 生活 [comp: 生 living + 活 alive] v & N live a life; life 日常生活 **rìcháng shēnghuó** daily life

shēnghuófèi 生活费 N cost of living, living expenses

shēnghuó shuǐpíng 生活水平 N living standards

shēngmìng 生命 [comp: 生 living + 命 life] N life (条 **tiáo**)

shēngmìng kēxué 生命科学 N life science

shēngmìnglì 生命力 N life force

shēngqì 生气 v get angry, be offended

shēngrì 生日 [modif: 生 birth + 日 day] N birthday ▪ 祝你生日快乐! **Zhù nǐ shēngrì kuàilè!** *I wish you a happy birthday!*
过生日 **guò shēngrì** celebrate a birthday ▪ 你今年打算怎么过生日? **Nǐ jīnnián dǎsuàn zěnme guò shēngrì?** *How are you going to celebrate your birthday this year?*

shēngrì hèkǎ 生日贺卡 N birthday card

shēngrì lǐwù 生日礼物 N birthday present

shēngyi 生意 N business, trade

shēngzhǎng 生长 [comp: 生 living + 长 growing] v grow, grow up, be brought up

shēng 声 TRAD 聲 N sound, noise, voice

shēngdiào 声调 [modif: 声 voice + 调 tone] N tone of a Chinese word

shēngyīn 声音 [comp: 声 voice + 音 sound] N voice, sound

shéng 绳 TRAD 繩 N string, rope

shéngzi 绳子 [suffix: 绳 rope + 子 nominal suffix] N rope, cord (根 **gēn**, 条 **tiáo**)

shěng 省 v save, economize

shěngde 省得 CONJ in case, so as not to

shěnglüè 省略 v omit, leave out

shèng 胜 TRAD 勝 v triumph (over), be victorious, defeat

shènglì 胜利 [comp: 胜 triumph + 利

gain benefit] v & n win a victory; victory (ANTONYM 失败 shībài)

shèng 圣 TRAD 聖 ADJ holy, sacred

Shèngdànjié 圣诞节 n Christmas

shèng 剩 v be left over, have as surplus

shèngcài 剩菜 n leftovers

shī 失 v lose

shībài 失败 [comp: 失 lose + 败 be defeated] v be defeated, lose, fail (ANTONYMS 胜利 shènglì, 成功 chénggōng)

shīmián 失眠 [v+obj: 失 lose + 眠 sleep] n & v insomnia; suffer from insomnia

shīqù 失去 [comp: 失 lose + 去 go away] v lose (something valuable)

shīwàng 失望 [v+obj: 失 lose + 望 hope] ADJ disappointed
对 … 失望 duì … shīwàng be disappointed with …

shīyè 失业 [v+obj: 失 lose + 业 occupation, employment] v lose one's job, become unemployed

shī 师 TRAD 師 n master, teacher

shīfàn 师范 n teachers' education

shīfàn xuéyuàn 师范学院 n teachers' college, college of education

shīfu 师傅 [comp: 师 teacher + 傅 tutor] n master worker (位 wèi)

> NOTE: 师傅 **shīfu** is also a polite form of address to a *worker*. For example, an electrician or mechanic can be addressed as 师傅 **shīfu** or, if his family name is 李 **Lǐ**, 李师傅 **Lǐ shīfu**.

shī 诗 TRAD 詩 n poem, poetry (首 shǒu)

shīgē 诗歌 n poem, poetry

shīrén 诗人 n poet

shī 施 v carry out, execute

shīgōng 施工 [v+obj: 施 execute + 工 work] v (construction work) be underway, be in progress

shī 狮 TRAD 獅 n lion

shīzi 狮子 [suffix: 狮 lion + 子 nominal suffix] n lion (头 tóu)

shī 湿 TRAD 濕 ADJ damp, wet (ANTONYM 干 gān)

shīdù 湿度 [modif: 湿 wet + 度 degree] n humidity

shīrùn 湿润 [comp: 湿 wet + 润 moist] ADJ moist, damp

shí 十 NUMERAL ten
十五 shíwǔ fifteen (15) / 五十 wǔshí fifty (50)

shífēn 十分 [modif: 十 ten + 分 point] ADV one hundred percent, totally, fully

shí 石 n stone

shítou 石头 [suffix: 石 stone, rock + 头 nominal suffix] n stone, rock (块 kuài)

shíyóu 石油 [modif: 石 stone + 油 oil] n petroleum, oil

shí 识 TRAD 識 v know (See rènshi 认识, zhīshi 知识.)

shíbié 识别 v distinguish, identify, recognize
识别敌友 shíbié dí yǒu tell enemies from friends

shí 时 TRAD 時 n time, times

shíchā 时差 n time difference between time zones

shídài 时代 [comp: 时 time + 代 generation] n a historical period, epoch, age, times

shíhou 时候 [comp: 时 time + 候 a certain point in time] n (the duration of) time, (a certain point in) time, (the time) when

shíjiān 时间 [comp: 时 time + 间 moment] n time, a period of time

shíkè 时刻 [comp: 时 time + 刻 a point] n at a particular point in time

shíkèbiǎo 时刻表 n (railway, coach) timetable

shímáo 时髦 ADJ fashionable, in vogue

shíqī 时期 [comp: 时 time + 期 period] n period of time, stage

shíshàng 时尚 n fashion, fad, vogue

shízhuāng 时装 n fashionable dress, latest fashion

shí 实 TRAD 實 ADJ real, true

shíhuà 实话 [modif: 实 true + 话 words]

N true fact, truth

实话实说 **shíhuà shíshuō** tell the truth

shíjì 实际 I N reality, actual situation **II** ADJ practical, realistic

shíjiàn 实践 [comp: 实 fruit, fruition + 践 implement] V & N put into practice, apply; practice

shíxiàn 实现 [comp: 实 fruit, fruition + 现 materialize] V materialize, realize

shíyàn 实验 [modif: 实 practical + 验 testing] N experiment, test (项 **xiàng**, 次 **cì**)

shíyànshì 实验室 N laboratory

shíyànyuán 实验员 N laboratory technician

shíyòng 实用 [modif: 实 practical + 用 use] ADJ practical (for use), useful, handy

shízài 实在 ADJ 1 honest, truthful 2 indeed, really

shí 食 N food

shípǐn 食品 [modif: 食 food + 品 article] N foodstuff (as commodities) (件 **jiàn**)

shítáng 食堂 [modif: 食 food + 堂 hall] N dining hall, mess hall, canteen

shíwù 食物 [modif: 食 food + 物 things] N food

shǐ 史 N history (See **lìshǐ** 历史.)

shǐ 使 V make, enable

shǐjìngr 使劲儿 [v+obj: 使 apply + 劲 strength] V exert all one's strength

shǐyòng 使用 [comp: 使 use + 用 use] V use, apply

shǐ 始 V begin, start, commence

shǐzhōng 始终 [comp: 始 beginning + 终 end] ADV from beginning to end, throughout, ever

shìbīng 士兵 N rank-and-file soldier

shì 示 V show, indicate

shì 世 N 1 the world 2 lifetime 3 generation

shìjì 世纪 [modif: 世 generation + 纪 age] N century

shìjiè 世界 [comp: 世 world + 界

boundary] N the world

世界上 **shìjiè shang** in the world

shìjièguān 世界观 N world outlook, worldview

shì 事 N affair, matter, business (件 **jiàn**)

NOTE: In many cases 事 **shì** may be replaced by 事情 **shìqing**. 事 **shì** or 事情 **shìqing** is a noun that can be applied widely, denoting any affair, matter or business to be done or considered. Here are some examples: ■ 我今天晚上没有事情做。**Wǒ jīntiān wǎnshang méiyǒu shìqing zuò.** *I've nothing to do this evening.* ■ 我跟你说一件事。**Wǒ gēn nǐ shuō yí jiàn shì.** *I want to tell you something.* ■ 他们在路上出事了。**Tāmen zài lùshang chūshì le.** *They had an accident on the way.*

shìqing 事情 N See note on 事 **shì**

shìshí 事实 [comp: 事 thing + 实 truth] N fact, truth (件 **jiàn**)

shìwù 事物 N thing, object, reality

shìxiān 事先 N beforehand, in advance

shì 试 TRAD 試 V test, try

试试/试一下 **shìshì/shì yíxià** have a try

shìjuàn 试卷 N examination paper, test paper (份 **fèn**)

shì 视 TRAD 視 V watch (See **diànshì** 电视, **zhòngshì** 重视.)

shìlì 视力 [modif: 视 vision + 力 power] N eyesight, sight

视力测验 **shìlì cèyàn** eyesight test

shìpín 视频 N video frequency

视频光盘 **shìpín guāngpán** video compact disc, VCD

shì 市 N municipality, city

shìchǎng 市场 [modif: 市 market + 场 ground] N marketplace, market

菜市场 **cài shìchǎng** vegetable market, food market / 市场经济 **shìchǎng jīngjì** market economy

shì 式 N form, pattern (See **fāngshì** 方式, **xíngshì** 形式, etc.)

shì 似 as in 似的 **shìde**

shìde 似的 PARTICLE be like, as … as

shì 是 V 1 be, yes ■ "你们的中文老师

是不是北京人？" "是的。" "**Nǐmen de Zhōngwén lǎoshī shì bu shì Běijīngrén?**" "**Shì de.**" *Is your Chinese teacher from Beijing?" "Yes."* **2** (indicating existence of), (there) be ■ 小学旁边是一座公园。**Xiǎoxué pángbian shì yí zuò gōngyuán.** *There is a park by the primary school.* **3** (used to emphasize the words following it) ■ 那个电话是谁打来的？**Nàge diànhuà shì shéi dǎ lai de?** *Who rang?*

shìfǒu 是否 ADV whether or not, yes or no

shì 室 N room (See **bàngōngshì** 办公室, **jiàoshì** 教室, etc.)

shì 柿 N persimmon

shìzi 柿子 N persimmon

shì 适 TRAD 適 V suit, fit

shìdàng 适当 [comp: 适 suitable + 当 ought to] ADJ appropriate, proper, suitable

shìhé 适合 [comp: 适 suit + 合 be harmonious] V suit, fit

shìyìng 适应 V be able to adapt to

shìyòng 适用 [v+obj: 适 suit + 用 use, application] ADJ applicable, suitable

shì 逝 V pass, leave

shi 匙 See **yàoshi** 钥匙

shōu 收 V receive, accept 收到 **shōudào** receive / 收回 **shōuhuí** take back, recall / 收下 **shōuxia** accept

shōuhuò 收获 [comp: 收 collect + 获 gain] V & N gather in crops, harvest; gain (of work), achievement, reward

shōujù 收据 N receipt

shōurù 收入 [comp: 收 collect + 入 entry] V & N earn, receive; income 人均收入 **rén jūn shōurù** average income per capita

shōushi 收拾 [comp: 收 gather in + 拾 pick up] V put in order, tidy up

shōusuō 收缩 V contract, shrink

shǒu 手 N hand (只 **zhī**, 双 **shuāng**) 右手 **yòushǒu** the right hand / 左手 **zuǒshǒu** the left hand

shǒubiǎo 手表 [modif: 手 hand + 表 watch] N wristwatch (块 **kuài**)

shǒuduàn 手段 N means, measure, method

shǒugōng 手工 [modif: 手 hand + 工 work] N done by hand, made by hand; manual work

shǒugōngyè 手工业 N handicraft industry

shǒugōngyì 手工艺 N arts and crafts, handicraft

shǒujī 手机 [modif: 手 hand + 机 machine] N cell phone, mobile telephone (只 **zhī**)

shǒujuàn 手绢 N handkerchief (块 **kuài**)

shǒu shang 手上 ADV in the hand ■ 他手上拿着一本书。**Tā shǒu shang názhe yì běn shū.** *He's holding a book in his hand.*

shǒushù 手术 N surgical operation, operation 做手术 **zuò shǒushù** perform an operation, operate

shǒushùjiān 手术间 N operating room, operating theater

shǒutào 手套 [modif: 手 hand + 套 covering] N glove (只 **zhī**, 副 **fù**)

shǒuxù 手续 N formalities, procedure 办手续 **bàn shǒuxù** go through the formalities

shǒuzhǐ 手指 N finger, thumb

NOTE: In Chinese the thumb 拇指 **mǔzhǐ**, or 大拇指 **dàmǔzhǐ**, is considered just one of the fingers. So it is correct to say: 我有十个手指。**Wǒ yǒu shí ge shǒuzhǐ.** *I have ten fingers.*

shǒu 守 V **1** observe, abide by (See **zūnshǒu** 遵守.) **2** keep watch, guard

shǒuhù 守护 V guard and defend

shǒu 首 MEASURE WORD (for songs and poems) 一首歌 **yì shǒu gē** a song

shǒudū 首都 [modif: 首 the head, first + 都 metropolis] N capital city

shǒuxiān 首先 [comp: 首 first + 先 before] ADV first, first of all

shǒuyào 首要 [comp: 首 first + 要 important] ADJ of primary importance

shòu 受 v receive, accept
受不了 **shòu bu liǎo** cannot stand/ endure

shòudào 受到 v have received, have suffered
受到很好的教育 **shòudào hěn hǎo de jiàoyù** have received an excellent education, very well-educated / 受到公司的警告 **shòudào gōngsī de jǐnggào** have received a warning from the company

shòufá 受罚 [v+obj: 受 suffer + 罚 penalty] v be punished, be penalized

shòushāng 受伤 [v+obj: 受 suffer + 伤 wound] v be wounded, be injured

shòuzuì 受罪 v endure hardship, have a very hard time

shòu 瘦 ADJ thin, lean

shòuròu 瘦肉 N lean meat

shòu 售 v sell

shòuhuòyuán 售货员 [suffix: 售 sell + 货 goods + 员 nominal suffix] N salesperson

shòu 寿 TRAD 壽 N life, lifespan
长寿 **chángshòu** longevity

shòumìng 寿命 [comp: 寿 life + 命 life] N lifespan

shòu 兽 TRAD 獸 N beast, four-legged mammal (See **yěshòu** 野兽.)

shū 书 TRAD 書 N book (本 **běn**)
看书 **kàn shū** read, do reading

shūbāo 书包 [modif: 书 book + 包 bag] N schoolbag, satchel (只 **zhī**)

shūdiàn 书店 [modif: 书 book + 店 store, shop] N bookstore, bookshop (家 **jiā**)

shūjià 书架 [modif: 书 book + 架 shelf] N bookshelf

shū 叔 N father's younger brother

shūshu 叔叔 N father's younger brother, uncle

NOTE: 叔叔 **shūshu** is a form of address used by a child for a man around his/her father's age. It is common to put a family name before 叔叔 **shūshu**, e.g. 张叔叔 **Zhāng shūshu**. Also see note on 阿姨 **āyí**.

shū 殊 ADJ different (See 特殊 **tèshū**.)

shūzi 梳子 [suffix: 梳 comb + 子 nominal suffix] N comb (把 **bǎ**)

shū 舒 v stretch, unfold

shūfu 舒服 [comp: 舒 relaxing + 服 conceding] ADJ comfortable, be well
不舒服 **bù shūfu** (of a person) not very well, be under the weather

shūshì 舒适 ADJ comfortable, cosy

shū 蔬 N vegetable

shūcài 蔬菜 N vegetable ▪ 多吃蔬菜，少吃肉，对健康有利。**Duō chī shūcài, shǎo chī ròu, duì jiànkāng yǒulì.** *Eating lots of vegetables and little meat is good for your health.*

shū 输[1] TRAD 輸 v lose (a game, a bet) (ANTONYM 赢 **yíng**)

shū 输[2] TRAD 輸 v transport

shūchū 输出 v 1 output 2 send out, export

shūrù 输入 v 1 input 2 bring in, introduce

shūsòng 输送 v transport, convey

shūxuè 输血 N blood transfusion

shú 熟 ADJ 1 ripe, cooked 2 familiar with, know well

shúliàn 熟练 [comp: 熟 familiar with + 练 practiced] ADJ skilful, skilled

shúxī 熟悉 [comp: 熟 familiar with + 悉 knowing] ADJ & v familiar with; be familiar with, know well

shǔ 数 TRAD 數 v count

shǔ 暑 N heat

shǔjià 暑假 [modif: 暑 summer + 假 holiday, vacation] N summer holiday, summer vacation

shǔ 属 TRAD 屬 v belong to

shǔyú 属于 v belong to

shǔ 鼠 N rat, mouse

shǔbiāo 鼠标 N (computer) mouse

shù 术 TRAD 術 N skill, art, craft (See **jìshù** 技术, **měishù** 美术, etc.)

shù 述 v narrate (See **fùshù** 复述.)

shù 树 TRAD 樹 N tree (棵 **kē**)

shùlín 树林 [comp: 树 tree + 林 wood] N forest, woods

shù 数 TRAD 數 N number, figure

shùjù 数据 [modif: 数 number + 据 evidence] N datum, data

shùjùkù 数据库 N database

shùliàng 数量 [comp: 数 number + 量 quantity] N quantity, amount

shùmǎ 数码 ADJ digital

数码化 **shùmǎhuà** digitalize; digitalization

shùmù 数目 N number, amount

shùxué 数学 [modif: 数 number + 学 knowledge, study of] N mathematics, maths

shùzì 数字 [modif: 数 number + 字 written word] N 1 numeral (in writing) 2 figure, number

shuā 刷 v brush

shuāyá 刷牙 v brush teeth

shuāzi 刷子 N brush (把 **bǎ**)

shuāi 摔 v fall, fumble

shuāidǎo 摔倒 v fall, trip and fall

shuǎi 甩 v swing, throw

shuāng 双 TRAD 雙 MEASURE WORD a pair of (shoes, chopsticks, etc.)

一双鞋 yì **shuāng xié** a pair of shoes / 两双筷子 **liǎng shuāng kuàizi** two pairs of chopsticks

shuāngfāng 双方 [modif: 双 both + 方 side, party] N both sides, both parties

shuāng 霜 N frost

shuí 谁 TRAD 誰 PRON 1 who, whom 2 everyone, anybody, whoever, no matter who

shuǐ 水 N water

自来水 **zìláishuǐ** running water, tap water / 开水 **kāishuǐ** boiled water

shuǐdào 水稻 [modif: 水 water + 稻 paddy rice] N paddy rice, rice

shuǐguǒ 水果 [modif: 水 water + 果 fruit] N fruit

shuǐpíng 水平 N 1 level, standard

2 proficiency (in language)

提高 … 水平 **tígāo … shuǐpíng** raise the standard of … / 生活水平 **shēnghuó shuǐpíng** living standard / 文化水平 **wénhuà shuǐpíng** cultural level, educational experience

shuì 税 N tax, duty

关税 **guānshuì** tariff

shuìwùjú 税务局 N tax bureau, Inland Revenue Service

shuì 睡 v sleep

睡着 **shuìzháo** fall asleep

shuìjiào 睡觉 [comp: 睡 sleep + 觉 sleep] v sleep, go to bed

NOTES: (1) 睡 **shuì** and 睡觉 **shuìjiào** are often interchangeable. (2) 觉 is pronounced **jiào** in 睡觉 **shuìjiào**, but **jué** in 觉得 **juéde**.

shuìyī 睡衣 N pajamas, dressing gown

shùn 顺 TRAD 順 ADJ smooth

shùnbiàn 顺便 [comp: 顺 smooth + 便 convenient] ADV in passing, incidentally

shùnlì 顺利 [comp: 顺 smooth + 利 favorable] ADJ smooth, without a hitch, successful

shùnxù 顺序 N sequence, order

shuō 说 TRAD 說 v 1 say, speak 2 explain, tell

说笑话 **shuō xiàohua** tell a joke, kid

shuō bu dìng 说不定 ADV 1 probably, likely 2 not for sure, indefinitely

shuōfú 说服 [v+compl: 说 speak + 服 obey] v 1 persuade 2 convince

shuōhuà 说话 v speak, talk

shuōhuǎng 说谎 v tell a lie; lie

shuōmíng 说明 [v+compl: 说 say + 明 clear] v & N explain, show; explanation, manual

shuò 硕 TRAD 碩 ADJ large, big

shuòshì 硕士 [modif: 硕 big + 士 scholar] N holder of a master's degree

硕士学位 **shuòshì xuéwèi** master's degree, masterate

sī 司 v take charge of
sījī 司机 [v+obj: 司 take charge + 机 machine] n (professional) automobile driver, train driver
sī 撕 v tear (a piece of paper)
撕得粉碎 sī de fěnsuì tear into tiny pieces, tear up
sī 私 adj private
sīrén 私人 [modif: 私 private + 人 person] adj private, personal
sī 思 v think
sīkǎo 思考 [comp: 思 think + 考 examine] v ponder over, reflect on, think seriously
独立思考 dúlì sīkǎo think things out for oneself, think independently
sīxiǎng 思想 [comp: 思 think + 想 think] n thought, thinking
sīxù 思绪 n train of thought, thoughts
sī 丝 TRAD 絲 n silk
sīchóu 丝绸 [comp: 丝 silk + 绸 silk cloth] n silk, silk cloth
sīháo 丝毫 n the slightest, in the least
没有丝毫变化 méiyǒu sīháo biànhuà without the slightest change, haven't changed in the least

NOTE: 丝毫 **sīháo** is usually used alongside with a negative word.

sǐ 死 v die (ANTONYM 活 huó)

NOTE: See note on 去世 qùshì.

sǐwáng 死亡 v & n die, perish; death, doom (ANTONYM 生存 shēncún)
死亡证 sǐwáng zhèng death certificate
sì 四 NUMERAL four
四十四 sìshí sì forty-four (44) / 四海为家 sì hǎi wéi jiā IDIOM Make the four seas one's home (→ Make one's home wherever one is.)
sì 寺 n monastery, temple
sìmiào 寺庙 n temples and monasteries
sì 似 v seem
sìhū 似乎 ADV it seems, as if

sōng 松 TRAD 鬆 adj loose, slack, lax, weak (ANTONYM 紧 jǐn)
sòng 颂 TRAD 頌 v praise
sòng 送 v 1 give as a gift 2 deliver (goods) 3 accompany (somebody), take, escort
sòng 诵 TRAD 誦 v chant, recite (See bèisòng 背诵.)
sōu 搜 v search
sōuchá 搜查 [comp: 搜 search + 查 check] v search, ransack
搜查证 sōuchá zhèng search warrant
sōují 搜集 [comp: 搜 search + 集 gather] v collect, gather
搜集资料 sōují zīliào collect data, data-gathering
sōusuǒ 搜索 v search
搜索队 sōusuǒduì search party
sōusuǒ yǐnqíng 搜索引擎 n search engine
sòu 嗽 n cough (See késou 咳嗽.)
sù 诉 TRAD 訴 v tell (See gàosu 告诉.)
sù 肃 TRAD 肅 adj solemn, respectful (See yánsù 严肃.)
sù 速 n speed
sùdù 速度 [modif: 速 speed + 度 degree] n speed, velocity
sù 宿 v stay overnight
sùshè 宿舍 [modif: 宿 stay overnight + 舍 lodge] n hostel, dormitory
学生宿舍 xuésheng sùshè students' hostel (dormitory)
sù 塑 v mold
sùliào 塑料 n plastic
塑料袋 sùliào dài plastic bag
sù 素 n vegetarian (food)
suān 酸 adj sour, tart
suàn 算 v 1 calculate 2 may be considered as
suànle 算了 v let it be, forget it
suī 虽 TRAD 雖 CONJ although
suīrán 虽然 CONJ although, though
▪ 他虽然赚了很多钱，但是还不满足。 Tā suīrán zhuànle hěn duō qián, dànshì

hái bù mǎnzú. *Although he's earned a lot of money, he is still dissatisfied.*

NOTE: 虽然 **suīrán** is often used together with 但是 **dànshì** or 但 **dàn** to form the pattern 虽然 ... 但(是).

suí 随 TRAD 隨 v let (somebody do as he pleases), as you wish

suíbiàn 随便 ADJ casual, informal

NOTE: 随便 **suíbiàn** is often used in casual conversation to mean something like *as you wish, anything you like,* or *I have no objection whatsoever.* For example:
■ "你喝红茶还是绿茶？" "随便。"
"Nǐ hē hóngchá háishi lǜchá?" "Suíbiàn."
"Do you want to drink black tea or green tea?" "Anything's fine with me."

suíshēn 随身 ADV (carry) on one's person, bring with one

suíshí 随时 ADV whenever, at any moment

suíshǒu 随手 ADV 1 immediately 2 casually, without much thought
随手乱放 **suíshǒu luàn fàng** put ... somewhere casually and without much thought

suízhe 随着 PREP along with, in the wake of

suì 岁 TRAD 歲 MEASURE WORD year (of age)

NOTE: See 年纪 **niánjì**.

suì 碎 ADJ broken, fragmentary

sūn 孙 TRAD 孫 N grandchild

sūnnǚ 孙女 N granddaughter

sūnzi 孙子 N grandson

sǔn 损 TRAD 損 v damage

sǔnshī 损失 [comp: 损 damage + 失 loss] v & N lose, suffer from damage and/or loss; loss, damage

suō 缩 TRAD 縮 v shrink (ANTONYM 胀 **zhàng**)

suōduǎn 缩短 [v+compl: 缩 shrink + 短 short] v shorten

suǒ 所 MEASURE WORD (for houses or institutions housed in a building)
一所医院 **yì suǒ yīyuàn** a hospital / 两所大学 **liǎng suǒ dàxué** two universities

suǒwèi 所谓 ADJ what is called, so-called

suǒyǐ 所以 CONJ therefore, so

NOTE: See note on 因为 **yīnwèi**.

suǒyǒu 所有 ADJ all, without exception

NOTES: 所有 **suǒyǒu** is (1) used only as an attribute, (2) always followed by 的 **de**, and (3) often used together with 都 **dōu**.

suǒ 索 v search

suǒpéi 索赔 [v+obj: 索 search for + 赔 compensation] v claim damages, claim indemnity

suǒ 锁 TRAD 鎖 N & v lock; lock up

T

tā 他 PRON he, him

tāmen 他们 [suffix: 他 he, him + 们 suffix denoting a plural number] PRON they, them

tā 它 PRON it

tāmen 它们 [suffix: 它 it + 们 suffix denoting a plural number] PRON (non-human) they, them (plural form of 它 **tā**)

tā 她 PRON she, her

tāmen 她们 [suffix: 她 she, her + 们 suffix denoting a plural number] PRON (female) they, them

tāi 胎 N 1 fetus, embryo 2 padding, stuffing

tái 台 TRAD 檯 I N table, desk (张 **zhāng**) II MEASURE WORD (for machines, big instruments, etc.)
一台机器 **yì tái jīqì** a machine

táijiē 台阶 N flight of steps, step

táishìjī 台式机 N desktop PC

Táiwān 台湾 N Taiwan

tái 抬 v lift, raise

抬高 **táigāo** raise (prices)

tài 太 ADV 1 excessively, too 2 extremely, really

Tàijíquán 太极拳 N shadow boxing, Taichi

tàitai 太太 N 1 Mrs 2 wife

NOTE: (1) While Mrs is used in English-speaking countries regardless of class or social status, its Chinese counterpart 太太 **tàitai** is only used in middle-class or upper-class circles. (2) Although Chinese women often retain their family names after marriage, 太太 **tàitai** as a form of address must be prefixed by the husband's family name.

tàiyang 太阳 [modif: 太 big, super + 阳 open, overt, masculine] N the sun, sunshine

NOTE: (1) Put together, 太 **tài** (meaning *big, great* in classical Chinese) and 阳 **yáng** (meaning *Yang of ancient Chinese thought*) mean the ultimate Yang, as the sun is the ultimate symbol of Yang. The ultimate symbol of Yin is the *moon* 月 **yuè**. (2) In 太阳 **tàiyang**, 阳 **yang** is pronounced in the neutral tone.

tài 态 TRAD 態 N stance

tàidu 态度 [comp: 态 stance + 度 appearance, bearing] N manner, bearing, attitude, approach

tài 泰 ADJ peace, safe ■ 国泰民安。 **Guó tài mín ān.** *The country is safe and the people live in peace.*

tān 贪 TRAD 貪 I v be greedy II ADJ corrupt

tānguān 贪官 N corrupt official

tānwū 贪污 [comp: 贪 corrupt + 污 filthy] v & N embezzle, be involved in corruption; embezzlement, corruption 贪污犯 **tānwūfàn** embezzler, grafter / 贪污公款 **tānwū gōngkuǎn** embezzle public funds

tān 摊 TRAD 攤 N vendor's stand, stall 摊儿 **tānr** vendor's stand, stall

tán 谈 TRAD 談 v talk, discuss

谈一下 **tán yíxià** talk briefly about, give a brief talk about

tánhuà 谈话 [comp: 谈 talk + 话 talk] v & N have a (serious, formal) talk; talk

tánpàn 谈判 v & N negotiate; negotiation

tántiān 谈天 v chat, chitchat

tán 弹 TRAD 彈 v pluck, catapult

tán gāngqín 弹钢琴 v play the piano

tán 坛 TRAD 壇 N altar 天坛 **tiāntán** the Temple of Heaven (in Beijing)

tǎn 毯 N blanket, rug, tapestry, carpet 羊毛毯 **yángmáotǎn** woolen blanket

tǎnzi 毯子 [suffix: 毯 blanket + 子 nominal suffix] N blanket (条 **tiáo**)

tǎn 坦 ADJ 1 candid, frank 2 level, smooth 平坦 **píngtǎn** (of land) level and expansive

tǎnshuài 坦率 ADJ frank, candid 坦率地说 **tǎnshuài de shuō** to be frank with you, to tell the truth

tàn 碳 N carbon

tāng 汤 TRAD 湯 N soup (碗 **wǎn**) 喝汤 **hē tāng** eat soup

táng 堂 N hall, main room (See lǐtáng 礼堂, shítáng 食堂.)

táng 糖 N sugar, candy (块 **kuài**)

tángguǒ 糖果 N candy, sweets

táng húlu 糖葫芦 N sugar-coated haws, crab apples, etc. stringed on a stick

tǎng 躺 v lie, recline

tàng 趟 MEASURE WORD (for trips)

tàng 烫 TRAD 燙 ADJ boiling hot, scalding hot, burning hot

táo 逃 v flee, run away (from danger, punishment, etc.)

táobì 逃避 [comp: 逃 flee + 避 avoid] v evade, shirk 逃避责任 **táobì zérèn** evade responsibility

táo 陶 N pottery

táocí 陶瓷 [comp: 陶 pottery + 瓷 porcelain] N pottery and porcelain, ceramics

táoqì 陶器 N pottery, earthenware

táo 淘 v wash in a pan or basket

táoqì 淘气 ADJ naughty, mischievous

tǎo 讨 TRAD 討 v ask for

tǎo jià huán jià 讨价还价 v haggle over prices, bargain

tǎolùn 讨论 [comp: 讨 explore + 论 discuss] **v & N** discuss; discussion

tǎoyàn 讨厌 [v+obj: 讨 ask for + 厌 boredom, vexation] **v & ADJ** loathe, dislike; disgusting, annoying

tào 套 MEASURE WORD set, suit, suite (for a collection of things)

一套衣服 **yí tào yīfu** a suit of clothes / 两套家具 **liǎng tào jiājù** two sets of furniture

tè 特 ADV particularly, especially

tèbié 特别 [comp: 特 special + 别 other, unusual] **ADJ** special, especially

tèdiǎn 特点 [modif: 特 special + 点 point] **N** special features, characteristic

tèsè 特色 [modif: 特 special + 色 color] **N** salient feature, characteristic

tèshū 特殊 [comp: 特 special + 殊 different] **ADJ** special, unusual, exceptional

tèzhēng 特征 [modif: 特 special + 征 feature] **N** characteristic, feature

téng 疼 v 1 ache, hurt

头疼 **tóu téng** headache, have a headache

NOTE: 疼 **téng** in the sense of *ache, hurt* is a colloquial word. You can use 痛 **tòng** instead of 疼 **téng** to mean *ache, hurt.*

2 love dearly

téngài 疼爱 Same as 疼 **téng v 2**

tī 梯 N ladder, steps (See **diàntī** 电梯, **lóutī** 楼梯.)

tī 踢 v kick

踢球 **tī qiú** play soccer / 踢足球 **tī zúqiú** play soccer

tí 提 v 1 carry in the hand (with the arm down) **2** mention

提建议 **tí jiànyì** put forward a proposal, make a suggestion / 提问题 **tí wèntí** raise a question

tíchàng 提倡 [comp: 提 put forward + 倡 advocate] **v** advocate, recommend

tígāng 提纲 N outline

tígāo 提高 [v+compl: 提 raise + 高 high] **v** raise, advance

tígōng 提供 [comp: 提 put forward + 供 supply] **v** provide, supply

tíqián 提前 [v+obj: 提 put forward + 前 forward] **v** put ahead of schedule, advance

tíwèn 提问 v put questions to, quiz

tíxǐng 提醒 v remind, call attention to

tí 题 TRAD 題 N topic, question

tímù 题目 N 1 question for an examination, school exercises, etc. (道 **dào**) **2** title, subject

tǐ 体 TRAD 體 I N human body, body **II v** experience personally, feel intimately

tǐhuì 体会 [comp: 体 experience personally + 会 understand] **v & N** gain intimate knowledge through personal experience, realize; personal understanding through experience

tǐjī 体积 N volume (mathematics)

tǐtiē 体贴 v give every consideration to, give loving care to

tǐwēn 体温 N (body) temperature

NOTE: See the notes on 温度 **wēndù**.

tǐxiàn 体现 v give expressions to, embody

tǐyàn 体验 N & v personal experience; learn through one's personal experience

tǐyù 体育 [modif: 体 physical + 育 education] **N** physical education, sports

tǐyùchǎng 体育场 [modif: 体育 sports + 场 ground] **N** stadium, arena

tǐyùguǎn 体育馆 [modif: 体育 sports + 馆 building] **N** gymnasium, gym

tǐyù kè 体育课 N physical education (PE) lesson

tì 替 v 1 replace, substitute **2** Same as 给 **gěi PREP**

tiān 天 N 1 sky, heaven 2 day 3 weather 4 abode of gods, Heaven
老天爷 **Lǎotiānyé** Heavens (a colloquial term that denotes "God" or "Nature")

tiānkōng 天空 [comp: 天 sky + 空 empty] N sky

tiānqì 天气 [comp: 天 weather + 气 weather] N weather

tiānshang 天上 ADV in the sky

tiāntiān 天天 ADV every day, from day to day

tiānxià 天下 ADV under heaven, in the world, on earth

tiānzhēn 天真 [comp: 天 natural + 真 genuine] ADJ 1 simple and unaffected, ingenuous 2 naive, gullible

tiān 添 V add, increase

tián 田 N farmland (especially paddy fields), fields
种田 **zhòngtián** grow crops, farm

tián 填 V fill in (a form, blanks as in an exercise)

tiánkòng 填空 V fill in blanks

tián 甜 ADJ sweet, honeyed

tiánshí 甜食 N sweet food, dessert

tiāo 挑 V take one's pick, choose, select
东挑西拣 **dōng tiāo xī jiǎn** choose this and pick that, spend a long time choosing, be very choosy

tiāoxuǎn 挑选 [comp: 挑 take one's pick + 选 select] V select, choose, pick out

tiáo 条 TRAD 條 MEASURE WORD (for things with a long, narrow shape)
一条河 **yì tiáo hé** a river /
两条鱼 **liǎng tiáo yú** two fish

tiáojiàn 条件 N 1 condition
生活条件 **shēnghuó tiáojiàn** living conditions / 工作条件 **gōngzuò tiáojiàn** working conditions
2 requirement, prerequisite

tiáo 调 TRAD 調 V adjust

tiáohé 调和 V 1 mediate, reconcile 2 compromise

tiáojì 调剂 V adjust, regulate

tiáojié 调节 V regulate, adjust
调节器 **tiáojiéqì** regulator, conditioner

tiáojiě 调解 [comp: 调 adjust + 解 solve] V mediate, make peace
调解纠纷 **tiáojiě jiūfēn** mediate a dipute

tiáoliào 调料 N condiment, seasoning

tiáopí 调皮 ADJ naughty, mischievous

tiáozhěng 调整 [comp: 调 adjust + 整 rectify] V adjust, rectify

tiǎo 挑 V poke, pick up

tiǎobō 挑拨 [comp: 挑 poke + 拨 stir] V sow discord, instigate
挑拨同事之间的关系 **tiǎobō tóngshì zhījiān de guānxi** sow discord among colleagues

tiǎoxìn 挑衅 [v+obj: 挑 pick up + 衅 quarrel] V & N provoke; provocation
故意挑衅 **gùyì tiǎoxìn** deliberate provocation

tiǎozhàn 挑战 V & N challenge to battle, challenge to a contest, throw down the gauntlet; challenge

tiào 跳 V jump

tiàogāo 跳高 N high jump

tiàoshéng 跳绳 N rope-skipping, rope-jumping

tiàoshuǐ 跳水 V & N dive; diving

tiàowǔ 跳舞 [comp: 跳 jump + 舞 dance] V dance

tiàoyuǎn 跳远 N long jump

tiàoyuè 跳跃 V jump, leap

tiē 贴 TRAD 貼 V paste, stick

tiě 帖 N note, card

tiězi 帖子 N brief note, message
(张 **zhāng**, 份 **fèn**)

tiě 铁 TRAD 鐵 N iron

tiělù 铁路 [modif: 铁 iron + 路 road] N railway (条 **tiáo**)

tīng 厅 TRAD 廳 N hall (See **cāntīng** 餐厅)

tīng 听 TRAD 聽 V listen
听见 **tīngjiàn** hear ▪ 我听见有人在花园里叫我。 **Wǒ tīngjiàn yǒu rén zài huāyuán li jiào wǒ.** I heard somebody calling me in the garden.

tīnghuà 听话 v heed, be obedient

tīngshuō 听说 v hear of, people say

tīngxiě 听写 N & v dictation; do dictation

tíng 停 v stop, park (a vehicle)
　停下来 **tíng xiàlai** come to a stop

tíngbó 停泊 v (of ships) lie at anchor,
　anchor

tíngchē 停车 [v+obj: 停 park + 车 car] v
　stop a car, park a car

tíngchēchǎng 停车场 N parking lot,
　car park

tíngdùn 停顿 v pause, halt

tíngzhǐ 停止 [comp: 停 stop + 止 stop] v
　stop, cease

tíngzhì 停滞 v stagnate, come to a
　standstill

tíng 亭 N pavilion, kiosk

tíngzi 亭子 N pavilion, kiosk

tíng 庭 N front courtyard (See **jiātíng**
　家庭)

tǐng 挺[1] ADV very ■ 她学习挺认真。
　Tā xuéxí tǐng rènzhēn. *She studies
　conscientiously.*

NOTE: 挺 **tǐng** and 很 **hěn** share the same
meaning, but 挺 **tǐng** is a colloquial word.

tǐng 挺[2] ADJ hard and straight

tǐngbá 挺拔 ADJ tall and straight

tǐng 艇 N light boat
　救生艇 **jiù shēngtǐng** lifeboat

tōng 通 I v (of roads, railways) lead to,
　go to II ADJ logical, coherent, reasonable

tōngcháng 通常 ADV general, usual

tōngguò 通过 [comp: 通 go through +
　过 pass] I v pass through II PREP through,
　as a result of

tōnghuò 通货 N currency, money

tōnghuò péngzhàng 通货膨胀 N
　inflation
　抑制通货膨胀 **yìzhì tōnghuò péngzhàng**
　to check inflation

tōngjī 通缉 v list someone as wanted

tōngsú 通俗 ADJ easily understood and
　accepted by common folks, popular

通俗读物 **tōngsú dúwù** light reading

tōngxùn 通讯 [v+obj: 通 communicate
　+ 讯 message] N communications

tōngyòng 通用 v be in common use, be
　current

tōngzhī 通知 v & N notify, inform; notice,
　circular

tóng 同 PREP with, along with

tóngbāo 同胞 N fellow-countryman,
　compatriot

tóngqíng 同情 [modif: 同 same + 情
　emotion] v & N sympathize with; sym-
　pathy

tóngshí 同时 [modif: 同 same + 时
　time] N at the same time, simultaneously

tóngshì 同事 [modif: 同 same + 事 job]
　N colleague

tóngwū 同屋 [modif: 同 same + 屋
　room] N roommate, flatmate

tóngxué 同学 [modif: 同 together + 学
　study] N classmate, schoolmate
　老同学 **lǎotóngxué** former schoolmate

NOTE: In Chinese schools, teachers address
students as 同学们 **tóngxuémen**, e.g. ■ 同
学们，我们现在上课了。**Tóngxuémen,
wǒmen xiànzài shàngkè le.** *Class, we're
starting class now.*

tóngyàng 同样 [modif: 同 same + 样
　way] ADJ same

tóngyì 同意 [modif: 同 same + 意
　opinion] v agree, approve (ANTONYM 反
　对 **fǎnduì**)

tóngzhì 同志 [comp: 同 same + 志
　aspiration] N comrade

NOTE: 同志 **tóngzhì** used to be the most
common form of address in China before
1980. Now it is seldom used. 同志 **tóngzhì**
is almost never used between a Chinese
and a foreigner. The common forms of
address in China today are 先生 **xiānsheng**
(to men) and 小姐 **xiǎojiě** (to women,
especially young women). In some places
同志 **tóngzhì** has acquired the meaning of
a fellow homosexual.

tóng 铜 TRAD 銅 N copper (Cu)

tóngkuàng 铜矿 N copper mine

tóng 童 N child (See **értóng** 儿童.)

tónghuà 童话 N children's story, fairy tale

tóngnián 童年 N childhood

tǒng 桶 N bucket, pail (只 **zhī**)

tǒng 统 TRAD 統 ADJ together

tǒngjì 统计 [modif: 统 together + 计 calculate] V & N add up; statistics

tǒngtǒng 统统 ADV all, entirely

tǒngyī 统一 I V unify, integrate II ADJ unified

tǒngzhì 统治 [comp: 统 lead + 治 govern] V control and run a country, rule

tòng 痛 V Same as 疼 **téng** V 1

tòngkǔ 痛苦 [comp: 痛 painful + 苦 bitter] ADJ painful, bitter, tortuous

tòngkuai 痛快 [comp: 痛 to one's heart's content + 快 delight] ADJ 1 overjoyed, very delighted 2 to one's great satisfaction 3 direct, forthright

tōu 偷 V steal, pilfer

tōutōu 偷偷 ADV stealthily, on the quiet

tóu 头 TRAD 頭 I N 1 the head 2 foreman, chief II ADJ first, first few III MEASURE WORD (for cattle or sheep) 一头牛 **yì tóu niú** a head of cattle (or buffalo/cow) / 两头羊 **liǎng tóu yáng** two sheep

tóufa 头发 [modif: 头 head + 发 hair] N hair (of the human head) (根 **gēn**)

tóu 投 V throw

tóujī 投机[1] I V & N speculate, engage in speculation; speculation 货币投机 **huòbì tóujī** currency speculation II ADJ opportunistic 投机分子 **tóujīfènzǐ** opportunist

tóujī 投机[2] ADJ agreeable, congenial, of the same mind 谈得很投机 **tán de hěn tóujī** have a most agreeable conversation

tóupiào 投票 V cast a vote, vote

tóurù 投入 [comp: 投 throw + 入 enter] V put into, invest

tóuxiáng 投降 V surrender, capitulate

tóuzhì 投掷 [comp: 投 throw + 掷 throw] V throw, hurl

tóuzī 投资 [v+obj: 投 put + 资 capital] V & N invest; investment 投资在一家合资企业 **tóuzī zài yìjiā hézī qǐ yè** invest in a joint-venture / 投资的回报 **tóuzī de huíbào** return on an investment

tòu 透 I V penetrate, pass through II ADJ thorough

tòulù 透露 V let on about, leak, disclose

tòumíng 透明 [comp: 透 thorough + 明 clear, bright] ADJ transparent

tòumíngdù 透明度 N transparency

tū 秃 ADJ having no hair, bald

tū 突 ADJ protruding

tūchū 突出 [comp: 突 protrude + 出 out] I ADJ prominent, conspicuous II V give prominence, emphasize, highlight

tūpò 突破 [modif: 突 sudden + 破 break] V & N break through, make a breakthrough; breakthrough

tūrán 突然 [suffix: 突 sudden + 然 adjectival suffix] ADJ & ADV sudden; suddenly

tú 图 TRAD 圖 N picture, drawing, chart, diagram (张 **zhāng**)

tú'àn 图案 N pattern, design

túshūguǎn 图书馆 [modif: 图书 books + 馆 building] N library (座 **zuò**)

tú 涂 TRAD 塗 V smear, spread on

tú 徒 N apprentice

túdì 徒弟 [comp: 徒 apprentice + 弟 younger brother] N apprentice, pupil

tú 途 N way, route

tújìng 途径 [comp: 途 way + 径 footpath] N way, road, path

tǔ 土 N soil, earth

tǔdì 土地 [comp: 土 soil + 地 land] N land

tǔdòu 土豆 [modif: 土 soil + 豆 bean] N potato (只 **zhī**, 块 **kuài**)

tǔrǎng 土壤 N soil 肥沃的土壤 **féiwò de tǔrǎng** fertile soil

tǔ 吐 v spit, exhale

tù 吐 v vomit

tù 兔 N rabbit, hare

tùzi 兔子 [suffix: 兔 rabbit, hare + 子 nominal suffix] N rabbit, hare (只 zhī)

tuán 团 TRAD 團 N (military) regiment; group, team
代表团 dàibiǎotuán delegation / 旅行团 lǚxíngtuán tour group / 歌舞团 gēwǔtuán song and dance troupe

tuánjié 团结 [comp: 团 rally around + 结 tie up] v unite, be in solidarity with

tuántǐ 团体 N organization, group

tuányuán 团圆 v & N reunite with family members; family reunion

tuī 推 v push

tuīchí 推迟 [v+compl: 推 push + 迟 late] v postpone

tuīcí 推辞 v decline, turn down

tuīdòng 推动 [v+compl: 推 push + 动 move] v push forward, promote

tuīguǎng 推广 [v+compl: 推 push + 广 wide] v popularize, spread

tuījiàn 推荐 [comp: 推 push + 荐 recommend] v recommend

tuǐ 腿 N leg (条 tiáo)

tuì 退 v move back, retreat

tuìbù 退步 v retrogress, lag behind

tuìkuǎn 退款 v refund, ask for refund

tuìxiū 退休 v & N retire (from employment); retirement

tuìxiūjīn 退休金 N pension, superannuation

tūn 吞 v swallow

tūn tūn tǔ tǔ 吞吞吐吐 IDIOM hesitant in speech, hum and haw

tūnyàn 吞咽 v swallow, gulp down

tuō 托 v entrust, ask

tuōyùn 托运 v consign for shipment

tuō 拖 v drag on, defer, procrastinate

tuō 脱 v take off (clothes, shoes, etc.)
脱衣服 tuō yīfu take off clothes / 脱帽子 tuō màozi take off one's hat / 脱鞋 tuō xié take off one's shoes

tuǒyuán 椭圆 N oval
椭圆形 tuǒyuánxíng oval shape

tuò 唾 N saliva

tuòmo 唾沫 N saliva, spittle

tuòqì 唾弃 v spurn with contempt, disdain and reject

W

wā 蛙 N frog
青蛙 qīngwā frog

wā 挖 v evacuate, dig, unearth

wǎ 瓦 N tile (片 piàn)

wà 袜 TRAD 襪 N stocking

wàzi 袜子 [suffix: 袜 stocking + 子 nominal suffix] N stocking, sock (只 zhī, 双 shuāng)
穿袜子 chuān wàzi put on socks, wear socks / 脱袜子 tuō wàzi take off socks

wāi 歪 ADJ not straight, askew, crooked

wāiqū 歪曲 [comp: 歪 askew + 曲 bend] v distort, misinterpret

wài 外 N outside (ANTONYM 里 lǐ)

wàibian 外边 [modif: 外 outside + 边 side] N outside (ANTONYM 里边 lǐbian)

wàidì 外地 [modif: 外 outside + 地 place] N parts of the country other than where one is (ANTONYM 本地 běndì)

wàidìrén 外地人 N one who is from other parts of the country, not a native

wàigōng 外公 N (maternal) granddad

wàiguó 外国 [modif: 外 outside + 国 country] N foreign country

wàiguórén 外国人 N foreigner

wàiguóhuò 外国货 N foreign products, foreign goods

wàijiāo 外交 [modif: 外 external + 交 deal with] N foreign affairs, diplomacy

Wàijiāobù 外交部 N Ministry of Foreign Affairs

Wàijiāo bùzhǎng 外交部长 N Minister of Foreign Affairs

wàijiāoguān 外交官 N diplomat

wàimiàn 外面 N Same as 外边 wàibian

wàipó 外婆 N (maternal) grandma

wàiwén 外文 [modif: 外 foreign + 文 writing] N foreign language (especially its writing) (门 mén)

wàiyǔ 外语 [modif: 外 foreign + 语 language] N foreign language (门 mén) ■ 懂一门外语很有用。Dǒng yì mén wàiyǔ hěn yǒuyòng. *Knowing a foreign language is useful.*

wān 弯 TRAD 彎 ADJ curved, tortuous

wān 湾 TRAD 灣 N bay, gulf (See Táiwān 台湾.)

wán 丸 N bolus, pill (粒 lì, 颗 kē)

wán 完 V finish, end
吃完 chīwán finish eating, eat up / 看完 kànwán finish reading/watching / 做完 zuòwán finish doing / 用完 yòngwán use up

wánchéng 完成 [comp: 完 finish + 成 accomplish] V accomplish, fulfill, complete

wánměi 完美 ADJ perfect, flawless
不完美 bù wánměi imperfect

wánquán 完全 [comp: 完 finished + 全 all] ADJ complete, whole

wánshàn 完善 I ADJ complete and perfect, consummate II V make perfect, improve

wánzhěng 完整 [comp: 完 complete + 整 whole] ADJ complete, integrated, intact

wánr 玩儿 [suffix: 玩 play + 儿 suffix] V play; have fun

NOTE: Though 玩儿 **wánr** is often glossed as *to play*, its basic meaning is *to have fun* or *to have a good time*. It can refer to many kinds of activities and therefore has a very wide application. More examples: ■ 我们常常到小明家去玩儿。**Wǒmen chángcháng dào Xiǎo Míng jiā qu wánr.** *We often go to Xiao Ming's home to have a good time (e.g. singing, dancing, playing*

cards, playing games or just chatting). ■ 上星期天我们在海边玩儿得真高兴! **Shàng Xīngqītiān wǒmen zài hǎibiān wánr de zhēn gāoxìng.** *We had a wonderful time by the seaside last Sunday.* ■ 我想去香港玩儿。**Wǒ xiǎng qù Xiānggǎng wánr.** *I want to have a holiday in Hong Kong.*

wánjù 玩具 N toy

wǎn 晚 ADJ late, not early, not on time

wǎnfàn 晚饭 [modif: 晚 supper + 饭 meal] N evening meal, supper, dinner (顿 dùn)
做晚饭 zuò wǎnfàn cook supper, prepare dinner

wǎnhuì 晚会 [modif: 晚 evening + 会 assembly] N evening party, an evening of entertainment

wǎnnián 晚年 N old age
安度晚年 āndù wǎnnián enjoy one's old age in peace

wǎnshang 晚上 N evening
今天晚上(今晚) jīntiān wǎnshang (jīnwǎn) this evening / 昨天晚上(昨晚) zuótiān wǎnshang (zuówǎn) yesterday evening

wǎn 碗 N bowl (只 zhī)
菜碗 càiwǎn dish bowl, big bowl / 饭碗 fànwǎn rice bowl; livelihood, job

wàn 万 TRAD 萬 NUMERAL ten thousand
一万两千三百 yíwàn liǎngqiān sānbǎi twelve thousand and three hundred (12,300) / 二十万 èrshí wàn two hundred thousand (200,000) / 一百万 yì bǎiwàn one million (1,000,000)/ 一千万 yì qiānwàn ten million (10,000,000)

NOTE: 万 **wàn** (ten thousand) is an important number in Chinese. While English has four basic digits (one, ten, hundred and thousand), Chinese has five (个 **gè** one, 十 **shí** ten, 百 **bǎi** hundred, 千 **qiān** thousand, 万 **wàn** ten thousand). The Chinese use 万 **wàn** to mean *ten thousand*. Therefore *a hundred thousand* is 十万 **shí wàn**. In Chinese-speaking communities in

Southeast Asia, some people use 十千 **shíqiān** for ten thousand, e.g. 三十千 **sānshíqiān** 30,000. This is, however, not acceptable in standard Chinese.

wànyī 万一 CONJ in the unlikely event of, in case

wáng 王 N king
国王 **guówáng** king (of a kingdom)

wángguó 王国 N kingdom
丹麦王国 **Dānmài wángguó** the Kingdom of Denmark

wánghòu 王后 N queen (位 **wèi**)

wángzǐ 王子 N prince (位 **wèi**)

wáng 亡 V die, perish (See **sǐwáng** 死亡.)

wǎng 网 TRAD 網 N net

wǎngbā 网吧 [modif: 网 net, network + 吧 bar] N Internet café (座 **zuò**, 家 **jiā**)

wǎngguò 网购 V & N shop online; online shopping

wǎngluò 网络 [modif: 网 net + 络 net, network] N Internet, network
网络营销 **wǎngluò yíngxiāo** Internet marketing

wǎngmín 网民 N netizen

wǎngqiú 网球 [modif: 网 net + 球 ball] N tennis

wǎngqiúchǎng 网球场 N tennis court

wǎngzhàn 网站 [modif: 网 net, network + 站 station] N website

wǎngzhàn yùnyíng 网站运营 N website operation

wǎng 往 PREP towards, in the direction of

wǎngfǎn 往返 V journey to and from, make a round trip

wǎngshì 往事 N past events, the past
回忆往事 **huíyì wǎngshì** recollect past events, reflect upon the past

wàng 忘 V forget

wàngjì 忘记 V Same as 忘 **wàng**

wàng 望 V look at, gaze into the distance
■ 举头望明月。 **Jǔ tóu wàng míngyuè.**
I look up to gaze at the bright moon.
(A line from a poem by the Tang

Dynasty poet Li Bai)

wàng 旺 ADJ flourishing, thriving (See **xīngwàng** 兴旺.)

wēi 危 ADJ perilous

wēihài 危害 [comp: 危 endanger + 害 damage] V & N endanger; danger

wēixiǎn 危险 [comp: 危 perilous + 险 risky] N & ADJ danger, risk; dangerous, in danger

wēi 威 N an awesome force

wēixié 威胁 V & N pose a threat, threaten; threat

wēi 微 ADJ small

wēibó 微博 N microblog, microblogging

wēixiào 微笑 [modif: 微 small + 笑 smile, laugh] V smile

wēixìn 微信 N micro-channel, WeChat

wéi 围 TRAD 圍 V enclose, surround

wéirào 围绕 [comp: 围 enclose + 绕 around] V 1 move around, encircle 2 center on, focus on

wéi 违 TRAD 違 V disobey

wéifǎn 违反 [comp: 违 disobey + 反 counter] V run counter to, violate

wéi 唯 ADV only

NOTE: In some cases, 唯 is also written as 惟.

wéiwùlùn 唯物论 N materialism

wéixīnlùn 唯心论 N idealism

wéiyī 唯一 [comp: 唯 only + 一 one] ADJ the only one, sole

wéi 维 TRAD 維 V preserve, safeguard

wéishēng sù 维生素 N vitamins

wéixiū 维修 [comp: 维 preserve + 修 repair] V keep in good condition, maintain (a machine, a house, etc.)

wěi 伟 TRAD 偉 ADJ big

wěidà 伟大 [comp: 伟 big + 大 big] ADJ great, grand, outstanding

wěi 尾 N tail, end

wěiba 尾巴 N tail (条 **tiáo**)

wèi 卫 TRAD 衛 V defend, protect

wèishēng 卫生 [v+obj: 卫 defend +

生 life] N hygiene, sanitation
个人卫生 gèrén wèishēng hygiene, personal hygiene / 公共卫生 gōnggòng wèishēng sanitation, public sanitation / 环境卫生 huánjìng wèishēng environmental sanitation

wèishēngjiān 卫生间 N bathroom, washroom, toilet

wèishēngjú 卫生局 N Bureau of Public Health, Health Department,

wèi 为 TRAD 為 PREP (do, work) for the benefit of

wèile 为了 V & PREP in order to, for the purpose of ▪ 他这样辛辛苦苦地工作，都是为了孩子。Tā zhèyàng xīn-xīn-kǔ-kǔ de gōngzuò, dōu shì wèile háizi. *He works so hard, all for his children.*

NOTE: Both 为 **wèi** and 为了 **wèile** can be used as prepositions and have similar meanings, but 为了 **wèile** is more commonly used in everyday Chinese.

wèishénme 为什么 [v+obj: 为 for + 什么 what] ADV why, what for

wèi 未 ADJ have not, did not

NOTE: 未 **wèi** is only used in rather formal, written styles. In everyday Chinese, 没有 **méiyǒu** is used instead.

wèibì 未必 ADV not necessarily, may not

wèilái 未来 N future, next, the time to come

wèi 位[1] MEASURE WORD (a polite measure word used with people)
一位老师 yí wèi lǎoshī a teacher

wèi 位[2] N place, location

wèiyú 位于 V be located in, be situated

wèizhi 位置 [comp: 位 seat + 置 locate] N 1 place, location 2 (abstract) position, post

wèi 味 N taste, flavor

wèidao 味道 N taste, flavor

wèi 胃 N stomach

wèikǒu 胃口 N appetite, interest (in something)

wèi 谓 TRAD 謂 V be called (See suǒwèi 所谓.)

wèi 喂 INTERJ 1 hey ▪ 喂，你的票呢？Wèi, nǐ de piào ne? *Hey, where's your ticket?* 2 hello, hi ▪ 喂，这里是大华公司，您找谁？Wèi, zhèlǐ shì Dàhuá Gōngsī, nín zhǎo shuí? *Hello, this is Dahua Company. Who would you like to speak to?*

NOTE: In telephone conversation 喂 **wèi** is equivalent to *hello*. In other contexts, 喂 **wèi** is a rude way of getting people's attention. It is more polite to say 对不起 **duìbuqǐ**, e.g. ▪ 对不起，先生，您的票呢？**Duìbuqǐ, xiānsheng, nín de piào ne?** *Excuse me, sir, where's your ticket?*

wēn 温 ADJ warm, temperate, gentle

wēndù 温度 [modif: 温 warmth + 度 degree] N (atmospheric) temperature

NOTE: (1) 温度 **wēndù** generally refers to atmospheric temperature only. For body temperature the expression is 体温 **tǐwēn**, e.g. ▪ 人的正常体温是多少？**Rénde zhèngcháng tǐwēn shì duōshǎo?** *What is the normal temperature of a human being?* When a person has a fever, however, 热度 **rèdù** is used to refer to his/her temperature, e.g. ▪ 他今天热度还很高。**Tā jīntiān rèdù hái hěn gāo.** *He is still running a fever.* (2) The Chinese use the centigrade system, which is called 摄氏 **shèshì**, e.g. ▪ 今天最高温度摄氏二十八度。**Jīntiān zuì gāo wēndù shèshì èrshíbā dù.** *Today's maximum temperature is 28 degrees centigrade.* In everyday usage, however, people usually omit 摄氏 **shèshì**.

wēnnuǎn 温暖 [comp: 温 warm + 暖 warm] ADJ warm

wēnróu 温柔 [comp: 温 gentle + 柔 soft] ADJ (of people) gentle and soft, soothing

wén 文 N culture

wénběn 文本 N text file

wénhuà 文化 N culture, civilization; education, schooling

wénjiàn 文件 N document, file (份 fèn)
文件管理 wénjiàn guǎnlǐn file management

wénjù 文具 N stationery, writing material

wénmíng 文明 [comp: 文 culture + 明 enlightenment] N & ADJ civilization, culture; civilized, cultured

wénxué 文学 N literature
　文学家 **wénxuéjiā** (great) writer

wényì 文艺 [comp: 文 literature + 艺 art] N literature and art; performing arts
　文艺晚会 **wényì wǎnhuì** an evening of entertainment, soirée

wénzhāng 文章 [comp: 文 writing + 章 chapter] N essay, article (篇 **piān**)

wénzì 文字 [comp: 文 writing + 字 script] N written language, script, character
　文字处理 **wénzì chǔlǐ** word processing

wén 纹 TRAD 紋 N lines, veins

wén 蚊 N mosquito

wénzi 蚊子 [suffix: 蚊 mosquito + 子 nominal suffix] N mosquito (只 **zhī**)

wén 闻 TRAD 聞 N what is heard (See xīnwén 新闻.)

wěn 稳 TRAD 穩 ADJ steady, stable

wěndìng 稳定 [comp: 稳 stable + 定 fixed] ADJ stable

wěn 吻 V & N kiss

wèn 问 TRAD 問 V ask (a question), inquire

wèn hǎo 问好 V ask after, give greetings to

wènhòu 问候 V give regards to, send regards to, ask after

wènlù 问路 V ask the way

wèntí 问题 [comp: 问 inquiry + 题 question] N question, problem, issue

wǒ 我 PRON I, me

wǒmen 我们 [suffix: 我 I, me + 们 suffix denoting a plural number] PRON we, us

wò 卧 V lie
　卧床休息 **wòchuáng xiūxi** lie in bed and rest

wòshì 卧室 N bedroom (间 **jiān**)

wò 握 V hold, grasp

wòshǒu 握手 [v+obj: 握 hold + 手 hand] V shake hands

wū 污 N filth

wūrǎn 污染 [comp: 污 soil + 染 dye] V & N pollute; pollution

wūrǔ 污辱 V humiliate, insult, tarnish

wū 屋 N house, room

wūzi 屋子 [suffix: 屋 house, room + 子 nominal suffix] N room (间 **jiān**)

NOTE: 屋子 **wūzi** in the sense of *room* is only used in north China. To southern Chinese 屋子 **wūzi** may mean *house*. To avoid ambiguity, it is better to use the word 房间 **fángjiān** for *room*.

wú 无 TRAD 無 V have no (ANTONYM 有 **yǒu**)

wúcóng 无从 V have no way (of doing something), be not in a position (to do something)

wú kě fèng gào 无可奉告 IDIOM no comment

wú kě nàihé 无可奈何 IDIOM there is no way out, have no alternative, helpless

wúliáo 无聊 ADJ 1 bored 2 silly, meaningless

wúlùn 无论 CONJ Same as 不管 **bùguǎn**. Tends to be used in writing.

wúnài 无奈 ADV having no alternative, helplessly

wúshù 无数 [modif: 无 no + 数 number] ADJ innumerable, countless

wúsuǒwèi 无所谓 I V doesn't matter II ADJ indifferent, apathetic

wǔ 五 NUMERAL five, 5

wǔ 午 N noon

wǔfàn 午饭 [modif: 午 noon + 饭 meal] N lunch (顿 **dùn**)

wǔ 武 N military

wǔqì 武器 [modif: 武 military + 器 artifact] N weapon (件 **jiàn**)
　大规模杀伤武器 **dàguīmó shāshāng wǔqì** weapon of mass destruction (WMD)

wǔshù 武术 [modif: 武 martial + 术 arts] N martial arts

wǔ 舞 N dance

wǔtái 舞台 N stage, arena

wù 务 TRAD 務 v work

wùshí 务实 ADJ pragmatic, practical

wù 勿 v do not, don't ∎ 请勿吸烟。
Qǐngwù xīyān. *Please do not smoke*
(→ No smoking. Smoke-free.)

wù 物 N things, objects

wùjià 物价 [modif: 物 thing + 价 price]
N price, commodity price

wùlǐ 物理 [modif: 物 things, objects +
理 pattern, rule] N physics

wùtǐ 物体 N object, substance

wùzhì 物质 N matter, substance

wù 雾 霧 N fog, mist

wùmái 雾霾 N smog

wù 误 TRAD 誤 ADJ erroneous

wùhuì 误会 [modif: 误 mistaken + 会
understanding] V & N misunderstand,
misconstrue; misunderstanding

X

xī 西 N west, Western

xīběi 西北 [comp: 西 west + 北 north] N
northwest, the Northwest

xībian 西边 [modif: 西 west + 边 side] N
west side, to the west, in the west

xīcān 西餐 [modif: 西 West + 餐 meal] N
Western-style meal

xīcānguǎn 西餐馆 N Western-style
restaurant (家 jiā)

Xīfāng 西方 [modif: 西 West + 方
direction, part] N the West, Occident

xīfú 西服 [modif: 西 West + 服 clothes]
N 1 Western-style clothes 2 Western-
style coat (件 jiàn)

xīguā 西瓜 N watermelon (只 zhī)

xīhóngshì 西红柿 [modif: 西 Western +
红 red + 柿 persimmon] N tomato (只
zhī)

xīnán 西南 [comp: 西 west + 南 south]
N southwest, the Southwest

xī 吸 v inhale, suck

xīqǔ 吸取 [comp: 吸 absorb + 取 take] v
absorb, draw
吸取教训 xīqǔ jiàoxun learn a lesson
(from past experience)

xīshōu 吸收 [comp: 吸 suck + 收
receive] v suck up, absorb

xīyān 吸烟 v smoke (a cigarette, a cigar,
etc)

xīyǐn 吸引 [comp: 吸 suck + 引 guide]
v attract
吸引力 xīyǐnlì attraction, appeal / 有吸
引力 yǒu xīyǐnlì attractive, appealing

xī 希 v wish

xīwàng 希望 [comp: 希 wish + 望 look
forward to] V & N hope, wish

xī 惜 v 1 cherish, treasure (See zhēnxī 珍
惜.) 2 have pity on (See kěxī 可惜.)

xī 悉 v know (See shúxi 熟悉.)

xī 息 v cease (See xiūxi 休息.)

xí 习 TRAD 習 v practice

xíguàn 习惯 [comp: 习 be familiar
with + 惯 be accustomed to] V & N be
accustomed to, be used to; habit
习惯上 xíguàn shang habitually

xí 席 N seat (See chūxí 出席, zhǔxí 主席.)

xǐ 洗 v wash

xǐshǒujiān 洗手间 N toilet, restroom,
washroom

> NOTE: 洗手间 **xǐshǒujiān** is a common
> euphemism for *toilet.*

xǐyījī 洗衣机 [modif: 洗衣 wash clothes
+ 机 machine] N washing machine
(台 tái)

xǐzǎo 洗澡 [comp: 洗 wash + 澡 bath,
take a bath] v take a bath, take a shower
洗澡间 xǐzǎojiān bathroom, shower
room (Same as 浴室 yùshì.)

xǐ 喜 v be fond of

xǐhuan 喜欢 [comp: 喜 be fond of + 欢
pleasure] v like, be fond of

xì 戏 TRAD 戲 N drama, play (出 chū)

xìjù 戏剧 N drama, play, theater

xì 系 N department (of a university)

系主任 **xì zhǔrèn** chair of a (university) department

xìtǒng 系统 N a group of items serving a common purpose, system (套 tào)

xì 细 TRAD 細 ADJ thin, slender (of objects shaped like a strip) (ANTONYM 粗 cū)

xìjié 细节 N detail

xìxīn 细心 [modif: 细 tiny + 心 the heart] ADJ very careful, meticulous

xiā 瞎 ADJ blind

xià 下[1] N below, under, underneath (ANTONYM 上 shàng)
山下 **shānxia** at the foot of a mountain or hills

xià 下[2] V go/come down (ANTONYM 上 shàng)
下班 **xiàbān** get off work / 下车 **xiàchē** get off a vehicle / 下课 **xiàkè** finish class / 下来 **xiàlai** come down / 下去 **xiàqu** go down

xià 下[3] MEASURE WORD (used with certain verbs to indicate the number of times the action is done) ∎ 我试了几下，都不行。 **Wǒ shìle jǐ xià, dōu bù xíng.** *I tried several times, but it didn't work.* ... 一下 ... **yíxià** (used after a verb to indicate the action is done briefly or tentatively) ∎ 我看一下电视就去洗澡。 **Wǒ kàn yíxià diànshì, jiù qù xǐzǎo.** *I'll watch TV for a short while before taking a bath.*

xiàbian 下边 [modif: 下 below, underneath + 边 side] N below, under (ANTONYM 上边 shàngbian)

xiàmiàn 下面 N Same as 下边 xiàbian

xiàwǔ 下午 [modif: 下 lower half + 午 noon] N afternoon (ANTONYM 上午 shàngwǔ)

xiàzài 下载 [modif: 下 down, downward + 载 carry] V download

xià 吓 TRAD 嚇 V frighten, scare, be frightened, be scared

xià 夏 N summer

xiàlìngyíng 夏令营 N summer camp

xiàtiān 夏天 [modif: 夏 summer + 天 days] N summer

xiān 先 ADV first (in time sequence) (ANTONYM 后 hòu)
先 ... 再 ... **xiān ... zài ...** first ... and then...

xiānhòu 先后 [comp: 先 before + 后 later] ADV one after another, successively

xiānsheng 先生 [modif: 先 first, before + 生 born] N 1 Mr, mister 2 sir, gentleman 3 husband

xiān 仙 N immortal, fairy

xiān 鲜 TRAD 鮮 ADJ fresh

xiānhuā 鲜花 [modif: 鲜 fresh + 花 flower] N fresh flower, flower (朵 duǒ)

xiānyàn 鲜艳 [comp: 鲜 bright + 艳 fresh and attractive] ADJ bright-colored, gaily-colored

xián 咸 TRAD 鹹 ADJ salty

xián 闲 TRAD 閑 ADJ idle, unoccupied
清闲 **qīngxián** leisurely, carefree

xiánrén 闲人 N idler, uninvolved person

xiánshì 闲事 N matter that does not concern you

xiǎn 显 TRAD 顯 V appear, look

xiǎnde 显得 V appear to be, seem to be

xiǎnrán 显然 ADJ, ADV obvious; obviously

xiǎnshì 显示 [comp: 显 display + 示 show] V show, manifest

xiǎn 险 TRAD 險 ADJ dangerous (See wēixiǎn 危险.)

xiàn 县 TRAD 縣 N (rural) county

xiànchéng 县城 N county town, county seat

xiànzhǎng 县长 N mayor of a county

xiàn 现 TRAD 現 ADJ present, ready

xiàndài 现代 [modif: 现 present + 代 generation] N modern times, the contemporary age

xiàndàihuà 现代化 V & N modernize; modernization

xiànjīn 现金 [comp: 现 now, ready + 金 gold, money] N ready money, cash

xiànshí 现实 [comp: 现 present + 实 real] N & ADJ what is real, reality, actuality; realistic, practical

xiànxiàng 现象 N phenomenon

xiànzài 现在 [comp: 现 present + 在 being] N the present time, now

xiàn 线 TRAD 線 N string, thread, wire (根 gēn)

xiàn 限 v limit

xiànzhì 限制 [comp: 限 limit + 制 control] v limit, restrict, confine

xiàn 羡 TRAD 羨 v admire, envy

xiànmù 羡慕 [comp: 羡 envy + 慕 envy] v envy, admire

xiàn 献 TRAD 獻 v offer (See gòngxiàn 贡献.)

xiāng 乡 TRAD 鄉 N rural town

xiāngxia 乡下 N countryside, rural area

xiāng 相 ADV each other, mutually

xiāngchǔ 相处 v get along (with each other)

xiāngdāng 相当 I ADJ suitable, appropriate II ADV fairly, rather, quite

xiāngduì 相对 ADV relatively, comparatively (ANTONYM 绝对 juéduì) 相对来说 xiāngduì láishuō relatively speaking / 相对论 xiāngduìlùn the theory of relativity

xiāngfǎn 相反 ADJ opposite, contrary

xiāngguān 相关 v be related to, be interrelated

xiānghù 相互 ADJ mutual, each other

xiāngsì 相似 ADJ similar to, be alike

xiāngtóng 相同 ADJ identical, same

xiāngxìn 相信 v believe, believe in

xiāng 箱 N box, chest

xiāngzi 箱子 [suffix: 箱 trunk + 子 nominal suffix] N trunk, chest, box, suitcase

xiāng 香 ADJ fragrant, sweet-smelling, aromatic

xiāngcháng 香肠 [modif: 香 savory + 肠 intestine] N sausage (根 gēn)

Xiānggǎng 香港 [modif: 香 fragrant + 港 harbor] N Hong Kong

xiāngjiāo 香蕉 [modif: 香 fragrant + 蕉 banana] N banana (根 gēn)

xiāngyān 香烟 [modif: 香 fragrant + 烟 smoke] N cigarette, incense smoke

xiāngzào 香皂 [modif: 香 fragrant + 皂 soap] N toilet soap, bath soap (块 kuài)

xiáng 详 TRAD 詳 ADJ detailed

xiángxì 详细 [comp: 详 in detail + 细 tiny] ADJ in detail, detailed

xiǎng 享 v enjoy

xiǎngshòu 享受 [comp: 享 enjoy + 受 experience] v & N enjoy; enjoyment

xiǎng 响 TRAD 響 ADJ loud, noisy

xiǎngliàng 响亮 ADJ loud and clear, resounding

xiǎng 想 v think 想一下 xiǎng yíxià think for a while, give ... some thought / 想办法 xiǎng bànfǎ think of a way (to do something)

xiǎngfǎ 想法 [modif: 想 thinking + 法 way, method] N what one thinks, idea, opinion

xiǎngniàn 想念 [comp: 想 think + 念 miss (someone)] v miss, remember with longing

xiǎngxiàng 想象 [v+obj: 想 think + 象 image] v imagine

xiàng 项 TRAD 項 MEASURE WORD item of something (for things that are composed of items or things considered to be components) 一项任务 yí xiàng rènwù a mission / 两项文件 liǎng xiàng wénjiàn two documents

xiàngliàn 项链 N necklace (条 tiáo) 戴一条珍珠项链 dài yì tiáo zhēnzhū xiànglián wear a pearl necklace

xiàngmù 项目 [comp: 项 item + 目 item] N item, project

xiàng 象[1] Same as 大象 dàxiàng

xiàng 象[2] I N appearance, shape, image II v imitate

xiàngqí 象棋 N chess (副 fù, 盘 pán)

国际象棋 guójì xiàngqí Western chess / 中国象棋 Zhōngguó xiàngqí Chinese chess / 下一盘象棋 xià yìpán xiàngqí play a game of chess

xiàng shēng zì 象声字 N sound-imitating word, onomatopoeia

xiàng xíng zì 象形字 N pictographic character, pictograph

xiàngzhēng 象征 V & N symbolize; symbol

xiàng 像 I v resemble, bear resemblance to, be like II N likeness of (a human being), portrait

xiàng 橡 N oak

xiàngjiāo 橡胶 N rubber
橡胶树 xiàngjiāoshù rubber tree

xiàngpí 橡皮 N eraser (a piece of rubber) (块 kuài)

xiàng 向 PREP in the direction of, towards

xiāo 消 v vanish

xiāochú 消除 [comp: 消 remove + 除 get rid of] v clear up, dispel

xiāodú 消毒 [v+obj: 消 dispel + 毒 toxin] v disinfect, sterilize

xiāofáng 消防 N fire-prevention and fire-fighting
消防车 xiāofángchē fire engine / 消防队 xiāofángduì fire brigade, fire department

xiāofèi 消费 v consume
消费品 xiāofèipǐn consumer commodities, consumer goods / 消费者 xiāofèizhě consumer

xiāohuà 消化 [comp: 消 eliminate + 化 exterminate] v digest

xiāojí 消极 ADJ lacking enthusiasm, passive (ANTONYM 积极 jījí)

xiāoshī 消失 [comp: 消 vanish + 失 lose] v disappear, vanish

xiāoxi 消息 [comp: 消 information + 息 news] N news, information (条 tiáo)

xiāo 销 TRAD 銷 v sell, market

xiāoshòu 销售 [comp: 销 sell + 售 sell] V & N sell; market
销售部 xiāoshòu bù sales department /

销售额 xiāoshòu'é money sales bring to a company, sales, takings / 销售量 xiāoshòuliàng sales volume

xiǎo 小 ADJ 1 small, little (ANTONYM 大 dà) 2 young

NOTE: "小 xiǎo + family name," like 小李 Xiǎo Lǐ, is a casual, friendly form of address to a person younger than oneself. See note on 老 lǎo for forms of address like 老李 Lǎo Lǐ.

xiǎochī 小吃 N small and inexpensive dishes, snacks

xiǎofèi 小费 N tip, gratuity

xiǎoháir 小孩儿 N Same as 孩子 háizi

xiǎohuǒzi 小伙子 N young man, lad

NOTE: See note on 姑娘 gūniang.

xiǎojiě 小姐 [comp: 小 young + 姐 elder sister] N young lady; Miss

NOTE: 小姐 xiǎojiě is a common form of address to a young (or not so young) woman. If her family name is not known, just use 小姐 xiǎojiě. 小姐 xiǎojiě is also the form of address for a waitress or female attendant, e.g. ■ 小姐，请给我一杯水。Xiǎojiě, qǐng gěi wǒ yì bēi shuǐ. *Please give me a glass of water.*

xiǎomài 小麦 N wheat

xiǎopéngyou 小朋友 N (a friendly form of address or reference to a child)

xiǎoqì 小气 ADJ stingy, miserly

xiǎoshí 小时 [modif: 小 small + 时 time] N hour
半小时 bàn xiǎoshí half an hour

xiǎoshuō 小说 [modif: 小 small + 说 talk] N novel, fiction (本 běn, 篇 piān)
爱情小说 àiqíng xiǎoshuō romance novel / 长篇小说 chángpiān xiǎoshuō novel / 短篇小说 duǎnpiān xiǎoshuō short story, story / 历史小说 lìshǐ xiǎoshuō historical novel

xiǎoshuōjiā 小说家 N (accomplished) novelist

xiǎotōu 小偷 [modif: 小 small, petty + 偷 thief] N thief

xiǎoxīn 小心 [modif: 小 small + 心 the heart] ADJ careful, cautious

xiǎoxué 小学 [modif: 小 small + 学 school] N primary school (座 zuò, 所 suǒ)

xiǎozǔ 小组 N small group (for work or study)

xiǎo 晓 TRAD 曉 V know

xiǎode 晓得 V Same as 知道 zhīdào. Only used in colloquial Chinese.

xiào 孝 N filial piety

xiàoshùn 孝顺 [comp: 孝 filial piety + 顺 obedience] V & N perform one's filial duties faithfully, be obedient and considerate of one's parents; filial piety

xiào 效 N effect

xiàoguǒ 效果 [comp: 效 effect + 果 result] N effect, result

xiàolǜ 效率 [modif: 效 effect + 率 rate] N efficiency

xiào 校 N school

xiàozhǎng 校长 [modif: 校 school + 长 chief] N headmaster, principal, university president, university vice chancellor

xiào 笑 V laugh, smile (ANTONYM 哭 kū) 大笑 dàxiào laugh

xiàohua 笑话 [modif: 笑 laughing + 话 talk] I N joke II V laugh at, ridicule

xiē 些 MEASURE WORD some, a few, a little 好些 hǎoxiē lots of, quite a few

xiē 歇 V take a rest

xié 斜 ADJ oblique, slanting

xié 鞋 N shoes (只 zhī, 双 shuāng) 凉鞋 liáng xié sandals / 皮鞋 pí xié leather shoes / 拖鞋 tuō xié slippers / 雨鞋 yǔ xié rubber boots / 运动鞋 yùndòng xié sports shoes

xié dài 鞋带 N shoelace, shoestring (条 tiáo, 根 gēn)

xié 协 TRAD 協 V join, assist

xiédìng 协定 [comp: 协 joint + 定 decision] N agreement, treaty

xiéhuì 协会 N association (an organization), society 环境保护者协会 huánjìng bǎohù zhě xiéhuì Environmentalists' Association

xiéshāng 协商 V discuss and seek advice, consult

xiě 血 N Same as xuè 血. Used only in colloquial Chinese.

xiě 写 TRAD 寫 V write, write with a pen

xiězuò 写作 V & N write as a professional writer, compose essays; writing

xiè 械 N tool

xiè 谢 TRAD 謝 V thank

xièxie 谢谢 V thank ▪ "谢谢你." "不客气." "Xièxie nǐ." "Bú kèqi." "Thank you." "You're welcome."

NOTE: There are many ways of replying to 谢谢你 xièxie nǐ, e.g. ▪ 不客气. **Bú kèqi.** *You don't have to be so polite.* ▪ 不用谢. **Bú yòng xiè.** *You don't have to thank me.* ▪ 没关系。**Méi guānxi.** *It doesn't matter.*

xiè 卸 V unload, discharge (See zhuāngxiè 装卸.)

xīn 心 N the heart, mind, feeling 用心 yòngxīn apply oneself to / 开心 kāixīn be joyous / 痛心 tòngxīn pained, agonized / 伤心 shāngxīn heartbroken

xīnlǐ 心理 [comp: 心 the heart + 理 theory] N mentality, psychology 心理分析 xīnlǐfēnxī psychoanalysis / 心理咨询 xīnlǐ zīxún psychological consultation

xīnlǐxué 心理学 N (the science of) psychology

xīnqíng 心情 [comp: 心 the heart + 情 emotion] N state of mind, mood

xīnzàng 心脏 [modif: 心 the heart + 脏 human organ] N the heart (as a medical term)

xīn 辛 ADJ spicy hot

xīnkǔ 辛苦 [comp: 辛 spicy hot + 苦 bitter] ADJ 1 hard and toilsome (job) 2 harsh, difficult (life)

xīnqín 辛勤 ADJ industrious, hard-working

xīn 欣 I ADJ joyful II v enjoy

xīnshǎng 欣赏 [comp: 欣 enjoy + 赏 appreciate] v 1 admire and enjoy 欣赏美丽的风光 **xīnshǎng měilì de fēngguāng** admire and enjoy beautiful sceneries
2 appreciate, like

xīn 新 ADJ new (ANTONYM 旧 jiù)

Xīnjiāpō 新加坡 N Singapore

xīnnián 新年 [modif: 新 new + 年 year] N New Year ■ 新年好！ **Xīnnián hǎo!** *Happy New Year!*
新年贺卡 **Xīnnián hèkǎ** New Year card

xīnwén 新闻 [modif: 新 new + 闻 what is heard] N news (of current affairs)

Xīnxīlán 新西兰 N New Zealand

xīnxiān 新鲜 [comp: 新 new + 鲜 fresh] ADJ fresh

xīn 薪 N 1 firewood 2 salary

xīnshuǐ 薪水 [comp: 薪 firewood + 水 water] N salary, pay

xìn 信¹ v believe

xìnniàn 信念 N faith, conviction

xìnrèn 信任 [comp: 信 trust + 任 entrust] v & N have confidence in (somebody), trust; confidence (in somebody), trust

xìnxīn 信心 [modif: 信 believe + 心 the heart] N confidence

xìnyòng 信用 N trustworthiness, credit 讲信用 **jiǎng xìnyòng** keep one's word, trustworthy

xìnyòngkǎ 信用卡 N credit card

xìnyǎng 信仰 v & N firmly believe in, have faith in; faith, belief, conviction 宗教信仰 **zōngjiào xìnyǎng** religious belief

xìn 信² N 1 letter, epistle 寄信 **jì xìn** post a letter / 介绍信 **jièshàoxìn** letter of recommendation, reference / 收到信 **shōudào xìn** receive a letter / 祝贺信 **zhùhèxìn** letter of

congratulation / 信封 **xìnfēng** envelope
2 message

xìnhào 信号 N signal

xìnxī 信息 [comp: 信 message + 息 news, tiding] N information

xīng 兴 TRAD 興 ADJ flourishing

xīngfèn 兴奋 [comp: 兴 flourishing + 奋 excited] ADJ excited, overjoyed

xīngfènjì 兴奋剂 N stimulant, dope

xīng 星 N celestial body, star (颗 kē) 恒星 **héngxīng** fixed star, star / 流星 **liúxīng** meteor / 行星 **xíngxīng** planet

NOTE: In everyday Chinese 星星 **xīngxīng** is normally used instead of 星 **xīng**, e.g. ■ 今天晚上的星星真亮。**Jīntiān wǎnshang de xīngxīng zhēn liàng.** *Tonight the stars are really bright.*

xīngqī 星期 N week 星期一 **Xīngqīyī** Monday / 星期二 **Xīngqīʼèr** Tuesday / 星期三 **Xīngqīsān** Wednesday / 星期四 **Xīngqīsì** Thursday / 星期五 **Xīngqīwǔ** Friday / 星期六 **Xīngqīliù** Saturday / 星期日 **Xīngqīrì** Sunday / 星期天 **Xīngqītiān** Sunday / 上星期 **shàng xīngqī** last week / 下星期 **xià xīngqī** next week

xíng 刑 ADJ penal, criminal

xíngshì 刑事 [modif: 刑 penal + 事 affair] ADJ criminal, penal 刑事犯 **xíngshìfàn** criminal offender, convict / 刑事案件 **xíngshì ànjiàn** criminal case

xíng 行¹ I v 1 travel, go ■ 三人行，必有我师。（孔子）**Sān rén xíng, bì yǒu wǒ shī. (Kǒngzǐ)** *When three people are walking together, at least one of them must be my teacher (Confucius). (→ One can always find someone good enough to be one's teacher.)* 2 practice II N trip

xíng 行² I v all right, OK, (that) will do II ADJ competent, capable

xíngdòng 行动 [comp: 行 work + 动 move] v & N move around; action, behavior, movement

xíngli 行李 N luggage, baggage (件 **jiàn**)

xíngrén 行人 [modif: 行 travel, go + 人 person] N pedestrian
行人道 **xíngréndào** sidewalk / 行人横道线 **xíngrén héngdào xiàn** pedestrian crossing

xíngwéi 行为 N behavior, conduct, act

xíng 形 N form, shape

xíngchéng 形成 [v+obj: 形 form + 成 become] V take shape, form

xíngróng 形容 V describe

xíngshì 形式 [comp: 形 shape + 式 manner] N form, shape (ANTONYM 内容 **nèiróng**)

xíngshì 形势 [comp: 形 shape + 势 force] N situation

xíngxiàng 形象 [comp: 形 shape + 象 image] N image, imagery

xíngzhuàng 形状 [comp: 形 shape + 状 shape] N appearance, shape, form

xíng 型 N model, type (See **dàxíng** 大型.)

xǐng 醒 V wake, wake up
睡醒 **shuìxǐng** have enough sleep / 叫醒 **jiàoxǐng** wake somebody up

xìng 兴 TRAD 興 ADJ joyful

xìngqù 兴趣 [comp: 兴 joy + 趣 interest] N interest
对 ⋯ 感兴趣 **duì ... gǎn xìngqù** be interested in ... / 对 ⋯ 有兴趣 **duì ... yǒu xìngqù** be interested in ... / 对 ⋯ 不感兴趣 **duì ... bù gǎn xìngqù** be uninterested in ... / 对 ⋯ 没有兴趣 **duì ... méiyǒu xìngqù** be uninterested in ...

xìng 性 N 1 nature, character 2 sex, gender

xìngbié 性别 N gender, sex

xìnggé 性格 N person's character, disposition, temperament ▪ 她性格很坚强。**Tā xìnggé hěn jiānqiáng.** *She has a strong character.*

xìngmìng 性命 N (human) life

xìngnéng 性能 N function, performance
性能良好 **xìngnéng liánghǎo** (of a machine) perform well, with satisfactory performance

xìngqíng 性情 [comp: 性 nature + 情 emotion] N disposition, temperament

xìngyù 性欲 N sexual desire, sex urge

xìngzhì 性质 [comp: 性 nature + 质 substance] N nature (of a matter, an event, etc.), basic quality

xìng 幸 N good fortune

xìngfú 幸福 [comp: 幸 good fortune + 福 happiness] ADJ happy, fortunate

NOTE: 幸福 **xìngfú** is used in a sublime sense, denoting a profound and almost perfect happiness. So it has a much more limited use than its English equivalents *happy* or *fortunate*. The usual Chinese word for *happy*, as in "I'm happy to hear the news," is 高兴 **gāoxìng**, e.g. ▪ 听到这个消息，我很高兴。**Tīngdào zhège xiāoxi, wǒ hěn gāoxìng.** *I'm happy to hear the news.*

xìnghǎo 幸好 ADV fortunately, luckily

xìngkuī 幸亏 ADV fortunately, luckily

xìngyùn 幸运 N good fortune, good luck

xìng 姓 N family name
贵姓 **guìxìng** your family name (polite usage, normally in a question) ▪ "您贵姓？" "我姓王。" **"Nín guìxìng?" "Wǒ xìng Wáng."** *"What's your family name?" "Wang."*

NOTE: The character 姓 **xìng** has the signific graph of 女 **nǚ**, meaning *female*, an indication that the Chinese once had a matriarchal society.

xìngmíng 姓名 [comp: 姓 family name + 名 given name] N full name

xiōng 兄 N elder brother

xiōngdì 兄弟 [comp: 兄 elder brother + 弟 younger brother] N brother(s)

xiōng 胸 N the chest, thorax

xiōnghuái 胸怀[1] V cherish
胸怀大志 **xiōnghuái dàzhì** have lofty aspirations, cherish high ideals

xiōnghuái 胸怀[2] N mind, breadth of mind, heart

胸怀宽广 **xiōnghuái kuānguǎng** broad-minded

xiōngtáng 胸膛 N the chest (of the human body)

xióng 雄 ADJ male (of animals) (**ANTONYM** 雌 **cí**)

xióng 熊 N bear (只 **zhī**)

xióngmāo 熊猫 [comp: 熊 bear + 猫 cat] N panda, giant panda (只 **zhī**)

xiū 修 v 1 Same as 修理 **xiūlǐ** 2 build, construct (a building, bridge, road, etc.)

xiūgǎi 修改 [comp: 修 repair + 改 alter] v amend, revise

xiūlǐ 修理 v repair, fix

xiū 休 N leisure

xiūxi 休息 [comp: 休 leisure + 息 pause] v rest, take a rest, have a day off

xiūxián 休闲 [comp: 休 leisure + 闲 idle] N leisure

休闲服 **xiūxián fú** casual clothes

xiù 秀 ADJ elegant (See **yōuxiù 优秀**.)

xiù 袖 N sleeve

xiùzi 袖子 N sleeve

xū 须 TRAD 須 MODAL v must (See **bìxū 必须**.)

xū 虚 ADJ void

xūxīn 虚心 [modif: 虚 empty + 心 the heart] ADJ open-minded and modest

xū 需 v need

xūyào 需要 [comp: 需 need + 要 want] v need, be in need of

xǔ 许 TRAD 許 v Same as 允许 **yúnxǔ**

xǔduō 许多 [comp: 许 approximate + 多 many, much] ADJ many, much

xǔkě 许可 v permit, allow

许可证 **xǔkězhèng** permit, license

xù 畜 v keep domesticated animals

xùchǎnpǐn 畜产品 N animal products

xù 续 TRAD 續 v continue (See **jìxù 继续**, **liánxù 连续**, etc.)

xù 绪 TRAD 緒 N mood (See **qíngxù 情绪**.)

xù 叙 TRAD 敘 v 1 chat 2 narrate

xùshù 叙述 v narrate

xuān 宣 v declare, publicize

xuānbù 宣布 v declare, announce

xuānchuán 宣传 [comp: 宣 announce + 传 spread] v & N disseminate, publicize; dissemination of information, propaganda

xuān 喧 ADJ noisy

xuǎn 选 TRAD 選 v 1 vote for 2 select, choose

xuǎnjǔ 选举 [comp: 选 select + 举 recommend] v & N elect, vote; election, voting ■ 参加大会的代表必须由选举产生。**Cānjiā dàhuì de dàibiǎo bìxū yóu xuǎnjǔ chǎnshēng.** *The delegates to the congress must be chosen by election.*

xuǎnzé 选择 [comp: 选 select + 择 choose] v & N select, choose; choice, alternative

xuē 削 v cut

xuējiǎn 削减 [comp: 削 cut + 减 decrease] v cut down, reduce

xué 学 TRAD 學 v learn, study

xuéfèi 学费 [modif: 学 study + 费 fee] N tuition, tuition fee

xuélì 学历 N record of formal schooling, record of education

xuéqī 学期 [modif: 学 study + 期 period] N semester, term

xuésheng 学生 [modif: 学 study + 生 scholar] N student, pupil (个 **gè**, 名 **míng**)

xuéshù 学术 N learning, scholarship

学术会议 **xuéshù huìyì** (scholarly or scientific) conference, symposium

xuéwèi 学位 [modif: 学 study + 位 position] N academic degree

学士学位 **xuéshì xuéwèi** bachelor degree / 硕士学位 **shuòshì xuéwèi** master's degree, masterate / 博士学位 **bóshì xuéwèi** Ph.D. degree, doctorate

xuéwèn 学问 [comp: 学 study + 问 ask] N learning, knowledge

xuéxí 学习 [comp: 学 learn + 习 practice] v & N study, learn; study, studies

向 … 学习 **xiàng … xuéxí** learn from …, emulate … ■ 你工作很认真，我要

向你学习。**Nǐ gōngzuò hěn rènzhēn, wǒ yào xiàng nǐ xuéxí.** *You work conscientiously. I must emulate you.*

xuéxiào 学校 [comp: 学 study + 校 school] N school (座 **zuò**)

xuéyuàn 学院 [comp: 学 study + 院 place (for certain activities)] N college, institute

xuě 雪 N snow
下雪 **xià xuě** to snow

xuě bái 雪白 ADJ snow-white, pure white

xuè 血 N blood ▪ 流了一点血，不要紧。**Liúle yìdiǎn xuě, bú yàojǐn.** *It's just a little bleeding, nothing serious.*

xuèyā 血压 [modif: 血 blood + 压 pressure] N blood pressure
高血压 **gāoxuèyā** high blood pressure, hypertension / 低血压 **dīxuèyā** low blood pressure, hypotension

xuèyè 血液 [modif: 血 blood + 液 liquid] N blood (as a technical term)

xūn 熏 TRAD 燻 V treat with smoke, smoke
熏鱼 **xūnyú** smoked fish

xún 寻 TRAD 尋 V seek

xúnzhǎo 寻找 [comp: 寻 seek + 找 look for] V look for, seek

xún 巡 V patrol

xúnluó 巡逻 V patrol, go on patrol
巡逻艇 **xúnluótǐng** patrol boat

xún 询 TRAD 詢 V inquire

xúnwèn 询问 [comp: 询 inquire + 问 ask] V inquire, ask

xùn 迅 ADJ rapid

xùnsù 迅速 [comp: 迅 rapid, speedy + 速 swift] ADJ rapid, speedy, swift

xùn 训 TRAD 訓 V train

xùnliàn 训练 [comp: 训 train + 练 practice] V train, drill

Y

yā 压 TRAD 壓 V press, push down

yājià 压价 V undersell

yālì 压力 N pressure

yā 呀 INTERJ oh, ah (expressing surprise)

yā 押 V detain, take into custody

yājīn 押金 N cash pledge, deposit

yā 鸭 TRAD 鴨 N duck

yāzi 鸭子 N duck (只 **zhī**)

yā 鸦 TRAD 鴉 N crow
乌鸦 **wūyā** crow (只 **zhī**)

yá 牙 N tooth, teeth

yáchǐ 牙齿 [comp: 牙 tooth + 齿 tooth] N tooth, teeth (颗 **kē**)

yágāo 牙膏 [modif: 牙 tooth + 膏 paste, cream] N toothpaste (管 **guǎn**)

yáshuā 牙刷 [modif: 牙 tooth + 刷 brush] N toothbrush (把 **bǎ**)

yáyī 牙医 N dentist, dentistry

yá 芽 N sprout

yǎ 哑 TRAD 啞 ADJ mute

yǎba 哑巴 N speech-impaired person, dumb person

yǎ 雅 ADJ refined

yà 亚 TRAD 亞 ADJ inferior; Asia

Yàzhōu 亚洲 [modif: 亚 Asia + 洲 continent] N Asia

ya 呀 PARTICLE Same as 啊 **ā** II PARTICLE. Used after a, e, i, o, u.

yān 烟 TRAD 煙 N 1 smoke 2 Same as 香烟 **xiāngyān** ▪ 请勿吸烟。**Qǐngwù xīyān.** *No smoking.*
禁烟区 **jìnyān qū** smoke-free area

yán 延 V extend

yáncháng 延长 [v+compl: 延 extend + 长 long] V prolong, extend

yán 严 TRAD 嚴 ADJ strict, severe

yángé 严格 ADJ strict, stringent, rigorous

yánsù 严肃 [comp: 严 severe + 肃 solemn] ADJ serious, solemn, earnest

yánzhòng 严重 [comp: 严 severe + 重 weighty] ADJ serious, grave, critical

yán 言 n speech

yánlùn 言论 n opinion on public affairs, expression of one's political views
言论自由 **yánlùn zìyóu** freedom of speech

yán 研 v study, research

yánjiū 研究 [comp: 研 research + 究 investigate] v & n consider carefully, research, study; research, study

yánjiūshēng 研究生 n graduate student, post-graduate student
研究生院 **yánjiūshēng yuàn** graduate school (of a university)

yánjiūsuǒ 研究所 n research institute, research unit

yánjiūyuàn 研究院 n research institute

yán 盐 TRAD 鹽 n salt

yán 颜 TRAD 顔 n complexion

yánsè 颜色 [comp: 颜 complexion + 色 color] n color

yǎn 眼 n the eye, eye
左眼 **zuǒyǎn** the left eye / 右眼 **yòuyǎn** the right eye

yǎnkē yīshēng 眼科医生 n ophthalmologist

yǎnjìng 眼镜 [modif: 眼 eye + 镜 mirror] n glasses, spectacles (副 **fù**)
太阳眼镜 **tàiyang yǎnjìng** sunglasses

yǎnjing 眼睛 [comp: 眼 eye + 睛 eyeball] n eye

yǎnlèi 眼泪 [modif: 眼 eye + 泪 tear] n tears (滴 **dī**)
流眼泪 **liú yǎnlèi** shed tears

yǎnqián 眼前 n 1 before one's eyes 2 at present, at this moment

yǎnxià 眼下 n at present, at this moment, now

yǎn 演 v 1 act, perform, show 2 show (a film)

yǎnchū 演出 v & n put on a theatrical performance, perform; theatrical performance

yǎnjiǎng 演讲 [comp: 演 perform + 讲 speak] v & n deliver a formal speech, give a formal lecture; public lecture, speech

yǎnyuán 演员 [modif: 演 act + 员 person] n actor, actress

yàn 咽 v swallow

yàn 宴 n feast

yànhuì 宴会 [modif: 宴 feast + 会 meet] n banquet, feast
参加宴会 **cānjiā yànhuì** attend a banquet / 告别宴会 **gàobié yànhuì** farewell banquet / 欢迎宴会 **huānyíng yànhuì** welcome banquet / 结婚宴会 **jiéhūn yànhuì** wedding banquet

yáng 羊 n sheep, goat, lamb (头 **tóu**)
山羊 **shānyáng** goat / 小羊 **xiǎoyáng** lamb

yáng 阳 TRAD 陽 n what is open, overt, masculine, the sun

yángguāng 阳光 [modif: 阳 the sun + 光 light] n sunshine, sunlight

yángtái 阳台 n balcony

yángxìng 阳性 ADJ (of medical test result) positive (ANTONYM 阴性 **yīnxìng**)

yáng 扬 TRAD 揚 v raise, make known (See biǎoyáng 表扬.)

yáng 洋 n ocean (See hǎiyáng 海洋.)

yǎng 养 TRAD 養 v 1 provide for, support 2 raise, keep as pet

yǎng 痒 v itch, tickle
发痒 **fāyǎng** itch

yàng 样 TRAD 樣 MEASURE WORD kind, category, type

yàngpǐn 样品 n sample, sample product, specimen

yàngzi 样子 n appearance, shape, manner

yāoqiú 要求 [comp: 要 ask + 求 request] v & n ask, demand, require; demand, requirement
满足顾客的要求 **mǎnzú gùkè de yāoqiú** meet our clients' demands

yāo 腰 n waist, small of the back

yāo 邀 v invite

yāoqǐng 邀请 [comp: 邀 invite + 请 ask] v & n invite; invitation
邀请信 **yāoqǐngxìn** letter of invitation

yáo 摇 v shake, wave

yáohuàng 摇晃 v sway, swing, rock

yáo 遥 ADJ faraway

yáokòng 遥控 v remote control
遥控器 **yáokòngqì** (a device of) remote control

yáoyuǎn 遥远 [comp: 遥 faraway + 远 distant] ADJ faraway, remote, distant

yǎo 咬 v bite

yào 药 TRAD 藥 N medicine, drug
草药 **cǎoyào** herbal medicine / 吃药 **chī yào** take medicine / 配药 **pèi yào** fill a prescription / 西药 **xīyào** Western medicine / 中药 **zhōngyào** traditional Chinese medicine

yàofāng 药方 N prescription
开药方 **kāi yàofāng** write a prescription

yàofáng 药房 N pharmacist's, pharmacy

yàopiàn 药片 N pill

yàoshuǐ 药水 N liquid medicine

yào 要¹ I want, ask for, would like
II MODAL v should, must

yào 要² ADJ important, essential

yàobu 要不 CONJ otherwise, or else

yàoburán 要不然 Same as 要不 **yàobu**

yàojǐn 要紧 ADJ important, urgent, serious
不要紧 **búyàojǐn** it doesn't matter

yàoshì 要是 CONJ if

NOTE: Both 如果 **rúguǒ** and 要是 **yàoshì** mean *if*. While 如果 **rúguǒ** is for general use, 要是 **yàoshì** is a colloquialism.

yào 钥 TRAD 鑰 See **yàoshi** 钥匙

yàoshi 钥匙 N key (把 **bǎ**)

yé 爷 TRAD 爺 N paternal grandfather

yéye 爷爷 N Same as 祖父 **zǔfù**. Used in colloquial Chinese.

yě 也 I ADV also, too II CONJ neither, nor

yěxǔ 也许 ADV perhaps, maybe

NOTE: See note on 恐怕 **kǒngpà**.

yě 野 ADJ open country, wild

yěshēng 野生 [modif: 野 wild + 生 living] ADJ wild (animal or plant)

野生动物 **yěshēng dòngwù** wildlife / 野生植物 **yěshēng zhíwù** wild plant

yěshòu 野兽 [modif: 野 wild + 兽 beast] N wild beast, wild animal

yěwài 野外 N open country, field
野外作业 **yěwàizuòyè** field work

yè 业 TRAD 業 N industry

yèwù 业务 [comp: 业 occupation + 务 business] N 1 professional work, vocational work 2 business

yèyú 业余 ADJ spare time, amateur

yè 叶 TRAD 葉 N leaf

yèzi 叶子 [suffix: 叶 leaf + 子 nominal suffix] N leaf (片 **piàn**)

yè 页 TRAD 頁 N page

yè 夜 N night, evening.
夜班 **yèbān** night shift / 夜车 **yèchē** night train / 半夜 **bànyè** midnight

yèli 夜里 N at night

yèwǎn 夜晚 N Same as 夜里 **yèli**

yī 一 NUMERAL one ■ 一万一千一百一十一 **yíwàn yìqiān yìbǎi shíyī** *eleven thousand, one hundred and eleven (11,111)*

NOTES: (1) 一 undergoes tone changes (tone sandhi). When standing alone, 一 is pronounced with the first tone, i.e. **yī**. When followed by a sound in the fourth tone, 一 changes to the second tone, e.g. 一定 **yídìng**. 一 is pronounced in the fourth tone in all other circumstances, e.g. 一般 **yìbān**, 一同 **yìtóng**, 一起 **yìqǐ**. Pay attention to the various tones of 一 here and in following words. (2) When saying a number (e.g. a telephone number) people may pronounce 一 as **yāo** for clarity, e.g. ■ 我的电话号码是五八一三九。 **Wǒ de diànhuà hàomǎ shì wǔ-bā-yāo-sān-jiǔ.** *My telephone number is 5-8-1-3-9.*

yíbàn 一半 N half, one half

yìbān 一般 ADJ 1 generally speaking, ordinarily 2 average, commonplace 3 same as, as ... as

yíbèizi 一辈子 N one's entire life

yìbiān 一边 N one side

CONJ while ... at the same time ...,
simultaneously

NOTE: 一边 … 一边 … yìbiān … yìbiān …
links two verbs to indicate that the two
actions denoted by the verbs take place
simultaneously. Another example: ▪ 他常
常一边做作业一边听音乐。 **Tā chángcháng
yìbiān zuò zuòyè yìbiān tīng yīnyuè.** *He
often does his homework while listening to
music.* When the verbs are monosyllabic,
边 … 边 … **biān ... biān** ... may be used
instead of 一边 … 一边 … **yìbiān ... yìbiān
...** , e.g. ▪ 孩子们边走边唱。 **Háizimen biān
zǒu biān chàng.** *The children sang while
walking.* ▪ 我们边吃边谈吧。 **Wǒmen
biān chī biān tán ba.** *Let's carry on the
conversation while eating.*

yìdàn 一旦 CONJ once, some day

yídào 一道 ADV Same as 一起 yìqǐ

yìdiǎnr 一点儿 N a tiny amount, a bit

yídìng 一定 ADJ 1 fixed, specified 2 to a
certain degree, fair, limited 3 certainly,
definitely

yìfāngmiàn … **yìfāngmiàn** … 一方面
… 一方面 … CONJ on the one hand …
on the other hand …

yígòng 一共 ADV in all, total, altogether

yíhuìr 一会儿 ADV in a very short time,
in a moment

yī … **jiù** … 一 … 就 … CONJ as soon as,
no sooner … than … ▪ 妈妈一回家，就
做晚饭。 **Māma yì huíjiā, jiù zuò wǎnfàn.**
*Mom cooks supper as soon as she gets
back home.*

yíkuàir 一块儿 ADV Same as 一起 yìqǐ.
Tends to be used in colloquial Chinese.

yílǜ 一律 ADV all, without exception

yìqí 一齐 ADV Same as 一起 yìqǐ

yìqǐ 一起 ADV together

yíqiè 一切 I ADJ all, every and each
without exception II PRON all, everything

yìshēng 一生 N all one's life, lifetime

yìshí 一时 N for the time being,
momentarily

yìtóng 一同 ADV Same as 一起 yìqǐ

yíxià 一下 ADV (used after a verb to
indicate the action is done briefly or
casually) ▪ 请您等一下，王先生马
上就来。 **Qǐng nín děng yíxià, Wáng
xiānsheng mǎshàng jiù lái.** *Please wait
for a while. Mr Wang will be here in a
moment.*

NOTE: It is very common in spoken Chinese
to use 一下 yíxià after a verb, especially
as an informal request. Some Northern
Chinese speakers use 一下儿 yíxiàr instead
of 一下 yíxià. More examples: ▪ 请您来
一下儿。 **Qǐng nín lái yíxiàr.** *Please come
over for a while.* ▪ 我们在这里停一下儿
吧。 **Wǒmen zài zhèlǐ tíng yíxiàr ba.** *Let's
stop here for a while.* ▪ 让我想一下儿再回
答。 **Ràng wǒ xiǎng yíxiàr zài huídá.**
Let me think a while before I answer.

yíxiàzi 一下子 ADV all at once, all at a
sudden

yìxiē 一些 MEASURE WORD a small amount
of, a bit of

yíyàng 一样 ADJ same, identical

yízài 一再 ADV time and again, repeatedly

yìzhí 一直 ADV always, all the time

yízhì 一致 ADJ unanimous, identical

yī 衣 N clothing

yīfu 衣服 [comp: 衣 clothing + 服
clothing] N clothes, a piece of clothing
(件 jiàn)

NOTE: 衣服 yīfu may denote *clothes* or *a
piece of clothing.* 一件衣服 yí jiàn yīfu may
be a jacket, a coat, a dress or a sweater, but
not a pair of trousers, which is 一条裤子 yì
tiáo kùzi.

yī 依 V rely on

yīcì 依次 V in proper order, one by one

yītuō 依托 V rely on, depend on

yī 医 TRAD 醫 V heal, cure

yīshēng 医生 [modif: 医 medicine + 生
scholar] N medical doctor (位 wèi)

yīwùshì 医务室 [modif: 医 medical +
务 affair + 室 room] N clinic (in a
school, factory, etc.)

yīxué 医学 [modif: 医 medical + 学

study] N medical science, medicine
医学院 **yīxuéyuàn** medical school
yīyuàn 医院 [modif: 医 medicine + 院 place (for certain activities)] N hospital (座 **zuò**)
送 … 去医院 **sòng … qù yīyuàn** take … to the hospital / 住(医)院 **zhù (yī) yuàn** be hospitalized
yí 仪 TRAD 儀 N instrument
yíqì 仪器 [comp: 仪 instrument + 器 utensil] N instrument (件 **jiàn**)
yíshì 仪式 N ceremony, function, rite
举行仪式 **jǔxíng yíshì** hold a ceremony
yí 移 V move, shift
yídòng 移动 [comp: 移 move + 动 move] V move, shift
yídòng diànhuà 移动电话 N cordless telephone
yímín 移民 V & N immigrate, emigrate; immigrant, emigrant; immigration
移民局 **Yímínjú** Immigration Services
yí 疑 V doubt
yíwèn 疑问 [comp: 疑 doubt + 问 inquire] N doubt ■ 这个计划一定要实现，这是毫无疑问的。 **Zhège jìhuà yídìng yào shíxiàn, zhè shì háowú yíwèn de.** *It is beyond any doubt that this plan will materialize.*
yǐ 已 ADJ Same as 已经 **yǐjīng**. Used in written Chinese.
yǐjīng 已经 ADJ already
yǐ 乙 N the second of the ten Heavenly Stems, second
yǐ 以[1] PREP **1** with, in the manner of **2** for, because of
yǐ 以[2] CONJ in order to, so as to
yǐhòu 以后 N after, later (ANTONYM 以前 **yǐqián**)
yǐjí 以及 CONJ Same as 和[2] **hé** CONJ. Used in formal Chinese.
yǐlái 以来 PARTICLE since, in the past …
yǐnèi 以内 N within, during
yǐqián 以前 N before, some time ago (ANTONYM 以后 **yǐhòu**)

不久以前 **bùjiǔ yǐqián** not long ago
yǐshàng 以上 N over, more than (ANTONYM 以下 **yíxià**)
yǐwài 以外 N beyond, outside, other than
yǐwéi 以为 V think (usually incorrectly)
yǐxià 以下 N below, less than (ANTONYM 以上 **yǐshàng**) ■ 他们的年收入在一万元以下。 **Tāmen de nián shōurù zài yíwàn yuán yǐxià.** *Their annual income is less than 10,000 yuan.*
yǐ 椅 N chair
yǐzi 椅子 [suffix: 椅 chair + 子 nominal suffix] N chair (把 **bǎ**) ■ 房间里有一张桌子和四把椅子。 **Fángjiān li yǒu yì zhāng zhuōzi hé sì bǎ yǐzi.** *There are a table and four chairs in the room.*
yì 亦 ADV also
yì 谊 TRAD 誼 N friendship (See yǒuyì 友谊.)
yì 义 TRAD 義 ADJ righteous
yìwù 义务 N duty, obligation
yìwù gōngzuò (yìgōng) 义务工作 (义工) N voluntary work
yìwù jiàoyù 义务教育 N compulsory education
yì 亿 TRAD 億 NUMERAL one hundred million
十亿 **shíyì** billion / 万亿 **wànyì** trillion
yì 忆 TRAD 憶 V recall (See huíyì 回忆, jìyì 记忆.)
yì 艺 TRAD 藝 N art
yìshù 艺术 [modif: 艺 art + 术 craft, skill] N art
艺术作品 **yìshù zuòpǐn** a work of art
yìshùjiā 艺术家 N (accomplished, recognized) artist
yì 译 TRAD 譯 V translate (See fānyì 翻译.)
yì 易[1] ADJ easy, not difficult (See róngyì 容易.)
yì 易[2] V exchange (See màoyì 贸易.)
yì 意 N idea, meaning
yìjiàn 意见 [comp: 意 idea + 见 viewpoint] N **1** opinion, view (条 **tiáo**) **2** complaint, objection

提意见 tí yìjiàn make a comment (on an issue, a proposal etc.), make a complaint

yìsi 意思 [comp: 意 meaning + 思 thought] N meaning

yìwài 意外 I ADJ unexpected, unforeseen **II** N mishap, accident

yìyì 意义 [comp: 意 meaning + 义 meaning] N significance, meaning

yì 益 N benefit (See lìyì 利益.)

yì 毅 ADJ firm, resolute

yìlì 毅力 [modif: 毅 resolute + 力 strength] N indomitable will, strong willpower

yìrán 毅然 ADV resolutely

yì 议 TRAD 議 V discuss

yìlùn 议论 [comp: 议 discuss + 论 comment] V comment, discuss, talk

yì 抑 V press down

yìzhì 抑制 V & N inhibit, restrain; inhibition, restraint

yīn 因 CONJ because

yīncǐ 因此 CONJ therefore, so

yīn'ér 因而 same as 因此 yīncǐ

yīnsù 因素 N factor, element

yīnwèi 因为 CONJ because ◼ 因为没有时间，所以我很少去看朋友。 Yīnwèi méiyǒu shíjiān, suǒyǐ wǒ hěnshǎo qù kàn péngyou. *I seldom go visiting friends because I don't have the time.*

NOTE: 因为 **yīnwèi** is usually followed by 所以 **suǒyǐ**: 因为 ⋯ 所以 ⋯ **yīnwèi ... suǒyǐ...** *because ... so/therefore*

yīn 阴 TRAD 陰 ADJ cloudy, overcast

yīntiān 阴天 cloudy day

yīnxìng 阴性 ADJ (of test result) negative (ANTONYM 阳性 yángxìng)

yīn 姻 N marriage (See hūnyīn 婚姻.)

yīn 音 N sound

yīnyuè 音乐 [comp: 音 sound + 乐 music] N music
轻音乐 qīng yīnyuè light music

yīnyuè huì 音乐会 N musical performance, concert

yīnyuè jiā 音乐家 N (accomplished) musician

yīnyuè xuéyuàn 音乐学院 N music school, conservatory

yín 银 TRAD 銀 N silver

yínháng 银行 [modif: 银 silver, money + 行 firm] N bank (家 jiā)

yǐn 引 V lead, provoke

yǐndǎo 引导 V guide, lead

yǐnqǐ 引起 V give rise to, lead to, cause, arouse

yǐnqíng 引擎 N engine, especially heat engine

yǐn 饮 TRAD 飲 V drink

yǐnliào 饮料 [modif: 饮 drink + 料 stuff] N drink, beverage

yǐnshíyè 饮食业 N catering industry, catering

yǐnyòngshuǐ 饮用水 N drinking water
非饮用水 fēi yǐnyòngshuǐ non-drinking water

yìn 印 V print, engrave
影印 yǐngyìn photocopy / 影印机 yǐngyìnjī photocopier

yìnshuā 印刷 [comp: 印 print + 刷 brush] V print (books, pamphlets, etc.)
印刷厂 yìnshuāchǎng print shop / 印刷机 yìnshuājī printing machine, press / 印刷品 yìnshuāpǐn printed matter

yìnxiàng 印象 [comp: 印 print + 象 image] N impression
给 ⋯ 留下印象 gěi ... liúxià yìnxiàng leave an impression on ...

yīng 应 TRAD 應 MODAL V Same as 应该 yīnggāi

yīngdāng 应当 MODAL V Same as 应该 yīnggāi

yīnggāi 应该 MODAL V should, ought to

yīng 英 ADJ heroic

Yīngguó 英国 N Britain, the UK

yīngjùn 英俊 ADJ (of men) handsome, attractive
英俊青年 yīngjùn qīngnián handsome young man

yīngtèwǎng 英特网 [modif: 英特 Internet + 网 net] N Same as 互联网 hùliánwǎng

Yīngwén 英文 [modif: 英 English + 文 writing] N the English language (especially the writing)

yīngxióng 英雄 N talented and brave person, hero

Yīngyǔ 英语 [modif: 英 English + 语 language] N the English language

yíng 迎 v meet

yíngjiē 迎接 [comp: 迎 meet + 接 receive] v meet, greet

yíng 营 TRAD 營 v operate

yíngyǎng 营养 N nutrition, nourishment

yíngyè 营业 v (of a commercial or service establishment) do business
营业时间 yíngyè shíjiān business hours

yíngyèyuán 营业员 N shop assistant, salesperson

yíng 蝇 TRAD 蠅 N fly

yíng 赢 v win (a game), beat (a rival)

yǐng 影 N shadow

yǐngxiǎng 影响 [comp: 影 shadow + 响 sound] v & N influence, affect; influence

yǐngzi 影子 N shadow, reflection

yìng 应 TRAD 應 v respond

yìngfu 应付 v 1 cope with 2 act perfunctorily

yìngpìn 应聘 v accept an offer of an employment

yìngyòng 应用 v apply, use
应用程序 yìngyòng chéngxù app, application (program) / 应用科学 yìngyòng kēxué applied science

yìng 映 v reflect (See fǎnyìng 反映.)

yìng 硬 ADJ (of substance) hard, tough (ANTONYM 软 ruǎn)

yìngjiàn 硬件 N (in computing) hardware

yōng 拥 TRAD 擁 v embrace

yōngbào 拥抱 [comp: 拥 embrace + 抱 hold in arms] v embrace, hug

yōngjǐ 拥挤 I v push, push and shove II ADJ crowded, be packed

yōng 佣 TRAD 傭 v employ, hire
女佣 nǚyōng woman servant, maid

yōngrén 佣人 N servant

yǒng 永 ADV forever

yǒngyuǎn 永远 [comp: 永 forever + 远 remote] ADV forever

yǒng 勇 N courage

yǒnggǎn 勇敢 [comp: 勇 bold + 敢 daring] ADJ brave, bold, fearless

yǒngqì 勇气 [modif: 勇 courage + 气 quality] N courage
勇于认错 yǒngyú rèncuò have the courage to admit one's own mistake

yǒng 泳 v swim (See yóuyǒng 游泳.)

yòng 用 v use, employ, (do something) with

yòngbuzháo 用不着 IDIOM 1 there is no need to 2 useless

yòngchu 用处 [modif: 用 use + 处 place] v use, advantage

yònggōng 用功 [v+obj: 用 use + 功 efforts] ADJ hardworking, studious, diligent (student)

yònglì 用力 [v+obj: 用 use + 力 strength] v exert oneself (physically)

yòngtú 用途 N use, function

yōu 优 TRAD 優 ADJ excellent

yōudiǎn 优点 [modif: 优 excellent + 点 point] N strong point, merit (ANTONYM 缺点 quēdiǎn)

yōuhuì 优惠 ADJ preferential, favorable
优惠价 yōuhuìjià preferential price

yōuliáng 优良 [comp: 优 excellent + 良 good] ADJ fine, good

yōuměi 优美 [comp: 优 excellent + 美 beautiful] ADJ beautiful, graceful

yōushèng 优胜 ADJ winning, superior
优胜者 yōushèngzhě winner

yōushì 优势 [modif: 优 superior + 势 power] N superiority, advantage, dominant position

yōuxiù 优秀 [comp: 优 excellent + 秀 elegant] ADJ outstanding, excellent

yōu 悠 ADJ remote

yōujiǔ 悠久 [comp: 悠 remote + 久 long] ADJ very long, long-standing, time-honored

yōu 幽 ADJ quiet, serene

yōumò 幽默 N humor

有幽默感 **yǒu yōumògǎn** have a sense of humor

yōu 忧 TRAD 憂 V worry

yóu 尤 ADV especially

yóuqí 尤其 ADV especially

yóu 由 PREP (introducing the agent of an action), by

yóuyú 由于 PREP & CONJ because of, owing to, due to; because, as

yóu 邮 TRAD 郵 N post

yóujú 邮局 [modif: 邮 post + 局 office] N post office

yóupiào 邮票 [modif: 邮 post + 票 ticket] N postal stamp (张 **zhāng**)

yóu 犹 TRAD 猶 PREP like, as

yóuyù 犹豫 ADJ hesitant, wavering, procrastinating

yóu 油 I N oil II ADJ greasy (food)

食油 **shíyóu** edible oil, cooking oil / 石油 **shíyóu** petroleum, oil

yóuhuà 油画 [modif: 油 oil + 画 painting] N oil painting (幅 **fú**)

yóutián 油田 [modif: 油 oil + 田 field] N oil field

yóuzhà 油炸 V & ADJ deep-fry; deep-fried

yóu 游 V play

yóulǎn 游览 [comp: 游 play + 览 see] V go sightseeing, tour for pleasure

游览者 **yóulǎnzhě** tourist

yóuyǒng 游泳 V swim

游泳池 **yóuyǒngchí** swimming pool / 游泳裤 **yóuyǒng kù** swimming trunks / 游泳衣 **yóuyǒng yī** swimsuit / 温水游泳池 **wēnshuǐ yóuyǒngchí** heated swimming pool

yóuxì 游戏 [modif: 游 play + 戏 have fun] N game

电脑游戏 **diànnǎo yóuxì** computer game

yóuxìjī 游戏机 N play station, console

yǒu 友 N friend

yǒuhǎo 友好 [comp: 友 friendly + 好 amiable] ADJ friendly

yǒuyì 友谊 [comp: 友 friendly + 谊 friendship] N friendship, amity

yǒu 有 V 1 possess, have 2 exist, there is (are)

没有 **méiyǒu** do not possess, have no; do not exist, there is no

yǒude 有的 PRON some

yǒudeshì 有的是 V be plenty of, be abundant, not in short supply

yǒu(yì)diǎnr 有(一)点儿 ADV slightly, a little, somewhat

NOTE: 有点 **yǒudiǎn**, 有点儿 **yǒudiǎnr**, 有一点 **yǒuyìdiǎn**, 有一点儿 **yǒuyìdiǎnr** mean the same thing. 有点儿 **yǒudiǎnr** and 有一点儿 **yǒuyìdiǎnr** are only used in colloquial Chinese.

yǒuguān 有关 V have a bearing on, have something to do with, be related to

yǒulì 有力 [v+obj: 有 have + 力 force] ADJ forceful, powerful, strong

yǒulì 有利 [v+obj: 有 have + 利 benefit] ADJ favorable, advantageous (ANTONYM 不利 **búlì**)

yǒumíng 有名 [v+obj: 有 have + 名 name, fame] ADJ famous, well-known

yǒuqián 有钱 [v+obj: 有 have + 钱 money] ADJ rich, wealthy

NOTE: See note on 富 **fù**.

yǒuqù 有趣 [v+obj: 有 have + 趣 fun] ADJ interesting, amusing

yǒushí 有时 ADV Same as 有时候 **yǒushíhou**

yǒushíhou 有时候 ADV sometimes, occasionally

yǒuxiào 有效 [v+obj: 有 have + 效 effect] ADJ 1 effective, efficacious 2 valid

有效期 **yǒuxiàoqī** term of validity, expiry date

yǒuxiē 有些 PRON Same as 有的 **yǒude**

yǒu yìsi 有意思 [v+obj: 有 have + 意思 meaning] ADJ meaningful, interesting

没有意思 **méiyǒu yìsi** uninteresting, meaningless

yǒuyòng 有用 [v+obj: 有 have + 用 use]
ADJ useful
没有用 **méiyǒu yòng** useless
yòu 右 N the right side (ANTONYM 左 **zuǒ**)
yòubian 右边 [modif: 右 right + 边 side]
N the right side, the right-hand side
yòu 幼 ADJ very young
yòu'ér 幼儿 [modif: 幼 very young + 儿
child] N young child between 2 and 6
years old
yòu'éryuán 幼儿园 [modif: 幼儿 young
child + 园 garden] N kindergarten
yòu 又 ADV 1 again 2 moreover,
additionally
又 … 又 … **yòu … yòu …** and also …,
both … and …

NOTE: See note on 再 **zài**.

yú 于 TRAD 於 PREP in, at (used only in
written Chinese)
yúshì 于是 CONJ as a result, consequently
yú 余 TRAD 餘 V spare (See 业余 **yèyú**.)
yú 鱼 TRAD 魚 N fish (条 **tiáo**)
yú 渔 TRAD 漁 N fishing, fishery ■ 授人以
鱼，不如授之以渔。(老子) **Shòu rén yǐ
yú, bùrú shuò zhī yǐ yú. (Lǎozǐ)** *Giving
someone a fish is not so good as teaching
him how to fish. (Laozi)*
yúchuán 渔船 N fishing boat (艘 **sōu**)
yúwǎng 渔网 N fishing net (张 **zhāng**)
yú 娱 TRAD 娛 V amuse, give pleasure to
yúlè 娱乐 [comp: 娱 amuse + 乐 amuse]
V & N entertain, amuse; entertainment,
amusement
娱乐活动 **yúlè huódòng** recreation,
recreational activities
yú 愉 N pleasure
yúkuài 愉快 [comp: 愉 pleasant + 快
delightful] ADJ 1 pleasant, joyful
2 pleased, happy
yǔ 与 TRAD 與 Same as 和 **hé** and 跟 **gēn**.
Used only in written Chinese.
yǔ cǐ tóng shí 与此同时 IDIOM at the
same time

yǔhuì 与会 V be present at a meeting
(conference)
yǔqí … bùrú 与其 … 不如 CONJ would
rather …than ■ 与其坐着谈，不如起而
行。**Yǔqí zuòzhe tán, bùrú qǐ ér xíng.** *We
would rather get up and do something
than sit here talking.*

NOTE: Pay attention to the different word
orders of 与其 … 不如 **yǔqí ... bùrú** *would
rather… than*: while it is 与其 A 不如 B
in Chinese, in English it is *would rather B
than A.*

yǔ 屿 TRAD 嶼 N small island, isle (See
dǎoyǔ 岛屿.)
yǔ 雨 N rain, precipitation
雨天 **yǔtiān** rainy day / 雨衣 **yǔyī**
raincoat / 下雨 **xià yǔ** to rain
yǔ 羽 N feather
yǔmáoqiú 羽毛球 [modif: 羽毛 feather
+ 球 ball] V badminton, shuttlecock
(只 **zhī**)
yǔ 语 TRAD 語 N language
yǔdiào 语调 [modif: 语 speech +
调 tune] N intonation
yǔfǎ 语法 [modif: 语 language + 法 law,
rule] N grammar
yǔqì 语气 [modif: 语 speech + 气
quality] N tone, manner of speaking
yǔyán 语言 [comp: 语 language + 言
speech] N language (门 **mén**, 种 **zhǒng**)
yǔyǐ 予以 V grant, give
yù 玉 N jade
yùmǐ 玉米 [modif: 玉 jade + 米 rice] N
corn, maize (根 **gēn**)
yùqì 玉器 N jade article, jadeware
yù 育 V educate, nurture (See **jiàoyù 教
育, tǐyù 体育**, etc.)
yù 浴 V bathe
yùshì 浴室 [modif: 浴 bathe + 室 room]
N bathroom (间 **jiān**)
yù 狱 TRAD 獄 N prison
地狱 **dìyù** hell
yù 遇 V encounter

yùdào 遇到 v encounter, come across

yùjiàn 遇见 v meet (someone)
unexpectedly, come across, run into

yù 预 TRAD 預 ADV in advance

yùbào 预报 [modif: 预 in advance +
报 report] N forecast, prediction

yùbèi 预备 [modif: 预 in advance +
备 prepare] v prepare, get ready
预备会议 yùbèi huìyì preparatory
meeting / 预备学校 yùbèi xuéxiào
preparatory school

yùdìng 预订 v book, place an order
■ 我已经在餐馆预订了席位。 Wǒ yǐjīng
zài cānguǎn yùdìng le xíwèi. *I've booked
seats in the restaurant.*

yùfáng 预防 [modif: 预 in advance
+ 防 defend] v & N take precautionary
measures to prevent, prevent; prevention

yùxí 预习 [modif: 预 preparatory + 习
study] v prepare lessons before class,
preview

yù 欲 N desire
食欲 shíyù desire for food, appetite /
性欲 xìngyù sexual desire, sex drive

yù 豫 N comfort

yuán 元¹ ADJ first, primary

yuándàn 元旦 [modif: 元 first + 旦
dawn] N the New Year's Day

yuánjiàn 元件 N component part,
component

yuánxiāo 元宵 [modif: 元 first +
宵 night] N 1 also known as 元宵节
Yuánxiāojié, the Lantern Festival (the
15th of the first month in the Chinese
Lunar Calendar, when the full moon
appears for the first time in a year.)
2 the traditional sweet dumpling for the
Lantern Festival

yuán 元² MEASURE WORD (the basic unit
of Chinese currency: 1 元 yuán = 10 角
jiǎo/毛 máo = 100 分 fēn), yuan, dollar
美元 Měiyuán US dollar / 日元 Rìyuán
Japanese yen

NOTE: 元 **yuán** is the formal word for the
basic unit of Chinese currency. In spoken
Chinese 块 **kuài** is more common. For
instance, the sum of 50 yuan is usually
written as 五十元 **wǔshí yuán**, but spoken
of as 五十块 **wǔshí kuài** or 五十块钱
wǔshí kuài qián.

yuán 员 TRAD 員 N member

yuángōng 员工 N staff, personnel

yuán 园 TRAD 園 N garden

yuán 原 ADJ original, former

yuánlái 原来 ADJ original, former

yuánliàng 原谅 v pardon, excuse, forgive

yuánliào 原料 [modif: 原 original + 料
material] N raw material

yuányīn 原因 [modif: 原 origin + 因
cause] N cause, reason

yuánzé 原则 N principle

yuán 圆 TRAD 圓 ADJ round, circular

yuán 援 v help

yuǎn 远 TRAD 遠 ADJ far, distant, remote
(ANTONYM 近 jìn)
离 ··· 远 ··· ... lí ... yuǎn ... is far from ...

yuàn 院 N courtyard

yuànzi 院子 [suffix: 院 courtyard + 子
nominal suffix] N courtyard, compound

yuàn 愿 TRAD 願 v wish, hope

yuànwàng 愿望 [comp: 愿 wish + 望
hope] N wish, aspiration, desire

yuànyì 愿意 [comp: 愿 wish + 意 desire]
I MODAL V be willing, will II v wish, want

yuàn 怨 v resent, complain (See **bàoyuàn**
抱怨.)

yuē 约 TRAD 約 ADV Same as 大约 dàyuē.
Used in written Chinese.

yuēhuì 约会 [v+obj: 约 arrange +
会 meeting] N (social) appointment,
engagement, date

yuè 月 N 1 month 2 the moon

yuèliang 月亮 N the moon

yuèqiú 月球 N the Moon (as a scientific
term)

yuè 乐 TRAD 樂 N music

yuèduì 乐队 [modif: 乐 music + 队

team] N band, orchestra

yuèqì 乐器 [modif: 乐 music + 器 implement] N musical instrument

yuèqǔ 乐曲 N melody

yuè 越 ADV even more

yuè ··· yuè ··· 越 ··· 越 ··· ADV the more ... the more ...

yuèlaiyuè 越来越 ADV more and more

yuè 阅 TRAD 閱 V read

yuèdú 阅读 [comp: 阅 read + 读 read] V read (seriously), peruse

yuèlǎnshì 阅览室 [modif: 阅览 read, browse + 室 room] N reading room (间 jiān)

yuè 跃 TRAD 躍 V leap

yuè 岳 N high mountain

yuèfù 岳父 N wife's father

yuèmǔ 岳母 N wife's mother

yūn 晕 TRAD 暈 V dizzy, giddy
头晕 tóu yūn feel dizzy

yún 云 TRAD 雲 N cloud
多云 duōyún cloudy, overcast

yǔn 允 V allow

yǔnxǔ 允许 [comp: 允 allow + 许 permit] V allow, permit

yùn 孕 ADJ pregnant

yùnyù 孕育 V be pregnant, breed, give rise to

yùn 运 TRAD 運 V transport, carry

yùndòng 运动 [comp: 运 move + 动 move] V & N do physical exercises; physical exercises

yùndònghuì 运动会 [modif: 运动 sports + 会 meeting] N sports meet, games

yùndòngxié 运动鞋 N sport shoes

yùndòngyuán 运动员 [modif: 运动 sports + 员 person] N athlete, sportsperson

yùnqi 运气 N good luck

yùnshū 运输 [comp: 运 transport + 输 transport] V & N transport, carry; transportation

yùnyòng 运用 V use, apply, put into use

Z

zá 杂 TRAD 雜 ADJ miscellaneous, sundry, all sorts of

záfèi 杂费 N sundry charges

zázhì 杂志 [modif: 杂 miscellaneous + 志 record] N magazine, journal (本 běn, 种 zhǒng)

zāi 灾 TRAD 災 N disaster, calamity
火灾 huǒzāi fire disaster, fire /
水灾 shuǐzāi flooding, floods

zāihài 灾害 [comp: 灾 disaster + 害 damage] N disaster, calamity
自然灾害 zìrán zāihài natural disaster

zài 再 ADV again

NOTE: 再 zài and 又 yòu are both glossed as *again*, but they have different usage: 又 yòu is used in the context of a past situation while 再 zài is used for a future situation. Here is another pair of examples: ▪ 她昨天又迟到了。 **Tā zuótiān yòu chídào le.** *She was late (for work, school, etc.) again yesterday.* ▪ 明天你不要再迟到了。 **Míngtiān nǐ bú yào zài chídào le.** *Please do not be late again tomorrow.*

zàijiàn 再见 [modif: 再 again + 见 see] V see you again, goodbye

zàisān 再三 [comp: 再 again + 三 three (times)] ADV over and over again

zài 在[1] I PREP in, on, at II V be in ▪ "你爸爸在家吗？" "他不在家。" **"Nǐ bàba zài jiā ma?" "Tā bú zài jiā."** *"Is your father home?" "No, he isn't."*
在 ··· 里 zài ... li in ▪ 在房间里 zài fángjiān li *in the room*
在 ··· 上 zài ... shang on ▪ 在桌子上 zài zhuōzi shang *on the desk*
在 ··· 下 zài ... xia under ▪ 在床下 zài chuáng xia *under the bed*
在 ··· 之间 zài ... zhī jiān between ▪ 在这两棵树之间 zài zhè liǎng kē shù zhī jiān *between the two trees*

zài 在[2] ADV (used to indicate an action

in progress) ■ 你在做什么? **Nǐ zài zuò shénme?** *What are you doing?*

zàihu 在乎 v care, care about

NOTE: 在乎 **zàihu** is normally used in a negative sentence, or a question.

zàiyú 在于 v lie in, rest with

zán 咱 PRON Same as 咱们 **zánmen**

zánmen 咱们 [suffix: 咱 we, us + 们 suffix denoting a plural number] PRON we, us (including the person or persons spoken to)

NOTE: 咱们 **zánmen** is only used in colloquial Chinese, and has a northern dialect flavor. You can always just use 我们 **wǒmen**, even to include the person(s) spoken to. The following examples are perfectly acceptable: ■ 你在学中文, 我也在学中文, 我们都在学中文。 **Nǐ zài xué Zhōngwén, wǒ yě zài xué Zhōngwén, wǒmen dōu zài xué Zhōngwén.** *You're learning Chinese. I'm learning Chinese. We're both learning Chinese.* ■ 我们去吃饭吧! **Wǒmen qù chīfàn ba!** *Let's go and have a meal.*

zàn 暂 TRAD 暫 ADJ temporary

zànshí 暂时 [comp: 暂 temporary + 时 time] ADJ temporary, for the time being

zàn 赞 TRAD 贊 v support

zànchéng 赞成 v approve of, support, be in favor of

zànměi 赞美 [comp: 赞 praise + 美 beautify] v eulogize, praise highly

zàntóng 赞同 v heartily approve of, agree with

zànyáng 赞扬 v speak highly of, praise, applaud

zànzhù 赞助 [comp: 赞 praise + 助 help] v support, sponsor
赞助人 **zànzhù rén** sponsor

zāng 脏 TRAD 髒 ADJ dirty (ANTONYM 干净 **gānjìng**)

zàng 脏 TRAD 臟 N internal organs of the body

zāo 遭 v meet with (misfortune)

zāodào 遭到 v suffer, encounter, meet with

zāo 糟 ADJ messy

zāogāo 糟糕 [modif: 糟 messy + 糕 cake] ADJ in a mess, terrible, very bad

zāota 糟蹋 v waste, ruin

zǎo 早 ADJ early

NOTE: A common greeting among the Chinese when they meet in the morning is 早 **zǎo** or 你早 **Nǐ zǎo**.

zǎochén 早晨 [modif: 早 early + 晨 early morning] N early morning (approximately 6–9 a.m.)

zǎofàn 早饭 [modif: 早 early + 饭 meal] N breakfast (顿 **dùn**)

zǎoshang 早上 N Same as 早晨 **zǎochén**

zǎo 澡 N bath (See 洗澡 **xǐzǎo**.)

zào 皂 N soap (See 香皂 **xiāngzào**.)

zào 造 v make, build

zàofǎn 造反 V & N rebel; rebellion

zàojù 造句 V & N make sentences; sentence-making
用所给的词语造句 **yòng suǒ gěi de cíyǔ zàojù** make sentences with the given words

zào 噪 ADJ noisy

zàoyīn 噪音 N noise
噪音污染 **zàoyīnwūrǎn** noise pollution, white pollution

zào 燥 ADJ dry (See 干燥 **gānzào**.)

zé 则 TRAD 則 CONJ in that case, then ■ 不进则退。 **Bú jìn zé tuì.** *If you don't make progress, then you'll fall behind.*

NOTE: 则 **zé** is used only in formal Chinese. In everyday Chinese, use 那 **nà** or 那么 **nàme** instead. See note on 那么 **nàme**.

zé 责 TRAD 責 N duty

zébèi 责备 v reproach, blame
责备的口气 **zébèi de kǒuqì** reproachful tone

zérèn 责任 N responsibility, duty

zérèngǎn 责任感 N sense of responsibility

zé 择 TRAD 擇 v choose, select (See xuǎnzé 选择.)

zěnme 怎么 PRON 1 how, in what manner ▪ 这个汉字怎么写? *Zhège Hànzi zěnme xiě? How do you write this Chinese character?* 2 no matter how (used with 都 **dōu** or 也 **yě**) ▪ 他怎么也找不到那本书。*Tā zěnme yě zhǎo bu dào nà běn shū. No matter how hard he tried, he couldn't find the book.* 3 why, how come ▪ 你怎么又迟到了? *Nǐ zěnme yòu chídào le? Why are you late again?* 4 how can ... ▪ 这么多作业，我今天怎么做得完? *Zhème duō zuòyè, wǒ jīntiān zěnme zuò de wán? How can I finish so many assignments today?*

zěnmebàn 怎么办 PRON what's to be done?

zěnmele 怎么了 PRON what happened?

zěnmeyàng 怎么样 PRON 1 (Same as 怎么 **zěnme**) 2 how ▪ 你今天觉得怎么样? *Nǐ jīntiān juéde zěnmeyàng? How are you feeling today?* 3 how's that? is it OK? ▪ 我晚上开车来接你，怎么样? *Wǒ wǎnshang kāichē lái jiē nǐ, zénmeyàng? I'll pick you up this evening. Is it OK?*

zěnyàng 怎样 PRON Same as 怎么样 **zěnmeyàng** (used in writing)

zēng 增 v increase

zēngjiā 增加 [comp: 增 increase + 加 add] v increase, add

zēngzhǎng 增长 [comp: 增 increase + 长 grow] v increase, grow

zèng 赠 TRAD 贈 v present a gift

zèngsòng 赠送 v present as a gift 向主人赠送礼物 *xiàng zhǔrén zèngsòng lǐwù* present a gift to the host

zhà 炸 v 1 blow up, blast, bomb 2 deep fry (See **yóuzhá** 油炸.)

zhà 榨 v squeeze

zhāi 摘 v pick, pluck

zhāiyào 摘要 [v+obj: 摘 pick + 要 what is important] V & N make a summary; abstract, summary 论文摘要 *lùnwén zhāiyào* abstract of an academic or scholarly paper

zhái 宅 N residence

zhǎi 窄 ADJ narrow (ANTONYM 宽 **kuān**)

zhài 债 TRAD 債 N debt 还债 *huánzhài* to pay off a debt, to settle a debt / 借债 *jièzhài* to borrow money, to ask for a loan / 欠债 *qiànzhài* to owe a debt

zhàiwù 债务 N debt, liabilities 债务人 *zhàiwùrén* debtor

zhàizhǔ 债主 N creditor

zhān 瞻 v look up

zhānyǎng 瞻仰 v look up with reverence, pay homage to

zhǎnxīn 崭新 ADJ brand-new, nascent

zhǎn 展 v display

zhǎnchū 展出 [v+compl: 展 show + 出 out] v be on show, put on display

zhǎnkāi 展开 v carry out, launch

zhǎnlǎn 展览 [modif: 展 display + 览 view] V & N put on display, exhibit; exhibition, show

zhǎnlǎnhuì 展览会 N exhibition, show

zhǎnxiāo 展销 v show and advertise (products)

zhǎnxiāohuì 展销会 N commodities fair 汽车展销会 *qìchē zhǎnxiāohuì* auto fair, car show

zhàn 占 v occupy, seize, take

zhàn piányi 占便宜 v gain unfair advantage

zhànxiàn 占线 v (of a telephone line) engaged, busy

zhànyǒu 占有 v own, possess

zhàn 站[1] v stand 站起来 *zhàn qǐlai* stand up

zhàn 站[2] N station, stop 站长 *zhànzhǎng* railway/coach stationmaster / 出租汽车站 *chūzū qìchē zhàn* taxi stand / 火车站 *huǒchē zhàn* railway station / 汽车站 *qìchē zhàn* coach/bus station; bus stop

zhàn 战 TRAD 戰 v battle

zhànshèng 战胜 [v+compl: 战 fight + 胜 victorious] N triumph over, defeat

zhànshi 战士 [modif: 战 fighting + 士 person] N soldier, fighter

zhànzhēng 战争 [comp: 战 fight + 争 strife] N war

zhāng 张¹ TRAD 張 MEASURE WORD (for paper, bed, table etc.)
一张纸 yì zhāng zhǐ a piece of paper / 两张床 liǎng zhāng chuáng two beds / 三张桌子 sān zhāng zhuōzi three tables / desks

Zhāng 张² TRAD 張 N common family name ▪ 张先生/太太/小姐 Zhāng xiānsheng/tàitai/xiǎojiě Mr/Mrs/Miss Zhang

zhǎng 长¹ TRAD 長 v 1 grow 2 grow to be, look

zhǎng 长² TRAD 長 N chief

zhǎngbèi 长辈 N people of the older generation, elder member of a family, elder

zhǎng 涨 TRAD 漲 v rise, go up

zhǎng 掌 N hand, palm

zhǎngwò 掌握 [comp: 掌 be in charge + 握 take ... in one's hands] v have a good command of, know well

zhàng 丈 N senior

zhàngfu 丈夫 N husband (ANTONYM 妻子 qīzi)

zhàng 账 TRAD 賬 N account
查账 cházhàng examine an account, audit / 算账 suàn zhàng compute income and expense, settle accounts

zhàngdān 账单 N bill
付电话账单 fù diànhuà zhàngdān pay phone bills

zhànghù 账户 N account
账户号 zhànghù hào account number

zhàngmù 账目 N items of an account
账目不清 zhàngmù bùqīng accounts in disorder

zhàng 胀 TRAD 脹 v expand (ANTONYM 缩 suō)

热胀冷缩 rè zhàng lěng suō expand when heated, and contract when cooled

zhàng 仗 N battle, war

zhāo 招 v beckon, attract

zhāodài 招待 v receive or entertain (a guest)

zhāodàihuì 招待会 N reception
记者招待会 jìzhě zhāodàihuì press conference, news conference

zhāohu 招呼 [comp: 招 beckon + 呼 call] v call, shout at
打招呼 dǎ zhāohu 1 greet 2 inform casually, tell

zhāopìn 招聘 [comp: 招 attract + 聘 invite for service] v advertise for a position, recruit (employees)
招聘广告 zhāopìn guǎnggào advertisement for staff (e.g. a teacher, a chef)

zhāo 朝 N early morning

zháo 着 v touch, catch

zháohuǒ 着火 v catch fire, be on fire ▪ 着火了！着火了！Zháohuǒ le! Zháohuǒ le! Fire! Fire!

zháojí 着急 v be anxious, be worried
别着急 bié zháojí don't worry, don't be so anxious

zháoliáng 着凉 v catch a cold

zhǎo 找 v look for, search for
找到 zhǎodào find

zhào 召 v summon

zhàokāi 召开 [comp: 召 summon + 开 open] v convene (a conference)

zhào 照¹ v 1 take a photo 2 look in a mirror 3 shine, light up

zhào 照² PREP according to, in the manner of

zhàocháng 照常 [v+obj: 照 according to + 常 usual] ADJ as usual

zhàogù 照顾 [comp: 照 look after + 顾 attend to] v look after, care for

zhàoliào 照料 v take care of, look after

zhàopiàn 照片 N photograph, picture, snapshot (张 zhāng)

zhàoxiàng 照相 [v+obj: 照 illuminate +

相 photograph] v take a picture ▪ 请你
给我们照个相。*Qǐng nǐ gěi wǒmen zhào
ge xiàng. Please take a picture of us.*
▪ 人们喜欢站在那幅画前照相。
**Rénmen xǐhuan zhàn zài nà fù huà qián
zhàoxiàng.** *People like to take photos
standing in front of that painting.*
zhàoxiàngguǎn 照相馆 N photographic
studio
zhàoxiàngjī 照相机 N camera
zhàoying 照应 v look after, take care of
zhào 罩 v cover, overspread
zhé 哲 ADJ wise
zhéxué 哲学 N philosophy
zhéxuéjiā 哲学家 N philosopher
zhě 者 SUFFIX (a nominal suffix denoting
a person or people) (See **dúzhě** 读者,
jìzhě 记者, etc.)
zhè 这 TRAD 這 PRON this
zhège 这个 [modif: 这 this + 个 one]
PRON this one, this
zhèli 这里 PRON this place, here

NOTE: In spoken Chinese 这里 **zhèli** can be
replaced by 这儿 **zhèr**.

zhème 这么 PRON like this, in this
manner, so
zhèxiē 这些 PRON these
zhèyàng 这样 PRON 1 Same as 这么
zhème. Used only in writing. 2 such
zhe 着 PARTICLE (used after a verb to
indicate the action or state is going on)
▪ 门开着，灯亮着，可是房间里没有
人。**Mén kāizhe, dēng liàngzhe, kěshì
fángjiān li méiyǒu rén.** *The door was
open and the light was on but there was
no one in the room.*
zhèi 这 TRAD 這 PRON Same as 这 zhè.
Used colloquially.
zhēn 真[1] ADV really, truly, indeed
zhēn 真[2] ADJ true, real (ANTONYM 假 jiǎ)
zhēnhuà 真话 N truth
zhēnkōng 真空 N vacuum
真空包装 **zhēnkōng bāozhuāng**
vacuum-packed

zhēnlǐ 真理 [modif: 真 true + 理
reasoning, principle] N truth
zhēnshí 真实 [comp: 真 real + 实
substance] ADJ true, real, authentic
zhēnxiàng 真相 N the real situation,
actual facts
zhēnxīn 真心 N sincerity
zhēnzhèng 真正 ADJ true, real, genuine
zhēnzhì 真挚 ADJ sincere, truthful
zhēn 侦 TRAD 偵 v detect, investigate
zhēnchá 侦察 v reconnoiter, scout
侦察卫星 **zhēnchá wèixīng**
reconnaissance (spy) satellite
zhēn 珍 ADJ valuable
zhēnxī 珍惜 [modif: 珍 valuable + 惜
cherish] v cherish dearly, value highly
zhēnzhū 珍珠 [modif: 珍 valuable +
珠 bead] N pearl (颗 kē)
珍珠项链 **zhēnzhū xiàngliàn** pearl
necklace
zhēn 针 TRAD 針 N 1 needle (根 gēn)
2 stitch
打针 **dǎzhēn** give an injection, get an
injection
zhēnduì 针对 v aim at, be aimed at
zhēnjiǔ 针灸 [comp: 针 needle + 灸
moxibustion] v & N give or receive
acupuncture and moxibustion treatment;
acupuncture and moxibustion
zhěn 诊 TRAD 診 v examine (a patient)
zhěnduàn 诊断 V & N diagnose; diagnosis
诊断为良性肿瘤 **zhěnduàn wéi
liángxìngzhǒngliú** diagnosed as benign
tumor / 做出诊断 **zuòchū zhěnduàn**
make a diagnosis
zhěn 枕 N pillow
zhěntou 枕头 n pillow (只 zhī)
zhèn 阵 TRAD 陣 MEASURE WORD (for an
action or event that lasts for some time)
一阵大风 **yí zhèn dà fēng** a gust of
strong wind
zhènyǔ 阵雨 N brief period of rain,
shower
zhèn 振 v arouse to action

zhèndòng 振动 V & N vibrate, oscillate; vibration, oscillation

zhèn 震 V shake, shock

地震 **dìzhèn** earthquake

zhènhàn 震撼 [v+compl: 震 shake + 撼 move] V shake, vibrate

zhèn 镇[1] TRAD 鎮 N rural town

zhèn 镇[2] TRAD 鎮 V suppress

zhèndìng 镇定 ADJ unperturbed, calm,

zhènyā 镇压 V (politically) suppress, repress, put down

zhēng 争 TRAD 爭 V argue, contend, vie

zhēnglùn 争论 [comp: 争 argue + 论 comment] V dispute, debate

zhēngqǔ 争取 [comp: 争 strive + 取 obtain] V strive for, fight for

zhēng 征 TRAD 徵 V solicit

zhēngqiú 征求 [comp: 征 solicit + 求 request] V solicit, ask for

zhēng 睁 TRAD 睜 V open (the eyes)

zhěng 整[1] ADJ whole, full, entire

zhěngge 整个 ADJ whole, entire

zhěng 整[2] V put in order

zhěnglǐ 整理 [comp: 整 put in order + 理 tidy up] V put in order, tidy up

zhěngqí 整齐 [comp: 整 neat + 齐 orderly] ADJ in good order, neat and tidy (ANTONYM 乱 luàn)

zhěngtǐ 整体 N whole, entirety, (something) as a whole

从整体上说 **cóng zhěngtǐ shàng shuō** on the whole

zhěngtiān 整天 N the whole day, all the time

整天抱怨 **zhěngtiān bàoyuàn** grumble all the time

zhèng 正 ADJ straight, upright (ANTONYMS 歪 wāi, 斜 xié)

zhèngcháng 正常 [comp: 正 normal + 常 usual] ADJ normal, regular

zhènghǎo 正好 [modif: 正 just + 好 good] ADJ 1 just right 2 chance to, by coincidence

zhèngquè 正确 [comp: 正 proper + 确 true] ADJ correct, accurate (ANTONYM 错误 cuòwù)

zhèngshì 正式 [modif: 正 formal + 式 manner] ADJ formal, official

zhèngzài 正在 ADV (used before a verb to indicate the action is in progress)
▪ 他正在看电视。**Tā zhèngzài kàn diànshì.** *He's watching TV.*

NOTE: 正在 … 呢 **zhèngzài … ne** is the same as 正在 **zhèngzài**, but with a casual, friendly tone.

zhèng 证 TRAD 證 N proof, certificate

zhèngjiàn 证件 [modif: 证 proof + 件 article] N paper or document proving one's identity, e.g an a passport, an ID card

zhèngjù 证据 N evidence, proof

zhèngmíng 证明 [v+compl: 证 prove + 明 clear] V & N prove, testify; proof, certificate

出证明 **chū zhèngmíng** issue a certificate

zhèngshū 证书 N certificate (份 fèn, 张 zhāng)

毕业证书 **bìyè zhèngshū** diploma / 结婚证书 **jiéhūn zhèngshū** marriage license, marriage certificate

zhèng 政 N governance

zhèngfǔ 政府 [modif: 政 governance + 府 building] N government

zhèngzhì 政治 [comp: 政 governance + 治 administering] N politics, governance

zhèng 症 N disease

急症 **jízhèng** acute disease, (medical) emergency / 急症室 **jízhèng shì** emergency room (ER)

zhèng 挣 V work to earn (money)

挣钱养活全家 **zhèngqián yǎnghuo quánjiā** work to earn money so as to provide for the family

zhī 之 PARTICLE Same as 的 **de**. Used in written Chinese or certain set expressions.

之后 zhī hòu after, behind / 之前 zhī qián before, prior to / 之外 zhī wài outside, apart from / 之下 zhī xià below, under / 之一 zhī yī one of

zhī 支[1] MEASURE WORD (for stick-like things) 一支笔 yì zhī bǐ a pen

zhī 支[2] v support, prop

zhīchí 支持 [comp: 支 prop up, support + 持 hold] v support

zhīpiào 支票 N (in banking) check, cheque (张 zhāng) 兑现支票 duìxiàn zhīpiào cash a check

zhī 枝 N twig, branch (根 gēn)

zhī 只 TRAD 隻 MEASURE WORD (used with certain nouns denoting animals or utensils, or objects normally occurring in pairs) 一只手 yì zhī shǒu a hand / 两只狗 liǎng zhī gǒu two dogs

zhī 汁 N juice (See guǒzhī 果汁.)

zhī 知 v know

zhīdào 知道 v know

zhīshi 知识 N knowledge

zhī 织 TRAD 織 v weave (See zǔzhī 组织.)

zhí 执 TRAD 執 v grasp, persist

zhízhào 执照 N license, permit 驾驶执照 jiàshǐ zhízhào driver's license

zhí 直 I ADJ straight (ANTONYM 弯 wān) II ADV straight, directly

zhídào 直到 [modif: 直 straight + 到 arrive] PREP until, till

zhíjiē 直接 [modif: 直 direct + 接 join] ADJ direct, immediate, straight away

zhí 值 N value

zhíde 值得 v be worth, be worthwhile

zhí 职 TRAD 職 N job

zhígōng 职工 [comp: 职 clerk + 工 worker] N staff (of a factory, a company, an enterprise, etc.), employee(s)

zhíyè 职业 [comp: 职 job + 业 occupation] N occupation, profession, vocation 职业介绍所 zhíyè jièshàosuǒ employment agency

zhíyèbìng 职业病 N occupational disease

zhí 殖 v breed

zhímín 殖民 v colonize 殖民地 zhímíndì colony / 殖民主义 zhímín zhǔyì colonialism

zhí 植 v plant, grow

zhíwù 植物 [modif: 植 plant + 物 thing] N plant, flora

zhíwùxué 植物学 N botany 植物学家 zhíwùxuéjiā botanist

zhíwùyuán 植物园 N botanical garden

zhí 侄 N one's brother's child

zhínǚ 侄女 N one's brother's daughter, niece

zhízi 侄子 N one's brother's son, nephew

zhǐ 只 TRAD 祇 ADV only, no more than

zhǐhǎo 只好 ADV have no choice/ alternative but, can only

zhǐshì 只是 ADV only, merely, simply

zhǐyào 只要 CONJ so long as, provided that, if only

zhǐyǒu 只有 I ADV can only, have no choice but II CONJ only, only if ■ 只有认真地学，才能学好中文。Zhǐyǒu rènzhēn de xué, cáinéng xuéhǎo Zhōngwén. *Only if you study in earnest, can you gain a good command of Chinese.*

zhǐ 纸 TRAD 紙 N paper (张 zhāng)

zhǐ 止 v stop, suspend (See tíngzhǐ 停止.) 止痛片 zhǐ tòng piàn painkiller

zhǐ 址 N location (See dìzhǐ 地址.)

zhǐ 指 v 1 point at, point to 2 refer to, allude to, mean

zhǐchū 指出 [v+obj: 指 point + 出 out] v point out

zhǐdǎo 指导 [comp: 指 point + 导 guide] v guide, direct, supervise

zhǐhuī 指挥 v command, direct, conduct 指挥部 zhǐhuībù headquarters

zhǐzhēn 指针 N (needle) indicator, pointer

zhì 至 v to, until (only used in written Chinese)

zhìjīn 至今 [v+obj: 至 to, until + 今 today] ADV till now, to this day, so far

zhìshǎo 至少 ADV at least

zhì 志 N will, willpower

zhìyuàn 志愿 I v volunteer II N wish, ideal

zhìyuànzhě 志愿者 N volunteer (a person)

zhì 制[1] TRAD 製 v make, work out

zhìzào 制造 [comp: 制 make + 造 make] v make, manufacture
制造业 zhìzàoyè manufacturing industry

zhìzuò 制作 v Same as 制造 zhìzào

zhì 制[2] I v control, rule II N system
公制 gōng zhì the metric system (of measurements)

zhìdìng 制定 [comp: 制 work out + 定 decide] v lay down, draw up

zhìdù 制度 N system, institution

zhì 治 v treat (a disease)

zhìliáo 治疗 v treat (a disease); treatment
治疗无效 zhìliáo wúxiào medical treatment failed

zhì 致 v reach (See yízhì 一致.)

zhì 质 TRAD 質 N nature, character

zhìliàng 质量 N quality (ANTONYM 数量 shùliàng)

zhì 秩 N order, rank

zhìxù 秩序 [comp: 秩 order + 序 sequence] N order, proper sequence

zhì 智 ADJ wise, intelligent
智者 zhìzhě wise man

zhìhuì 智慧 N wisdom

zhìnéng 智能 [modif: 智 intelligent + 能 ability] N intelligence and capability
人工智能 réngōng zhìnéng artificial intelligence (AI)

zhìnéng shǒujī 智能手机 N smartphone

zhì 置 v place (See wèizhì 位置.)

zhōng 中 I N center, middle
东南西北中 dōng, nán, xī, běi, zhōng the east, the south, the west, the north and the center
II ADJ middle, medium

zhōngcān 中餐 [modif: 中 Chinese + 餐 meal] N Chinese cuisine, Chinese food

Zhōngguó 中国 [modif: 中 middle, central + 国 kingdom, country] N China

Zhōnghuá 中华 N China, Chinese

NOTE: Both 中国 **Zhōngguó** and 中华 **Zhōnghuá** may refer to *China*, but 中华 **Zhōnghuá** has historical and cultural connotations.

zhōngjiān 中间 N center, middle, among

zhōngjiè 中介 N 1 medium, intermedium 2 Same as 中介人 **zhōngjièrén**

zhōngjièrén 中介人 N agent, intermediary

zhōngnián 中年 N middle age
中年人 zhōngniánrén middle-aged person

Zhōngqiūjié 中秋节 N the Mid-Autumn Festival (the 15th day of the 8th month in the Chinese lunar calendar)

Zhōngwén 中文 [modif: 中 China + 文 writing] N the Chinese language (especially the writing)

NOTE: See note on 汉语 **Hànyǔ**.

zhōngwǔ 中午 [modif: 中 middle + 午 noon] N noon

zhōngxīn 中心 [modif: 中 central + 心 the heart] N central part, center
市中心 shìzhōngxīn city center, CBD / 研究中心 yánjiū zhōngxīn research center

zhōngxué 中学 [modif: 中 middle + 学 school] N secondary school, high school, middle school (座 zuò, 所 suǒ)

zhōngxún 中旬 N middle ten days of a month (11th to 20th)

zhōngyào 中药 [modif: 中 Chinese + 药 medicine, drug] N traditional Chinese medicine (e.g. herbs)

zhōngyī 中医 [modif: 中 Chinese + 医 medicine, medical science] N traditional Chinese medicine

zhōng 钟 TRAD 鐘 N clock (座 zuò)

zhōnglóu 钟楼 N clock tower

zhōngtóu 钟头 **N** Same as 小时 **xiǎoshí** (used in spoken Chinese)

zhōng 终 **TRAD** 終 **N** end, finish

zhōngduān 终端 [modif: 终 end + 端 extreme] **N** terminal

zhōngnián 终年 **ADV** all year round, throughout the year

zhōngyú 终于 **ADV** finally, in the end

zhǒng 肿 **TRAD** 腫 **V** swell

zhǒngliú 肿瘤 **N** tumor
恶性肿瘤 **èxìng zhǒngliú** malignant tumor, cancer / 良性肿瘤 **liángxìng zhǒngliú** benign tumor

zhǒng 种 **TRAD** 種 **I MEASURE WORD** kind, sort, type **II N** seed

zhǒnglèi 种类 **N** kind, category

zhòng 众 **TRAD** 眾 **N** crowd (See **guānzhòng** 观众.)

zhòng 种 **TRAD** 種 **V** plant, grow

zhòng 重 **ADJ 1** heavy (**ANTONYM** 轻 **qīng**) **2** important

zhòngdà 重大 [comp: 重 weighty + 大 big] **ADJ** major, great, significant

zhòngdiǎn 重点 [comp: 重 weighty + 点 point] **N** main point, focal point, emphasis

zhòngliàng 重量 [modif: 重 heavy + 量 amount] **N** weight

zhòngshì 重视 [modif: 重 weighty + 视 view] **V** attach importance to, value

zhòngyào 重要 [comp: 重 heavy + 要 (in this context) important] **ADJ** important, significant

zhōu 洲 **N** continent (See **Yàzhōu** 亚洲, **Ōuzhōu** 欧洲 etc.)

zhōu 周 **TRAD** 週 **N** week

NOTES: (1) 周 **zhōu** and 星期 **xīngqī** both mean *week*, but 周 **zhōu** is usually used in writing only. Normally 星期 **xīngqī** is the word to use. (2) 周 **zhōu** is not used with any measure word.

zhōudào 周到 [modif: 周 circumference, all sides + 到 reach] **ADJ** thorough,

thoughtful, considerate

zhōumò 周末 [modif: 周 week + 末 end] **N** weekend

zhōuwéi 周围 [comp: 周 circuit + 围 encircle] **N** surrounding area, all around

zhōu 粥 **N** porridge, gruel
喝粥 **hē zhōu** eat porridge / 小米粥 **xiǎomǐzhōu** millet gruel

zhū 猪 **TRAD** 豬 **N** pig, hog, swine (头 **tóu**)

zhú 竹 **N** bamboo

zhúzi 竹子 [suffix: 竹 bamboo + 子 nominal suffix] **N** bamboo (棵 **kē**)

zhú 逐 **ADV** successive

zhúbù 逐步 [modif: 逐 successive + 步 step] **ADV** step by step, progressively, gradually

zhújiàn 逐渐 [comp: 逐 successive, one by one + 渐 gradual] **ADV** gradually, step by step

zhǔ 主 **N** master, owner

zhǔcài 主菜 **N** main course (of a dinner)

zhǔchí 主持 **V** be in charge of, host (a TV program), chair (a meeting)
节目主持人 **jiémù zhǔchírén** host/hostess of a TV/radio show

zhǔdòng 主动 [modif: 主 self + 动 act] **ADJ** of one's own accord, taking the initiative

zhǔguān 主观 [modif: 主 subjective + 观 view] **ADJ** subjective

zhǔrén 主人 [modif: 主 master + 人 person] **N** host (**ANTONYM** 客人 **kèren**)

zhǔrèn 主任 [modif: 主 principal + 任 appointed] **N** chairman (of a committee), director (of a department)
主任医生 **zhǔrèn yīshēng** chief physician, chief surgeon / 办公室主任 **bàngōngshì zhǔrèn** office manager / 车间主任 **chējiān zhǔrèn** head of a workshop (in a factory)

zhǔshí 主食 **N** staple food (usually cereal)

zhǔtí 主题 **N** theme
(电影的)主题歌 **(diànyǐng de) zhǔtígē** theme song (of a movie)

zhǔxí 主席 [modif: 主 principal + 席 seat] N chairman, chairperson

zhǔyào 主要 [comp: 主 major + 要 (in this context) important] ADJ major, chief, main

zhǔyi 主意 [comp: 主 major + 意 idea] N definite view, idea

zhǔzhāng 主张 V & N advocate, stand for; proposition, idea, what one stands for

zhǔ 煮 V boil, cook

zhǔ 嘱 TRAD 囑 V advise

zhǔfù 嘱咐 [comp: 嘱 advice + 咐 tell] V exhort, tell (somebody to do something) earnestly, advise

zhù 助 V assist (See **bāngzhù** 帮助.)

zhù 住 V live, stay

zhùyuàn 住院 N be hospitalized

zhù 注 V add, pour

zhùcè 注册 V register
注册商标 zhùcè shāngbiāo registered trademark

zhùjiě 注解 V & N annotate, explain with notes; explanatory note, note

zhùyì 注意 V pay attention to, take notice of

zhù 祝 V express good wishes, wish
■ 祝你生日快乐! Zhù nǐ shēngrì kuàilè! *I wish you a happy birthday!*

zhùfú 祝福 V give one's blessing to, wish somebody happiness

zhùhè 祝贺 [comp: 祝 wish well + 贺 congratulate] V congratulate

zhù 著 V write

zhùmíng 著名 ADJ famous, well-known

zhù 筑 TRAD 築 V build, construct (See **jiànzhù** 建筑.)

zhuā 抓 V grab, seize

zhuājǐn 抓紧 [v+obj: 抓 grab + 紧 tight] V grasp firmly

zhuān 专 TRAD 專 ADJ concentrated, focused

zhuānjiā 专家 [modif: 专 specialist + 家 expert] N expert, specialist

zhuānkē 专科 N special field of study, specialty
专科医生 zhuānkē yīshēng medical specialist

zhuānmén 专门 ADJ specialized, specialist

zhuānxīn 专心 [modif: 专 concentrate + 心 the heart] ADJ focused, be absorbed in

zhuānyè 专业 [modif: 专 specialist + 业 profession] N specialist field of study, specialty

zhuān 砖 TRAD 磚 N brick
砖头 zhuāntóu brick (块 kuài)

zhuānwǎ 砖瓦 N bricks and tiles, building material

zhuǎn 转 TRAD 轉 V 1 turn, change 2 pass on, forward
转车 zhuǎnchē transfer to another train (or bus) / 转学 zhuǎnxué transfer to another school

zhuǎnbiàn 转变 [comp: 转 turn + 变 change] V change, transform (usually for the better)

zhuǎngào 转告 [modif: 转 transfer + 告 tell] V pass along (word), pass on (a message)

zhuǎn jīyīn 转基因 ADJ genetically modified
转基因食品 zhuǎn jīyīn shípǐn genetically modified food

zhuàn 赚 TRAD 賺 V make money, make a profit

zhuāng 装 TRAD 裝 V pretend

zhuāngshì 装饰 V & N decorate; decoration ■ 他们用中国工艺品装饰客厅。Tā men yòng Zhōngguó gōngyìpǐn zhuāngshì kètīng. *They decorated their living room with Chinese handicrafts.*
装饰品 zhuāngshì pǐn article for decoration, ornament

zhuānxiū 装修 V fit up (e.g. a house)

zhuàng 状 TRAD 狀 N form, shape

zhuàngkuàng 状况 [comp: 状 shape (of things) + 况 situation] N shape (of things), situation, condition

zhuàngtài 状态 [comp: 状 shape (of things) + 态 condition] **N** state (of affairs), appearance

zhuàng 撞 v bump against, collide

zhuī 追 v chase, run after, try to catch up

zhuīdào 追悼 v mourn over (the death of somebody)

zhuīdàohuì 追悼会 N memorial service, memorial meeting

zhuīqiú 追求 [comp: 追 chase + 求 seek] **v** pursue, seek ■ 人人追求幸福。**Rénrén zhuīqiú xìngfú.** *Everyone pursues happiness.*

zhǔn 准 TRAD 準 **ADJ** accurate, exact

zhǔnbèi 准备 v & N prepare; preparation 准备好 **zhǔnbèi hǎo** be well prepared

zhǔnquè 准确 [comp: 准 accurate + 确 verified] **ADJ** accurate, exact

zhǔnshí 准时 ADJ punctual, on time

zhuō 捉 v catch, capture

zhuōzi 桌子 [suffix: 桌 table + 子 nominal suffix] **N** table, desk (张 **zhāng**)

zī 咨 v consult

zīxún 咨询 [comp: 咨 consult + 询 inquire] **v & N** seek advice from, consultation

zī 姿 N looks, appearance

zīshì 姿势 N posture, carriage

zī 资 TRAD 資 **N** money, property

zīběn 资本 [comp: 资 capital + 本 principal] **N** capital 资本主义 **zīběn zhǔyì** capitalism

zīgé 资格 N qualification

zījīn 资金 [comp: 资 capital + 金 gold, fund] **N** fund, capital

zīliào 资料 [comp: 资 capital + 料 material] **N** material, data

zīyuán 资源 [modif: 资 capital + 源 source] **N** natural resources

zī 滋 v grow

zīzhǎng 滋长 v grow, develop, engender

zǐ 子 N son 长子 **zhǎngzi** the first son, eldest son

zǐdì 子弟 N children and younger family members

zǐsūn 子孙 N children and grandchildren, descendants 子孙后代 **zǐsūn hòudài** descendants, posterity

zǐ-nǚ 子女 N sons and daughters, one's children

zǐ 仔 ADJ careful

zǐxì 仔细 ADJ very careful, paying attention to details

zǐ 紫 ADJ purple

zì 自 PREP Same as 从 **cóng**. Used only in written Chinese.

zìcóng 自从 [comp: 自 from + 从 from] **PREP** from, since

zìdòng 自动 [modif: 自 self + 动 act] **ADJ** automatic

zìfèi 自费 [modif: 自 self + 费 cost] **ADJ** self-supporting, paid by oneself 自费留学生 **zìfèi liúxuéshēng** self-supporting foreign student, fee-paying foreign student

zìháo 自豪 [modif: 自 self + 豪 pride] **v** be very proud of oneself

zìjǐ 自己 PRON self, one's own 你自己 **nǐ zìjǐ** yourself / 你们自己 **nǐmen zìjǐ** yourselves / 他/她自己 **tā zìjǐ** himself/herself / 他们自己 **tāmen zìjǐ** themselves / 我自己 **wǒ zìjǐ** myself / 我们自己 **wǒmen zìjǐ** ourselves

zìjué 自觉 [modif: 自 self + 觉 conscious, aware] **ADJ** being aware of, being conscious of, voluntary, conscientious

zìrán 自然 I N nature **II ADJ** natural

zìshā 自杀 v & N attempt or commit suicide; suicide

zìsī 自私 [comp: 自 self + 私 private] **ADJ** selfish, egoistic

zìxìn 自信 ADJ self-confident 缺乏自信 **quēfá zìxìn** lacking in self-confidence

zìxíngchē 自行车 [modif: 自 self + 行 walking + 车 vehicle] **N** bicycle (辆 **liàng**)

zìxué 自学 [modif: 自 self + 学 study] **v**

study independently, teach oneself

zìyóu 自由 ADJ & N free, unrestrained; freedom, liberty

zìyuàn 自愿 [modif: 自 self + 愿 willing] ADJ voluntary, of one's own accord

zìzhùcān 自助餐 [modif: 自助 self-help + 餐 meal] N buffet dinner, buffet

zì 字 N Chinese character ■ 这个字是什么意思? 怎么念? **Zhège zì shì shénme yìsi? zěnme niàn?** *What is the meaning of this Chinese character? How is it pronounced?*

zìmǔ 字母 N letter (of an alphabet) 字母表 **zìmǔbiǎo** alphabet

zìmù 字幕 N caption, subtitle

zi 子 SUFFIX (forming a noun, e.g. **bēizi 杯子**, **xiāngzi 箱子**, etc.)

zōng 宗 N ancestor

zōngjiào 宗教 N religion 宗教信仰 **zōngjiào xìnyǎng** religious belief

zōng 综 TRAD 綜 ADJ comprehensive

zōnghé 综合 ADJ comprehensive, synthesized

zǒng 总 TRAD 總 ADV always, invariably

zǒngcái 总裁 N CEO, director general

zǒnggòng 总共 [comp: 总 total + 共 altogether] ADV in all, altogether

zǒngjié 总结 [modif: 总 general + 结 conclude, conclusion] V & N sum up, do a review of one's past work or life experiences; summary, a general view of one's past work or life experiences

zǒnglǐ 总理 [modif: 总 general + 理 administer] N premier, prime minister

zǒngshì 总是 ADV Same as 总 **zǒng**

zǒngsuàn 总算 ADV at long last, finally

zǒngtǒng 总统 [modif: 总 general + 统 rule, command] N president (of a country)

zǒngzhī 总之 ADV in a word, in short

zǒu 走 V walk; leave

zòu 奏 V play a musical instrument

zū 租 V & N rent, hire, charter; rent (money) 房租 **fángzū** (housing) rent

zūjīn 租金 [modif: 租 rent + 金 gold] N money paid for lease or hiring, rent

zú 足 N foot

zúqiú 足球 [modif: 足 foot + 球 ball] N soccer, football

zú 族 N clan, nationality (See **mínzú 民族**.)

zǔ 阻 V 1 resist, prevent 2 hinder, block

zǔlì 阻力 [modif: 阻 resist + 力 strength, force] N resistance, obstacle

zǔzhǐ 阻止 [comp: 阻 stop + 止 stop] V prevent, stop, hold back

zǔ 祖 N ancestor

zǔfù 祖父 [modif: 祖 ancestor + 父 father] N grandfather

zǔguó 祖国 [modif: 祖 ancestor + 国 country] N motherland, fatherland

zǔmǔ 祖母 [modif: 祖 ancestor + 母 mother] N grandmother

zǔ 组 TRAD 組 N group

zǔchéng 组成 V make up, compose, consist of

zǔhé 组合 I V make up, compose, constitute II N association, combination

zǔzhī 组织 [comp: 组 to group + 织 to weave] V & N organize, arrange for; organization, organized system

zuǐ 嘴 N mouth

zuì 最 ADV most (used before an adjective to indicate the superlative degree)

zuìchū 最初 N the initial stage, initially

zuìhǎo 最好 [modif: 最 most + 好 good] ADV had better

zuìhòu 最后 N & ADV the final stage; finally

zuìjìn 最近 ADV & N recently; recent time

zuì 醉 V get drunk, be intoxicated

zūn 尊 V respect

zūnjìng 尊敬 [comp: 尊 respect + 敬 respect] V respect, honor

zūnzhòng 尊重 [comp: 尊 respect + 重 value] v respect, esteem, value

zūn 遵 v obey

zūnshǒu 遵守 [comp: 遵 obey + 守 abide by] v observe, abide by

zuó 昨 N yesterday

zuótiān 昨天 [modif: 昨 past + 天 day] N yesterday

zuó 琢 as in 琢磨 **zuómo**

zuómo 琢磨 v turn over in one's mind, think over, consider

zuǒ 左 N the left side

zuǒbian 左边 [modif: 左 left + 边 side] N the left side, the left-hand side

zuǒyòu 左右 [comp: 左 left + 右 right] ADV approximately, nearly, about

zuò 坐 v sit, be seated

zuò 作 v Same as 做 **zuò**

NOTE: 做 **zuò** and 作 **zuò** have the same pronunciation and often the same meaning, but 做 **zuò** is much more commonly used while 作 **zuò** occurs only in certain set expressions.

zuòjiā 作家 [modif: 作 create + 家 expert] N writer (especially of literary works, e.g. novels, stories)

zuòpǐn 作品 [modif: 作 create + 品 article] N literary or artistic work

zuòwéi 作为 PREP as, in the capacity of

zuòwén 作文 [modif: 作 create + 文 writing] N (student's) composition

zuòyè 作业 N school assignment, homework

zuòyòng 作用 [comp: 作 work + 用 use] N function, role
在 ··· 中起作用 zài ... zhōng qǐ zuòyòng play a role in …, perform a function in …

zuòzhě 作者 [suffix: 作 create + 者 nominal suffix] N author

zuò 座 MEASURE WORD (for large and solid objects, such as a large building)
一座城市 yí zuò chéngshì a city / 一座

大楼 yí zuò dàlóu a big building / 一座大学 yí zuò dàxué a university / 一座工厂 yí zuò gōngchǎng a factory / 一座桥 yí zuò qiáo a bridge / 一座山 yí zuò shān a mountain, a hill

zuòtán 座谈 [comp: 座 seat + 谈 talk] v have an informal discussion, have an informal meeting

zuòtánhuì 座谈会 N an informal discussion, forum

zuòwèi 座位 [comp: 座 seat + 位 seat] N seat

zuò 做 v 1 do 2 make

NOTE: See note on 作 **zuò**.

zuòdōng 做东 v play host, stand the treat

zuòfǎ 做法 [modif: 做 do + 法 method] N way of doing things, method, practice

zuòfàn 做饭 N cook, prepare a meal

zuògōng 做工 v do manual work, work

zuòkè 做客 v be a guest, visit

zuòmèng 做梦 N & v 1 dream; have a dream 2 daydream; have a pipe dream
■ 别做梦了。Bié zuòmèng le. Don't be daydreaming.

English-Chinese Word Finder

A

a decade of a century **niándài** 年代 80

a good many, a large number of, lots of **hǎoxiē** 好些 44

a good many, much **hǎo duō** 好多 43

a large amount of, a large number of **dàliàng** 大量 19

a large quantity of, lots of **dàpī** 大批 19

a long period of time **chángqī** 长期 12, **hǎojiǔ** 好久 43

a nominal suffix (denoting a person or people) **zhě** 者 135

a period of time felt to be very long, a very long time **bàntiān** 半天 3

a person or animal (colloquial Chinese) **dōngxi** 东西 25

a short while ago, just **gāngcái** 刚才 35

a small amount of, a bit of **yìxiē** 一些 124, **yìdiǎnr** 一点儿 124

a true man, true men **nánzǐhàn** 男子汉 79

a young child between 2 and 6 years old **yòu'ér** 幼儿 129

abandon, give up **fàngqì** 放弃 31

abdomen, stomach, belly **dùzi** 肚子 26

ability, capacity **nénglì** 能力 79

able, capable, efficient (of people) **nénggàn** 能干 79

abode of gods, Heaven **tiān** 天 105

about, on **guānyú** 关于 39

above, high up **shàngbian** 上边 93, **shàngmiàn** 上面 93

absent from work without leave **kuànggōng** 旷工 65

absolute **juéduì** 绝对 61

absorb, draw **xīqǔ** 吸取 113

absorb, take in **shèqǔ** 摄取 94

abstract (adj.) **chōuxiàng** 抽象 15

abundant, ample, adequate **chōngfèn** 充分 14

abundant, rich, plenty **fēngfù** 丰富 32

academic degree **xuéwèi** 学位 120

accept, take **jiēshòu** 接受 57

accept an offer of an employment **yìngpìn** 应聘 127

accidentally, by chance **ǒurán** 偶然 81

accompany (somebody), take, escort **sòng** 送 101

accomplish, fulfill, complete **wánchéng** 完成 109

according to a fixed time, on time **ànshí** 按时 2

according to, in accordance with **àn** 按 2

according to, in the manner of **zhào** 照 134

account **zhànghù** 账户 134

accounting; accountant **kuàijì** 会计 65

accumulate, build up **jīlěi** 积累 50

accurate, exact **zhǔnquè** 准确 141

ache, hurt (v.) **téng** 疼 104, **tòng** 痛 (v.) 107

achievement, examination result **chéngjì** 成绩 13

acknowledge, recognize **chéngrèn** 承认 14

acrobatics, juggery **bǎxì** 把戏 2

act as referee or umpire (in sports) **cáipàn** 裁判 10

act in the capacity of **dānrèn** 担任 20

act perfunctorily **yìngfu** 应付 127

active, brisk **huóyuè** 活跃 49

actor, actress **yǎnyuán** 演员 122

actually, as a matter of fact, in fact **qíshí** 其实 85

acupuncture and moxibustion **zhēnjiǔ** 针灸 135

acute (disease) **jíxìng** 急性 51

add fuel, fuel up **jiāyóu** 加油 52

add up; statistics **tǒngjì** 统计 107

address **dìzhǐ** 地址 23

address or reference to a child (friendly) **xiǎopéngyou** 小朋友 116

address: to an old man (a respectful form) **lǎoxiānsheng** 老先生 67; to an old woman (a respectful form) **lǎotàitai** 老太太 67

adjudicate, judge (in law) **cáipàn** 裁判 10

adjust, rectify **tiáozhěng** 调整 105

adjust, regulate **tiáojì** 调剂 105

admire **pèifu** 佩服 82

admire and enjoy **xīnshǎng** 欣赏 118

admit (mistakes, errors, etc.) **chéngrèn** 承认 14

adolescents and young people **qīngshàonián** 青少年 87

adopt (a policy, a measure, an attitude, etc.) **cǎiqǔ** 采取 10

adult **chéngrén** 成人 13

adult, grown-up **dàren** 大人 19

advance **qiánjìn** 前进 86

advanced, high-level **gāojí** 高级 35

advancing a step further **jìnyíbù** 进一步 58

advertise for a position, recruit (employees) **zhāopìn** 招聘 134

advertisement, (TV) commercial **guǎnggào** 广告 40

advocate, recommend **tíchàng** 提倡 104

advocate, stand for; what one stands for **zhǔzhāng** 主张 140

affair, matter, business **shì** 事 97

affect, have bearing on **guānxi** 关系 39

affection, love **gǎnqíng** 感情 34

affirm, confirm **quèrèn** 确认 89

Africa **Fēizhōu** 非洲 31

after, later **yǐhòu** 以后 125

after all, anyway **bìjìng** 毕竟 6

after this, ever after **cǐhòu** 此后 17, **cǐkè** 此刻 17

afternoon **xiàwǔ** 下午 114

afterwards, ... and then **ránhòu** 然后 89

afterwards, later on **hòulái** 后来 45

again **yòu** 又 129, **zài** 再 131

again, once again **chóngxīn** 重新 15

age (of a person) **niánlíng** 年龄 80, **niánjì** 年纪 80

agent, intermediary **zhōngjièrén** 中介人 138

agree, approve **tóngyì** 同意 106

agreeable, of the same mind **tóujī** 投机 107

agreement, treaty **xiédìng** 协定 117

agriculture, farming **nóngyè** 农业 80

aim, purpose **mùdì** 目的 77

aim at **zhēnduì** 针对 135

air, atmosphere **kōngqì** 空气 64

air conditioner **kōngtiáojī** 空调机 64

aircraft, airplane **fēijī** 飞机 31

airport, airfield **fēijī chǎng** 飞机场 31, **jīchǎng** 机场 49

alcoholic beverage, wine **jiǔ** 酒 60

all, both, every and each, without exception **dōu** 都 25

all, entire, each and every one (of a group of people) **quántǐ** 全体 89

all, entire, without exception **quánbù** 全部 89, **yíqiè** 一切 124, **yìtóng** 一同 124, **suǒyǒu** 所有 102, **yílǜ** 一律 124

all, entirely **tǒngtǒng** 统统 107

all, everybody **dàjiā** 大家 19

all, everything **yíqiè** 一切 124

all at once, all at a sudden **yíxiàzi** 一下子 124

all one's life, lifetime **yìshēng** 一生 124

all right, OK, (that) will do **xíng** 行 118

all the year round **chángnián** 常年 12, **zhōngnián** 终年 139

all-round, comprehensive **quánmiàn** 全面 89

alleviate, relieve **huǎnjiě** 缓解 47

allow, permit **yǔnxǔ** 允许 131

allow display, give free rein to **fāhuī** 发挥 29

allowance, pocket money, small change **língqián** 零钱 70

almost **chàbuduō** 差不多 12

almost, nearly **chàdiǎnr** 差点儿 12, **jīhū** 几乎 49

alone, on one's own **dāndú** 单独 20

along with, in the wake of **suízhè** 随着 102

already **yǐjīng** 已经 125

also, too **yě** 也 123

altar **tán** 坛 103

alter, change, correct **gǎi** 改 34

although **suīrán** 虽然 101

altitude, height **gāodù** 高度 35

altogether, in total **gòng** 共 37

always, all the time **yìzhí** 一直 124

always, constantly **lǎoshi** 老是 67

always, ever **cónglái** 从来 17

always, invariably **zǒngshì** 总是 142

ambassador **dàshǐ** 大使 19

amend, revise **xiūgǎi** 修改 120

Americas (continent of) **Měizhōu** 美洲 74

among them, in it **qízhōng** 其中 85

amuse, give pleasure to **yú** 娱 129

analyze; analysis **fēnxī** 分析 32

ancestor **zǔ** 祖 142

ancient **gǔ** 古 38

ancient, time-honored **gǔlǎo** 古老 38

ancient times, antiquity **gǔdài** 古代 38

and, with **hé** 和 44, **jí** 及 50

and so on and so forth, et cetera **děng** 等 23, **shénmede** 什么的 95

angle (maths) **jiǎo** 角 56

angle (to fish) **diào** 钓 25

angle, point of view **jiǎodù** 角度 56

animal (as verbal abuse) **chùsheng** 畜生 16

animal **dòngwù** 动物 25

animated cartoon, cartoons **dònghuà piàn** 动画片 25

annotate; explanatory note, note **zhùjiě** 注解 140

annoyed and angry, vexed **fánnǎo** 烦恼 29

answer (to a list of questions) **dá'àn** 答案 18

answer, reply **dāying** 答应 18

anthropology **rénlèi xué** 人类学 90

anxious, worried, impatient **jí** 急 51

any, whatever **rènhé** 任何 90

anyway, at any rate **fǎnzheng** 反正 30

apartment house, housing complex **gōngyù** 公寓 37

apologetic, sorry, regretful **bàoqiàn** 抱歉 4

apologize, say sorry; apology **dàoqiàn** 道歉 22

apology, regret **qiànyì** 歉意 86

appeal, call on **hūyù** 呼吁 46

appear to be, seem to be **xiǎnde** 显得 114

appearance, look **múyàng** 模样 77

appearance, shape, form **xíngzhuàng** 形状 119

appearance, shape, manner **yàngzi** 样子 122

appetite, interest (in something) **wèikǒu** 胃口 111

apple **píngguǒ** 苹果 84

applicable, suitable **shìyòng** 适用 98

apply, use **yìngyòng** 应用 127

apply for (a visa, a job, a permit, etc.) **shēnqǐng** 申请 94

appointment (social), engagement, date **yuēhuì** 约会 130

appraise, evaluate; appraisal, evaluation **píngjià** 评价 84

appreciate, like **xīnshǎng** 欣赏 118

apprentice, pupil **túdì** 徒弟 107

appropriate, proper, suitable **shìdàng** 适当 98

approve, ratify **pīzhǔn** 批准 83

approve of, support, be in favor of **zànchéng** 赞成 132

approximately, about **dàyuē** 大约 19, **múyàng** 模样 77

approximately, nearly, about **zuǒyòu** 左右 143

Arabic language (especially the writing), the **Ālābówén** 阿拉伯文 1

Arabic language, the **Ālābóyǔ** 阿拉伯语 1

architect **jiànzhùshī** 建筑师 54

architecture (as a discipline) **jiànzhùxué** 建筑学 54

area (in mathematics) **miànjī** 面积 75

arm **gēbo** 胳膊 35

armed forces, troops **jūnduì** 军队 61

arms and ammunition **jūnhuǒ** 军火 61

army uniform **jūnzhuāng** 军装 61

arouse, stir up **jīfā** 激发 50

arrange, make arrangements; plan **ānpái** 安排 1

arrange, put in order **páiliè** 排列 81

arrest, take into custody **dàibǔ** 逮捕 20

arrive, reach **dàodá** 到达 21

art **yìshù** 艺术 125

artificial leg **jiǎtuǐ** 假腿 53

artificial, man-made **réngōng** 人工 90

artillery man **pàobīng** 炮兵 82

artist **yìshùjiā** 艺术家 125

arts and crafts, handicraft **shǒugōngyì** 手工艺 98

as, in the capacity of **zuòwéi** 作为 143

as a result, consequently **yúshì** 于是 129

as a result, consequently, finally **jiéguǒ** 结果 57

as far as possible, to the best of one's ability **jǐnliàng** 尽量 58

as luck would have it, fortunately **qiàqiǎo** 恰巧 86

as soon as possible, as fast as possible **jǐn kuài** 尽快 58

as usual **zhàocháng** 照常 134

Asia **Yàzhōu** 亚洲 121

ask, demand, require; demand, requirement **yāoqiú** 要求 122

ask, request **qǐng** 请 88

ask (a question), inquire **wèn** 问 112

ask after, give greetings to **wèn hǎo** 问好 112

ask for leave **qǐngjià** 请假 88

ask the way **wènlù** 问路 112

assemble, get together **jù** 聚 61

assembly, congress, rally **dàhuì** 大会 19

assign (a job) **pài** 派 82

assignment, mission **rènwù** 任务 90

associate with, be in contact with **jiāowǎng** 交往 55

association (an organization), society **xiéhuì** 协会 117

association, combination **zǔhé** 组合 142

at a particular point in time **shíkè** 时刻 96

at least **zhìshǎo** 至少 138

at long last, finally **zǒngsuàn** 总算 142

at night **yèlǐ** 夜里 123, **yèwǎn** 夜晚 123

at once, immediately **mǎshàng** 马上 72, **lìkè** 立刻 68

at present, at this moment, now **mùqián** 目前 77, **yǎnqián** 眼前 122

at that time, then **dāngshí** 当时 21

at the beginning, for the first time **chū** 初 15

at the heels of (a previous action or event) **jiēzhe** 接着 57

at the place in question, local **dāngdì** 当地 21

at the same time **yǔ cǐ tóng shí** 与此同时 129, **tóngshí** 同时 106

at the time of, when **dāng** 当 21

athlete, sportsperson **yùndòngyuán** 运动员 131

atlas **dìtúcè** 地图册 23

atmosphere, ambiance **qìfēn** 气氛 85

atmospheric temperature **qìwēn** 气温 85

attach, add **fù** 附 33

attach importance to, value **zhòngshì** 重视 139

attempt or commit suicide; suicide **zìshā** 自杀 141

attend (a meeting, a court trial, etc.) **chūxí** 出席 15

attend (a school), study (in a school) **dú** 读 26

attend (school), go to (work) **shàng** 上 93

attend/hold a meeting **kāihuì** 开会 62

attendant, waiter/waitress **fúwù yuán** 服务员 32

attract **xīyǐn** 吸引 113

auction, sell at a reduced price **pāimài** 拍卖 81

audience (in a theater, of TV, etc.), spectator **guānzhòng** 观众 39

audio/sound recorder **lùyīnjī** 录音机 71

auditorium, assembly hall **lǐtáng** 礼堂 67

Australia **Àodàlìyà** 澳大利亚 2

author **zuòzhě** 作者 143

authorities, the **dāngjú** 当局 21

authority, power **quánlì** 权力 89

autograph, sign one's name **qiānmíng** 签名 86

automatic **zìdòng** 自动 141

automobile, car **qìchē** 汽车 86

average **píngjūn** 平均 84

average, commonplace **yìbān** 一般 123

aviation **hángkōng** 航空 43

avoid, avert **bìmiǎn** 避免 6

award (v.) **shǎng** 赏 93

award; prize, award **jiǎng** 奖 55

B

back (of the body), the **hòubèi** 后背 45

back, rear **hòubian** 后边, **hòumiàn** 后面 45

background **bèijǐng** 背景 5

backpack **bèibāo** 背包 5

backward, outdated **luòhòu** 落后 72

bad **huài** 坏 47

bad, evil **è** 恶 28

badminton, shuttlecock **yǔmáoqiú** 羽毛球 129

bake, roast, toast **kǎo** 烤 63

bakery **miànbāo fáng** 面包房 76

balcony **yángtái** 阳台 122

ball **qiú** 球 88

balloon **qìqiú** 气球 85

ballroom dancing **jiāojìwǔ** 交际舞 55

bamboo **zhúzi** 竹子 139

banana **xiāngjiāo** 香蕉 115

band, orchestra **yuèduì** 乐队 130

bandit, robber **qiángdào** 强盗 86

bank/shore (of a river, lake, or sea) **àn** 岸 2

bank **yínháng** 银行 126

banquet, feast **yànhuì** 宴会 122

bar, pub **jiǔbā** 酒吧 60

barber, hairdresser, hairstylist **lǐfàshī** 理发师 68

barbershop, hair salon **lǐfàdiàn** 理发店 68

base **jīdì** 基地 50

basic knowledge **chángshí** 常识 12

basketball **lánqiú** 篮球 66

bathroom **yùshì** 浴室 129

bathroom, washroom, toilet **wèishēngjiān** 卫生间 111

battery, electrical cell **diànchí** 电池 24

bay, gulf **wān** 湾 109

be a guest, visit **zuòkè** 做客 143

be a pity, be a shame **kěxī** 可惜 64

be able to adapt to **shìyìng** 适应 98

be accustomed/used to; habit **xíguàn** 习惯 113

be alarmed, be panic-stricken **jīnghuāng** 惊慌 59

be anxious, be worried **zháojí** 着急 134

be ashamed **cánkuì** 惭愧 11

be at a loss what to do, be at one's wit's end **méizhé** 没辙 74

be bashful, be shy **hàixiū** 害羞 43

be born **chūshēng** 出生 15

be bound to, be sure to, must **bìdìng** 必定 6

be called, be known as, be referred to as **jiàozuò** 叫做 56

be cautious, take care **dāngxīn** 当心 21

be close to, be near **jiējìn** 接近 57

be concerned about, care for **guānxīn** 关心 39

be defeated, lose, fail **shībài** 失败 96

be deficient in, lack **quēfá** 缺乏 89

be determined, make up one's mind **juéxīn** 决心 17

be discharged from hospital **chūyuàn** 出院 15

be distributed (over an area); distribution **fēnbù** 分布 32

be dressed in **chuānzhe** 穿着 16

be equal to, equal **děngyú** 等于 23

be faced with **miànduì** 面对 75

be faced with, be up against **miànlín** 面临 75

be fashionable, be popular **liúxíng** 流行 71

be flustered, panic **huāng** 慌 47

be fond of eating, be gluttonous **hào chī** 好吃 44

be fooled, be duped **shàngdàng** 上当 93

be free, not occupied **kòngxián** 空闲 64

be good at **shànyú** 善于 92

be good, be well-behaved (of children) **guāi** 乖 39

be grateful, thank **gǎnxiè** 感谢 35

be greedy **tān** 贪 103

be hospitalized **zhùyuàn** 住院 14

be in accord **fú** 符 33

be in charge of, host (a TV program), chair (a meeting) **zhǔchí** 主持 139

be in common use, be current **tōngyòng** 通用 106

be in romantic love, be courting **liàn'ài** 恋爱 69

be independent **dúlì** 独立 26

be interested (in) **gǎn xìngqù** 感兴趣 35

be jealous; envy **dùjì** 妒忌 26

be left over, have as surplus **shèng** 剩 96

be like, as **rútóng** 如同 91

be like, as alike **fǎngfú** 仿佛 31

be like, be similar to **hǎoxiàng** 好像 44

be located in, be situated **wèiyú** 位于 111

be no good (at something), be poor in **bùxíng** 不行 10

be not as good as, be not as ... as **bùrú** 不如 9

be on a business trip **chūchāi** 出差 15

be on holiday, have the day off **fàngjià** 放假 27

be on show, put on display **zhǎnchū** 展出 133

be particular about, pay much attention to **jiǎngjiu** 讲究 55

be plenty of, not in short supply **yǒudeshì** 有的是 131

be pregnant **huáiyùn** 怀孕 47

be pregnant, give rise to **yùnyù** 孕育 131

be present at a meeting (conference) **yǔhuì** 与会 129

be present, come **guānglín** 光临 (a polite expression) 40

be punished, be penalized **shòufá** 受罚 99

be related to, be interrelated **xiāngguān** 相关 115

be responsible, be in charge **fùzé** 负责 33

be shocked, be startled, be alarmed **chījīng** 吃惊 14

be short of, lack in **chà** 差 12, **quēshǎo** 缺少 89

be stranded, be in a tough spot **kùn** 困 65

be sure to, must never **qiānwàn** 千万 (used for emphasis) 86

be underway, be in progress (construction work) **shīgōng** 施工 96

be unwilling to give up, hate to part with **shěbudé** 舍不得 94

be very proud of oneself **zìháo** 自豪 141

be willing to part with, not grudge **shědé** 舍得 94

be willing, will **yuànyì** 愿意 130

be worth, be worthwhile **zhíde** 值得 137

be worthy of, deserve **pèi** 配 82

be wounded, be injured **shòushāng** 受伤 99

be, yes **shì** 是 97

beam (in structure) **liáng** 梁 69

bean curd, tofu **dòufu** 豆腐 26

bear (animal) **xióng** 熊 120

beautiful **měilì** 美丽 74

beautiful, bright (of abstract things) **měihǎo** 美好 74

beautiful, graceful **yōuměi** 优美 127

because of, owing to, due to **yóuyú** 由于 128

because **yīnwèi** 因为 126

beckon, attract **zhāo** 招 134

become **chéngwéi** 成为 13

become famous **chéngmíng** 成名 13

becomes liquid, condense (of gas or hot air) **níngjié** 凝结 80

bed **chuáng** 床 16

bedroom **wòshì** 卧室 *112*

bee **mìfēng** 蜜蜂 *75*

beef **niúròu** 牛肉 *80*

beer **píjiǔ** 啤酒 *83*

before, some time ago **yǐqián** 以前 *125*

before one's eyes **yǎnqián** 眼前 *122*

beforehand, in advance **shìxiān** 事先 *97*

begin, start, commence; beginning, start **kāishǐ** 开始 *62*

begin construction **dònggōng** 动工 *25*

behavior, conduct, act **xíngwéi** 行为 *119*

Beijing (Peking) **běijīng** 北京 *5*

Beijing (Peking) opera **jīngjù** 京剧 *59*

being aware of, being conscious of; voluntary, conscientious **zìjué** 自觉 *141*

being certain and assured; confidence **bǎwò** 把握 *2*

believe, believe in **xiāngxìn** 相信 *115*

bell **líng** 铃 *70*

belong to **shǔyú** 属于 *99*

below, less than **yǐxià** 以下 *125*

below, under **xiàbian** 下边 *114*, **xiàmiàn** 下面 *114*

benefit, interest **lìyì** 利益 *68*

benefit; being beneficial **hǎochu** 好处 *43*

beseech, beg, ask for humbly **qiú** 求 *88*

besides, apart from (that), as well **cǐwài** 此外 *17*

between-meal nibbles **língshí** 零食 *70*

beyond, outside, other than **yǐwài** 以外 *125*

bicycle **zìxíngchē** 自行车 *141*

bid farewell to, part with **gàobié** 告别 *35*

big and powerful **qiángdà** 强大 *86*

big, imposing building **dàshà** 大厦 *19*

big, large **dà** 大 *19*

bill **zhàngdān** 账单 *134*

bird **niǎo** 鸟 *80*

birthday **shēngrì** 生日 *95*

birthday card **shēngrì hèkǎ** 生日贺卡 *95*

birthday present **shēngrì lǐwù** 生日礼物 *95*

bite (v.) **yǎo** 咬 *123*

bitter (food) **kǔ** 苦 *65*

black, dark **hēi** 黑 *45*

blackboard **hēibǎn** 黑板 *45*

blame (v.) **guài** 怪 *39*

blanket **tǎnzi** 毯子 *103*

blind **máng** 盲 *73*, **xiā** 瞎 *114*

blind person **mángrén** 盲人 *73*

block up, stop up **dǔ** 堵 *26*

block, keep off **dǎng** 挡 *21*

blood **xuè** 血 *121*

blood (technical term) **xuèyè** 血液 *121*

blood pressure **xuèyā** 血压 *121*

blood transfusion **shūxuè** 输血 *99*

blow (of a wind), be windy **guā fēng** 刮风 *39*

blue, indigo **lán** 蓝 *66*

bluish green **bì** 碧 *6*

boarding card **dēngjīpái** 登机牌 *23*

boat, ship **chuán** 船 *16*

boil, cook (v.) **zhǔ** 煮 *140*

boiled water **kāishuǐ** 开水 *62*

boiling hot, scalding hot **tàng** 烫 *103*

bold, courageous **dàdǎn** 大胆 *19*

bolus, pill **wán** 丸 *109*

bone **gǔtou** 骨头 *38*

book **shū** 书 *99*

book, place an order **yùdìng** 预订 *130*

bookshelf **shūjià** 书架 *99*

bookstore, bookshop **shūdiàn** 书店 *99*

bored **wúliáo** 无聊 *112*

borrow, lend **jiè** 借 *57*

boss, one in charge **lǎobǎn** 老板 *66*

botanical garden **zhíwùyuán** 植物园 *137*

botany **zhíwùxué** 植物学 *137*

both sides, both parties **shuāngfāng** 双方 *100*

bottle **píngzi** 瓶子 *84*

boundary, border **jì** 际 *52*, **jiāng** 疆 *55*

bow (archer's) **gōng** 弓 *37*

bowl **wǎn** 碗 *109*

box, case **hézi** 盒子 *44*

box, chest **xiāng** 箱 *115*

boy **nán háizi** 男孩子 *78*

brain, mind **nǎozi** 脑子 *79*

brand name, brand **páizi** 牌子 *82*

brand-new, nascent **zhǎnxīn** 崭新 *133*

brave, bold **dǎndà** 胆大 *20*

brave, bold, fearless **yǒnggǎn** 勇敢 *127*

bread **miànbāo** 面包 *76*

break **dǎpò** 打破 *18*

break down, be out of order **huài** 坏 *47*

break through; breakthrough **tūpò** 突破 *107*

breakfast **zǎofàn** 早饭 *132*

breast **rǔfáng** 乳房 *91*

breathe, inhale and exhale **hūxī** 呼吸 *46*

bricks and tiles, building material **zhuānwǎ** 砖瓦 *140*

bridge **qiáo** 桥 *87*

brief note, message **tiězi** 帖子 *105*

brief period of rain, shower **zhènyǔ** 阵雨 *136*

briefly or casually **yíxià** 一下 *124*

bright-colored, gaily-colored **xiānyàn** 鲜艳 *114*

bright, well-lit **míngliàng** 明亮 *76*

brilliant, splendid **huīhuáng** 辉煌 *48*

brilliant, thrilling, wonderful (theatrical performance or sports event) **jīngcǎi** 精彩 *59*

bring, take **dài** 带 *20*

bring in, introduce **shūrù** 输入 *99*

bring up, nurture **péiyù** 培育 *82*

Britain, the UK **Yīngguó** 英国 *126*

broadband **kuāndài** 宽带 *65*

broadcast (radio or TV programs) **bōfàng** 播放 *8*, **guǎngbō** 广播 *40*

brother(s) **xiōngdì** 兄弟 *119*

browse **liúlǎn** 浏览 *71*

brush (n.) **shuāzi** 刷子 *100*

brush (v.) **shuā** 刷 *100*

Buddha **fó** 佛 *32*

Buddhism **fójiào** 佛教 *32*

buffet dinner **zìzhùcān** 自助餐 *142*

build, construct **jiànlì** 建立 *54*, **jiànshè** 建设 *54*

build, erect; building, edifice **jiànzhù** 建筑 *54*

building (for a specific purpose) **guǎn** 馆 *40*

building with two or more stories **lóu** 楼 *71*

bullet **dàn** 弹 *21*

bump against, collide **zhuàng** 撞 *141*

bump into, touch **pèng** 碰 *83*

Bureau of Public Health, Health Department **wèishēngjú** 卫生局 *111*

burn **ránshāo** 燃烧 *89*

burn the midnight oil **kāi yèchē** 开夜车 *62*

bus **gōnggòng qìchē** 公共汽车 *37*

bus stop, coach station, railway station **chēzhàn** 车站 *13*

business **yèwù** 业务 *123*

business, trade **shēngyi** 生意 *95*

business administration **shāngyè guǎnlǐ** 商业管理 *93*

business affairs **shāngwù** 商务 *93*

business district **shāngyè qū** 商业区 *93*

busy, fully occupied **máng** 忙 *73*

but, yet **búguò** 不过 *9*, **dànshì** 但是 *21*, **kěshì** 可是 *64*, **rán'ér** 然而 *89*

butter **huángyóu** 黄油 *48*

butterfly **húdié** 蝴蝶 *46*

buy, purchase (v.) **mǎi** 买 *73*

buying and sellinng, trade, business **mǎimài** 买卖 *73*

by (the agent of an action) **yóu** 由 *128*

by oneself **qīnzì** 亲自 *87*, **qīnshēn** 亲身 *87*, **gèzì** 各自 *36*

C

cabbage **báicài** 白菜 *2*

cabin (in ship or airplane) **cāng** 舱 *11*

cadre, official **gànbù** 干部 *35*

cake **dàngāo** 蛋糕 *21*

cakes and pastries **gāodiǎn** 糕点 *35*

calculate **suàn** 算 *101*

calendar **rìlì** 日历 *91*

call, address, shout, cry out **jiào** 叫 *56*

call, address; form of address **chēnghu** 称呼 *13*

call, shout at **zhāohu** 招呼 *134*

call a taxi **dǎ chē** 打车, **dǎ dī** 打的 *18*

call on, pay a visit to **kànwàng** 看望 *63*

calm, quiet, uneventful **píngjìng** 平静 *84*

camera **zhàoxiàngjī** 照相机 *135*

can, be able to **néng** 能 *79*, **nénggòu** 能够 *79*

can only, have no choice but **zhǐyǒu** 只有 *137*

Canada **Jiānádà** 加拿大 *52*

cancel **qǔxiāo** 取消 *88*

cancer **áizhèng** 癌症 *1*

candid, frank **tǎnshuài** 坦率 *103*

capacity, volume **róngliàng** 容量 *91*

capital (for investment) **zīběn** 资本 *141*

capital city **shǒudū** 首都 *98*

caption, subtitle **zìmù** 字幕 *142*

carbon **tàn** 碳 *103*

card **kǎ** 卡 *62*

care, care about **zàihu** 在乎 *132*

care for and protect, cherish **àihù** 爱护 *1*

careful, cautious **xiǎoxīn** 小心 *117*, **jǐnshèn** 谨慎 *58*

careless **cūxīn** 粗心 *17*

careless, sloppy **mǎ mǎ hū hū** 马马虎虎 *72*

carpet **dìtǎn** 地毯 *23*

carriage (in a train) **chēxiāng** 车厢 *13*

carry in the hand **tí** 提 *104*

carry on the back **fù** 负 *33*

carry on the head, hit with the head **dǐng** 顶 *25*

carry on the shoulder, take on **dān** 担 *20*

carry out, execute **shī** 施 *96*

carry out, launch **zhǎnkāi** 展开 *133*

carry… on the back **bēi** 背 *5*

carve, engrave, cut **kè** 刻 *64*

cash pledge, deposit **yājīn** 押金 *121*

cast, spread out **sā** 撒 *92*

cast a vote, vote **tóupiào** 投票 *107*

castle, citadel **chéngbǎo** 城堡 *14*

casual, informal **suíbiàn** 随便 *102*

casually, without much thought **suíshǒu** 随手 *102*

cat **māo** 猫 *73*

catalog **mùlù** 目录 *77*

catch a cold **zháoliáng** 着凉 *134*, **gǎnmào** 感冒 *34*

catch cold, have a cold **shāngfēng** 伤风 *92*

catch fire, be caught fire **zháohuǒ** 着火 *134*

catering industry, catering **yǐnshíyè** 饮食业 *126*

cattle, ox, cow, calf, buffalo **niú** 牛 *80*

Caucasian **báirén** 白人 *2*

cause, reason **yuányīn** 原因 *130*

cave (for hiding), cavern **dòngxué** 洞穴 *25*

celebrate; celebration **qìngzhù** 庆祝 *88*

celestial body, star **xīng** 星 *118*

cell phone, mobile phone **shǒujī** 手机 *98*

center, middle, among **zhōngjiān** 中间 *138*

center on, focus on **wéirào** 围绕 *110*

centimeter **gōngfēn** 公分 *37*

central part, center **zhōngxīn** 中心 *138*

century **shìjì** 世纪 *97*

CEO, director general **zǒngcái** 总裁 *142*

cereal, grain **gǔ** 谷 *38*

ceremony, function, rite **yíshì** 仪式 *125*

certainly, definitely **yídìng** 一定 *124*

certificate **zhèngshū** 证书 *136*

chair **yǐzi** 椅子 *125*

chairman, chairperson **zhǔxí** 主席 *140*

chairman, director **zhǔrèn** 主任 *139*

chalk **fěnbǐ** 粉笔 *32*

challenge (to a battle, contest), throw down the gauntlet; challenge **tiǎozhàn** 挑战 *105*

champion, championship **guànjūn** 冠军 *40*

chance to, by coincidence **zhènghǎo** 正好 *136*

change, replace **huàn** 换 *47*

change, transform (usually for the better) **zhuǎnbiàn** 转变 *140*

change a scheduled time, change the date (of an event) **gǎiqī** 改期 *34*

change into, turn into **biànchéng** 变成 *7*

change one's profession (or trade) **gǎiháng** 改行 *34*

characteristic, feature **tèzhēng** 特征 *104*

charge, rush, dash **chōng** 冲 *15*

charger (battery's) **chōngdiànqì** 充电器 *14*

charm, enchantment **mèilì** 魅力 *74*

chase, run after, try to catch up **zhuī** 追 *141*

chat, chitchat **tántiān** 谈天 *103*

chat, shoot the bull/breeze **liáotiān** 聊天 *70*

cheap goods, bargain **piányihuò** 便宜货 *83*

check, cheque (in banking) **zhīpiào** 支票 *137*

check, look up **chá** 查 *11*

cheek **sāi** 腮 *92*

chemical industry **huàgōng** 化工 *46*

chemical test, laboratory test **huàyàn** 化验 *47*

chemistry **huàxué** 化学 *47*

cherish **xiōnghuái** 胸怀 *119*

cherish dearly, value highly **zhēnxī** 珍惜 *135*, **àixī** 爱惜 *1*

cherish the memory of, think of tenderly **huáiniàn** 怀念 *47*

chess **xiàngqí** 象棋 *115*

chest (human body), the **xiōngtáng** 胸膛 *120*

chew, munch, masticate **jiáo** 嚼 *56*, **jué** 嚼 *61*

chicken, hen, rooster **jī** 鸡 *50*

chief (n.) **zhǎng** 长 *134*

child, children **értóng** 儿童 *28*, **háizi** 孩子 *42*

child, son **ér** 儿 *28*

childhood **tóngnián** 童年 *107*

children and grandchildren, descendants **zǐsūn** 子孙 *141*

children and younger family members **zǐdì** 子弟 *141*

children's story, fairy tale **tónghuà** 童话 *107*

China **Zhōngguó** 中国 *138*

China, Chinese **Zhōnghuá** 中华 *138*

Chinese character **Hànzì** 汉字 *43*

Chinese cuisine, Chinese food **zhōngcān** 中餐 *138*

Chinese currency, Renminbi **Rénmínbì** 人民币 *90*

Chinese language (especially the writing), the **Zhōngwén** 中文 *138*

Chinese language, the **Hànyǔ** 汉语 *43*

Chinese New Year's Eve **chúxī** 除夕 *16*

chocolate **qiǎokèlì** 巧克力 *87*

chopsticks **kuàizi** 筷子 *65*

Christmas **Shèngdànjié** 圣诞节 *96*

chronic (disease) **mànxìng** 慢性 *73*

cinema, movie theater **diànyǐngyuàn** 电影院 *24*

circulate, spread **liúchuán** 流传 *71*

circumstance, situation **qíng** 情 *87*

city, town **chéng** 城 *14*

city, urban area **chéngshì** 城市 *14*

civilization, culture; civilized, cultured **wénmíng** 文明 *112*

civilized, enlightened **kāimíng** 开明 *62*

claim damages, claim indemnity **suǒpéi** 索赔 *102*

clan, nationality **zú** 族 *142*

clap one's hands, applaud **gǔzhǎng** 鼓掌 *38*, **pāishǒu** 拍手 *81*

class (in school) **bān** 班 *3*

classic, classical **gǔdiǎn** 古典 *38*

classics, classical works **jīngdiǎn** 经典 *59*

classification **kē** 科 *63*

classmate, schoolmate **tóngxué** 同学 *106*

classroom **jiàoshì** 教室 *56*

clear, plain, obvious **míngbai** 明白 *76*

clear (of speech or image),

distinct **qīngchu** 清楚 *87*

clear up, dispel **xiāochú** 消除 *116*

clean (adj.) **gānjìng** 干净 *34*

clean up **dǎsǎo** 打扫 *18*

clever, bright, intelligent **cōngming** 聪明 *17*

climate **qìhòu** 气候 *85*

climb, scale **pāndēng** 攀登 *82*

climb a hill or mountain; mountaineering **páshān** 爬山 *81*

clinic (in a school, factory, etc.) **yīwùshì** 医务室 *124*

clock **zhōng** 钟 *139*

clock tower **zhōnglóu** 钟楼 *139*

close, intimate **mìqiè** 密切 *75*

close, seal up **fēng** 封 *32*

close, shut; turn off, switch off **guān** 关 *39*

close by one's side, on one's person **shēnbiān** 身边 *94*

close down, shut down **guānbì** 关闭 *39*

close to, close by **jìn** 近 *59*

close together, inseparable **jǐnmì** 紧密 *58*

clothes, a piece of clothing **yīfu** 衣服 *124*

clothes, garments, apparel **fúzhuāng** 服装 *33*

cloud **yún** 云 *131*

cloudy day **yīntiān** 阴天 *126*

club **jùlèbù** 俱乐部 *61*

coach, tutor **fǔdǎo** 辅导 *33*

coal **méi** 煤 *74*, **méitàn** 煤炭 *74*

coal gas **méiqì** 煤气 *74*

coal mine **méikuàng** 煤矿 *74*

Coca-Cola **kěkǒukělè** 可口可乐 *64*

cocktail party, reception **jiǔhuì** 酒会 *60*

coffee **kāfēi** 咖啡 *62*

cold (referring to weather) **hán** 寒 *43*

cold **lěng** 冷 *67*

cold, indifferent, apathetic **lěngdàn** 冷淡 *67*

colleague **tóngshì** 同事 *106*

collect, gather **sōují** 搜集 *101*

collective **jítǐ** 集体 *51*

college, institute **xuéyuàn** 学院 *121*

colonize **zhímín** 殖民 *137*

color **yánsè** 颜色 *122*

color, hue **sècǎi** 色彩 92

comb (n.) **shūzi** 梳子 99

combine, integrate **jiéhé** 结合 57

come from **láizì** 来自 66

come into view, appear, emerge **chūxiàn** 出现 15

come late, be late (for work, school, etc.) **chídào** 迟到 14

comfort, console **ānwèi** 安慰 9

comfortable, be well **shūfu** 舒服 99

comfortable, cosy **shūshì** 舒适 99

command, direct, conduct **zhǐhuī** 指挥 137

commemorate; commemoration **jìniàn** 纪念 51

comment, discuss, talk **yìlùn** 议论 126

commerce, business **shāngyè** 商业 93

commercial firm, company, corporation **gōngsī** 公司 37

commit a crime, break the law **fàn zuì** 犯罪 30

commit treason **pànguó** 叛国 82

commodities fair **zhǎnxiāohuì** 展销会 133

commodity **shāngpǐn** 商品 93

common, commonplace, ordinary **pǔtōng** 普通 84

common, shared **gòngtóng** 共同 38

common people, ordinary folk **lǎobǎixìng** 老百姓 66

common sense **chángshí** 常识 12

common understanding, consensus **gòngshí** 共识 37

communications **tōngxùn** 通讯 106

communist party **gòngchǎndǎng** 共产党 37

compact disc (CD) **guāngdié** 光碟, **guāngpán** 光盘 40

comparatively, relatively, to some degree **bǐjiào** 比较 6

compare **bǐjiào** 比较 6

compare and contrast **duìbǐ** 对比 27

compensate for; compensation for **péicháng** 赔偿 82

compete, have a match; match,

game, competition **bǐsài** 比赛 6

compete; competition **jìngzhēng** 竞争 60

competent, capable **xíng** 行 118

compile, edit, compose **biān** 编 6

complacent, deeply pleased with oneself **déyì** 得意 22

complain, grumble **bàoyuàn** 抱怨 5

complaint, objection **yìjiàn** 意见 125

complete, whole **wánquán** 完全 109

complete and perfect, consummate **wánshàn** 完善 109

complete, integrated, intact **wánzhěng** 完整 109

complicated, complex **fùzá** 复杂 33

compliment, praise **chēngzàn** 称赞 13

component part, component **yuánjiàn** 元件 130

component part, ingredient **chéngfèn** 成分 13

composition (student's) **zuòwén** 作文 143

comprehensive, synthesized **zōnghé** 综合 142

compromise **tiáohé** 调和 105

compulsory education **yìwù jiàoyù** 义务教育 125

compute, count, calculate **jìsuàn** 计算 51

computer **diànnǎo** 电脑 24, **jìsuànjī** 计算机 51

computer programming **chéngxù** 程序 14

computer software **ruǎnjiàn** 软件 92

concentrate, focus **jízhōng** 集中 51

concentrate on, be absorbed in **zhuānxīn** 专心 140

concept, notion **gàiniàn** 概念 34

concept, sense **guānniàn** 观念 39

conclude and sign (a contract, an agreement, etc.) **qiāndìng** 签订 86

condiment, seasoning **tiáoliào** 调料 105

condition **tiáojiàn** 条件 105

(poor) condition **dìbù** 地步 23

conduct, carry out **jìnxíng** 进行 58

confidence **xìnxīn** 信心 118

confirm, acknowledge; affirmative **kěndìng** 肯定 64

confirm, fix, determine **quèdìng** 确定 89

conform to, accord with **fúhé** 符合 33

conform with, correspond to **héhu** 合乎 44

Confucianism, Confucianists **rújiā** 儒家 91

congratulate **zhùhè** 祝贺 140, **gōngxǐ** 恭喜 37

connection, relation **guānxi** 关系 39

consequences, (bad) results **hòuguǒ** 后果 45

consider carefully, research, study **yánjiū** 研究 122

consign for shipment **tuōyùn** 托运 108

consul (diplomatic) **lǐngshì** 领事 70

consulate **lǐngshìguǎn** 领事馆 70

consult, refer to **cānkǎo** 参考 11

consume **xiāofèi** 消费 116

contain, have as ingredients **bāohán** 包含 4

content, substance **nèiróng** 内容 79

continent **zhōu** 洲 139

continent, mainland **dàlù** 大陆 19

continue, go on **jìxù** 继续 52

continue, sustain, persist **chíxù** 持续 14

contract, agreement **hétóng** 合同 44

contract, shrink **shōusuō** 收缩 98

contradiction, disunity **máodùn** 矛盾 73

contrary to expectations, instead **fǎn'ér** 反而 30

contribute, dedicate **gòngxiàn** 贡献 38

contribute money; financial donation **juānkuǎi** 捐款 61

control, command **kòngzhì** 控制 64

control and run a country, rule **tǒngzhì** 统治 *107*

convene (a conference) **zhàokāi** 召开 *134*

convenient, easy **biànlì** 便利 *7*

convenient, handy **fāngbiàn** 方便 *30*

convince **shuōfú** 说服 *100*

cook, bake **shāo** 烧 *93*

cook, prepare a meal **zuòfàn** 做饭 *143*

cooked dish **cài** 菜 *11*

cooked rice **mǐfàn** 米饭 *75*

cookie(s), biscuit(s) **bǐnggān** 饼干 *8*

cool-headed, calm, sober **lěngjìng** 冷静 *67*

cool, relaxed and fashionable, attractive **kù** 酷 *65*

cooperate, coordinate **pèihé** 配合 *82*

cooperate; cooperation **hézuò** 合作 *44*

cope with **yìngfu** 应付 *127*

copper mine **tóngkuàng** 铜矿 *107*

copy **chāo** 抄, **chāoxiě** 抄写 *12*

copy, clone (n.) **fùzhì** 复制 *33*

cordial **qīnqiè** 亲切 *87*

cordless telephone **yídòng diànhuà** 移动电话 *125*

corner; horn **jiǎo** 角 *56*

correct, accurate **zhèngquè** 正确 *136*

correct, true **duì** 对 *27*

corrupt official **tānguān** 贪官 *103*

cost of living, living expenses **shēnghuófèi** 生活费 *95*

cotton **mián** 棉 *75*

cotton or linen cloth **bù** 布 *10*

cough **késou** 咳嗽 *63*

count (v.) **shǔ** 数 *99*

counter, bar **guìtái** 柜台 *41*

counterfeit, forge **màopái** 冒牌 *73*

country, state, nation **guójiā** 国家 *41*

countryside, rural area **xiāngxia** 乡下 *115*

county (rural) **xiàn** 县 *114*

county town, county seat **xiànchéng** 县城 *114*

courage **dǎnzi** 胆子 *21*, **yǒngqì** 勇气 *127*

courage, guts **dǎnliàng** 胆量 *20*

course, a program of study **kèchéng** 课程 *64*

courtyard, compound **yuànzi** 院子 *130*

cover, lid,, top **gài** 盖 *34*

cow's milk, milk **niúnǎi** 牛奶 *80*

coward **dǎxiǎo guǐ** 胆小鬼 *21*

crawl, climb **pá** 爬 *81*

create **chuàngzào** 创造 *16*

create (art and literature); work of art or literature **chuàngzuò** 创作 *16*

creativity **chuàngzàoxìng** 创造性 *16*

credit card **xìnyòngkǎ** 信用卡 *118*

creditor **zhàizhǔ** 债主 *133*

creep, crawl **páxíng** 爬行 *81*

criminal, penal **xíngshì** 刑事 *118*

crisp **cuì** 脆 *17*

criticize, scold; criticism **pīpíng** 批评 *83*

crow **yā** 鸦 *121*

crowd (n.) **zhòng** 众 *139*

crowded, be packed **yōngjǐ** 拥挤 *127*

cruel and vicious **hěndú** 狠毒 *45*

cruel **kù** 酷 *65*

cruel, relentless **hěn** 狠 *45*

cry, weep, sob **kū** 哭 *64*

cucumber **huángguā** 黄瓜 *48*

cultivate, breed **péiyǎng** 培养 *82*

culture, civilization; education, schooling **wénhuà** 文化 *111*

cunning, crafty **jiǎohuá** 狡猾 *56*

cup, mug, glass **bēizi** 杯子 *5*

curious **hào qí** 好奇 *44*

currency **huòbì** 货币 *49*

currency, money **tōnghuò** 通货 *106*

currency exchange rate **huìlǜ** 汇率 *48*

curse, swear (v.) **mà** 骂 *72*

curtain **lián** 帘 *69*

curved, tortuous **wān** 弯 *109*

custom, social customs **fēngsú** 风俗 *32*

customer, client **gùkè** 顾客 *39*

customs, customs house **hǎiguān** 海关 *42*

cut **xuē** 削 *120*, **qiē** 切 *87*

cut (with scissors), shear **jiǎn** 剪 *54*

cut down, reduce **xuējiǎn** 削减 *120*

cut into parts, cut down **cái** 裁 *10*

cut open **pōu** 剖 *84*

D

daddy, papa **bàba** 爸爸 *2*

daily, routine **rìcháng** 日常 *91*

daily necessities **rìyòngpǐn** 日用品 *91*

daily schedule, schedule **rìchéng** 日程 *91*

dairy product **rǔzhìpǐn** 乳制品 *91*

damp, humid **cháoshī** 潮湿 *12*

dance (v.) **tiàowǔ** 跳舞 *105*

danger, risk; dangerous **wēixiǎn** 危险 *110*

dare (v.) **gǎn** 敢 *34*

dark **hēi'àn** 黑暗 *45*

data (for a thesis, a report, etc.) **cáiliào** 材料 *10*

date (especially of an event) **rìqī** 日期 *91*

daughter **nǚ'ér** 女儿 *81*

dawn, morning **dàn** 旦 *21*

day, date **rìzi** 日子 *91*

day and night, round the clock **rìyè** 日夜 *91*

day after tomorrow **hòutiān** 后天 *45*

day before yesterday **qiántiān** 前天 *86*

daydream; have a pipe dream **zuòmèng** 做梦 *143*

daytime **báitiān** 白天 *2*

deal with, go through **bànlǐ** 办理 *3*

dear, beloved, darling **qīn'ài** 亲爱 *87*

debate **biànlùn** 辩论 *7*

debt, liabilities **zhàiwù** 债务 *133*

deceive, dupe, cheat **qīpiàn** 欺骗 *85*

decide, make up one's mind; decision **juédìng** 决定 *61*

decisive, not hesitant, straight to the point **gāncuì** 干脆 *34*

declare, announce **xuānbù** 宣布 *120*

decline, turn down **tuīcí** 推辞 108

decorate; decoration **zhuāngshì** 装饰 140

deep, profound **shēnhòu** 深厚 95

deep fry; deep-fried **yóuzhà** 油炸 128

deeply concern, be at pains **cāoxīn** 操心 11

deeply grieved **bēitòng** 悲痛 5

deeply grieved, in deep sorrow **chéntòng** 沉痛 13

definite and explicit; make definite and explicit **míngquè** 明确 76

definite view, idea **zhǔyi** 主意 140

delay **dānwù** 耽误 20

delete, remove, cross out **shānchú** 删除 92

deliberate, intentional, on purpose **gùyì** 故意 39

delicious, palatable **hǎochī** 好吃 43

deliver (goods) **sòng** 送 101

deliver a formal speech; public lecture, speech **yǎnjiǎng** 演讲 122

dentist, dentistry **yáyī** 牙医 121

deny, repudiate **fǒurèn** 否认 32

depart, leave **líkāi** 离开 67

department, branch **bùmén** 部门 10

department (of a university) **xì** 系 114

department of internal medicine (in a hospital) **nèikē** 内科 79

deputy, vice-... **fù** 副 33

descend, land **jiàngluò** 降落 55

describe **xíngróng** 形容 119

describe (in writing) **miáoxiě** 描写 76

desert **shāmò** 沙漠 92

design **shèjì** 设计 94

desire (n.) **yù** 欲 130

desktop PC **táishìjī** 台式机 103

detail **xìjié** 细节 114

detain, take into custody **yā** 押 121

develop (into a state) **fā** 发 28

develop (resources, products, etc.), open up and exploit **kāifā** 开发 62

develop, expand, grow **fāzhǎn** 发展 29

developed, well-developed **fādá** 发达 29

deviation, error **piānchā** 偏差 83

diagnose; diagnosis **zhěnduàn** 诊断 135

diary book **rìjìběn** 日记本 91

dictation; do dictation **tīngxiě** 听写 106

dictionary **cídiǎn** 词典 17

die, pass away (polite) **qùshì** 去世 88

die, perish; death, doom **sǐwáng** 死亡 101

difference, discrepancy **chā** 差 11

difficult **nán** 难 79

difficult to understand, profound **shēn** 深 95

difficult, hard, tough **jiānkǔ** 艰苦 53

difficulty; difficult **kùnnan** 困难 65

digest **xiāohuà** 消化 116

digital **shùmǎ** 数码 100

diligent and conscientious **qínkěn** 勤恳 87

diligent, hard-working **qín** 勤 87

diligent, applying oneself to **qínfèng** 勤奋 87

dining hall, mess hall, canteen **shítáng** 97

diplomat **wàijiāoguān** 外交官 109

direct (a film or play); director (of films or plays) **dǎoyǎn** 导演 21

direct, forthright **tòngkuai** 痛快 107

direct, immediate, straight away **zhíjiē** 直接 137

direction, orientation **fāngxiàng** 方向 30

director/chief of a bureau **júzhǎng** 局长 60

dirty **zāng** 脏 132

disappear, vanish **xiāoshī** 消失 116

disappointed **shīwàng** 失望 96

disaster **huò** 祸 49

disaster, calamity **zāihài** 灾害 131

disbelieve, doubt **huáiyí** 怀疑 47

discipline **jìlù** 纪律 51

discover, find, find out **fāxiàn** 发现 29

discuss, consult **shāngliang** 商量 93

discuss; discussion **tǎolùn** 讨论 104

discuss and seek advice, consult **xiéshāng** 协商 117

discussion (informal), forum **zuòtánhuì** 座谈会 143

disease, illness **jíbìng** 疾病 50

dish, plate **pán** 盘 82

disheartened, discouraged **huīxīn** 灰心 48

disinfect, sterilize **xiāodú** 消毒 116

dispatch (v.) **pài** 派 82

disperse, distribute **sàn** 散 92

display **chén** 陈 13

display **zhǎn** 展 133

display, show **biǎoxiàn** 表现 7

disposition, temperament **xìngqíng** 性情 119

dispute, debate **zhēnglùn** 争论 136

disseminate, publicize; propaganda **xuānchuán** 宣传 120

dissertation, thesis, essay **lùnwén** 论文 72

distance **jùlí** 距离 61

distinguish, differentiate **fēnbié** 分别 32

distinguish, identify, recognize **shíbié** 识别 96

distinguish between, differentiate **qūbié** 区别 88

distort, misinterpret **wāiqū** 歪曲 108

distribute, allocate **fēnpèi** 分配 32

district (urban) **qū** 区 88

disturb, interrupt **dǎrǎo** 打扰 18

ditch, trench **gōu** 沟 38

dive; diving **tiàoshuǐ** 跳水 105

divide, point, mark **fēn** 分 31

divorce **líhūn** 离婚 67

dizzy, giddy **yūn** 晕 131

do, be engaged in, carry on **gǎo** 搞 35

do, work **gàn** 干 35

do; make **zuò** 作 143, **zuò** 做 143

do something willingly **gānxīn** 甘心 34

do according to, on the basis of **gēnjù** 根据 36

do advanced studies, undergo in-service advanced training **jìnxiū** 进修 58

do all one can, do one's utmost **jìnlì** 尽力 58

do business (of a commercial or service establishment) **yíngyè** 营业 127

do manual labor **láodòng** 劳动 66

do manual work, work **zuògōng** 做工 143

do not (as imperative or advice) **búyào** 不要 10, **bié** 别 7

do not have **méiyǒu** 没有 74

do one's utmost, do everything within one's power **jiélì** 竭力 57

do physical exercise, move about; activity, purposeful action **huódòng** 活动 49

do physical exercises, have a work-out **jiànshēn** 健身 55, **yùndòng** 运动 131

doctor **dàifu** 大夫 (colloquialism) 19

doctor, Ph.D. **bóshì** 博士 8

document, file **wénjiàn** 文件 111

doesn't matter; indifferent, apathetic **wúsuǒwèi** 无所谓 112

dog **gǒu** 狗 38

donate (something of considerable value) **juānxiàn** 捐献 61

done by hand, manual work **shǒugōng** 手工 98

door, gate **mén** 门 75

dosage **jìliàng** 剂量 52

Double Ninth Festival (9th day of the 9th lunar month), the **Chóngyáng Jié** 重阳节 15

doubt (n.) **yíwèn** 疑问 125

download **xiàzài** 下载 114

downstairs **lóu xia** 楼下 71

doze, doze off **dǎ kēshui** 打瞌睡 18

draft, sketch, manuscript **gǎozi** 稿子 35

drag on, defer, procrastinate **tuō** 拖 108

dragon **lóng** 龙 71

drama, play, theater **xìjù** 戏剧 113

drape over the shoulder **pī** 披 83

draw, paint **huà** 画 47

drawer **chōuti** 抽屉 15

dream; have a dream **zuòmèng** 做梦 143

dream of, have a pipe dream **mèngxiǎng** 梦想 75

dress up, make up **dǎban** 打扮 18

dress, the way of dressing, attire **chuānzhuó** 穿着 16

drink (v.) **hē** 喝 44

drink, beverage **yǐnliào** 饮料 126

drink a toast, "Bottoms up!" **gānbēi** 干杯 34

drinking water **yǐnyòngshuǐ** 饮用水 126

drive (a vehicle), pilot (a plane) **kāi** 开 62

drive (v.) **qū** 驱 88

drive, pilot **jià** 驾 53, **jiàshǐ** 驾驶 53

driver, pilot **jiàshǐyuán** 驾驶员 53

drop (used with liquids) **dī** 滴 23

drop, point, dot **diǎn** 点 24

drop bombs, attack with bombs **hōngzhà** 轰炸 45

dry, arid **gānzào** 干燥 34

dry in the air, air-dry **liàng** 晾 69

dry in the sun, bask **shài** 晒 92

dry land, land **lùdì** 陆地 71

dry spell, drought **hàn** 旱 43

dry up, exhausted **kūjié** 枯竭 65

duck **yāzi** 鸭子 121

dumb, stupid **bèn** 笨 5

during the period of **qījiān** 期间 85

dust **huīchén** 灰尘 48

duty, obligation **yìwù** 义务 125

dynasty **cháo** 朝 12

E

e-mail **diànzǐ yóujiàn** 电子邮件 24

each, every **gè** 各 36

each other **bǐcǐ** 彼此 6

each other, one another **hùxiāng** 互相 46

ear **ěr** 耳 28, **ěrduo** 耳朵 28

early **zǎo** 早 132

early morning (approximately 6–9 a.m.) **zǎochén** 早晨 132, **zǎoshang** 早上 132

earn, receive; income **shōurù** 收入 98

earnest, conscientious, serious **rènzhēn** 认真 90

earnest, sincere **kěnqiè** 恳切 64

earrings **ěrhuán** 耳环 28

Earth, globe, the **dìqiú** 地球 23

earth, ground **dì** 地 23

earth's surface, the **dìmiàn** 地面 23

earthquake, seism **dìzhèn** 地震 23

easily understood and accepted by common folks, popular **tōngsú** 通俗 106

east; eastern **dōng** 东 25

east side, in/to the east **dōngbian** 东边 25, **dōngmiàn** 东面 25

easy, not difficult **róngyì** 容易 91

easy, not requiring much effort (of a job) **qīngsōng** 轻松 87

eat, take (food or medicine) **chī** 吃 14

economize, cut down on, be frugal with **jiéshěng** 节省 57

economy **jīngjì** 经济 59

edit, compile; editor **biānjí** 编辑 6

educate, teach; education **jiàoyù** 教育 56

effect, result **xiàoguǒ** 效果 117

effective, efficacious **yǒuxiào** 有效 128

efficiency **xiàolǜ** 效率 117

efforts **gōngfu** 工夫 36

efforts, ability **lìliàng** 力量 68

egg (especially chicken egg) **dàn** 蛋 21

eight **bā** 八 2

elbow out, push aside, squeeze out **páijǐ** 排挤 81

elder brother, older brother **gēge** 哥哥 35

elder sister **jiějie** 姐姐 57

elect, vote; election, voting **xuǎnjǔ** 选举 120

electric fan **diànshàn** 电扇 24

electric light **diàndēng** 电灯 24

electron **diànzǐ** 电子 24

elegant and natural **dàfang** 大方 19

elementary, initial **chūjí** 初级 16

elephant **dàxiàng** 大象 19

elevator, lift **diàntī** 电梯 24

embassy **dàshǐguǎn** 大使馆 19

embezzlement, corruption **tānwū** 贪污 103

embrace, hug (v.) **yōngbào** 拥抱 127

emerge from, get out of **chū** 出 15

emit, send forth, give off **mào** 冒 73

emotion, affection **qíng** 情 87

emphasize, lay stress on **qiángdiào** 强调 86

empty, void, hollow **kōng** 空 64

enclose, surround **wéi** 围 110

encounter, come across **yùdào** 遇到 130

encourage **gǔlì** 鼓励 38

end, finish, wind up, terminate **jiéshù** 结束 57

endanger; danger **wēihài** 危害 110

endure, bear **chéngshòu** 承受 14

endure, tolerate, put up with **rěn** 忍 90

endure hardship, have a very hard time **shòuzuì** 受罪 99

enemy, those who are hostile **dírén** 敌人 23

energy, vigor, stamina **jīnglì** 精力 59

energy sources **néngyuán** 能源 79

engage in business **jīngshāng** 经商 59

engaged, busy (of a telephone line) **zhànxiàn** 占线 133

engine, especially heat engine **yǐnqíng** 引擎 126

engineer **gōngchéngshī** 工程师 36

English language (especially the writing), the **Yīngwén** 英文 127

English language, the **Yīngyǔ** 英语 127

enjoy; enjoyment **xiǎngshòu** 享受 115

enlighten, arouse; enlightenment, inspiration **qǐfā** 启发 85

enough, sufficient **gòu** 够 38

enraged, angry **fènnù** 愤怒 32

enroll (students), appoint (job applicants) **lùqǔ** 录取 71

enter, enter into **jìnrù** 进入 58

enter deeply into **shēnrù** 深入 95

enter one's name, sign up, apply for (a place in school) **bàomíng** 报名 4

enterprise **qǐyè** 企业 85

entertain, amuse; entertainment, amusement **yúlè** 娱乐 129

entertainment expense **jiāojìfèi** 交际费 55

enthusiastic, active, energetic **jījí** 积极 50

enthusiastic, warm-hearted **rèqíng** 热情 90

entrepreneur **qǐyèjiā** 企业家 85

entry, entrance **rùkǒu** 入口 92

environment, surroundings, ecology **huánjìng** 环境 47

envy, admire **xiànmù** 羡慕 115

envy, be jealous, hate **jìdu** 忌妒 52

epidemic **liúxíngbìng** 流行病 71

equal, equality **píngděng** 平等 84

equipment, installation **shèbèi** 设备 94

eraser **xiàngpí** 橡皮 116

error, mistake **miùwù** 谬误 77

especially **yóuqí** 尤其 128

essay, article **wénzhāng** 文章 112

essence, fundamentals; essential, fundamental, basic **gēnběn** 根本 36

establish, set up **jiànlì** 建立 54, **chénglì** 成立 13

estimate, reckon, size up; estimate, appraisal **gūjì** 估计 38

ethnic group, nationality **mínzú** 民族 76

ethnic minority (non-Han ethnic people in China) **shǎoshù mínzú** 少数民族 94

eulogize, praise highly **zànměi** 赞美 132

Euro **Ōuyuán** 欧元 81

Europe **Ōuzhōu** 欧洲 81

European Union, the (= 欧洲 联盟 **Ōuzhōu Liánméng**) **Ōuméng** 欧盟 81

evade, shirk **táobì** 逃避 103

even, so much so **shènzhì** 甚至 95

even if, even **jiùshì** 就是 60

even if, even though **jíshǐ** 即使 51, **jǐnguǎn** 尽管 58, **nǎpà** 哪怕 78

even more **yuè** 越 131

even number **ǒushù** 偶数 81

evening **wǎnshang** 晚上 109

evening meal, supper, dinner **wǎnfàn** 晚饭 109

evening party, an evening of entertainment **wǎnhuì** 晚会 109

every, each **měi** 每 74

every day, from day to day **tiāntiān** 天天 105

everyone, anybody, whoever, no matter who **shuí** 谁 100

everywhere **dàochù** 到处 21

evidence, proof **zhèngjù** 证据 136

exaggerate, boast **kuāzhāng** 夸张 65

examine, inspect, check **jiǎnchá** 检查 54

examine, test; examination, test **jiǎnyàn** 检验 54, **kǎoshì** 考试 63

examination paper, test paper **shìjuàn** 试卷 97

examine and repair (a machine), maintain **jiǎnxiū** 检修 54

example **lìzi** 例子 68

excellent **yōu** 优 127

except, besides **chúle ... (yǐwài)** 除了 ... (以外) 16

exceptionally, unusually **géwài** 格外 35

excessive, going too far **guòfèn** 过分 42

exchange, communicate **jiāoliú** 交流 55

exchange, convert (currency) **duìhuàn** 兑换 27

exchange, swap (v.) **jiāohuàn** 交换 55

excited, overjoyed **xīngfèn** 兴奋 118

exciting, stirring, moving, excited **jīdòng** 激动 50

Excuse me, ... **qǐngwèn** 请问 88

exercise, train, drill **liànxí** 练习 69

exert all one's strength **shǐjìnr** 使劲儿 97

exert oneself (physically) **yònglì** 用力 127

exhausted, dog tired **jīn pí lì jìn** 筋疲力尽 58

exhausted, tired **lèi** 累 67

exhibition, show **zhǎnlǎnhuì** 展览会 133

exhort, tell (somebody to do something) earnestly, advise **zhǔfù** 嘱咐 140

exist **cúnzài** 存在 18

exist, there is (are) **yǒu** 有 128

exist side by side, co-exist **bìngcún** 并存 8

exit **chūkǒu** 出口 15

expand, enlarge **kuòdà** 扩大 65

expect, look forward to **qīdài** 期待 85

expense, cost **fèiyòng** 费用 31

expensive, of great value **guì** 贵 41

experience, lesson (learnt from experiences) **jīngyàn** 经验 59

experience, undergo; personal experience **jīnglì** 经历 59

experiment, test **shíyàn** 实验 97

expert, specialist **zhuānjiā** 专家 140

explain, account for; explanation, interpretation **jiěshì** 解释 57

explain, show; explanation, manual **shuōmíng** 说明 100

export **chūkǒu** 出口 15

expose (wrongdoing), bring to light **jiēfā** 揭发 56

express, show, manifest **biǎoshì** 表示 7

express (thoughts or emotions) **biǎodá** 表达 7

express good wishes, wish **zhù** 祝 140

expression, look **shénsè** 神色 95

exquisite, of very high standard **jiǎngjiu** 讲究 55

extend, swell, expand **péngzhàng** 膨胀 83

extent **dìbù** 地步 23

extinguish, put out, go out **miè** 灭 76

extremely easy to do, a piece of cake **qīng ér yì jǔ** 轻而易举 87

extremely, highly **jíqí** 极其 50

extremely, very **jíle** 极了 50

eye, the **yǎnjing** 眼睛 122

eyebrow **méimao** 眉毛 74

eyesight, sight **shìlì** 视力 97

F

face (n.) **liǎn** 脸 69

face, honor **miànzi** 面子 76

face, surface **miàn** 面 75

face; towards, to **cháo** 朝 12

facial expression **biǎoqíng** 表情 7

facial expression, look, air **shénqíng** 神情 95

facilities, equipment **shèshī** 设施 94

fact, truth **shìshí** 事实 97

faction, school (of thought) **pài** 派 82

factor, element **yīnsù** 因素 126

factory, works **gōngchǎng** 工厂 36

fair, impartial **gōngpíng** 公平 37

faith, conviction **xìnniàn** 信念 118

fake (goods), forgery **jiǎhuò** 假货 53

fall, autumn **qiūtiān** 秋天 88

fall, drop (v.) **diào** 掉 24

fall, lower **jiàng** 降 55

fall, trip and fall (v.) **shuāidǎo** 摔倒 100

fall ill, get sick **shēngbìng** 生病 95

fall into a coma **hūnmí** 昏迷 48

false, untrue, fake **jiǎ** 假 53

false tooth, dentures **jiǎyá** 假牙 53

familiar with; know well **shúxī** 熟悉 99

family, household **jiātíng** 家庭 53

family name **xìng** 姓 119

famous, well-known **yǒumíng** 有名 128, **zhùmíng** 著名 140

famous brand, name brand **míngpái** 名牌 76

famous scenic spot **míngshèng** 名胜 76

famous scenic spots and cultural relics **míngshèng gǔjì** 名胜古迹 76

fan (of ball games) **qiúmí** 球迷 88

fan **shànzi** 扇子 92

fantasize, have an illusion; fantasy, illusion **huànxiǎng** 幻想 47

faraway, remote, distant **yáoyuǎn** 遥远 123

farm **nóngchǎng** 农场 80

farming area, rural area, countryside **nóngcūn** 农村 80

farmland (especially paddy fields), fields **tián** 田 105

fashion, fad, vogue **shíshàng** 时尚 96

fashionable dress, latest fashion **shízhuāng** 时装 96

fashionable, in vogue **shímáo** 时髦 96

fate, destiny **mìngyùn** 命运 77

father **fùqin** 父亲 33

father's elder brother **bófù** 伯父 8

father's elder brother's wife **bómǔ** 伯母 8

father's younger brother **shū** 叔 99

fatigued, tired **píláo** 疲劳 83

favorable, advantageous **yǒulì** 有利 128

fax **chuánzhēn** 传真 16

fear, be fearful **hàipà** 害怕 43

fearsome, frightening, terrible, terrifying **kěpà** 可怕 64

fed up with **nì** 腻 80

fee, charge **fèi** 费 31

feel (v.) **gǎn** 感, **gǎndào** 感到 34

feel, find, think **juéde** 觉得 61

feel; feeling, impression **gǎnjué** 感觉 34

feel deeply grateful **gǎnjī** 感激 34

feel ill, uncomfortable; feel sorry, sad **nánshòu** 难受 79

feelings, emotion **gǎnqíng** 感情 34

fellow-countryman, compatriot **tóngbāo** 同胞 106

female (humans) **nǚ** 女 81

female (of certain animals) **mǔ** 母 77

female student/pupil **nǚshēng** 女生 81

fertilizer **féiliào** 肥料 31

festival day, red-letter day **jiérì** 节日 57

festival, (public) holiday **jié** 节 57

field (of activity or thinking) **lǐngyù** 领域 70

fierce, intense **jīliè** 激烈 50

fight, struggle, strive **fèndòu** 奋斗 32

figure, number **shùzì** 数字 100

filial piety **xiàoshùn** 孝顺 117

fill (a bowl/plate) with rice **chéngfàn** 盛饭 14

fill (water, air), pour **guàn** 灌 40

fill in blanks **tiánkòng** 填空 105

film, movie **diànyǐng** 电影 24

filter **guòlǜ** 过滤 42

final game (of a match), finals **juésài** 决赛 61

(the) final stage, finally **zuìhòu** 最后 142

finally, in the end **zhōngyú** 终于 139

fine, clear (of weather) **qíng** 晴 88

fine, good **yōuliáng** 优良 127

fine (weather), sunny **qínglǎng** 晴朗 88

fine arts **měishù** 美术 74

fine arts specialist, artist **měishùjiā** 美术家 74

fine long hair **háo** 毫 43

finger, thumb **shǒuzhǐ** 手指 98

finish, end (v.) **wán** 完 109

fire **huǒ** 火 49

fire disaster, fire **huǒzāi** 火灾 49

fire-prevention and fire-fighting **xiāofáng** 消防 116

firecracker **biānpào** 鞭炮 7

firewood **xīn** 薪 118

firmly believe in, have faith in; faith, belief, conviction **xìnyǎng** 信仰 118

first (in time sequence) **xiān** 先 114

first, first of all **shǒuxiān** 首先 98

fish (n.) **yú** 鱼 129

fishing boat **yúchuán** 渔船 129

fishing net **yúwǎng** 渔网 129

fishing, fishery **yú** 渔 129

fit up (e.g. a house) **zhuānxiū** 装修 140

fit well, have the proper size

and shape (of clothes) **héshēn** 合身 44

five **wǔ** 五 112

fix, make immovable **gùdìng** 固定 39

fixed, specified **yídìng** 一定 124

flag, banner **qízi** 旗子 85

flat, level, smooth **píng** 平 84

flatulence, fart **pì** 屁 83

flavor or taste of food **kǒuwèi** 口味 64

flee, run away (from danger, punishment, etc.) **táo** 逃 103

flesh, meat **ròu** 肉 91

flight of steps, step **táijiē** 台阶 103

flight, flight number **hángbān** 航班 43

float **fú** 浮 33

flood **hóngshuǐ** 洪水 45

floor **lóu** 楼 71

flour **miànfěn** 面粉 76

flow **liú** 流 70

flower **huā** 花 46

fluctuate (like a wave) **bōdòng** 波动 8

fluent **liúlì** 流利 71

fly (insect) **yíng** 蝇 127

fly, flutter **fēi** 飞 31

fog, mist **wù** 雾 113

-fold, times **bèi** 倍 5

follow **gēn** 跟 36

following, from **cóng** 从 17

fond of learning, thirsty for knowledge **hào xué** 好学 44

food **shíwù** 食物 97

foodstuff (as commodities) **shípǐn** 食品 97

foolish, stupid **shǎ** 傻 92

foot, feet **jiǎo** 脚 56

for civil use, civil **mínyòng** 民用 76

for example **bǐrú** 比如 6

for example, such as **lìrú** 例如 68

for the most part, mostly **dàduō** 大多 19

for the purpose of **wèile** 为了 111

for the time being, momentarily **yìshí** 一时 124

forbid, prohibit, ban **jìnzhǐ** 禁止 59

forceful, powerful, strong **yǒulì** 有力 128

forecast, prediction **yùbào** 预报 130

forehead **é** 额 28

foreign affairs, diplomacy **wàijiāo** 外交 108

foreign country **wàiguó** 外国 108

foreign language (especially its writing) **wàiwén** 外文 109

foreign language **wàiyǔ** 外语 109

foreign products, foreign goods **wàiguóhuò** 外国货 108

foreigner **wàiguórén** 外国人 108

forest **sēnlín** 森林 92

forever **yǒngyuǎn** 永远 127

forge, shape metal **duàn** 锻 26

forget **wàng** 忘 110, **wàngjì** 忘记 110

fork **chāzi** 叉子 11

form, diagram, table **biǎo** 表 7

form, shape **xíngshì** 形式 119

form a line, line up, queue up **páiduì** 排队 81

formal talk **huìtán** 会谈 48

formal, official **zhèngshì** 正式 136

formalities, procedure **shǒuxù** 手续 98

fortunately, luckily **xìnghǎo** 幸好 119, **xìngkuī** 幸亏 119

foul (in sports), break a rule **fàn guī** 犯规 30

foundation, base, basis **jīchǔ** 基础 50

fountain pen **gāngbǐ** 钢笔 35

four **sì** 四 101

fowl, poultry **qín** 禽 87

fragile, frail **cuìruò** 脆弱 17

fragrant, sweet-smelling, aromatic **xiāng** 香 115

France **Fǎguó** 法国 29

free, unrestrained; freedom, liberty **zìyóu** 自由 142

free from worries **kuàng** 旷 65

free of charge **miǎnfèi** 免费 75

free time, unoccupied space **kòng** 空 64

freezing cold **hánlěng** 寒冷 43

French language (especially the writing), the **Fǎwén** 法文 29

French language, the **Fǎyǔ** 法语 29

fresh **xīnxiān** 新鲜 118

fresh flower **xiānhuā** 鲜花 114

friend **péngyou** 朋友 *83*
friendly **yǒuhǎo** 友好 *128*
friendship, amity **yǒuyì** 友谊 *128*
frighten, scare, be frightened, be scared **xià** 吓 *114*
frog **qīngwā** 青蛙 *87*
from, since **zìcóng** 自从 *141*
from … to …, from … till … **cóng … dào …** 从 … 到 … *17*
from beginning to end, throughout, ever **shǐzhōng** 始终 *97*
from today, from now on **jīnhòu** 今后 *58*
front (n.) **qiánbian** 前边 *86*, **qiánmiàn** 前面 *86*
frost **shuāng** 霜 *100*
fruit **shuǐguǒ** 水果 *100*
fruit, fruits **guǒshí** 果实 *41*
fruit juice **guǒzhī** 果汁 *41*
fuel **ránliào** 燃料 *89*
full name **xìngmíng** 姓名 *119*
function **gōngnéng** 功能 *37*
function, performance **xìngnéng** 性能 *119*
function, role **zuòyòng** 作用 *143*
fund, capital **zījīn** 资金 *141*
fundamental, basic **jīběn** 基本 *50*
funeral arrangement, funeral **sāngshì** 丧事 *92*
fungus, bacterium **jūn** 菌 *61*
furniture **jiājù** 家具 *53*
future **jiānglái** 将来 *55*
future, next, the time to come **wèilái** 未来 *111*
future, prospects, future prospects **qiántú** 前途 *86*
fuzzy, blurred **móhú** 模糊 *77*

G

gain unfair advantage **zhàn piányi** 占便宜 *133*
gallery, art museum **měishùguǎn** 美术馆 *74*
game **yóuxì** 游戏 *128*
game of mahjong, mahjong **májiàng** 麻将 *72*
gap, disparity **chājù** 差距 *11*
garage **chēkù** 车库 *13*
garden **huāyuán** 花园 *46*
gas station, service station **jiāyóuzhàn** 加油站 *52*

gasoline, gas, petrol **qìyóu** 汽油 *86*
gather together, assemble **jíhé** 集合 *51*
gender, sex **xìngbié** 性别 *119*
gene **jīyīn** 基因 *50*
general, more or less **dàgài** 大概 *19*
general, usual **tōngcháng** 通常 *106*
generally speaking, ordinarily **yìbān** 一般 *123*
generation **shì** 世 *97*
generation; dynasty **dài** 代 *20*
generous, liberal **dàfang** 大方 *19*
genetically modified **zhuǎn jīyīn** 转基因 *140*
gentle and soft, soothing (of people) **wēnróu** 温柔 *111*
gentleman, gentry **shēnshì** 绅士 *94*
geography **dìlǐ** 地理 *23*
German language (especially the writing), the **Déwén** 德文 *22*
German language, the **Déyǔ** 德语 *22*
Germany **Déguó** 德国 *22*
get, obtain **dé** 得 *22*
get along (with each other) **xiāngchǔ** 相处 *115*
get angry, be offended **shēngqì** 生气 *95*
get drunk, be intoxicated **zuì** 醉 *142*
get in touch (with), come into contact with **jiēchù** 接触 *56*
get in touch, contact; connection, being related **liánxì** 联系 *69*
get on (a vehicle), go aboard (a plane, ship) **shàng** 上 *93*
get on the Internet, surf the Internet **shàngwǎng** 上网 *93*
get rid of **chú** 除 *16*
get up (out of bed) **qǐchuáng** 起床 *85*
get up (out of bed), stand up, rise **qǐlai** 起来 *85*
get worried, fret **fāchóu** 发愁 *29*
ghost, phantom **guǐ** 鬼 *41*
gift, present **lǐwù** 礼物 *67*
give, provide **gěi** 给 *36*

give (or get) an injection **dǎzhēn** 打针 *18*
give a discount **dǎzhé** 打折 *18*
give birth to, grow **shēng** 生 *95*
give every consideration to, give loving care to **tǐtiē** 体贴 *104*
give expressions to, embody **tǐxiàn** 体现 *104*
give first aid, rescue **jiùhù** 救护 *60*
give one's blessing to, wish somebody happiness **zhùfú** 祝福 *140*
give regards to, ask after **wènhòu** 问候 *112*
give rise to, lead to, cause, arouse **yǐnqǐ** 引起 *126*
giving permission, may, can, be allowed **kěyǐ** 可以 *64*
glass **bōli** 玻璃 *8*
glasses, spectacles **yǎnjìng** 眼镜 *122*
glorious, honorable **guāngróng** 光荣 *40*
glove **shǒutào** 手套 *98*
glue, mucilage **jiāoshuǐ** 胶水 *56*
go abroad, go overseas **chūguó** 出国 *15*
go and see a doctor, visit a clinic **kànbìng** 看病 *62*
go bankrupt; bankruptcy **pòchǎn** 破产 *84*
go beyond, exceed **chāo** 超 *12*
go by, base on **píng** 凭 *84*
go into hiding **duǒcáng** 躲藏 *28*
go rotten, go bad; rotten **làn** 烂 *66*
go sightseeing, tour for pleasure **yóulǎn** 游览 *128*
go through, pass **jīngguò** 经过 *59*
go to, attend **fù** 赴 *33*
go upwards, ascend **shàng** 上 *93*
go/come down **xià** 下 *114*
god, supernatural being **shén** 神 *95*
gold **jīn** 金 *58*, **jīnzi** 金子 *58*, **huángjīn** 黄金 *48*
good, all right **hǎo** 好 *43*
good, fine, commendable **liánghǎo** 良好 *69*
good fortune, good luck **xìngyùn** 幸运 *119*

good luck **yùnqi** 运气 *131*
good-for-nothing **fèiwù** 废物 *31*
goods **huò** 货 *49*
goose **é** 鹅 *28*
government **zhèngfǔ** 政府 *136*
government office, state organ **jīguān** 机关 *49*
gown **páo** 袍 *82*
grab, seize **zhuā** 抓 *140*
gradually, by and by **jiànjiàn** 渐渐 *55*
gradually, step by step **zhújiàn** 逐渐 *139*
graduate from school **bìyè** 毕业 *6*
graduate student, post-graduate student **yánjiūshēng** 研究生 *122*
grain, cereal, staple food **liángshí** 粮食 *69*
grammar **yǔfǎ** 语法 *129*
granddaughter **sūnnǚ** 孙女 *102*
grandfather **yéye** 爷爷 *123*, **zǔfù** 祖父 *142*
grandmother **zǔmǔ** 祖母 *142*
grandson **sūnzi** 孙子 *102*
grant, give **yǔyǐ** 予以 *129*
grape **pútao** 葡萄 *84*
grape wine, wine **pútaojiǔ** 葡萄酒 *84*
grasp firmly **zhuājǐn** 抓紧 *140*
grassland, steppe, pasture **cǎoyuán** 草原 *11*
greasy **nì** 腻 *80*
great, grand, outstanding **wěidà** 伟大 *110*
great achievement **chéngjiù** 成就 *13*
great fun **hǎowánr** 好玩儿 *44*
great majority, overwhelming majority **dàduōshù** 大多数 *19*
great personage, big shot, very important person (VIP) **dàrénwù** 大人物 *19*
green **lǜ** 绿 *72*, **qīng** 青 *87*
green card (permanent residency permit) **lǜkǎ** 绿卡 *72*
green jade **bìyù** 碧玉 *6*
Green Party, the **lǜdǎng** 绿党 *72*
greet, say hello to **dǎ zhāohu** 打招呼 *18*
greeting card **hèkǎ** 贺卡 *45*
groan, moan (v.) **shēnyín** 呻吟 *94*

ground, field **chǎng** 场 *12*
grounds, basis **gēnjù** 根据 *36*
group (n.) **zǔ** 组 *142*
group photo **héyǐng** 合影 *44*
grow, develop, engender **zīzhǎng** 滋长 *141*
grow, grow up, be brought up **shēngzhǎng** 生长 *95*
grow up **chéngzhǎng** 成长 *14*
guarantee, pledge, warrant **bǎozhèng** 保证 *4*
guard and defend (a military installation, a VIP, etc.) **jǐngwèi** 警卫 *59*
guard and defend **shǒuhù** 守护 *98*
guess, speculate **cāi** 猜 *10*
guest, visitor **kèren** 客人 *64*
guesthouse, hotel **bīnguǎn** 宾馆 *8*
guide, direct, supervise **zhǐdǎo** 指导 *137*
guide, lead **yǐndǎo** 引导 *126*
gymnasium, gym **tǐyùguǎn** 体育馆 *104*

H

hacker **hēikè** 黑客 *45*
had better **zuìhǎo** 最好 *142*
haggle over prices, bargain **tǎojià huán jià** 讨价还价 *104*
hail, hailstone **báo** 雹 *5*
hair (on human head) **tóufa** 头发 *107*
hair **máo** 毛 *73*
half **bàn** 半 *3*
half a day **bàntiān** 半天 *3*
hall **tīng** 厅 *105*
hand **shǒu** 手 *98*
hand, palm **zhǎng** 掌 *134*
handicraft industry **shǒugōngyè** 手工业 *98*
handkerchief **shǒujuàn** 手绢 *98*
handle, deal with **chǔlǐ** 处理 *16*
handsome, attractive (men) **yīngjùn** 英俊 *126*
handsome, pretty, good-looking **piàoliang** 漂亮 *83*
hang up, put up **guà** 挂 *39*
happy, fortunate **xìngfú** 幸福 *119*
hard, suffering, miserable (life) **kǔ** 苦 *65*
hard, tough (substance) **yìng** 硬 *127*

hard and straight **tǐng** 挺 *106*
hard and toilsome (job) **xīnkǔ** 辛苦 *117*
hardly avoidable, almost inevitable **nánmiǎn** 难免 *79*
hardware (in computing) **yìngjiàn** 硬件 *127*
hardworking, assiduous, painstaking **kèkǔ** 刻苦 *64*
hardworking, studious, diligent (student) **yònggōng** 用功 *127*
harm (n.) **hàichu** 害处 *42*
harm, hurt (v.) **shānghài** 伤害 *93*
harsh, difficult (life) **xīnkǔ** 辛苦 *117*
harvest; gain (of work), achievement, reward **shōuhuò** 收获 *98*
hasten (to do something) **gǎnjǐn** 赶紧 *34*, **gǎnkuài** 赶快 *34*
hat, cap **màozi** 帽子 *73*
hate, be angry with **hèn** 恨 *45*
have ... for hire, rent **chūzū** 出租 *15*
have, possess, be provided with **jùyǒu** 具有 *61*
have a (serious, formal) talk; talk **tánhuà** 谈话 *103*
have a bearing on, be related to **yǒuguān** 有关 *128*
have a dialogue; dialogue **duìhuà** 对话 *27*
have a good command of, know well **zhǎngwò** 掌握 *134*
have an informal discussion, have an informal meeting **zuòtán** 座谈 *143*
have bad luck, be out of luck **dǎoméi** 倒霉 *21*
have confidence in (somebody), trust; confidence (in somebody), trust **xìnrèn** 信任 *117*
have dealings with, negotiate with, to **dǎ jiāodao** 打交道 *18*
have no choice but to ..., simply must ... **fēi ... bùkě** 非 ... 不可 *31*
have no choice/alternative but, can only **zhǐhǎo** 只好 *137*
have no way (of doing something), be not in a position (to do something) **wúcóng** 无从 *112*

have one's hair done **lǐfà** 理发 68

have received **jiēdào** 接到 56

have received, have suffered **shòudào** 受到 99

have to, have got to **děi** 得 22, **bùdébù** 不得不 9

having a tendency to, likely **róngyì** 容易 91

having eaten one's fill, full **bǎo** 饱 4

having no alternative, helplessly **wúnài** 无奈 112

having no hair, bald **tū** 秃 107

he, him **tā** 他 102

head (part of body), the **tóu** 头 107

headmaster, principal, university president, university vice chancellor **xiàozhǎng** 校长 117

heal, cure (v.) **yī** 医 124

health; healthy, in good health **jiànkāng** 健康 54

hear of, people say **tīngshuō** 听说 106

(the) heart, mind, feeling **xīn** 心 117

heart (as a medical term), the **xīnzàng** 心脏 117

heartbreaking, heartbroken **shāngxīn** 伤心 93

heartily approve of, agree with **zàntóng** 赞同 132

heavy **zhòng** 重 139

heed, be obedient **tīnghuà** 听话 106

height and size (of a person), build **gèzi** 个子 36

help, assist; help, assistance **bāngzhù** 帮助 3

help, help out **bāngmáng** 帮忙 3

hemp **má** 麻 72

hen's egg **jīdàn** 鸡蛋 50

herdsman **mùmín** 牧民 77

here **cǐ** 此 17

hesitant in speech, hum and haw **tūn tūn tǔ tǔ** 吞吞吐吐 108

hesitant, wavering, procrastinating **yóuyù** 犹豫 128

hey, hello, hi **wèi** 喂 111

hide, avoid, keep away from **duǒbì** 躲避 28

high jump **tiàogāo** 跳高 105

high mountain **yuè** 岳 131

highland, plateau **gāoyuán** 高原 35

hinder, hamper, disturb **fáng'ài** 妨碍 30

historian **lìshǐxuéjiā** 历史学家 68

historic site, place of historic interest **gǔjì** 古迹 38

historical period, epoch, age, times **shídài** 时代 96

history **lìshǐ** 历史 68

hoax, fraud **piànjú** 骗局 83

hobby, interest **àihào** 爱好 1

hold (carry in hand) **ná** 拿 77

hold, grasp (v.) **wò** 握 112

hold (a meeting, a ceremony) **jǔxíng** 举行 60

hold concurrent post, do part-time job **jiānzhí** 兼职 54

hold high, raise, lift **jǔ** 举 60

hold in the mouth, contain, have … as ingredients **hán** 含 43

holder of a master's degree **shuòshì** 硕士 100

hole, cave, cavity **dòng** 洞 25

holiday, holiday period, leave **jiàqī** 假期 53

home **jiā** 家 52

honest, sincere **chéngshí** 诚实

honest, truthful **shízài** 实在 97

honest person, simple-minded person, gullible person **lǎoshi rén** 老实人 67

honest to goodness, faithful **lǎoshi** 老实 67

Hong Kong **Xiānggǎng** 香港 115

honored guest **jiābīn** 嘉宾 52

hook **gōu** 钩 38

hope, wish (n.) **xīwàng** 希望 113

horrible, extremely serious; extremely **bùdéliǎo** 不得了 9

horse **mǎ** 马 72

hospitable **hào kè** 好客 44

hospital **yīyuàn** 医院 125

host **zhǔrén** 主人 139

hostel, dormitory **sùshè** 宿舍 101

hot **rè** 热 90

hot and stifling, muggy, sultry **mēnrè** 闷热 75

hot pepper **làjiāo** 辣椒 66

hotel **jiǔdiàn** 酒店 60, **lǚguǎn** 旅馆 71

hotel guest, passenger (of coach, train, plane, etc.) **lǚkè** 旅客 71

hour **xiǎoshí** 小时 116

house, home; room **fáng** 房 30

house, housing **fángzi** 房子 31

household chores, housework **jiāwù** 家务 53

hometown, home village **jiāxiāng** 家乡 53

how, in what manner **zěnme** 怎么 133, **zěnmeyàng** 怎么样 133

how … wish to **hènbude** 恨不得 45

how can ... **zěnme** 怎么 133

how many **jǐ** 几 51

how many, how much **duōshǎo** 多少 27

huge, enormous **pángdà** 庞大 82

huge, gigantic, tremendous **jùdà** 巨大 61

human being, person **rén** 人 90

human body **shēntǐ** 身体 94

human resources affairs **rénshì** 人事 90

humankind, mankind **rénlèi** 人类 90

humidity **shīdù** 湿度 96

humiliate, insult, tarnish **wūrǔ** 污辱 112, **wǔrǔ** 侮辱 112

humor **yōumò** 幽默 128

hundred **bǎi** 百 2

hungry, famished **è** 饿 28

hunter **lièrén** 猎人 70

hurried and confused, in a great rush **huāngmáng** 慌忙 47

hurried, hastily **jímáng** 急忙 51

hurriedly, in a rush **cōngcōng** 匆匆 17

husband **xiānsheng** 先生 114, **zhàngfu** 丈夫 134

husband and wife **fūqī** 夫妻 32

husband or wife **àirén** 爱人 1

husband's mother **pópo** 婆婆 84

husband's parents **gōngpó** 公婆 37

hydrogen (H) **qīng** 氢 87

hygiene, sanitation **wèishēng** 卫生 111

I

I, me **wǒ** 我 *112*

I'm afraid, perhaps **kǒngpà** 恐怕 *64*

I'm embarrassed **bù hǎo yìsi** 不好意思 *9*

I'm sorry, I beg your pardon **duìbuqǐ** 对不起 *27*

ice cream **bīngjīlíng** 冰激凌, **bīngqílín** 冰淇淋 *8*

ideal, aspiration **lǐxiǎng** 理想 *68*

idealism **wéixīnlùn** 唯心论 *110*

identical, same **xiāngtóng** 相同 *115*

idiom, idiomatic expression, set phrase **chéngyǔ** 成语 *13*

idler, uninvolved person **xiánrén** 闲人 *114*

if **yàoshì** 要是 *123*

if, in case **jiǎshǐ** 假使 *53*, **rúguǒ** 如果 *91*

if … **de huà** … 的话 *22*

illness **bìng** 病 *8*, **máobìng** 毛病 *73*

illustrated magazine, pictorial **huàbào** 画报 *47*

image, imagery **xíngxiàng** 形象 *119*

imagine **xiǎngxiàng** 想象 *115*

imitate, ape, be a copycat **mófǎng** 模仿 *77*

immediately **suíshǒu** 随手 *102*

immediately, promptly, without delay **lìjí** 立即 *68*, **jíshí** 及时 *50*

immigrate, emigrate; immigrant, emigrant; immigration **yímín** 移民 *125*

immortal, fairy **xiān** 仙 *114*

impartial, without bias **kèguān** 客观 *64*

impatient **búnàifán** 不耐烦 *9*

(an) impatient or impetuous person, a quick-tempered person **jíxìngzi** 急性子 *51*

important, significant **zhòngyào** 重要 *139*

important, urgent, serious **yàojǐn** 要紧 *123*

impression **yìnxiàng** 印象 *126*

impressions, reflections, thoughts **gǎnxiǎng** 感想 *34*

in, inside **lǐ** 里 *68*, **lǐbian** 里边, **lǐmiàn** 里面 *68*

in, on, at **zài** 在 *131*

in a hurry, in haste **cōngmáng** 匆忙 *17*

in a loud voice **dàshēng** 大声 *19*

in a mess, terrible, very bad **zāogāo** 糟糕 *132*

in a very short time, in a moment **yíhuìr** 一会儿 *124*

in a word, in short **zǒngzhī** 总之 *142*

in accordance with, based on **běnzhe** 本着 *5*

in advance **yù** 预 *130*

in all, altogether **zǒnggòng** 总共 *142*, **yígòng** 一共 *124*

in case, so as not to **shěngde** 省得 *95*

in charge of day-to-day business **chángwù** 常务 *12*

in detail, detailed **xiángxì** 详细 *115*

in frantic haste, flustered, flurried **huāngzhāng** 慌张 *47*

in good order, neat and tidy **zhěngqí** 整齐 *136*

in order to, so as to **yǐ** 以 *125*

in passing, incidentally **shùnbiàn** 顺便 *100*

in proper order, one by one **yīcì** 依次 *124*

in succession, in a row **liánxù** 连续 *69*

in that case, then **nàme** 那么 *78*, **zé** 则 *132*

in the direction of, towards **xiàng** 向 *116*

in the end, finally, after all **dàodǐ** 到底 *21*, **jiūjìng** 究竟 *60*

in the face of, in front of, before **miànqián** 面前 *75*

in the past (referring to something) **guòqù** 过去 *41*

in the sky **tiānshang** 天上 *105*

in the sky, in the air **kōngzhōng** 空中 *64*

in the unlikely event of, in case **wànyī** 万一 *110*

in those years, then **dāngnián** 当年 *21*

in town, downtown **chénglǐ** 城里 *14*

inadequate, insufficient **bùzú** 不足 *10*

incisive, insightful, profound **shēnkè** 深刻 *95*

include, embrace **bāokuò** 包括 *4*

increase, add **zēngjiā** 增加 *133*

increase, grow **zēngzhǎng** 增长 *133*

indeed, really **shíyòng** 实用 *97*

indicator (needle), pointer **zhǐzhēn** 指针 *137*

individual, one-to-one **gèbié** 个别 *36*

individual, personal **gèrén** 个人 *36*

indomitable will, strong will-power **yìlì** 毅力 *126*

industrious, hard-working **xīnqín** 辛勤 *118*

industry (manufacturing) **gōngyè** 工业 *36*

inevitable, bound to **bìrán** 必然 *6*

inexpensive, cheap **piányi** 便宜 *83*

inflation **tōnghuò péngzhàng** 通货膨胀 *106*

influence, affect; influence **yǐngxiǎng** 影响 *127*

influenza, flu **liúxíngxìng gǎnmào (liúgǎn)** 流行性感冒 (流感) *71*

information **xìnxī** 信息 *118*

ingenious, very clever **qiǎomiào** 巧妙 *87*

inhale, suck **xī** 吸 *113*

inhibit, restrain; inhibition, restraint **yìzhì** 抑制 *126*

(the) initial stage, initially **zuìchū** 最初 *142*

initiative, enthusiasm, zeal **jījíxìng** 积极性 *50*

ink **mòshuǐ** 墨水 *77*

innate character, true nature **běnzhì** 本质 *5*

innumerable, countless **wúshù** 无数 *112*

input **shūrù** 输入 *99*

inquire, ask **dǎtīng** 打听 *18*, **xúnwèn** 询问 *121*

insane, frenzied **fēngkuáng** 疯狂 *32*

insect **kūnchóng chóngzi** 虫子 *15*, 昆虫 *65*

inside, within **nèi** 内 *79*

insomnia; suffer from insomnia **shīmián** 失眠 *96*

inspire, fire up … with enthusiasm, hearten **gǔwǔ** 鼓舞 38

install, fix **ānzhuāng** 安装 2

instant noodles **fāngbiàn miàn** 方便面 30

instrument **yíqì** 仪器 125

insult (v.) **rǔ** 辱 91

insure; insurance **bǎoxiǎn** 保险 4

intelligence and capability **zhìnéng** 智能 138

intensity, strength **qiángdù** 强度 87

intensive care ward 重病房 **zhòngbìngfáng** 8

interest (n.) **xìngqù** 兴趣 119

interest, delight **qùwèi** 趣味 89

interest (on a loan) **lìxī** 利息 68

interest rate **lìlǜ** 利率 68

interesting, absorbing (book, movie, etc.) **hǎokàn** 好看 44

interesting, amusing **yǒuqù** 有趣 128

interior, inside **nèibù** 内部 79

intermittent, sporadic, off and on **duàn duàn xù xù** 断断续续 26

internal organs of the body **zàng** 脏 132

international **guójì** 国际 41

international students (especially in a university) **liúxuéshēng** 留学生 71

Internet, network **wǎngluò** 网络 110

Internet, World Wide Web **hùliánwǎng** 互联网 46, **yīngtèwǎng** 英特网 126

Internet café **wǎngbā** 网吧 110

interrupt (somebody's talk), cut in **dǎchà** 打岔 18

interview (of mass media) **cǎifǎng** 采访 10

intestine **cháng** 肠 12

intonation **yǔdiào** 语调 129

introduce, present, recommend **jièshào** 介绍 57

invent; invention **fāmíng** 发明 29

invest; investment **tóuzī** 投资 107

investigate; investigation **diàochá** 调查 25

invite; invitation **yāoqǐng** 邀请 122

invite and appoint to a (professional or managerial) position **pìnqǐng** 聘请 84

invite to dinner, host a dinner party **qǐngkè** 请客 88

involve, have something to do with **shèjí** 涉及 94

iron (n.) **tiě** 铁 105

iron and steel, steel **gāngtiě** 钢铁 35

irrigate, water **jiāoguàn** 浇灌 56

irrigate; irrigation **guàngài** 灌溉 40

irritate; irritation **cìjī** 刺激 17

island, islet **dǎoyǔ** 岛屿 21

isolated, without support or sympathy **gūlì** 孤立 38

it **tā** 它 102

it can be seen, it is thus clear **kějiàn** 可见 63

it is said, they say, rumor has it **jùshuō** 据说 61

it looks as if, it seems as if **kànlái** 看来 63, **kànyàngzi** 看样子 63

it seems, as if **sìhū** 似乎 101

itch, tickle **yǎng** 痒 122

item, project **xiàngmù** 项目 115

items of an account **zhàngmù** 账目 134

J

jacket **jiākèshān** 夹克衫 52

jade article, jadeware **yùqì** 玉器 129

Japan **Rìběn** 日本 91

Japanese currency, yen **Rìyuán** 日元 91

Japanese language, the **Rìyǔ** 日语 91

Japanese language (especially the writing), the **Rìwén** 日文 91

jeans **niúzǎi kù** 牛仔裤 80

job **zhí** 职 137

jog, run (physical exercise) **pǎobù** 跑步 82

joke (n.) **xiàohua** 笑话 117

joke, crack a joke, make fun of, kid **kāi wánxiào** 开玩笑 62

journey, travel **lǚtú** 旅途 71

journey to and from, make a round trip **wǎngfǎn** 往返 110

joyful, delighted, glad, willing **gāoxìng** 高兴 35

joyful, happy **kuàilè** 快乐 65

joyous festival **jiājié** 佳节 52

judge, decide; judgment, verdict **pànduàn** 判断 82

juice **zhī** 汁 137

jump (v.) **tiào** 跳 105

jump, leap (v.) **tiàoyuè** 跳跃 105

junk, reject, useless product **fèipǐn** 废品 31

just, barely **gāng** 刚 35

just right **zhènghǎo** 正好 136

K

keep, maintain **bǎochí** 保持 4

keep, save, conserve **bǎocún** 保存 4

kernel, core, nucleus **hé** 核 45

kettle **hú** 壶 46

key **yàoshi** 钥匙 123

keyboard **jiànpán** 键盘 55

kick (v.) **tī** 踢 104

kill, slay, put to death **shā** 杀 92

kilogram **gōngjīn** 公斤 37

kilometer **gōnglǐ** 公里 37

kind, category, type **lèi** 类 67, **yàng** 样 122, **zhǒnglèi** 种类 139

kind-hearted, good-hearted **shànliáng** 善良 92

kind-hearted, with good intention **hǎoxīn** 好心 43

kindergarten **yòu'éryuán** 幼儿园 129

king, monarch **guówáng** 国王 41

kingdom **wángguó** 王国 110

kiss **wěn** 吻 112

kitchen **chúfáng** 厨房 16

knead dough **róumiàn** 揉面 91

knitting wool, woolen yarn **máoxiàn** 毛线 73

knock, beat, strike **qiāo** 敲 87

knot **jié** 结 57

know **zhīdào** 知道 137

know, understand **rènde** 认得 90, **rènshi** 认识 90, **xiǎode** 晓得 (only used in colloquial Chinese) 117

know, understand, find out **liǎojiě** 了解 70

know how to, can **huì** 会 48

knowledge **zhīshi** 知识 137

knowledge, experience **jiànshi** 见识 54

L

Labor Day (May 1st) **Láodòng Jié** 劳动节 66

labor union, trade union **gōnghuì** 工会 36

laboratory **shíyànshì** 实验室 97

laboratory technician **shíyànyuán** 实验员 97

lack, be short of **quē** 缺 89

lacking enthusiasm, passive **xiāojí** 消极 116

ladder, steps **tī** 梯 104

ladle, spoon **sháozi** 勺子 93

lake **hú** 湖 46, **pō** 泊 84

lamp, lighting **dēng** 灯 22

land **tǔdì** 土地 107

landlord, landlady **fángdōng** 房东 31

landscape **shānshuǐ** 山水 92

landscape, scenery **fēngjǐng** 风景 32

language **yǔyán** 语言 129

Lantern Festival, the **yuánxiāo** 元宵 (also known as 元宵节 **Yuánxiāojié**) 130

lap, overlap **dié** 叠 25

large-scale, large-sized **dàxíng** 大型 19

last year **qùnián** 去年 88

late, not early, not on time **wǎn** 晚 109

laugh, smile **xiào** 笑 117

laugh at, ridicule **xiàohua** 笑话 117

laughable, ridiculous **kěxiào** 可笑 64

law **fǎlǜ** 法律 29

law, regular pattern **guīlǜ** 规律 40

law court, court **fǎyuàn** 法院 29

lawn **cǎodì** 草地 11

lawyer, solicitor, barrister **lǜshī** 律师 72

lay down, draw up **zhìdìng** 制定 138

lead, exercise leadership; leader, leadership **lǐngdǎo** 领导 70

lead to, cause **dǎozhì** 导致 21

lead to, go to (of roads, railways) **tōng** 通 106

leader (of a class in school, a squad in the army, etc.) **bānzhǎng** 班长 3

leaf **yèzi** 叶子 123

leak **lòu** 漏 71

lean meat **shòuròu** 瘦肉 99

leap (v.) **yuè** 跃 131

learn, study **xué** 学 120

learning, knowledge **xuéwèn** 学问 120

learning, scholarship **xuéshù** 学术 120

leather shoes **píxié** 皮鞋 83

leave application, a leave form **jiàtiáo** 假条 53

leave empty or blank **kòng** 空 64

leave for, go to **qù** 去 88

leave of absence, holiday, vacation **jià** 假 53

lecture, course of lectures **jiǎngzuò** 讲座 55

lecture, talk down to **jiàoxùn** 教训 56

left side, the **zuǒ** 左 143

left side/left-hand side, the **zuǒbiān** 左边 143

leftovers **shèngcài** 剩菜 96

leg **tuǐ** 腿 108

legal, legitimate **héfǎ** 合法 44

legend, folktale **chuánshuō** 传说 16

leisure **xiūxián** 休闲 120

lesson, class, lecture **kè** 课 64

lesson (learnt from mistakes or experience) **jiàoxùn** 教训 56

lesson learned (from personal experiences) **gǎnshòu** 感受 34

let, allow **ràng** 让 89

let alone **hékuàng** 何况 44

let it be, forget it **suànle** 算了 101

let know, notify **dǎ zhāohu** 打招呼 18

let on about, leak, disclose **tòulù** 透露 107

letter, epistle **xìn** 信 118

letter (of an alphabet) **zìmǔ** 字母 142

letter received, incoming letter **láixìn** 来信 66

level, degree **chéngdù** 程度 14

level, standard **shuǐpíng** 水平 100

library **túshūguǎn** 图书馆 107

license, permit **zhízhào** 执照 137

license plate (vehicle's) **chē pái** 车牌 13

lie, falsehood **huǎngyán** 谎言 48, **jiǎhuà** 假话 53

lie, recline **tǎng** 躺 103

lie at anchor, anchor (of ships) **tíngbó** 停泊 106

lie in, rest with **zàiyú** 在于 132

life **shēngmìng** 生命 95

life, livelihood **rìzi** 日子 91

life (human) **xìngmìng** 性命 119

life (one's entire) **rénshēng** 人生 90

life force **shēngmìnglì** 生命力 95

life science **shēngmìng kēxué** 生命科学 95

lifespan **shòumìng** 寿命 99

lifetime **shì** 世 97

lift, raise **tái** 抬 103

light (of weight) **qīng** 轻 87

light (ray) **guāng** 光 40

light, bright, promising **guāngmíng** 光明 40

light, bright, shining **liàng** 亮 69

light and delicate (color, smell or taste) **qīngdàn** 清淡 87

light boat **tǐng** 艇 106

light hair, down **róng** 绒 91

lighten, alleviate **jiǎnqīng** 减轻 54

lightning **shǎndiàn** 闪电 92

like, as … as **shì** 似 97

like, be fond of **xǐhuan** 喜欢 113

like that, so **nàme** 那么 78, **nàyàng** 那样 78

like this, in this manner, so **zhème** 这么 135, **zhèyàng** 这样 135 (used only in writing)

likeness of (a human being), portrait **xiàng** 像 116

limit, extent **dù** 度 26

limit, restrict, confine **xiànzhì** 限制 115

line, row, queue **háng** 行 43

lines, veins **wén** 纹 112

lining, underwear **chèn** 衬 13

link up, connect **gōutōng** 沟通 38

lion **shīzi** 狮子 96

liquid medicine **yàoshuǐ** 药水 123

list someone as wanted **tōngjī** 通缉 106

listen **tīng** 听 *105*

literary or artistic work **zuòpǐn** 作品 *143*

literature **wénxué** 文学 *112*

literature and art; performing arts **wényì** 文艺 *112*

live, stay **zhù** 住 *140*

live a life; life **shēnghuó** 生活 *95*

live and work in peace and contentment **ān jū lè yè** 安居乐业 *1*

lively, vivacious **huópo** 活泼 *49*

liver, the **gān** 肝 *34*

living room, sitting room **kètīng** 客厅 *64*

living standards **shēnghuó shuǐpíng** 生活水平 *95*

loan money to/from; loan **dàikuǎn** 贷款 *20*

loathe, dislike; disgusting, annoying **tǎoyàn** 讨厌 *104*

lock, lock up **suǒ** 锁 *102*

logic **luójì** 逻辑 *72*

lonely **jìmò** 寂寞 *52*

long, lengthy **cháng** 长 *12*

long distance **chángtú** 长途 *12*

long distance running **chángpǎo** 长跑 *12*

long jump **tiàoyuǎn** 跳远 *105*

look, see **kàn** 看 *62*

look after, care for **zhàogù** 照顾 *134*

look after, take care of **zhàoying** 照应 *135*

look down upon, despise **kànbuqǐ** 看不起 *62*

look for, seek **xúnzhǎo** 寻找 *121*

look forward to, long for **pànwàng** 盼望 *82*

look in a mirror **zhào** 照 *134*

look on **pángguān** 旁观 *82*

look up with reverence, pay homage to **zhānyǎng** 瞻仰 *133*

look up words in a dictionary **chá cídiǎn** 查词典 *11*

loose, slack, lax, weak **sōng** 松 *101*

lorry, truck **kǎchē** 卡车 *62*

lose (something valuable) **shīqù** 失去 *96*

lose, suffer from damage/loss; loss, damage **sǔnshī** 损失 *102*

lose (a game, a bet) **shū** 输 *99*

lose (one's way), take a wrong turning **míshī** 迷失 *75*, **mílù** 迷路 *75*

lose one's job, become unemployed **shīyè** 失业 *96*

lose one's temper, flare up **fāhuǒ** 发火 *29*

loud, noisy **xiǎng** 响 *115*

loud and clear, resounding **xiǎngliàng** 响亮 *115*

lovable, lovely **kě'ài** 可爱 *63*

love, compassion **àixīn** 爱心 *1*

love, like, be fond of **ài** 爱 *1*

love ardently, be in deep love with **rè'ài** 热爱 *90*

love dearly **téng** 疼 *104*, **téngài** 疼爱 *104*

low, soft (of voice) **qīng** 轻 *87*

low-priced, inexpensive **liánjià** 廉价 *69*

lower, cut, reduce **jiàngdī** 降低 *55*

luckily, as luck would have it **còuqiǎo** 凑巧 *17*

luckily, fortunately **duōkuī** 多亏 *27*

lucky, auspicious **jíxiáng** 吉祥 *51*

luggage, baggage **xíngli** 行李 *119*

lunch **wǔfàn** 午饭 *112*

lungs, the **fèi** 肺 *31*

luxurious, sumptuous **háohuá** 豪华 *43*

M

machine, machinery **jīqì** 机器 *49*

machine tool **jīchuáng** 机床 *49*

mad, crazy **kuáng** 狂 *65*

Madam, Ms, lady, woman (respectful form of address) **nǚshì** 女士 *81*

magazine, journal **zázhì** 杂志 *131*

magnetic card (for telephone calls, etc.) **cíkǎ** 磁卡 *17*

magnetic disc **cípán** 磁盘 *17*

main course (of a dinner) **zhǔcài** 主菜 *139*

main point, focal point, emphasis **zhòngdiǎn** 重点 *139*

main street **dàjiē** 大街 *19*

maintain (a machine, a house, etc.) **wéixiū** 维修 *110*

major, chief, main **zhǔyào** 主要 *140*

major, great, significant **zhòngdà** 重大 *139*

majority **duōshù** 多数 *27*

make, manufacture **zhìzào** 制造 *138*, **zhìzuò** 制作 *138*

make ... better/more favorable; improvement, amelioration. **gǎishàn** 改善 *34*

make ... more advanced/sophisticated, improve; improvement **gǎijìn** 改进 *34*

make (wine), brew (beer) **niàng** 酿 *80*

make a big noise, be noisy **chǎo** 吵 *12*

make a detour, bypass **rào** 绕 *90*

make a laughing stock of oneself, be held up for mockery **chū yángxiàng** 出洋相 *15*

make a photocopy of, photocopy **fùyìn** 复印 *33*

make a public announcement, publish **gōngbù** 公布 *36*

make a sound recording (e.g. music, reading) **lùyīn** 录音 *71*

make a summary; abstract, summary **zhāiyào** 摘要 *133*

make a video recording **shèxiàng** 摄像 *94*

make clear, demonstrate **biǎomíng** 表明 *7*

make extra efforts **jiāyóu** 加油 *52*

make false claims **mào** 冒 *73*

make fewer, reduce **jiǎnshǎo** 减少 *54*

make haste, hasten without the slightest delay **liánmáng** 连忙 *69*

make money/profit **zhuàn** 赚 *140*

make perfect, improve **wánshàn** 完善 *109*

make sentences; sentence-making **zàojù** 造句 *132*

make social contacts; social intercourse, communication **jiāojì** 交际 *55*

make trouble, create a disturbance **nào** 闹 *79*

make up for missed lessons **bǔkè** 补课 *9*

make up, compose, consist of **gòuchéng** 构成 *38*, **zǔchéng** 组成 *142*, **zǔhé** 组合 *142*

make use of, benefit from, exploit **lìyòng** 利用 *68*

making great efforts **nǔlì** 努力 *81*

male (humans) **nán** 男 *78*

male (of animals) **xióng** 雄 *120*

male (of certain animals) **gōng** 公 *36*

male student/pupil **nánshēng** 男生 *78*

man, men **nánrén** 男人 *78*

man-made, artificial **rénzào** 人造 *90*

manage, administer; management, administration **guǎnlǐ** 管理 *40*

manage financial affairs; fund management **lǐcái** 理财 *68*

manage to find time (to do something) **chōukòng** 抽空 *15*

manager **jīnglǐ** 经理 *59*

manner, bearing, attitude, approach **tàidu** 态度 *103*

manner, way **fāngshì** 方式 *30*

manpower, man-day **réngōng** 人工 *90*

many, much **xǔduō** 许多 *120*

map **dìtú** 地图 *23*

marketplace, market **shìchǎng** 市场 *97*

marriage **hūnyīn** 婚姻 *49*

marriage partner, fiancé(e) **duìxiàng** 对象 *27*

marry (of a man) **qǔ** 娶 *88*

marry (of a woman) **jià** 嫁 *53*

marry, get married **jiéhūn** 结婚 *57*

martial arts **gōngfu** 功夫 *37*, **wǔshù** 武术 *112*

martial arts film **gōngfu piàn** 功夫片 *37*

marvelous, intriguing **qímiào** 奇妙 *85*

mascot **jíxiángwù** 吉祥物 *51*

master, owner **zhǔ** 主 *139*

master, teacher **shī** 师 *96*

master worker **shīfu** 师傅 *96*

match (for starting a fire) **huǒchái** 火柴 *49*

matchmaker **méiren** 媒人 *74*

matchmaker, go-between **jièshào rén** 介绍人 *57*

material, data **zīliào** 资料 *141*

materialism **wéiwùlùn** 唯物论 *110*

materialize, realize **shíxiàn** 实现 *97*

materials **cáiliào** 材料 *10*

maternal, of a mother **mǔ** 母 *77*

maternal granddad **wàigōng** 外公 *108*

maternal grandma **wàipó** 外婆 *109*, **lǎolao** 姥姥 *66*

maternal instinct, maternity **mǔxìng** 母性 *77*

mathematics, maths **shùxué** 数学 *100*

matter, substance **wùzhì** 物质 *113*

matter of importance, a **dàshì** 大事

mature, ripen; mature, ripe **chéngshú** 成熟 *13*

may, possible, possibly; possibility **kěnéng** 可能 *64*

mayor of a county **xiànzhǎng** 县长 *114*

meal **cān** 餐 *11*

meals (provided by a school, a factory, etc.) **huǒshí** 伙食 *49*

meaning **yìsi** 意思 *126*

meaningful, interesting **yǒu yìsi** 有意思 *128*

means, measure, method **shǒuduàn** 手段 *98*

measure, gauge **cè** 测 *11*

measure, step (n.) **cuòshī** 措施 *18*

measure, take measurements **liáng** 量 *69*

meat dish (animal, fowl, fish meat) **hūncài** 荤菜 *48*

mediate, make peace **tiáojiě** 调解 *105*

mediate, reconcile **tiáohé** 调和 *105*

medical doctor **yīshēng** 医生 *124*

medical emergency **jízhěn** 急诊 *51*

medical science, medicine **yīxué** 医学 *125*

medicine, drug **yào** 药 *123*

medium, media **méitǐ** 媒体 *74*

medium, intermedium **zhōngjiè** 中介 *138*

meet, greet **yíngjiē** 迎接 *127*

meet, receive (formal) **huìjiàn** 会见 *48*

meet, see (a person) **jiànmiàn** 见面 *54*

meet (someone) unexpectedly, run into **yùjiàn** 遇见 *130*

meet the needs of, satisfy **mǎnzú** 满足 *73*

meet unexpectedly, run into **pèngdao** 碰到 *83*

meeting, conference **huìyì** 会议 *48*

melody **yuèqǔ** 乐曲 *131*

melon, gourd **guā** 瓜 *39*

member (of a family or group) **chéngyuán** 成员 *14*

memorial service, memorial meeting **zhuīdàohuì** 追悼会 *141*

mend, patch **bǔ** 补 *9*

mental illness, psychosis **jīngshén bìng** 精神病 *59*

mentality, psychology **xīnlǐ** 心理 *117*

mention **tí** 提 *104*

menu **càidān** 菜单 *11*

metal **jīnshǔ** 金属 *58*

meteorological observatory **qìxiàngtái** 气象台 *85*

meteorological phenomena, weather **qìxiàng** 气象 *85*

meteorology **qìxiàngxué** 气象学 *85*

meter (colloquial) **mǐ** 米 *75*

meter **gōngchǐ** 公尺 *36*

method, way, means **fāngfǎ** 方法 *30*

metropolis, big city **dūshì** 都市 *26*

microblog, microblogging **wēibó** 微博 *110*

micro-channel, WeChat **wēixìn** 微信 *110*

Mid-Autumn Festival (the 15th day of the 8th Chinese lunar month) **Zhōngqiūjié** 中秋节 *138*

middle, medium **zhōng** 中 *138*

middle age **zhōngnián** 中年 *138*

middle ten days of a month (11th to 20th) **zhōngxún** 中旬 *138*

midnight, at midnight **bànyè** 半夜 *3*

mildew, mold **méi** 霉 *74*

military affairs **jūnshì** 军事 *61*

military regiment; group, team **tuán** 团 *108*

milk **nǎi** 奶 *78*

mind, breadth of mind, heart **xiōnghuái** 胸怀 *119*

mine (coal, gold, etc.) **kuàng** 矿 *65*

miner **kuànggōng** 矿工 *65*

mineral water **kuàngquánshuǐ** 矿泉水 *65*

minibus, van **miànbāochē** 面包车 *76*

minister (in government) **bùzhǎng** 部长 *10*

Minister of Foreign Affairs **Wàijiāo bùzhǎng** 外交部长 *109*

Ministry of Foreign Affairs **Wàijiāobù** 外交部 *108*

minority **shǎoshù** 少数 *93*

minute (of an hour) **fēnzhōng** 分钟 *32*

miracle, wonder **qíjì** 奇迹 *85*

mirror **jìngzi** 镜子 *60*

mishap, accident **yìwài** 意外 *126*

miss, remember with longing **xiǎngniàn** 想念 *115*

mistake, error; wrong, mistaken **cuòwù** 错误 *18*

misunderstand, misconstrue; misunderstanding **wùhuì** 误会 *113*

model **mótè** 模特 *77*

model, type (n.) **xíng** 型 *119*

modern times (usually from the year 1840) **jìndài** 近代 *59*

modern times, the contemporary age **xiàndài** 现代 *114*

modernize; modernization **xiàndàihuà** 现代化 *114*

modest **kèqi** 客气 *64*

modest, self-effacing **qiānxū** 谦虚 *86*

moist, damp **shīrùn** 湿润 *96*

mold (v.) **sù** 塑 *101*

mold (fungi) **méijūn** 霉菌 *74*

mold, matrix **mú** 模 *77*

monastery, temple **sì** 寺 *101*

money **qián** 钱 *86*

money, currency **jīnqián** 金钱 *58*

money paid for lease or hiring, rent **zūjīn** 租金 *142*

monkey **hóuzi** 猴子 *45*

monopoly **lǒngduàn** 垄断 *71*

monotonous **dāndiào** 单调 *20*

month **yuè** 月 *130*

mood, feelings **qíngxù** 情绪 *88*

Moon (as a scientific term) **yuèqiú** 月球 *130*

moon, the **yuèliang** 月亮 *130*

moral quality and conduct, behavior **pǐnxíng** 品行 *84*

moral, ethics **dàodé** 道德 *21*

more and more **yuèláiyuè** 越来越 *131*

more or less the same **chàbuduō** 差不多 *12*

moreover, additionally **yòu** 又 *129*

moreover, what's more **érqiě** 而且 *28*, **bìngqiě** 并且 *8*

morning (usually from 8 a.m. to noon) **shàngwǔ** 上午 *93*

mosquito **wénzi** 蚊子 *112*

most (used before an adjective to indicate the superlative degree) **zuì** 最 *142*

mother **māma** 妈妈 *72*, **mǔqin** 母亲 *77*

mother's brother, uncle **jiùfù** 舅父 *60*, **jiùjiù** 舅舅 *60*

mother's brother's wife, aunt **jiùmǔ** 舅母 *60*, **jiùmā** 舅妈 *60*

mother's sister **āyí** 阿姨 *1*

motherland, fatherland **zǔguó** 祖国 *142*

motorcycle **mótuōchē** 摩托车 *77*

mountain, hill **shān** 山 *92*

mourn over (the death of somebody) **zhuīdào** 追悼 *141*

mouse (computer's) **shǔbiāo** 鼠标 *99*

mouse, mice, rat, rats **lǎoshǔ** 老鼠 *67*

mouth **kǒu** 口 *64*, **zuǐ** 嘴 *142*

move, shift (v.) **yídòng** 移动 *125*

move, touch emotionally **gǎndòng** 感动 *35*

move (house); house moving **bānjiā** 搬家 *3*

move around, encircle **wéirào** 围绕 *110*

move around; action, behavior, movement **xíngdòng** 行动 *118*

movement (of the body) **dòngzuò** 动作 *25*

movie star, star **míngxīng** 明星 *76*

moving, touching (adj.) **dòngrén** 动人 *25*

moxibustion **jiǔ** 灸 *60*

Mr, mister **xiānsheng** 先生 *114*

Mrs; wife **tàitai** 太太 *103*

much, very much **shèn** 甚 *95*

mud **ní** 泥 *79*

muddle-headed, muddled, confused **hútu** 糊涂 *46*

multi-colored **cǎisè** 彩色 *10*

multi-storied building **lóu fáng** 楼房 *71*

multiply **chéng** 乘 *14*

municipality, city **shì** 市 *97*

muscle **jīròu** 肌肉 *50*

muscle, tendon, sinew **jīn** 筋 *58*

museum **bówùguǎn** 博物馆 *9*

music **yīnyuè** 音乐 *126*

music school, conservatory **yīnyuè xuéyuàn** 音乐学院 *126*

musical instrument **yuèqì** 乐器 *131*

musical performance, concert **yīnyuè huì** 音乐会 *126*

musician (one who is accomplished) **yīnyuè jiā** 音乐家 *126*

must, have to, have got to **bìxū** 必须 *6*

mute (adj.) **yǎ** 哑 *121*

mutual, each other **xiānghù** 相互 *115*

myopia, near-sightedness, short-sightedness **jìnshì** 近视 *59*

mysterious, mythical **shénmì** 神秘 *95*

mythology, fairy-tales **shénhuà** 神话 *95*

N

nail **dīngzi** 钉子 *25*

naive, gullible **tiānzhēn** 天真 *105*

name, given name **míngzi** 名字 *76*

name card, visiting card **míngpiàn** 名片 *76*

narrate **xùshù** 叙述 *120*

National Day (October 1 in China) **Guóqìngjié** 国庆节 *41*

nationality, citizenship **guójí** 国籍 *41*

native place, hometown, home village **gùxiāng** 故乡 *39*

natural resources **zīyuán** 资源 *141*

nature (of a matter, an event, etc.), basic quality **xìngzhì** 性质 *119*

nature; natural **zìrán** 自然 *141*

naughty, mischievous **táoqì** 淘气 *104*, **tiáopí** 调皮 *105*

necessary, requisite, indispensable **bìyào** 必要 *6*

neck **bózi** 脖子 *8*, **jǐng** 颈 *59*

necklace **xiàngliàn** 项链 *115*

necktie, tie **lǐngdài** 领带 *70*

need, be in need of **xūyào** 需要 *120*

need not, not have to, unnecessarily **búbì** 不必 *9*

needle **zhēn** 针 *135*

negate, deny **fǒudìng** 否定 *32*

negative (test result) **yīnxìng** 阴性 *126*

negative effect, disadvantage **huàichu** 坏处 *47*

negotiate **jiāoshè** 交涉 *55*

negotiate; negotiation **tánpàn** 谈判 *103*

neighbor **línjū** 邻居 *70*

neither, nor **yě** 也 *123*

net **wǎng** 网 *110*

netizen **wǎngmín** 网民 *110*

never **cóngbù** 从不 *17*

new **xīn** 新 *118*

new word (language) **shēngcí** 生词 *95*

New Year **xīnnián** 新年 *118*

New Year's Day, the **yuándàn** 元旦 *130*

New Zealand **Xīnxīlán** 新西兰 *118*

news (current affairs) **xīnwén** 新闻 *118*

news, information **xiāoxi** 消息 *116*

news reporter, correspondent **jìzhě** 记者 *51*

newspaper **bàozhǐ** 报纸 *4*

newspaper office **bàoshè** 报社 *4*

next, secondary, secondly **qícì** 其次 *85*

next door **gébì** 隔壁 *36*

next in importance, of secondary importance **cìyào** 次要 *17*

next year **míngnián** 明年 *76*

night, evening **yè** 夜 *123*

nine **jiǔ** 九 *60*

no, not **bù** 不 *9*

no comment **wú kě fèng gào** 无可奉告 *112*

no matter (what, how, who, etc.) **bùguǎn** 不管 *9*, **búlùn** 不论 *9*, **wúlùn** 无论 *112*

no matter how **zěnme** 怎么 *133*

no need, there's no need, don't have to **búyòng** 不用 *10*

no wonder **nánguài** 难怪 *79*, **guàibudé** 怪不得 *39*

noise **zàoyīn** 噪音 *132*

noisy and exciting, boisterous, bustling, lively (scene or occasion) **rènao** 热闹 *90*

nonsense, rubbish **fèihuà** 废话 *31*

noodle **miàn** 面 *76*, **miàntiáor** 面条儿 *76*

noon **zhōngwǔ** 中午 *138*

normal, nothing wrong **hǎohǎor** 好好儿 *43*

normal, regular **zhèngcháng** 正常 *136*

north, northern **běi** 北 *5*

north side, to/in the north **běibian** 北边, **běimiàn** 北面 *5*

northeast, the Northeast **dōngběi** 东北 *25*

northern region **běifāng** 北方 *5*

northwest, the Northwest **xīběi** 西北 *113*

nose **bízi** 鼻子 *5*

not allow, must not **bùxǔ** 不许 *10*

not bad, quite good **búcuò** 不错 *9*

not enough time (to do something) **láibují** 来不及 *66*

not for sure, indefinitely **shuō bu dìng** 说不定 *100*

not in the least, not at all **háo bù** 毫不 *43*

not long afterwards, near future, soon **bùjiǔ** 不久 *9*

not necessarily, may not **wèibì** 未必 *111*

not necessarily, unlikely **bú jiàndé** 不见得 *9*

not often, seldom **shǎo** 少 *93*

not only ... but also **búdàn ... érqiě** 不但 ... 而且 *9*

not salty, tasteless, bland **dàn** 淡 *21*

not straight, askew, crooked **wāi** 歪 *108*

not the same, different **bùtóng** 不同 *10*

not very, not much **búdà** 不大 *9*

not wrong; quite right **búcuò** 不错 *9*

notebook **běnzi** 本子 *5*

notebook computer, laptop **bǐjìběn diànnǎo** 笔记本电脑 *6*

notes (class or reading) **bǐjì** 笔记 *6*

nothing serious, it's nothing, it doesn't matter **méishénme** 没什么 *74*

notify, inform; notice, circular **tōngzhī** 通知 *106*

novel, fiction **xiǎoshuō** 小说 *116*

novelist **xiǎoshuōjiā** 小说家 *116*

now that, since, as **jìrán** 既然 *52*

nuclear power plant **hédiànzhàn** 核电站 *45*

nuclear weapon **héwǔqì** 核武器 *45*

number, amount **shùmù** 数目 *100*

number of times (of doing something) **huí** 回 *48*

number recorded when grading, mark, grade **fēnshù** 分数 *32*

numeral (in writing) **shùzì** 数字 *100*

nurse **hùshi** 护士 *46*

nutrition, nourishment **yíngyǎng** 营养 *127*

O

o'clock **diǎnzhōng** 点钟 *24*

obey, submit to **fúcóng** 服从 *32*

object, substance **wùtǐ** 物体 *113*

object (of an action or feeling) **duìxiàng** 对象 *27*

objective **kèguān** 客观 *64*

oblique, slanting **xié** 斜 *117*

observe, abide by **zūnshǒu** 遵守 *143*

observe, watch **guānchá** 观察 39

observe the (Chinese) New Year's Day **guònián** 过年 42

obtain, achieve **qǔdé** 取得 88

obvious, apparent, evident **míngxiǎn** 明显 76

obvious; obviously **xiǎnrán** 显然 114

occasionally, once in a long while **ǒu'ěr** 偶尔 81

occupation, profession, vocation **zhíyè** 职业 137

occupational disease **zhíyèbìng** 职业病 137

ocean **yáng** 洋 122

Oceania **Dàyángzhōu** 大洋洲 19

odd number **dānshù** 单数 20

of course, that goes without saying **dāngrán** 当然 21

of high speed **gāosù** 高速 35

of one's own accord, taking the initiative **zhǔdòng** 主动 139

of primary importance **shǒuyào** 首要 98

of the Christian/common era, AD (anno Domini) **gōngyuán** 公元 37

office **bàngōngshì** 办公室 3, **jú** 局 60

official (in government) **guān** 官 39

official, officer, mandarin **guānyuán** 官员 40

often **chángcháng** 常常 12

often, day-to-day **jīngcháng** 经常 59

oh, ah (expressing surprise) **yā** 呀 121

oil **yóu** 油 128

oil field **yóutián** 油田 128

oil painting **yóuhuà** 油画 128

old, elderly **lǎo** 老 66

old, past, second-hand (of things) **jiù** 旧 60

old age **wǎnnián** 晚年 109

old person, elderly person **lǎorén** 老人 66

omit, leave out **shěnglüè** 省略 95

on one's person, bring with one **suíshēn** 随身 102

on one's way (to) **lùshang** 路上 71

on the one hand … on the

other hand … **yìfāngmiàn** … **yìfāngmiàn** … 一方面 … 一方面 … 124

on top of, on, above **shàng** 上 93

once, formerly **céngjīng** 曾经 11

once, some day **yídàn** 一旦 124

once upon a time (used in story-telling) **cóngqián** 从前 17

one **yī** 一 123

one after another, in succession **lùxù** 陆续 71, **xiānhòu** 先后 114

one after another, numerous and disorderly **fēnfēn** 纷纷 32

one hundred million **yì** 亿 125

one hundred percent, totally, fully **shífēn** 十分 96

one percentage **bǎifēndiǎn** 百分点 3

one side **yìbiān** 一边 123

one who is from other parts of the country, not a native **wàidìrén** 外地人 108

one who owns a farm, farmer **nóngchǎngzhǔ** 农场主 80

one-sided, unilateral **piànmiàn** 片面 83

one's brother's daughter, niece **zhínǚ** 侄女 137

one's brother's son, nephew **zhízi** 侄子 137

one's entire life **yíbèizi** 一辈子 123

one's father's sister, aunt **gūgu** 姑姑 38

one's taste **kǒuwèi** 口味 64

only, merely, simply **zhǐshì** 只是 137

only, only if **zhǐyǒu** 只有 137

open, open up **kāifàng** 开放 62

open (the eyes) **zhēng** 睁 136

open, public; make public, reveal **gōngkāi** 公开 37

open, start (of a play, a ceremony, conference, etc.) **kāimù** 开幕 62

open country, field **yěwài** 野外 123

open for business **kāimén** 开门 62

open up (land, space etc.) **kāikuò** 开阔 62

open-minded and modest **xūxīn** 虚心 120

opening ceremony **kāimù shì** 开幕式 62

operate (a business) **jīngyíng** 经营 59

operating room, operating theater **shǒushùjiān** 手术间 98

ophthalmologist **yǎnkē yīshēng** 眼科医生 122

opinion, view **yìjiàn** 意见 125

opinion on public affairs, expression of one's political views **yánlùn** 言论 122

opponent **duìshǒu** 对手 27

opportunistic **tóujī** 投机 107

opportunity, chance **jīhuì** 机会 49

oppose, object **fǎnduì** 反对 30

opposite, contrary **xiāngfǎn** 相反 115

opposite, the opposite side **duìmiàn** 对面 27

optimistic **lèguān** 乐观 67

or **huòzhě** 或者 49, **háishì** 还是 42

orchid **lánhuā** 兰花 66

order, command **mìnglìng** 命令 77

order, proper sequence **zhìxù** 秩序 138

order of sequence **hào** 号 44

ordinary, common **píngcháng** 平常 84

ordinary time, usually, normally **píngcháng** 平常 84

organism **jītǐ** 机体 50

organization, group **tuántǐ** 团体 108

organize, arrange for; organization, organized system **zǔzhī** 组织 142

original, former **yuánlái** 原来 130

originally, at first **běnlái** 本来 5

orphan **gū'ér** 孤儿 38

other **qítā** 其他 85

other, another **biéde** 别的 7, **lìngwài** 另外 70

other people, others **biérén** 别人 7

other side, other party, the **duìfāng** 对方 27

otherwise, or **bùrán** 不然 9, **fǒuzé** 否则 32

otherwise, or else **yàobu** 要不 123, **yàoburán** 要不然 123

out of town, suburban area **chéngwài** 城外 *14*

outline (n.) **tígāng** 提纲 *104*

outpatient service (in a hospital) **ménzhěn** 门诊 *75*

output **shūchū** 输出 *99*

output (in production), yield **chǎnliàng** 产量 *12*

outside **wàibian** 外边 *108*

outstanding, excellent **yōuxiù** 优秀 *127*, **chūsè** 出色 *15*

oval **tuǒyuán** 椭圆 *108*

over, more than **yǐshàng** 以上 *125*

over and over again **zàisān** 再三 *131*

over-sensitive, allergic **guòmǐn** 过敏 *42*

overcoat **dàyī** 大衣 *19*

overcome, conquer **kèfú** 克服 *64*

overjoyed, very delighted **tòngkuai** 痛快 *107*

overlook, negelect **hūshì** 忽视 *46*

oversexed, lewd **hào sè** 好色 *44*

overtake, exceed **chāoguò** 超过 *12*

owe a debt of gratitude **qiàn rénqíng** 欠人情 *86*

own, possess **zhànyǒu** 占有 *133*

P

padding, stuffing **tāi** 胎 *102*

paddy rice, rice **shuǐdào** 水稻 *100*

page **yè** 页 *123*

painful, bitter, tortuous **tòngkǔ** 痛苦 *107*

painter, artist **huàjiā** 画家 *47*

pair, two (matching people or things) **duì** 对 *27*

pajamas, dressing gown **shuìyī** 睡衣 *100*

panda, giant panda **xióngmāo** 熊猫 *120*

paper or document proving one's identity (passport, ID card, etc.) **zhèngjiàn** 证件 *136*

paper **zhǐ** 纸 *137*

parcel, package **bāoguǒ** 包裹 *4*

pardon, excuse, forgive **yuánliàng** 原谅 *130*

parking lot, car park **tíngchēchǎng** 停车场 *106*

part, spare part **língjiàn** 零件 *70*

part of, aspect **dìfang** 地方 *23*

part with, be separated from **fēnbié** 分别 *32*

participate, attend **cānjiā** 参加 *11*

participate, involve **cānyú** 参与 *11*

partner, mate **huǒbàn** 伙伴 *49*

parts of the country other than where one is **wàibian** 外边 *108*, **wàimiàn** 外面 *109*

party member **dǎngyuán** 党员 *21*

pass (a test, an examination, etc.) **jígé** 及格 *50*

pass along (word), pass on (a message) **zhuǎngào** 转告 *140*

pass through **tōngguò** 通过 *106*

passport **hùzhào** 护照 *46*

password (in computing), secret code, cipher code **mìmǎ** 密码 *75*

past events, the past **wǎngshì** 往事 *110*

past the sell-by date **guòqī** 过期 *42*

past time, in the past **cóngqián** 从前 *17*

paste, stick (v.) **tiē** 贴 *105*

pastureland, pastoral area **mùqū** 牧区 *77*

paternal grandmother, granny **nǎinai** 奶奶 *78*

patient (adj.) **nàifán** 耐烦 *78*

patient **bìngrén** 病人 *8*

patient; patience **nàixīn** 耐心 *78*

patrol, go on patrol **xúnluó** 巡逻 *121*

pattern, design **tú'àn** 图案 *107*

pause, halt **tíngdùn** 停顿 *106*

pavilion, kiosk **tíngzi** 亭子 *106*

pay a sum of money, make a payment **fùkuǎn** 付款 *33*

pay attention to, take notice of **zhùyì** 注意 *140*

pay out, contribute **fùchù** 付出 *33*

pay taxes **nàshuì** 纳税 *78*

peace **hépíng** 和平 *44*

peaceful and quiet, still **jìjìng** 寂静 *52*

peanut **huāshēng** 花生 *46*

pear **lí** 梨 *67*

pearl **zhēnzhū** 珍珠 *135*

peasant, farmer **nóngmín** 农民 *80*

pedestrian **xíngrén** 行人 *119*

pellet **kēlì** 颗粒 *63*

pencil **qiānbǐ** 铅笔 *86*

pencil box **qiānbǐ hé** 铅笔盒 *86*

pencil sharpener **qiānbǐ dāo** 铅笔刀 *86*

pension, superannuation **tuìxiūjīn** 退休金 *108*

people, the public **rénmen** 人们 *90*

people (of a country) **rénmín** 人民 *90*

people of the older generation, family elder, elder **zhǎngbèi** 长辈 *134*

people of the same generation **bèi** 辈 *5*

percentage **bǎifēnbǐ** 百分比 *3*

perfect, flawless **wánměi** 完美 *109*

perform; theatrical performance **yǎnchū** 演出 *122*

performance, show **biǎoyǎn** 表演 *7*

perhaps, maybe **huòxǔ** 或许 *49*, **yěxǔ** 也许 *123*

period, stage **jiēduàn** 阶段 *56*

period of time, stage **shíqī** 时期 *96*

permit, allow **xǔkě** 许可 *120*

persimmon **shìzi** 柿子 *98*

person of Chinese descent **Huáyì** 华裔 *46*

person's character, disposition, temperament **xìnggé** 性格 *119*

personal experience; learn through one's personal experience **tǐyàn** 体验 *104*

personal understanding through experience **tǐhuì** 体会 *104*

personality **gèxìng** 个性 *36*

personnel, staff **rényuán** 人员 *90*

persuade **shuōfú** 说服 *100*

pessimistic **bēiguān** 悲观 *5*

pest (insect) **hàichóng** 害虫 *42*

petroleum, oil **shíyóu** 石油 *96*

Ph.D. degree **bóshì xuéwèi** 博士学位 *8*

pharmacist's, pharmacy **yàofáng** 药房 *123*

phenomenon **xiànxiàng** 现象 *115*

philosopher **zhéxuéjiā** 哲学家 *135*

philosophy **zhéxué** 哲学 *135*

photocopier **fùyìnjī** 复印机 *33*

photocopy (n.) **fùyìnjiàn** 复印件 *33*

photograph, picture, snapshot **zhàopiàn** 照片 *134*

photographer **shèyǐngshī** 摄影师 *94*

physical education, sports **tǐyù** 体育 *104*

physical education (PE) lesson **tǐyù kè** 体育课 *104*

physical strength **lìqi** 力气 *68*

physics **wùlǐ** 物理 *113*

pictographic character, pictograph **xiàng xíng zì** 象形字 *116*

pig, hog, swine **zhū** 猪 *139*

pill (medicine) **yàopiàn** 药片 *123*

pillow **zhěntou** 枕头 *135*

pipeline, conduit **guǎndào** 管道 *40*

pitiful, pitiable **kělián** 可怜 *63*

place, location **wèizhi** 位置 *111*, **dìfang** 地方 *23*

place of an event or activity, venue **dìdiǎn** 地点 *23*

place of one's birth or origin **jíguàn** 籍贯 *51*

plain boiled water **báikāishuǐ** 白开水 *2*

plain truth **lǎoshihuà** 老实话 *67*

plan, intend **dǎsuàn** 打算 *18*

plan, program (for a major project) **fāng'àn** 方案 *30*

plan, program, project **jìhuà** 计划 *51*

plant, flora **zhíwù** 植物 *137*

plant, grow **zhòng** 种 *139*

plastic **sùliào** 塑料 *101*

plate, dish, tray **pánzi** 盘子 *82*

play; have fun **wánr** 玩儿 *109*

play baseball/basketball/volleyball, etc. **dǎ qiú** 打球 *18*

play host, stand the treat **zuòdōng** 做东 *143*

play station, (game) console **yóuxìjī** 游戏机 *128*

play the piano **tán gāngqín** 弹钢琴 *103*

play tricks, get up to mischief **gǎo guǐ** 搞鬼 *35*

pleasant, joyful **yúkuài** 愉快 *129*

pleasant to the ear, melodious **hǎotīng** 好听 *44*

pleasant to the eye, good-looking, pretty **hǎokàn** 好看 *44*

pleasantly cool, nice and cool **liángkuai** 凉快 *69*

pleasantly warm, mild **nuǎnhuo** 暖和 *81*

pleased, happy **yúkuài** 愉快 *129*

pleasing to the eye **měiguān** 美观 *74*

plot for murder **móuhài** 谋害 *77*

pluralizer (for people) **men** 们 *75*

pocket **kǒudài** 口袋 *64*

poem, poetry **shīgē** 诗歌 *96*

poet **shīrén** 诗人 *96*

point out **zhǐchū** 指出 *137*

poke, pick up **tiǎo** 挑 *105*

pole **gān** 杆 *34*

police station **pàichūsuǒ** 派出所 *82*

policeman, police **jǐngchá** 警察 *59*

polite, courteous **lǐmào** 礼貌 *67*

polite, courteous, stand on ceremony **kèqi** 客气 *64*

political party **dǎng** 党 *21*

politics, governance **zhèngzhì** 政治 *136*

pollute; pollution **wūrǎn** 污染 *112*

pond **chítáng** 池塘 *14*

ponder over, reflect on, think seriously **sīkǎo** 思考 *101*

poor in, short of **pínfá** 贫乏 *84*

poor person, poor people **qióngrén** 穷人 *88*

popularize, spread **tuīguǎng** 推广 *108*

population (human) **rénkǒu** 人口 *90*

pornography; pornographic **huángsè** 黄色 *48*

porridge, gruel **zhōu** 粥 *139*

portion, part **bùfen** 部分 *10*

pose a threat, threaten; threat **wēixié** 威胁 *110*

position, post **wèizhi** 位置 *111*

positive **jījí** 积极 *50*

positive (of medical test result) **yángxìng** 阳性 *122*

positive result, achievement **chéngguǒ** 成果 *13*

possess, be provided with **jùbèi** 具备 *61*

possess, have **yǒu** 有 *128*

post office **yóujú** 邮局 *128*

postal stamp **yóupiào** 邮票 *128*

postpone **tuīchí** 推迟 *108*

posture, carriage **zīshì** 姿势 *141*

pot, pan, wok **guō** 锅 *41*

potato **tǔdòu** 土豆 *107*

pottery, earthenware **táoqì** 陶器 *104*

pour (water), make (tea) **dào** 倒 *21*

powder **fěn** 粉 *32*

pragmatic, practical **wùshí** 务实 *113*

praise, commend; praise, commendation **biǎoyáng** 表扬 *7*

preferential, favorable **yōuhuì** 优惠 *127*

premier, prime minister **zǒnglǐ** 总理 *142*

prepare lessons before class, preview **yùxí** 预习 *130*

prepare, get ready **yùbèi** 预备 *130*

prepare; preparation **zhǔnbèi** 准备 *141*

prescription **yàofāng** 药方 *123*

present as a gift **zèngsòng** 赠送 *133*

(the) present time, now **xiànzài** 现在 *115*

president (of a country) **zǒngtǒng** 总统 *142*

pressure **yālì** 压力 *121*

pretend, feign **jiǎzhuāng** 假装 *53*

prevent, stop, hold back **zǔzhǐ** 阻止 *142*

previous, last **shàng** 上 *93*

price **jiàgé** 价格 *53*, 价钱 *53*

price quotations **hángqíng** 行情 *43*

price, commodity price **wùjià** 物价 *113*

prick; thorn **cì** 刺 *17*

primary school **xiǎoxué** 小学 *117*

prince **wángzǐ** 王子 *110*

princess **gōngzhǔ** 公主 *37*

principle **yuánzé** 原则 *130*

printer **dǎyìnjī** 打印机 *18*

printing plate **bǎn** 版 *3*

prison, jail **láofáng** 牢房 *66*

private, personal **sīrén** 私人 101

probably **dàgài** 大概 19

probably, likely **shuō bu dìng** 说不定 100

probably, will **huì** 会 48

procedure **chéngxù** 程序 14

procedure, steps **bùzhòu** 步骤 10

process, course **guòchéng** 过程 42

process (unfinished products) **jiāgōng** 加工 52

produce, emit, give off **fāchū** 发出 29

produce, give rise to **chǎnshēng** 产生 12

produce, manufacture **shēngchǎn** 生产 95

product, produce **chǎnpǐn** 产品 12

professional automobile driver, train driver **sījī** 司机 101

professional work, vocational work **yèwù** 业务 123

proficiency (in language) **shuǐpíng** 水平 100

profit **lìrùn** 利润 68

progress, progressive **jìnbù** 进步 58

project, construction work, engineering **gōngchéng** 工程 36

prolong, extend **yáncháng** 延长 121

prominent, conspicuous; give prominence, emphasize, highlight **tūchū** 突出 107

promise **dāying** 答应 18

promote (to a higher position) **jìnshēng** 晋升 58

promote, advance **cùjìn** 促进 17

pronunciation **fāyīn** 发音 29

propagate, disseminate **chuánbō** 传播 16

property, belongings **cáichǎn** 财产 10

propose a toast, toast **jìngjiǔ** 敬酒 60

pros and cons **lìbì** 利弊 68

prosperous, thriving **fánróng** 繁荣 29

protect, safeguard, conserve **bǎohù** 保护 4

protruding **tū** 突 107

proud, conceited, arrogant **jiāo'ào** 骄傲 55

prove, testify; proof, certificate **zhèngmíng** 证明 136

provide, supply **tígōng** 提供 104

provide an answer, give an explanation **jiědá** 解答 57

provoke; provocation **tiǎoxìn** 挑衅 105

psychology (as a science) **xīnlǐxué** 心理学 117

puberty **qīngchūnqī** 青春期 87

public, communal **gōnggòng** 公共 37

public expense, at public expense **gōngfèi** 公费 37

public garden, park **gōngyuán** 公园 37

public relations **gōnggòng guānxi** 公共关系 37

public road, highway **gōnglù** 公路 37

public telephone, payphone **gōngyòng diànhuà** 公用电话 37

publicize, make known, publish **fābiǎo** 发表 29

publish **chūbǎn** 出版 15

publish (in a newspaper, a journal, etc.) **dēng** 登 23

punch a card, record presence at work by punching a time clock **dǎ kǎ** 打卡 18

punctual, on time **zhǔnshí** 准时 141

punctuation mark **biāodiǎn** 标点 7

punish, penalize **fá** 罚 29

purchase **gòumǎi** 购买 38

pure, clean-minded, unselfish **chúnjié** 纯洁 16

pure nonsense, drivel **hú shuō bā dào** 胡说八道 46

purple **zǐ** 紫 141

pursue, seek **zhuīqiú** 追求 141

push, push and shove **yōngjǐ** 拥挤 127

push forward, promote **tuīdòng** 推动 104

put, place, arrange **bǎi** 摆 3

put, place, put in **fàng** 放 31

put ... right, rectify **gǎizhèng** 改正 34

put ahead of schedule, advance **tíqián** 提前 104

put in order, tidy up **shōushi** 收拾 98, **zhěnglǐ** 整理 136

put into, invest **tóurù** 投入 107

put into practice, apply; practice **shíjiàn** 实践 97

put on (a show), perform, demonstrate **biǎoyǎn** 表演 7

put on (clothes or shoes) **chuān** 穿 16

put on display, exhibit; exhibition, show **zhǎnlǎn** 展览 133

put out a fire; fire fighting **jiùhuǒ** 救火 60

put questions to, quiz **tíwèn** 提问 104

put somebody to trouble, bother **máfan** 麻烦 72

put together, pool **còu** 凑 17

put upside down **dào** 倒 21

Q

qualification **zīgé** 资格 141

qualified, up to standard **hégé** 合格 44

quality **zhìliàng** 质量 138

quantity, amount **shùliàng** 数量 100

quarrel **chǎojià** 吵架 12

quarter of an hour **kè** 刻 64

queen **wánghòu** 王后 110

question, problem, issue **wèntí** 问题 112

question for an examination, school exercises, etc. **tímù** 题目 104

quick, fast, speedy **kuài** 快 65

quiet, peaceful, serene **ānjìng** 安静 1

quietly, on the quiet **qiāoqiāo** 悄悄 87

quilt, blanket **bèizi** 被子 5

quite a few **bùshǎo** 不少 9

R

rabbit, hare **tùzi** 兔子 108

radio station **diàntái** 电台 24

railway **tiělù** 铁路 105

rain, precipitation **yǔ** 雨 129

rainbow **cǎihóng** 彩虹 10

raise, advance **tígāo** 提高 104

raise, keep as pet **yǎng** 养 122

RAM, memory **nèicún** 内存 79

rank-and-file soldier **shìbīng** 士兵 97

rapid, speedy, swift **xùnsù** 迅速 121

rashly, carelessly **húluàn** 胡乱 46

rate (n.) **lǜ** 率 72

ratio, percentage **bǐlì** 比例 6

raw, not cooked; unripe **shēng** 生 95

raw material **yuánliào** 原料 130

reach, achieve **dádào** 达到 18

reach, attain **dá** 达 18

read, study **dúshū** 读书 26

read (a book, newspaper, etc.) **kàn** 看 62

read (seriously), peruse **yuèdú** 阅读 131

read in a loud and clear voice **lǎngdú** 朗读 66

reader **dúzhě** 读者 26

reading room **yuèlǎnshì** 阅览室 131

ready money, cash **xiànjīn** 现金 114

real situation, actual facts, the **zhēnxiàng** 真相 135

reality, actual situation; practical, realistic **shíjì** 实际 97

really, truly **díquè** 的确 23

reason, basis **dàolǐ** 道理 22

reason, justification, ground **lǐyóu** 理由 68

reasonable, logical **hélǐ** 合理 44

rebel; rebellion **zàofǎn** 造反 132

recall, recollect; recollection, memory **huíyì** 回忆 48

receipt **fāpiào** 发票 29, **shōujù** 收据 98

receive, accept **shōu** 收 98, **shòu** 受 99

receive (a visitor) **jiēdài** 接待 56

receive/meet (somebody), give an audience **jiējiàn** 接见 56

receive or entertain (a guest) **zhāodài** 招待 134

receive visitors **huìkè** 会客 48

recently, recent times **zuìjìn** 最近 142

reception **zhāodàihuì** 招待会 134

recommend **tuījiàn** 推荐 108

reconnoiter, scout **zhēnchá** 侦察 135

record, memory **jì** 纪 51

record, register **jìlù** 记录 51

record of formal schooling/education **xuélì** 学历 120

record with a video camera or video recorder **lùxiàng** 录像 71

recover, restore **huīfù** 恢复 48

red **hóng** 红 45

red envelope (containing money) for children on Chinese New Year's Day **hóngbāo** 红包 45

reduce weight **jiǎnféi** 减肥 54

referee, umpire **cáipàn** 裁判 10

reference book(s) **cānkǎoshū** 参考书 11

reflect, mirror **fǎnyìng** 反映 30

reform **gǎigé** 改革 34

refrigerator, freezer **bīngxiāng** 冰箱 8

refund, ask for refund **tuìkuǎn** 退款 108

refuse, reject **jùjué** 拒绝 61

regarding **duìyú** 对于 27

region, area **dìqū** 地区 23

register **zhùcè** 注册 140

register, check in **dēngjì** 登记 23

register (at a hospital) **guàhào** 挂号 39

regret, feel sorry (for having done something) **hòuhuǐ** 后悔 45

regulate, adjust **tiáojié** 调节 105

relative, relation **qīnqi** 亲戚 87

relatively, comparatively **xiāngduì** 相对 115

relax, rest and relax **fàngsōng** 放松 31

relaxed and content **ānxīn** 安心 1

reliable, trustworthy **kěkào** 可靠 63

religion **zōngjiào** 宗教 142

rely on, depend on **yītuō** 依托 124

remain (in the same place), stay behind, retain **liú** 留 71

remember, memorize; memory **jìyì** 记忆 51

remind, call attention to **tíxǐng** 提醒 104

remit money, send remittance; remittance **huìkuǎn** 汇款 48

remold, rebuild; remolding, rebuilding **gǎizào** 改造 34

remote control **yáokòng** 遥控 123

remuneration **dàiyù** 待遇 20

rent, hire, charter; rent (money) **zū** 租 142

repair, fix **xiūlǐ** 修理 120

repeat **chóngfù** 重复 15

repeatedly, over and over again **fǎnfù** 反复 30

replace, substitute **tì** 替 104

report, make known **bàogào** 报告 4

report, make known, convey **fǎnyìng** 反映 30

report (news), cover; news story **bàodào** 报道 4

report for duty, register **bàodào** 报到 4

represent, indicate; representative **dàibiǎo** 代表 20

reproach, blame **zébèi** 责备 132

reptile **páxíng dòngwù** 爬行动物 81

republic **gònghéguó** 共和国 37

request, ask for; request **qǐngqiú** 请求 88

requirement, prerequisite **tiáojiàn** 条件 105

rescue, salvage **qiǎngjiù** 抢救 87

research institute **yánjiūyuàn** 研究院 122

research institute, research unit **yánjiūsuǒ** 研究所 122

reside; residency **jūzhù** 居住 60

residence **zhái** 宅 133

resident, inhabitant **jūmín** 居民 60

resign **cízhí** 辞职 17

resistance, obstacle **zǔlì** 阻力 142

resolute, determined **jiānjué** 坚决 53

resolutely **yìrán** 毅然 126

respect, esteem, value **zūnzhòng** 尊重 143

respect, honor **zūnjìng** 尊敬 142

respect and love **jìng'ài** 敬爱 60

response, reaction **fǎnyìng** 反应 30

responsibility, duty **zérèn** 责任 132

rest, take a rest, have a day off **xiūxi** 休息 120

restaurant **cāntīng** 餐厅 11

restaurant; hotel **fàndiàn** 饭店 30

result, outcome, consequence **jiéguǒ** 结果 57

résumé, curriculum vitae **jiǎnlì** 简历 54, **lǚlì** 履历 72

retail, sell retail **língshòu** 零售 70

retain, reserve **bǎoliú** 保留 4

retell, repeat **fùshù** 复述 33

retire (from employment); retirement **tuìxiū** 退休 108

retrogress, lag behind **tuìbù** 退步 108

return, pay back **huán** 还 47

return to one's home country **huíguó** 回国 48

reverse, opposite **fǎn** 反 29

review (one's lesson) **fùxí** 复习 33

revolution **gémìng** 革命 35

rice **dàmǐ** 大米 19

rice, paddy rice **mǐ** 米 75

rice bowl; way of making a living, job **fànwǎn** 饭碗 30

rich, wealthy **yǒuqián** 有钱 128

riddle **míyǔ** 谜语 75

ride a horse **qí mǎ** 骑马 85

ridge **lǒng** 垄 71

right (n.) **quánlì** 权利 89

right now **cǐshí** 此时 17

right side/right-hand side, the **yòubian** 右边 129

rights and interests **quányì** 权益 89

ring (on finger) **jièzhi** 戒指 57

ripe, cooked **shú** 熟 99

ripple, wave **bō** 波 8

rise in an uprising; uprising **qǐyì** 起义 85

risk **fēngxiǎn** 风险 32

risk, take a risk **màoxiǎn** 冒险 73

river **hé** 河 44, **jiāng** 江 55

road, path **dàolù** 道路 22

roast duck **kǎo yā** 烤鸭 63

role, part **juésè** 角色 61

roll (v.) **gǔn** 滚 41

Romanized Chinese writing, *pinyin* **pīnyīn** 拼音 83

romantic **làngmàn** 浪漫 66

romantic love **àiqíng** 爱情 1

room **fángjiān** 房间 31, **wūzi** 屋子 112

room (hotel) for a single person **dānrén fángjiān** 单人房间 20

roommate, flatmate **tóngwū** 同屋 112

root **gēn** 根 36

rope, cord **shéngzi** 绳子 95

rope-skipping, rope-jumping **tiàoshéng** 跳绳 105

route, itinerary **lùxiàn** 路线 71

rubber **xiàngjiāo** 橡胶 116

rubbish, garbage **lājī** 垃圾 65

rubbish disposal **lājī chǔlǐ** 垃圾处理 65

rule, established practice **guīju** 规矩 40

rule, law, regulation **guīzé** 规则 41

ruler (tool) **chǐ** 尺 14

run a fever **fāshāo** 发烧 29

run counter to, violate **wéifǎn** 违反 110

runway, track (in a sports ground) **pǎodào** 跑道 82

rural town **xiāng** 乡 115, **zhèn** 镇 136

Russia **Éluósī** 俄罗斯 28

Russia, the state of Russia **Éguó** 俄国 28

Russian language (especially the writing), the **Éwén** 俄文 28

Russian language, the **Éyǔ** 俄语 28

S

sack, bag **dài** 袋 20

sad, grieved **nánguò** 难过 79

safe, risk-free **bǎoxiǎn** 保险 4

safe, secure; security, safety **ānquán** 安全 1

safe and sound **píng'ān** 平安 84

sailboat **fānchuán** 帆船 29

salary, pay **xīnshuǐ** 薪水 118

salesperson **shòuhuòyuán** 售货员 99

salient feature, characteristic **tèsè** 特色 104

saliva, spittle **tuòmo** 唾沫 108

salt **yán** 盐 122

salty **xián** 咸 114

same **tóngyàng** 同样 106

same, identical **yíyàng** 一样 124

same as, as … as **yìbān** 一般 123

sample, sample product, specimen **yàngpǐn** 样品 122

sand, grit **shāzi** 沙子 92

sandy beach **shātān** 沙滩 92

satirize, ridicule, mock; satire **fěngcì** 讽刺 32

satisfied, satisfactory **mǎnyì** 满意 73

sausage **xiāngcháng** 香肠 115

save, practice thrift **jiéyuē** 节约 60

save, rescue, salvage **jiù** 救 60

save (money), deposit (money) **chǔxù** 储蓄 16

say, speak **shuō** 说 100

scale, scope, dimension **guīmó** 规模 41

scar **shāngbā** 伤疤 92

scene, occasion **qíngjǐng** 情景 87

scenery, sight **fēngguāng** 风光 32

scholarship **jiǎngxuéjīn** 奖学金 55

school **xuéxiào** 学校 121

school assignment, homework **zuòyè** 作业 143, **gōngkè** 功课 37

schoolbag, satchel **shūbāo** 书包 99

science **kēxué** 科学 63

scientist **kēxuéjiā** 科学家 63

scissors, shears **jiǎndāo** 剪刀 54

scope, range, limits **fànwéi** 范围 30

scratch/scrape (with a sharp object) **huá** 划 46

screw **luósīdīng** 螺丝钉 72

sea, ocean, seas and oceans **hǎiyáng** 海洋 42

seafood **hǎixiān** 海鲜 42

seaport **hǎigǎng** 海港 42

search (v.) **sōusuǒ** 搜索 101

search, ransack **sōuchá** 搜查 101

search; searching **cházhǎo** 查找 12

search engine **sōusuǒ yǐnqíng** 搜索引擎 101

season **jìjié** 季节 52

seat **zuòwèi** 座位 143

second (in order) **yǐ** 乙 125

second, two **èr** 二 28

secondary school, high school, middle school **zhōngxué** 中学 *138*

secret, confidential **mìmì** 秘密 *75*

secretary **mìshu** 秘书 *75*

section (of something long) **duàn** 段 *26*

security guard **bǎo'ān** 保安 *4*

see, get sight of **kànjiàn** 看见 *62*

see you again, goodbye **zàijiàn** 再见 *131*

seek advice from, consult **zīxún** 咨询 *141*

seize (an opportunity) **bǎwò** 把握 *2*

select, choose, pick out **tiāoxuǎn** 挑选 *105*

select, choose; choice, alternative **xuǎnzé** 选择 *120*

self, one's own **zìjǐ** 自己 *141*

self-confident **zìxìn** 自信 *141*

self-supporting, paid by oneself **zìfèi** 自费 *141*

selfish, egoistic **zìsī** 自私 *141*

sell **mài** 卖 *73*, sell **shòu** 售 *99*

sell; market **xiāoshòu** 销售 *116*

semester, term **xuéqī** 学期 *120*

send by mail, post **.jì** 寄 *52*

send off (people) **huānsòng** 欢送 *47*

send out **fāchū** 发出 *29*

send out, export **shūchū** 输出 *99*

sense of responsibility **zérèngǎn** 责任感 *133*

sensitive **mǐn'gǎn** 敏感 *76*

sentence **jùzi** 句子 *61*

sequence, order **shùnxù** 顺序 *100*

serial number **hàomǎ** 号码 *44*

serious, grave, critical **yánzhòng** 严重 *121*

serious, solemn, earnest **yánsù** 严肃 *121*

servant **yōngrén** 佣人 *127*

serve, work for **fúwù** 服务 *32*

server (for computers) **fúwù qì** 服务器 *32*

service industry **fúwù yè** 服务业 *32*

set off (on a journey), start (a journey) **chūfā** 出发 *15*

set one's mind at ease, be at ease **fàngxīn** 放心 *31*

settle accounts, balance the books **jiézhàng** 结账 *57*

seven **qī** 七 *85*

several, some **jǐ** 几 *51*

severe, formidable, redoubtable **lìhai** 厉害 *68*

sex, gender **xìng** 性 *119*

sex urge, eroticism **sèqíng** 色情 *92*

sexual desire, sex urge **xìngyù** 性欲 *119*

shadow, reflection **yǐngzi** 影子 *127*

shadow boxing, Taichi **Tàijíquán** 太极拳 *103*

shaft **gǎn** 杆 *35*

shake, vibrate **zhènhàn** 震撼 *136*

shake hands **wòshǒu** 握手 *112*

shallow **qiǎn** 浅 *86*

shape (of things), situation, condition **zhuàngkuàng** 状况 *140*

share, stock **gǔpiào** 股票 *38*

she, her **tā** 她 *102*

shed tears **liúlèi** 流泪 *71*

sheep, goat, lamb **yáng** 羊 *122*

shell (of shellfish) **bèiké** 贝壳 *5*

shift (in a workplace) **bān** 班 *3*

shirt **chènshān** 衬衫 *13*

shirt or similar underwear **chènyī** 衬衣 *13*

shoelace, shoestring **xié dài** 鞋带 *117*

shoot, fire **shèjī** 射击 *94*

shop, store **shāngdiàn** 商店 *93*

shop; shopping **gòuwù** 购物 *38*

shop assistant, salesperson **yíngyèyuán** 营业员 *127*

shop online; online shopping **wǎngguò** 网购 *110*

shopping center, mall **shāngchǎng** 商场 *93*

short (length, time) **duǎn** 短 *26*

short (person or plant) **ǎi** 矮 *1*

short-term **duǎnqī** 短期 *26*

shortcoming, defect **quēdiǎn** 缺点 *89*

shorten **suōduǎn** 缩短 *102*

should, must **yào** 要 *123*

should, ought to **gāi** 该 *34*, **yīnggāi** 应该 *126*, **yīngdāng** 应当 *126*

shoulder **jiānbǎng** 肩膀 *53*

shout, cry out, yell **hǎn** 喊 *43*

show, manifest **xiǎnshì** 显示 *114*

show and advertise (products) **zhǎnxiāo** 展销 *133*

shower (bath) **línyù** 淋浴 *70*

shroud, envelope (v.) **lǒngzhào** 笼罩 *71*

shut up, say no more **bì zuǐ** 闭嘴 *6*

sick leave **bìng jià** 病假 *8*

side, aspect **fāngmiàn** 方面 *30*

side, by the side **pángbiān** 旁边 *82*

side effect **fù zuòyòng** 副作用 *33*

sign, mark **biāozhì** 标志 *7*

sign (a treaty, a contract, etc.) **qiānshǔ** 签署 *86*

signal **xìnhào** 信号 *118*

signboard **páizi** 牌子 *82*

significance, meaning **yìyì** 意义 *126*

silent, reticent **chénmò** 沉默 *13*

silk, silk cloth **sīchóu** 丝绸 *101*

silly, meaningless **wúliáo** 无聊 *112*

silver **yín** 银 *126*

similar to, be alike **xiāngsì** 相似 *115*

simple and convenient, handy **jiǎndān** 简单 *54*

simple and unaffected, ingenuous **tiānzhēn** 天真 *105*

simple-minded, ingenuous **dānchún** 单纯 *20*

simple-minded, naive **lǎoshi** 老实 *67*

simplified Chinese character **jiǎntǐzì** 简体字 *54*

simply, virtually **jiǎnzhí** 简直 *54*

since, in the past … **yǐlái** 以来 *125*

since then, from then on **cóngcǐ** 从此 *17*

sincere **chéngkěn** 诚恳 *14*

sincere, truthful **zhēnzhì** 真挚 *135*

sincerity **zhēnxīn** 真心 *135*

sing songs, sing **chànggē** 唱歌 *12*

Singapore **Xīnjiāpō** 新加坡 *118*

singer (professional) **gēshǒu** 歌手 *35*

single bed **dānrén chuáng** 单人床 *20*

single word, a **dāncí** 单词 20

single-parent family **dānqīn jiātíng** 单亲家庭 20

sir, gentleman **xiānsheng** 先生 114

sit, be seated **zuò** 坐 143

situation **xíngshì** 形势 119

situation, circumstance **qíngkuàng** 情况 87

six **liù** 六 71

size **dàxiǎo** 大小 19

size (of clothing, shoes, etc.) **hàomǎ** 号码 44

size, measurements **chǐcùn** 尺寸 14

size (of shoes, shirts, readymade clothing, etc.) **chǐmǎ** 尺码 14

skate; ice-skating **huábīng** 滑冰 46

ski; skiing **huáxuě** 滑雪 46

skilful, skilled **shúliàn** 熟练 99

skill, ability, capability **běnlǐng** 本领 5

skill, art, craft **shù** 术 99

skin (human) **pífū** 皮肤 83

skin, leather **pí** 皮 83

skirt **qúnzi** 裙子 89

sky **tiānkōng** 天空 105

sky, heaven **tiān** 天 105

sleep, go to bed **shuìjiào** 睡觉 100

sleeve **xiùzi** 袖子 120

slender, slim **miáotiáo** 苗条 76

slightly, a little, somewhat **lüèwēi** 略微 72 , **yǒu(yì)diǎnr** 有(一)点儿 128

slightly, just a little bit **shāowēi** 稍微 93

slogan **kǒuhào** 口号 64

sloppy, careless **mǎhu** 马虎 72

slow or indolent person, slow coach **mànxìngzi** 慢性子 73

small and inexpensive dishes, snacks **xiǎochī** 小吃 116

small group (for work or study) **xiǎozǔ** 小组 117

smartphone **zhìnéng shǒujī** 智能手机 138

smear, spread on **tú** 涂 107

smelly, stinking **chòu** 臭 15

smelt (v.) **liàn** 炼 69

smile **wēixiào** 微笑 110

smog **wùmái** 雾霾 113

smoke (a cigarette, a cigar, etc.) **chōuyān** 抽烟 15, **xīyān** 吸烟 113

smooth, glossy **guānghuá** 光滑 40

smooth, without a hitch, successful **shùnlì** 顺利 100

snack, light refreshments **diǎnxīn** 点心 24

snake **shé** 蛇 94

sneeze (v.) **dǎ pēntì** 打喷嚏 18

snow **xuě** 雪 121

snow-white, pure white **xuě bái** 雪白 121

so long as, provided that, if only **zhǐyào** 只要 137

so-so, not too bad, just managing **mǎ mǎ hū hū** 马马虎虎 72

soap **féizào** 肥皂 31, **xiāngzào** 香皂 115

soccer, football **zúqiú** 足球 142

social butterfly **jiāojìhuā** 交际花 55

social class **jiējí** 阶级 56

social contact, social life **shèjiāo** 社交 94

social gathering, (social) party **jùhuì** 聚会 61

social media **shèjiāo méitǐ** 社交媒体 94

social network **shèjiāo wǎngluò** 社交网络 94

social party **pàiduì** 派对 82

social status, identity **shēnfen** 身份 94, **shēnfèn** 身分 94

socialism **shèhuì zhǔyì** 社会主义 94

society **shèhuì** 社会 94

sociology **shèhuìxué** 社会学 94

socket (for electric items) **chāzuò** 插座 11

soda water, soft drink, soda, pop **qìshuǐ** 汽水 86

soft and mild, gentle **róuhé** 柔和 91

soil **tǔrǎng** 土壤 107

soldier **bīng** 兵 8, **jūnrén** 军人 61

soldier, fighter **zhànshi** 战士 134

solicit, ask for **zhēngqiú** 征求 136

solve (a problem), settle (an issue) **jiějué** 解决 57

some **yǒude** 有的 128, **yǒuxiē** 有些 128

some, a few, a little **xiē** 些 117

somersault **jīndǒu** 筋斗 58

sometimes, occasionally **yǒushíhou** 有时候 128

son **érzi** 儿子 28

song **gē** 歌 35

song, melody **qǔzi** 曲子 88

sons and daughters, one's children **zǐ-nǚ** 子女 141

sooner or later, eventually **chízǎo** 迟早 14

sound, noise, voice **shēng** 声 95

sound-imitating word, onomatopoeia **xiàng shēng zì** 象声字 116

soup **tāng** 汤 103

sour, tart **suān** 酸 101

south side, in/to the south **nánbian** 南边 79, **nánmiàn** 南面 79

south, southern **nán** 南 79

southeast **dōngnán** 东南 25

southern part/south of a country, the **nánfāng** 南方 79

southerner **nánfāngrén** 南方人 79

southwest, the Southwest **xīnán** 西南 113

sow discord, instigate **tiǎobō** 挑拨 105

soy paste **jiàng** 酱 55

soy sauce, sauce, paste **jiàngyóu** 酱油 55

space, room **kōngjiān** 空间 64

spare time, amateur **yèyú** 业余 123

speak, talk **shuōhuà** 说话 100

speak (at a meeting), make a speech; speech, talk **fāyán** 发言 29

speak highly of, praise, applaud **zànyáng** 赞扬

special, especially **tèbié** 特别 104

special, unusual, exceptional **tèshū** 特殊 104

special features, characteristic **tèdiǎn** 特点 104

special field of study, specialty **zhuānkē** 专科 140

specialist field of study, specialty **zhuānyè** 专业 140

specialized, specialist **zhuānmén** 专门 140

specific, concrete, particular **jùtǐ** 具体 61

speculate; speculation **tóujī** 投机 107

speech, talk **jiǎnghuà** 讲话 55

speech-impaired person, dumb person **yǎba** 哑巴 121

speed, velocity **sùdù** 速度 101

spell, phonetize **pīnyīn** 拼音 83

spend (a period of time) **dùguò** 度过 26

spend (time), live (a life), observe (a festival) **guò** 过 42

spirit, mind **jīngshén** 精神 59

spit, exhale **tǔ** 吐 108

spoken language, speech **kǒuyǔ** 口语 64

spokesperson **fāyánrén** 发言人 29

sponsor (for club membership, political party, association etc.) **jièshào rén** 介绍人 57

sport shoes **yùndòngxié** 运动鞋 131

sports coach **jiàoliàn** 教练 56

sports ground (especially for ball games) **qiúchǎng** 球场 88

sports ground, playground **cāochǎng** 操场 11

sports meet, games **yùndònghuì** 运动会 131

spring (season) **chūn** 春, **chūntiān** 春天 16

Spring Festival (the Chinese New Year), the **chūnjié** 春节 16

spurn with contempt, disdain and reject **tuòqì** 唾弃 108

square (in mathematics) **píngfāng** 平方 84

square, plaza **guǎngchǎng** 广场 40

stable **wěndìng** 稳定 112

stadium, arena **tǐyùchǎng** 体育场 104

staff, personnel **yuángōng** 员工 130

staff (of a factory, a company, an enterprise, etc.), employee(s) **zhígōng** 职工 137

stage, arena **wǔtái** 舞台 113

stagnate, come to a standstill **tíngzhì** 停滞 106

stairs, stairway, staircase **lóutī** 楼梯 71

stammer, stutter **kǒuchī** 口吃 64

stand (v.) **zhàn** 站 133

stand treat **qǐngkè** 请客 88

stand up **zhàn qǐlai** 站起来 133

standard, criterion; up to standard, perfect **biāozhǔn** 标准 7

Standard Modern Chinese, Mandarin, Putonghua **Pǔtōnghuà** 普通话 84

staple food (usually cereal) **zhǔshí** 主食 139

start (a performance, a film, etc.) **kāiyǎn** 开演 62

start (a school term/semester) **kāixué** 开学 62

starting from …**cóng … qǐ** 从 … 起 17

state (of affairs), appearance **zhuàngtài** 状态 141

state of mind, mood **xīnqíng** 心情 117

stationery, writing material **wénjù** 文具 112

stature, figure **shēncái** 身材 94

status, position **dìwèi** 地位 23

stealthily, on the quiet **tōutōu** 偷偷 107

steamed bun **mántou** 馒头 73

steamed bun with filling **bāozi** 包子 4

steel **gāng** 钢 35

step by step, progressively, gradually **zhúbù** 逐步 139

stick, club **bàng** 棒 4

still, as before **háishì** 还是 42, **réngrán** 仍然 91

still, yet **hái** 还 42

still more, even more **gèng** 更 36, **gèngjiā** 更加 36

stimulant, dope **xīngfènjì** 兴奋剂 118

stimulate, give incentive to; stimulation, incentive **cìjī** 刺激 17

stingy, miserly **xiǎoqì** 小气 116

stipulate, regulate, specify; stipulation, regulation, provision **guīdìng** 规定 40

stir-fry, sauté **chǎo** 炒 13

stock of money (for special purposes), fund, foundation **jījīn** 基金 50

stocking, sock **wàzi** 袜子 108

stomach **dù** 肚 26, **wèi** 胃 111

stone, rock **shítou** 石头 96

stop, cease (v.) **tíngzhǐ** 停止 106

stop a car, park a car **tíngchē** 停车 106

stopper, plug, cork **sāizi** 塞子 92

store, shop **diàn** 店 24

story (storey), level, floor **céng** 层 11

story, tale **gùshi** 故事 39

strange, unusual, odd **qíguài** 奇怪 85

stranger **mòshēng rén** 陌生人 77

straps, braces, suspenders **bēidài** 背带 5

street **jiēdào** 街道 57

street, avenue **mǎlù** 马路 72

strength (physical), power **lìliàng** 力量 68

strengthen, reinforce **jiāqiáng** 加强 52

stretch out, extend **shēn** 伸 94

strict, stringent, rigorous **yángé** 严格 121

strike down, overthrow, down with … **dǎdǎo** 打倒 18

strive for, fight for **zhēngqǔ** 争取 136

strong, heavy (of atmosphere, interest, etc.) **nónghòu** 浓厚 81

strong, intense, violent **qiángliè** 强烈 87

strong, staunch **jiānqiáng** 坚强 53

strong, very good **bàng** 棒 4

strong point, merit **yōudiǎn** 优点 127

structure **gòuzào** 构造 38

structure, construction, composition **jiégòu** 结构 57

student, pupil **xuésheng** 学生 120

study (in a school) **niàn** 念 80

study abroad **liúxué** 留学 71

study, learn; study, studies **xuéxí** 学习 120

sturdy, strong, robust **jiēshi** 结实 56

study independently, teach oneself **zìxué** 自学 141

style (of doing things) **fēnggé** 风格 32

subjective **zhǔguān** 主观 *139*

substandard product **cìpǐn** 次品 *17*

substitute for, replace, instead of **dàitì** 代替 *20*

suburbs, outskirts (of a city) **jiāoqū** 郊区 *55*

subway **dìtiě** 地铁 *23*

succeed; successful **chénggōng** 成功 *13*

succeed in getting/obtaining **dédào** 得到 *22*

such **zhèyàng** 这样 *135*

suck up, absorb **xīshōu** 吸收 *113*

sudden, suddenly **hūrán** 忽然 *46*, **tūrán** 突然 *107*

sue, file a lawsuit against **qǐsù** 起诉 *85*

suffer, encounter, meet with **zāodào** 遭到 *132*

suffer losses, be at a disadvantage **chīkuī** 吃亏 *14*

sufficient, full **chōng** 充 *14*

suffix (denoting an accomplished expert) **jiā** 家 *52*

sugar, candy, sweets **tángguǒ** 糖果 *103*

suggest, propose; suggestion, proposal **jiànyì** 建议 *54*

suit, fit (v.) **shìhé** 适合 *98*

suitable, appropriate **xiāngdāng** 相当 *115*, **héshì** 合适 *44*

sum up, induce; summing-up, induction **guīnà** 归纳 *41*

summarize, generalize **gàikuò** 概括 *34*

summary, a general view of one's past work or life experiences **zǒngjié** 总结 *142*

summer **xiàtiān** 夏天 *114*

summer camp **xiàlìngyíng** 夏令营 *114*

summer holiday, summer vacation **shǔjià** 暑假 *99*

sun, sunshine **tàiyang** 太阳 *103*

sundry charges **záfèi** 杂费 *131*

sunshine, sunlight **yángguāng** 阳光 *12*

super **chāojí** 超级 *12*

super-highway, motorway **chāojí gōnglù** 超级公路 *12*

superiority, advantage, dominant position **yōushì** 优势 *127*

supermarket **chāo(jí) shì(chǎng)** 超(级)市(场) *12*

supplement, add **bǔchōng** 补充 *9*

supply, provide **gōng** 供 *37*

support (v.) **zhīchí** 支持 *137*

support, sponsor **zànzhù** 赞助 *132*

support with the hand **fú** 扶 *33*

suppose, assume **jiǎshè** 假设 *53*

supposing, if **jiǎrú** 假如 *53*

suppress, repress, put down (politically) **zhènyā** 镇压 *136*

sure enough, as expected **guǒrán** 果然 *41*

surface **biǎomiàn** 表面 *7*

surgical operation, operation **shǒushù** 手术 *98*

surplus **duōyú** 多余 *28*

surrender, capitulate **tóuxiáng** 投降 *107*

surrounding area, all around **zhōuwéi** 周围 *139*

swallow, gulp down **tūnyàn** 吞咽 *108*

sway, swing, rock **yáohuàng** 摇晃 *123*

sweet food, dessert **tiánshí** 甜食 *105*

swim (v.) **yóuyǒng** 游泳 *128*

swindler, con man **piànzi** 骗子 *83*

switch (n.) **kāiguān** 开关 *62*

symbolize; symbol **xiàngzhēng** 象征 *116*

sympathize with; sympathy **tóngqíng** 同情 *106*

system **xìtǒng** 系统 *114*

system, institution **zhìdù** 制度 *138*

T

table, desk **zhuōzi** 桌子 *141*

table of contents **mùlù** 目录 *77*

table tennis, table tennis ball **pīngpāngqiú** 乒乓球 *84*

tablet (computer) **píngbǎn diànnǎo** 平板电脑 *84*

tactics **cèlüè** 策略 *11*

tail **wěiba** 尾巴 *110*

Taiwan **Táiwān** 台湾 *103*

take a bath, take a shower **xǐzǎo** 洗澡 *113*

take a picture **zhàoxiàng** 照相 *135*, **pāizhào** 拍照 *81*

take a picture, shoot a movie, photograph **shèyǐng** 摄影 *94*

take a short leisurely walk, stroll **sànbù** 散步 *92*

take care of, look after **zhàoliào** 照料 *134*

take off (clothes, shoes, etc.) **tuō** 脱 *108*

take off (of a plane) **qǐfēi** 起飞 *85*

take out to show, produce **chūshì** 出示 *15*

take place, happen, occur **fāshēng** 发生 *29*

take precautionary measures to prevent, prevent **yùfáng** 预防 *130*

take responsibility for, undertake **chéngdān** 承担 *13*

take shape, form **xíngchéng** 形成 *119*

take turns **lúnliú** 轮流 *72*

talented and brave person, hero **yīngxióng** 英雄 *127*

talented person, person of ability **réncái** 人才 *90*

talk, hold a conversation; conversation **huìhuà** 会话 *48*

talk nonsense; nonsense **húshuō** 胡说 *46*

tall, high **gāo** 高 *35*

tall and big **gāodà** 高大 *35*

tall and straight **tǐngbá** 挺拔 *106*

tangerine **júzi** 橘子 *60*

target, objective, goal **mùbiāo** 目标 *77*

taste (n.) **qùwèi** 趣味 *89*

taste, flavor **wèidao** 味道 *111*

tax bureau, Inland Revenue Service **shuìwùjú** 税务局 *100*

taxi **chūzūchē** 出租车 *15*

tea **chá** 茶 *11*

teach in school, be a teacher **jiāoshū** 教书 *55*

teacher **jiàoshī** 教师 *56*, **lǎoshī** 老师 *67*

teacher (in a particular school) **jiàoyuán** 教员 *56*

teachers' college, college of education **shīfàn xuéyuàn** 师范学院 *96*

teachers' education **shīfàn** 师范 *96*

teaching and studying, teaching **jiàoxué** 教学 *56*

teaching material, textbook, coursebook **jiàocái** 教材 *56*

teacup **chábēi** 茶杯 11

team (ball game) **qiúduì** 球队 88

team leader **duìzhǎng** 队长 27

tear (a piece of paper) **sī** 撕 101

tears, teardrops **yǎnlèi** 眼泪 122

technical ability **jìnéng** 技能 52

technician **jìshùyuán** 技术员 52

technique, technology, skill **jìshù** 技术 52

telegram, cable **diànbào** 电报 24

telephone, telephone call **diànhuà** 电话 24

television **diànshì** 电视 24

tell, inform **gàosu** 告诉 35

tell a lie; lie **shuōhuǎng** 说谎 100

temper, temperament, disposition **píqi** 脾气 83

temperature (atmospheric) **wēndù** 温度 111

temperature (body's) **tǐwēn** 体温 104

temples and monasteries **sìmiào** 寺庙 101

temporary, for the time being **zànshí** 暂时 132

ten **shí** 十 96

ten thousand **wàn** 万 109

tennis **wǎngqiú** 网球 110

tennis court **wǎngqiúchǎng** 网球场 110

tense, nervous **jǐnzhāng** 紧张 58

tentative, provisional, temporary **línshí** 临时 70

terminal (n.) **zhōngduān** 终端 139

territory, domain **lǐngyù** 领域 70

test (in a school), exam; examination **cèyàn** 测验 11

text **kèwén** 课文 64

text file **wénběn** 文本 111

text message (by cell phone), text **duǎnxìn** 短信 26

textbook, course book **kèběn** 课本 64

thank **xièxie** 谢谢 117

that **nà** 那 78

that one **nàge** 那个 78

the area nearby, neighborhood **fùjìn** 附近 33

the best **guàn** 冠 40

the curtain falls (of a theatrical performance, an event, etc.) **bìmù** 闭幕 6

the East, the Orient **Dōngfāng** 东方 25

the Great Wall (in Northern China) **Chángchéng** 长城 12

the Kuomintang (a major party in Taiwan) **Guómíndǎng** 国民党 41

the more … the more … **yuè … yuè …** 越 … 越 … 131

The onlooker sees most of the game. **pángguānzhě qīng** 旁观者清 82

the only one, sole **wéiyī** 唯一 110

the person in charge **fùzérén** 负责人 33

the rest, the remainder **qíyú** 其余 85

the slightest, in the least **sīháo** 丝毫 101

the West, Occident **Xīfāng** 西方 113

the world **shìjiè** 世界 97

theater **jùchǎng** 剧场 61

theme **zhǔtí** 主题 139

theory, thinking **lǐlùn** 理论 68

there is/are no **méiyǒu** 没有 74

there, over there, in that place **nàli** 那里 78, **nàr** 那儿 (used colloquially) 78

there is no need to **yòngbuzháo** 用不着 127

there is no need, why **hébì** 何必 44

there is no way out, have no alternative, helpless **wú kě nàihé** 无可奈何 112

therefore, so **suǒyǐ** 所以 102, **yīncǐ** 因此 126, **yīn'ér** 因而 126

thermos, thermos flask **rèshuǐpíng** 热水瓶 90

these **zhèxiē** 这些 135

they, them **tāmen** 他们 102

they, them (non-human) **tāmen** 它们 102

they, them (female) **tāmen** 她们 102

thick (of smoke, cloud, etc.) **nónghòu** 浓厚 81

thief **xiǎotōu** 小偷 117

thin and flat piece **piàn** 片 83

thing, object, reality **shìwù** 事物 97

thing, things **dōngxi** 东西 25

think (usually incorrectly) **yǐwéi** 以为 125

think, consider **rènwéi** 认为 90

think over carefully, consider, contemplate **kǎolǜ** 考虑 63

thirsty **kě** 渴 64

this **cǐ** 此 17, **zhè** 这 135

this, that **qí** 其 85

this locality **běndì** 本地 5

this moment **cǐkè** 此刻 17

this one, this **zhège** 这个 135

this place, here **zhèli** 这里 135

this year **jīnnián** 今年 58

thorough, thoughtful, considerate **zhōudào** 周到 139

those **nàxiē** 那些 78

thought, thinking **sīxiǎng** 思想 101

thousand **qiān** 千 86

three **sān** 三 92

thrifty, frugal **jiǎn** 俭 54

thrifty and simple **jiǎn pǔ** 俭朴 54

throat **sǎngzi** 嗓子 92

through, as a result of **tōngguò** 通过 106

throw, hurl (v.) **tóuzhì** 投掷 107

thunderstorm **léiyǔ** 雷雨 67

thus, thereby **cóng'ér** 从而 17

ticket **piào** 票 83

tiger **lǎohǔ** 老虎 66

till now, to this day, so far **zhìjīn** 至今 138

time, a period of time **zhōngtóu** 钟头 (used in spoken Chinese) 139

time, a period of time **shíjiān** 时间 96

time (the duration of), (a certain point in) time **shíhou** 时候 96

time and again, repeatedly **yízài** 一再 124

time difference between time zones **shíchā** 时差 96

timely, at the proper time **jíshí** 及时 50

timetable (for a railway, coach) **shíkèbiǎo** 时刻表 91

timetable (for a schedule), program **rìchéngbiǎo** 91

timid, cowardly **dǎnxiǎo** 胆小 20

tin, jar **guàntou** 罐头 40

tip, gratuity **xiǎofèi** 小费 116

tired, weary, exhausted **pífá** 疲乏 83

title, subject **tímù** 题目 104

to, towards **duìyú** 对于 27

to, until **zhì** 至 (only used in written Chinese) 138

to a certain degree, fair, limited **yídìng** 一定 124

to one's great satisfaction **tòngkuai** 痛快 107

today **jīntiān** 今天 58

today, now **rújīn** 如今 91

together **yìqǐ** 一起 124, **yídào** 一道 124, **yìqí** 一齐 124, **yíkuàir** 一块儿 124

toilet **cèsuǒ** 厕所 11

toilet, restroom, washroom **xǐshǒujiān** 洗手间 113

tomato **xīhóngshì** 西红柿 113

tomorrow **míngtiān** 明天 76

tone, manner of speaking **yǔqì** 语气 129

tone of a Chinese word **shēngdiào** 声调 95

tongs, clip **jiāzi** 夹子 52

tongue **shétou** 舌头 94

too, excessively **guòyú** 过于 42

tool, implement **gōngjù** 工具 36

tooth, teeth **yáchǐ** 牙齿 121

toothbrush **yáshuā** 牙刷 121

toothpaste **yágāo** 牙膏 121

top grade, high quality **gāodàng** 高档 35

topic of conversation, subject of a talk, theme **huàtí** 话题 47

totally ignore (a fact), deny **mǒshā** 抹杀 77

tourist guide **dǎoyóu** 导游 21

towards, in the direction of **wǎng** 往 110

towards evening, at dusk **bàngwǎn** 傍晚 3

towel **máojīn** 毛巾 73

toy **wánjù** 玩具 109

track; orbit **guǐdào** 轨道 41

trade, exchange **màoyì** 贸易 74

trade and profession, industry **hángyè** 行业 43

tradition, heritage **chuántǒng** 传统 16

traditional Chinese character **fántǐ zì** 繁体字 29

traditional Chinese medicine (e.g. herbs) **zhōngyào** 中药 138

traditional Chinese medicine **zhōngyī** 中医 138

traffic jam **dǔchē** 堵车 26, **sāichē** 塞车 92

traffic lights, stoplights **hónglǜdēng** 红绿灯 45

train (for transport) **lièchē** 列车 70, **huǒchē** 火车 49

train, develop **péiyǎng** 培养 82

train, drill **xùnliàn** 训练 121

train attendant **lièchē yuán** 列车员 70

train of thought, thoughts **sīxù** 思绪 101

training **péixùn** 培训 82

tranquil, quiet **níngjìng** 宁静 80

transform, change, alter **gǎibiàn** 改变 34

transform, change; transformation, change **biànhuà** 变化 7

transition **guòdù** 过渡 42

translate, interpret; translator, interpreter **fānyì** 翻译 29

transparency **tòumíngdù** 透明度 107

transparent **tòumíng** 透明 107

transport, carry; transportation **yùnshū** 运输 131

transport, convey **shūsòng** 输送 99

transport, transportation, traffic **jiāotōng** 交通 55

travel, journey, tour **lǚxíng** 旅行 71

travel for pleasure, tour, go sight-seeing **lǚyóu** 旅游 71

treasure **bǎo** 宝 4

treasured object, treasure **bǎobèi** 宝贝 4

treat (a disease); treatment **zhìliáo** 治疗 138

treat (people), approach (matters) **duìdài** 对待 27

treat as, regard as **dàngzuò** 当做 21

treatment **dàiyù** 待遇 20

tree **mù** 木 77, **shù** 树 100

tremble, shiver, shake **fādǒu** 发抖 29

triangle **sānjiǎo** 三角 92

trick, swindle **bǎxì** 把戏 2

triumph over, defeat **zhànshèng** 战胜 134

trolley bus, streetcar **diànchē** 电车 24

troops, the army **bùduì** 部队 10

troublesome, knotty **máfan** 麻烦 72

trousers **kùzi** 裤子 65

true, real, authentic **zhēnshí** 真实 135

true, real, genuine **zhēnzhèng** 真正 135

true fact, truth **shíhuà** 实话 96

trunk, chest, box, suitcase **xiāngzi** 箱子 115

trustworthiness, credit **xìnyòng** 信用 118

truth **zhēnhuà** 真话 135, **zhēnlǐ** 真理 135

try to talk … into (or out of) doing something, advise **quàn** 劝 89

tuition, tuition fee **xuéfèi** 学费 120

tumor **zhǒngliú** 肿瘤 139

tunnel, underpass **dìdào** 地道 23

turn a corner **guǎiwān** 拐弯 39

turn over in one's mind **zuómo** 琢磨 143

turn traitor, become a turncoat **pànbiàn** 叛变 82

turnip, radish, carrot **luóbo** 萝卜 72

TV program, item in a theatrical performance **jiémù** 节目 57

two **liǎng** 两 69

two people **liǎ** 俩 68

type (n.) **lèixíng** 类型 67

type (v.) **dǎzì** 打字 18

U

ugly, not good to look at **chǒu** 丑 15, **nánkàn** 难看 79

umbrella **sǎn** 伞 92

unanimous, identical **yízhì** 一致 124

uncover, expose **jiēlù** 揭露 56

under heaven, in the world, on earth **tiānxià** 天下 105

undergo physical training, do physical exercises **duànliàn** 锻炼 26

undergraduate course **běnkē** 本科 5

underground **dìxià** 地下 23

underneath, under **dǐxia** 底下 23

undersell **yājià** 压价 *121*

understand, comprehend **lǐjiě** 理解 *68*, **míngbai** 明白 *76*

unexpected, unforeseen **yìwài** 意外 *126*

unexpectedly, contrary to expectation **què** 却 *89*, **jìngrán** 竟然 *60*

unexpectedly, shockingly **jūrán** 居然 *60*

unfamiliar **mòshēng** 陌生 *77*

unfeeling, cold-blooded **lěngkù** 冷酷 *67*

unfortunate **búxìng** 不幸 *10*

unfrequented, desolate **lěngjìng** 冷静 *67*

unhurried, leisurely **cóngróng** 从容 *17*

unified **tǒngyī** 统一 *107*

unify, integrate **tǒngyī** 统一 *107*

unimportant, doesn't matter **búyàojǐn** 不要紧 *10*

unique, distinctive **dútè** 独特 *26*

unit (in an apartment house), apartment, flat **dānyuán** 单元 *20*

unite, be in solidarity with **tuánjié** 团结 *108*

unite, get together (to do something) **liánhé** 联合 *69*

United Nations Organization, the **Liánhéguó** 联合国 *69*

university, institution of higher education **dàxué** 大学 *19*

university professor **jiàoshòu** 教授 *56*

unless, only if **chúfēi** 除非 *16*

unload, discharge **xiè** 卸 *117*

unmarried young woman, girl, lass **gūniang** 姑娘 *38*

unperturbed, calm **zhèndìng** 镇定 *136*

unprecedented **kōngqián** 空前 *64*

until, till **zhídào** 直到 *137*

unusually, very **fēicháng** 非常 *31*

uphold, persist (in) **jiānchí** 坚持 *53*

upholstered chair, sofa, couch **shāfā** 沙发 *92*

upload **shàngzài** 上载 *93*

upper garment, jacket **shàngyī** 上衣 *93*

upset, disturbed **bù'ān** 不安 *9*

upstairs **lóu shang** 楼上 *71*

urgent, pressing **jǐnjí** 紧急 *58*, **pòqiè** 迫切 *84*

US dollar, greenback **Měiyuán** 美元 *74*

(the) USA, America **Měiguó** 美国 *74*

use, advantage **yòngchu** 用处 *127*

use, apply **shǐyòng** 使用 *97*, **yùnyòng** 运用 *131*

use, employ **cǎiyòng** 采用 *10*

use, function (n.) **yòngtú** 用途 *127*

use (transport), travel (by car, train, plane, etc.) **chéngzuò** 乘坐 *14*

use as an excuse; excuse, pretext **jièkǒu** 借口 *58*

useful **yǒuyòng** 有用 *129*

useless **méiyòng** 没用 *74*

V

vacuum **zhēnkōng** 真空 *135*

vague, ambiguous **hánhu** 含糊 *43*

valid **yǒuxiào** 有效 *128*

valley **gǔ** 谷 *38*

valuable, precious **bǎoguì** 宝贵 *4*

value, worth **jiàzhí** 价值 *53*

values **jiàzhíguān** 价值观 *53*

vandalize, damage **pòhuài** 破坏 *84*

vapor, steam **qì** 汽 *85*

vase **huāpíng** 花瓶 *46*

vast, extensive **guǎngdà** 广大 *40*

vegetables **cài** 菜 *11*, **shūcài** 蔬菜 *99*

vehicle, traffic **chē** 车 *13*

vendor's stand, stall **tān** 摊 *103*

venue (meeting, conference, assembly or rally) **huìchǎng** 会场 *48*

verdict, conclusion **jiélùn** 结论 *57*

verified to be true, indeed **quèshí** 确实 *89*

very **hěn** 很 *45*, **tǐng** 挺 *106*

very bad, abominable **èliè** 恶劣 *28*

very careful, meticulous **xìxīn** 细心 *114*

very careful, paying attention to details **zǐxì** 仔细 *141*

very difficult, strenuous (of a big and important task) **jiānjù** 艰巨 *53*

very few, exceptional **gèbié** 个别 *36*

very long, long-standing, time-honored **yōujiǔ** 悠久 *127*

very much to one's liking, find … satisfactory **chènxīn** 称心 *13*

vibrate, oscillate; vibration, oscillation **zhèndòng** 振动 *136*

vicious, malicious **èdú** 恶毒 *28*

video frequency **shìpín** 视频 *97*

video recorder **lùxiàngjī** 录像机 *71*

view, scenery **jǐng** 景 *59*, **jǐngsè** 景色 *59*

viewpoint, view **guāndiǎn** 观点 *39*

vigor, vitality, stamina **jīngshén** 精神 *59*

village **cūnzi** 村子 *18*

vineyard **pútaoyuán** 葡萄园 *84*

violate the law **fàn fǎ** 犯法 *30*

virus **bìngdú** 病毒 *8*

visa **qiānzhèng** 签证 *86*

visit (a place) **cānguān** 参观 *11*

visit, interview **fǎngwèn** 访问 *31*

vitamins **wéishēng sù** 维生素 *110*

vivid, lively **shēngdòng** 生动 *95*

vocabulary, lexicon **cíhuì** 词汇 *17*

voice **sǎngzi** 嗓子 *92*

voice, sound **shēngyīn** 声音 *95*

volcano **huǒshān** 火山 *49*

volleyball **páiqiú** 排球 *81*

volume (books) **cè** 册 *11*

volume (mathematics) **tǐjī** 体积 *104*

voluntary, of one's own accord **zìyuàn** 自愿 *142*

voluntary work **yìwù gōngzuò** (**yìgōng**) 义务工作（义工）*125*

volunteer (n.) **zhìyuànzhě** 志愿者 *138*

volunteer (v.) **zhìyuàn** 志愿 *138*

vomit (v.) **ǒu** 呕 *81*, **tù** 吐 *108*

W

wages, salary **gōngzī** 工资 *36*

waist, small of the back **yāo** 腰 *122*

wait **děngdài** 等待 (usually used in writing) *23*

wait a minute **děng yíxià** 等一下 *23*

wait on, serve **cìhou** 伺候 *17*

wake, wake up **xǐng** 醒 *119*

walk; leave (v.) **zǒu** 走 *142*

wall **qiáng** 墙 *87*

wallet, purse **qiánbāo** 钱包 *86*

want, ask for, would like **yào** 要 *123*

war **zhànzhēng** 战争 *134*

ward (in hospital) **bìngfáng** 病房 *8*

warm **wēnnuǎn** 温暖 *111*

warm-hearted, enthusiastic **rèxīn** 热心 *90*

wash (v.) **xǐ** 洗 *113*

washing machine **xǐyījī** 洗衣机 *113*

waste, ruin (v.) **zāota** 糟蹋 *132*

waste, squander **làngfèi** 浪费 *66*

waste gas **fèiqì** 废气 *31*

waste material **fèiwù** 废物 *31*

watch (TV, a movie, etc.) **kàn** 看 *62*

water **shuǐ** 水 *100*

watermelon **xīguā** 西瓜 *113*

wave **bōlàng** 波浪 *8*

way, road, path **tújìng** 途径 *107*

way of doing things, method, practice **bànfǎ** 办法 *3*, **zuòfǎ** 做法 *143*

way of looking at things, view **kànfǎ** 看法 *62*

we, us **wǒmen** 我们 *112*

we, us (including one(s) spoken to) **zánmen** 咱们 *132*

weak (of tea, coffee) **dàn** 淡 *21*

wean (a child) **duàn nǎi** 断奶 *26*

weapon **wǔqì** 武器 *112*

wear (clothes or shoes), be dressed in **chuān** 穿 *16*

wear, put on **dài** 戴 *20*

weather **tiānqì** 天气 *105*

webcam **shèxiàngtóu** 摄像头 *94*

website **wǎngzhàn** 网站 *110*

website operation **wǎngzhàn yùnyíng** 网站运营 *110*

wedding ceremony **hūnlǐ** 婚礼 *49*

week **xīngqī** 星期 *118*, **zhōu** 周 *139*

weekend **zhōumò** 周末 *139*

weight **zhòngliàng** 重量 *139*

welcome (v.) **huānyíng** 欢迎 *47*

well behaved, behaving within the norm **guīju** 规矩 *40*

well distributed, evenly applied **jūnyún** 均匀 *61*

west, western **xī** 西 *113*

west side, in/to the west **xībian** 西边 *113*

Western-style clothes, Western-style coat **xīfú** 西服 *113*

Western-style meal **xīcān** 西餐 *113*

Western-style restaurant **xīcānguǎn** 西餐馆 *113*

what **shénme** 什么 *95*

what happened? **zěnmele** 怎么了 *133*

what is called, so-called **suǒwèi** 所谓 *102*

what is crucial or critical **guānjiàn** 关键 *39*

what is open, overt, masculine, the sun **yáng** 阳 *122*

what is real, reality, actuality; realistic, practical **xiànshí** 现实 *115*

what one thinks, idea, opinion **xiǎngfǎ** 想法 *115*

what's more, moreover **hékuàng** 何况 *44*

what's to be done? **zěnmebàn** 怎么办 *133*

wheel **lún** 轮 *72*

when **dāng ... de shíhou** 当 ... 的时候 *21*

whenever, at any moment. **suíshí** 随时 *102*

where **nǎli** 哪里 *78*, **nǎr** 哪儿 (used colloquially) *78*

whether or not, yes or no **shìfǒu** 是否 *98*

which **nǎ** 哪 *77*

which, what **hé** 何 *44*

while ... at the same time ..., simultaneously **yìbiān ... yìbiān ... ** 一边 ... 一边 ... *123*

whip **biān** 鞭 *7*

white **bái** 白 *2*

who, whom **shuí** 谁 *100*, **shéi** 谁 (colloquialism) *94*

whole, entire **zhěngge** 整个 *136*

whole, entirety, (something) as a whole **zhěngtǐ** 整体 *136*

(the) whole day, all the time **zhěngtiān** 整天 *136*

whooping cough **bǎirìké** 百日咳 *3*

why, how come **zěnme** 怎么 *133*

why, what for **wèishénme** 为什么 *111*

widespread, commonplace **pǔbiàn** 普遍 *84*

widespread, wide-ranging, extensive **guǎngfàn** 广泛 *40*

wife **qīzi** 妻子 *85*

wife's father **yuèfù** 岳父 *131*

wife's mother **yuèmǔ** 岳母 *131*

wild (animal or plant) **yěshēng** 野生 *123*

wild beast, wild animal **yěshòu** 野兽 *123*

will, shall, be going to, be about to **jiāng** 将, **jiāngyào** 将要 *55*

will not do, be not allowed **bùxíng** 不行 *10*

win, obtain, get **huòdé** 获得 *49*

win a victory; victory **shènglì** 胜利 *95*

wind, draft **fēng** 风 *32*

wind direction **fēngxiàng** 风向 *32*

wind force, wind power **fēnglì** 风力 *32*

window **chuānghu** 窗户 *16*

window curtain **chuānglián** 窗帘 *16*

wine shop, restaurant **jiǔdiàn** 酒店 *54*

wing (bird's) **chìbǎng** 翅膀 *14*

winning, superior **yōushèng** 优胜 *127*

winter **dōng** 冬 *25*, **dōngtiān** 冬天 *25*

winter vacation, winter holiday **hánjià** 寒假 *43*

wiretap, bug **qiètīng** 窃听 *87*

wisdom **zhìhuì** 智慧 *138*

wise, intelligent **zhì** 智 *138*

wish, aspiration, desire **yuànwàng** 愿望 *130*

wish, want (v.) **yuànyì** 愿意 130

wish, ideal **zhìyuàn** 志愿 138

wit; sharp-witted **jīzhì** 机智 50

with **gēn** 跟 36

with, along with **tóng** 同 106

with, in the manner of **yǐ** 以 125

with a high degree **gāodù** 高度 35

with great difficulty **hǎo róngyì** 好容易 44

with regard to, concerning **jiù** 就 60

withdraw money **qǔkuǎn** 取款 88

within, during **yǐnèi** 以内 125

without interruption, continuously, incessantly **búduàn** 不断 9, **bùtíng** 不停 9

wolf **láng** 狼 66

wolf with short forelegs **bèi** 狈 5

woman, adult woman **nǚrén** 女人 81

woman, womankind **fùnǚ** 妇女 33

wonderful, terrific **liǎobuqǐ** 了不起 70

wood, timber **mùtou** 木头 77

wood, woods **shùlín** 树林 100

woolen sweater, woolen pullover **máoyī** 毛衣 73

word, phrase, wording **cíyǔ** 词语 17

words of a song **gēcí** 歌词 35

work, job **huór** 活儿 49

work (v.); work, job **gōngzuò** 工作 36

work (as manual laborer) **dǎgōng** 打工 18, **gàn huór** 干活儿 35

work (white-collar, office) **bàngōng** 办公 3

work overtime **jiābān** 加班 52

work to earn (money) **zhèng jǐ** 挣 136

work unit **dānwèi** 单位 20

workman, worker **gōngrén** 工人 36

workshop (in a factory) **chējiān** 车间 13

world outlook, worldview **shìjièguān** 世界观 97

worried and unhappy **fánmèn** 烦闷 29

worry, feel anxious **dānxīn** 担心 20

would rather …, would prefer **nìngkě** 宁可 80

would rather …than **yǔqí** … **bùrú** 与其 … 不如 129

wound, injure **shāng** 伤 92

wrap, bind **guǒ** 裹 41

wrap up; parcel, bag **bāo** 包 4

wristwatch **shǒubiǎo** 手表 98

write, write with a pen **xiě** 写 117

write and post a blog; web log, blog, blogger **bókè** 博客 8

write as a professional writer, compose essays; writing **xiězuò** 写作 117

write back, write in reply; letter in reply **huíxìn** 回信 48

writer (especially of literary works, e.g. novels, stories) **zuòjiā** 作家 143

writing instrument, pen, pencil **bǐ** 笔 6

written language, script, character **wénzì** 文字 112

wrong, mistaken **cuò** 错 18

Y

Yangtze River (China's longest river) **Chángjiāng** 长江 12

year **nián** 年 80

year after next **hòunián** 后年 45

year before last **qiánnián** 前年 86

yellow **huáng** 黄 47, **huángsè** 黄色 48

Yellow River, the **Huánghé** 黄河 48

yesterday **zuótiān** 昨天 143

you (honorific) **nín** 您 80

you (plural) **nǐmen** 你们 79

you (singular) **nǐ** 你 79

you're welcome, not at all **búkèqi** 不客气 9

young **niánqīng** 年轻 80

young, early youth **shào** 少 94

young and tender, tender **nèn** 嫩 79

young lady; Miss **xiǎojiě** 小姐 116

young man (around 10 to 16 years old), adolescent **shàonián** 少年 94

young man **nán qīngnián** 男青年 78

young man, lad **xiǎohuǒzi** 小伙子 116

young person, young people **niánqīngrén** 年轻人 80

young person, young people, youth (especially male) **qīngnián** 青年 87

young woman **nǚ qīngnián** 女青年 81

younger brother **dìdi** 弟弟 23

younger sister **mèimei** 妹妹 74

your family name **guìxìng** 贵姓 41

youth, quality of being young **qīngchūn** 青春 87

Z

zero **líng** 零 70

zipper, zip fastener **lāsuǒ** 拉锁 66

zoo **dòngwùyuán** 动物园 25

zoology **dòngwùxué** 动物学 25